WITHDRAWN

EUGENE O'NEILL
IN CHINA

EUGENE O'NEILL
IN CHINA

An International
Centenary Celebration

Edited by
Haiping Liu
and
Lowell Swortzell

Contributions in Drama and Theatre Studies, Number 44

Greenwood Press
New York • Westport, Connecticut • London

Library of Congress Cataloging-in-Publication Data

Eugene O'Neill in China : an international centenary celebration /
   edited by Haiping Liu and Lowell Swortzell.
      p.   cm.—(Contributions in drama and theatre studies, ISSN
   0163-3821 ; no. 44)
   Includes index.
   ISBN 0-313-27379-0 (alk. paper)
    1. O'Neill, Eugene, 1888-1953—Criticism and interpretation—
Congresses.   2. O'Neill, Eugene, 1888-1953—Stage history—
Congresses.   I. Liu, Hai-p' ing, 1944- II. Swortzell, Lowell.
III. Series.
   PS3529.N5Z6374   1992
   812'.52—dc20   91-28744

British Library Cataloguing in Publication Data is available.

Library of Congress Catalog Card Number: 91-28744
ISBN: 0-313-27379-0
ISSN: 0163-3821

First published in 1992

Greenwood Press, 88 Post Road West, Westport, CT 06881
An imprint of Greenwood Publishing Group, Inc.

Printed in the United States of America

The paper used in this book complies with the
Permanent Paper Standard issued by the National
Information Standards Organization (Z39.48-1984).

10 9 8 7 6 5 4 3 2 1

Copyright Acknowledgments

Permission to reprint the following copyrighted materials is gratefully acknowledged:

"O'Neill in China" by Lowell Swortzell. Published in *The Recorder*, a Journal of the American Irish Historical Society, vol. 3, no. 1, Summer 1989.

"Eternal Recurrence and the Shaping of O'Neill's Dramatic Structures" by Albert E. Kalson and Lisa M. Schwerdt. *Comparative Drama*, Summer 1990. Reprinted by kind permission of the Editors of *Comparative Drama*.

Extracts from *Eugene O'Neill: A World View* (1979); *Eugene O'Neill at Work: Newly Released Ideas for Plays* (1981); *The Plays of Eugene O'Neill: A New Assessment* (1985) by Virginia Floyd. Reprinted by permission of Crossroads/Continuum/Frederick Ungar.

Extracts from *Eugene O'Neill and Oriental Thought: A Divided Vision* by James A. Robinson. Copyright 1982 by the Board of Trustees, Southern Illinois University, Carbondale. Reprinted by permission of Southern Illinois University Press.

Extract from "Eugene O'Neill's Gorgeous Satire" by Brooks Atkinson. Copyright 1928 by the New York Times Company. Reprinted by permission.

Excerpts from *O'Neill: The Biography of Eugene O'Neill* by Arthur and Barbara Gelb. Copyright 1960, 1962 by Arthur and Barbara Gelb. Reprinted by permission of Harper Collins Publishers and Barbara Gelb.

Excerpts from the following plays of Eugene O'Neill:

Desire Under the Elms. Copyright 1931 by Eugene O'Neill. Renewed by Carlotta Monterey O'Neill. Reprinted from *The Plays of Eugene O'Neill*, vol. 2, by permission of Random House, Inc. and Jonathan Cape,

For Bob and Jerrie Runice who helped me to start,
endure, and enjoy the long journey to this book.
H. L.

This book is dedicated to the memory of
Virginia Floyd in appreciation of her many
contributions to O'Neill scholarship, the
last of which are published here.
L. S.

Contents

Part Five: O'Neill Abroad

Contents xiii

Illustrations

Illustrations are from the Jiangsu Art Theatre's production of *The Emperor Jones* and follow page xliii.

Acknowledgments

I would like to express my sincere gratitude to all those individuals and institutions who helped in one way or another in the preparation of the centennial celebration and the present book, and particularly to Frederick Wilkins, Arthur and Barbara Gelb, Travis Bogard, Jordan Miller and Cao Yu, who gave me inspiration and encouragement when I had in mind only a vague notion of the conference; to all my "pals" in *Choubeizhu* (the preparatory team), who helped enormously in developing and materializing the idea; to Yvonne Shafer, James Robinson, and John Scherting for their suggestions and contact with the U.S. Embassy and Consulate and some scholars in the United States; to the China Fund, the United Board, and Occidental Petroleum for the funding necessary for the project; to Margaret Ranald for proposing the fruitful contact with Greenwood Press for this book and for her valuable ideas on editing; to Marilyn Brownstein of Greenwood for her patience and understanding; to Lowell Swortzell for his kindness and courage in agreeing to co-edit this book with me far away across the Pacific Ocean; to Zhao Yu for her unfailing assistance in the work of editing, which must have seemed to her to have no end; and, finally, to Bob, Jerrie, Yun, Qian, and Fei, who gave me confidence, love, and backing to undertake and carry through the whole project.

Haiping Liu

I thank Eugene O'Neill for being the cause of my first visit to China--a wonderful experience in itself, filled with landscapes of great beauty and people of enormous graciousness with a well-maintained tradition of hospitality.

I thank Haiping Liu for organizing the conference and for his invitation to co-edit this volume. His vision and determination to honor O'Neill resulted in the largest international gathering of researchers and performers to be held anywhere during the centenary observances. He successfully appealed to bureaucrats for money, to officials for space, and to scholars and artists he thought should attend (and who, amazingly enough, for the most part did). He inspired educators to find the funds to take themselves to Nanjing. He challenged theatre companies to produce O'Neill's plays especially for the Festival. All these accomplishments may be termed cultural miracles, considering how monumentally underpaid teachers and artists are the world over. Yet, they arrived in Nanjing for four days of international celebration, ready to deliver their papers and to perform their productions, all because one professor believed that China was the ideal place to proclaim Eugene O'Neill a world playwright.

Of course, he was assisted. Among my fondest memories remain the faces of his many colleagues who greeted and escorted us about Nanjing. They also presented us with O'Neill's somber portrait on conference T-shirts which we still wear with pride and gratitude. To the students who took such great measures to make the daily operations run smoothly, we especially are indebted.

The purpose of this book is to capture the intellectual and artistic stimulation of that conference, allowing readers to share its impressive accomplishment in fostering international studies of O'Neill. Limitations of space, inevitably, make it impossible to include all the papers presented in Nanjing. The final selection represents the major areas of investigation explored by O'Neill scholars today. These papers are organized into divisions similar to the order in which they were originally delivered.

Missing, unfortunately, are the informal discussions that took place between sessions, on excursions about Nanjing, at theatres, at receptions, and during meals. It was these conversations which truly united delegates in their studying, sharing, and probing of O'Neill. Many of these impromptu meetings were with students whose enthusiasm for O'Neill, American theatre, and American life in general proved to be insatiable. To be certain, the Americans and Europeans also asked endless questions about Chinese theatre, education, and society-- sometimes well into the morning.

Some of that splendid collegiality is captured in the panel discussion, the last section of this book, in which the Festival productions were discussed in open forum. If one multiplies that lively exchange by a period of four days, the reader will gain a sense of the comaraderie of the entire conference.

I wish to thank, too, the editors of *The Recorder* for permission to reprint my article on the conference as my introduction to this book.

Richard Spencer has proved to be an exemplary research assistant, particularly in masterminding incompatible computer programs. His contributions include a mind that questions every sentence at least twice, for which both authors and readers should be doubly grateful.

Dr. Leslie White, a former student and O'Neill scholar in her own right, saw the manuscript through its final stages of preparation and, as with two previous books, I am once again indebted to her sharp vision and caustic wit with which she first attacks and then improves my work.

When mail service stopped at the outbreak of the student uprising in June 1989, the diskettes containing the complete conference presentations were hand-delivered to New York by Americans suddenly being recalled home. With their help and the ability of FAX machines to communicate even in the most troubled of times, *Eugene O'Neill in China* surmounted political and diplomatic obstacles that might have delayed or even prevented its publication. With improving United States-Chinese relations comes hope that conferences such as the one reported here will continue to disseminate knowledge and strengthen friendships throughout the world.

Lowell Swortzell

Letter of Greeting from the People's Republic of China

Dear Professor Haiping Liu,

Thank you for your kind invitation to the international conference in commemoration of Eugene O'Neill's centennial. I would indeed like to attend, yet I very much regret to say my poor health prevents me from coming to Nanjing. I hope you will understand and forgive me.

I am so glad to learn that the conference is extremely well planned and prepared. I can imagine how much time you and your colleagues must have put into it. But you can be assured that the conference will be a great, unprecedented event in the history of the exchange of drama and theatre between China and the United States. It will, I am sure, win glory for the academic and theatrical circles.

As for the papers to be presented at the conference, I hope they can be collected and published later as a book, so that other people, either O'Neill scholars or those merely interested in him, might also benefit from the conference and have a better understanding of this great dramatist's work. I avidly look forward to such a publication.

Thank you for inviting me to be an honorary adviser to the conference. I accept the honor with gratitude.

Best wishes for the success of the conference.

Sincerely,

Cao Yu,
President
Chinese Dramatists' Association

Letter of Greeting from
the United States

Dear Professor Liu:

    I write to salute you on the tremendous success of your monumental task of organizing the international conference *Eugene O'Neill: World Playwright*, which I know will be one of the most significant commemorations of the centennial of Eugene O'Neill's birth and to send officially an expression of admiration and respect from the membership of the Eugene O'Neill Society, which has been honored to co-sponsor the event.

    We know very well the massive difficulties involved in organizing so vast and complex an event and we congratulate you and your colleagues for surmounting all the potential obstacles so successfully. It is evidence both of your personal and tireless dedication to America's foremost dramatist and of the respect in which O'Neill is held throughout the world today. Eugene O'Neill was truly a "citizen of the world," and your conference underscores that fact, while also strengthening the warm bond of friendship between our two nations.

    The massive array of events and speakers you have succeeded in bringing together is the envy of conference directors everywhere. Having myself done some work in that area, I can say that very personally! And there is no way to express adequately the disappointment I feel in not being able to be present and congratulate you in person. But I hope that you will convey my greetings to the many who will attend and my best wishes for what I am confident will be an occasion of unequalled importance to the worldwide appreciation of Eugene O'Neill. The Eugene O'Neill Society doffs its collective hat in awe!

Sincerely yours,

Frederick C. Wilkins,
President
The Eugene O'Neill Society

O'Neill's Universal Brotherhood: A Theatre for Today's World

Keynote address at the opening ceremony for *Eugene O'Neill: World Playwright*, June 6, 1988, Nanjing

On this historic day when scholars of the East and of the West meet to celebrate the centennial of America's premier playwright, let us in the spirit of Eugene O'Neill extend to one another warm greetings of friendship and good fellowship. Let us also offer sincere thanks to our hosts, the University of Nanjing and the People's Republic of China, whose foresight made this meeting a reality and particularly to their representative, Professor Haiping Liu, the gracious conference coordinator who smoothed all paths that led here. The People's Republic of China is to be highly commended, as it is one of the few countries in the world that has mounted a massive international conference that is destined to be a learning experience for all who attend. The scope of the four-day program here and the eagerly anticipated plays to be presented here and in Shanghai indicate both a deep dedication to O'Neill and an appreciation of his stature as world dramatist.

How pleased O'Neill himself would be by the great intermingling of peoples from so many nations to pay tribute to him as they explore the many facets of his life and plays. Indeed, this international conference is a significant step forward in the realization of a cherished dream that became a major motif in his plays: the brotherhood of man. Inasmuch as he stood stalwartly Janus-masked, benevolently facing both East and West, throughout his creative career, let us select as the theme of our historic coming together: "O'Neill's Universal Brotherhood: A Theatre for Today's World."

From his years of early adulthood the dramatist sought to expand his mental horizons by signing on as seaman to sail beyond his country's boundaries and its narrow native provincialism. In the process he was exposed to the many nationalities and ethnic distinctions of his fellow crewmen and learned among these rough, uneducated seamen lessons about the value of friendship, sacrifice, and integrity. Later, when he wrote the early one-act sea plays in the Glencairn series, he was able accurately to depict his ethnic gallery of characters with compassion and understanding.

In the two decades that followed, the 1920s and 1930s, in the plays he actually wrote and in the ideas he conceived for others, O'Neill sought intently to improve the lot of suffering humanity as he explored numerous social issues: discrimination against nonwhites by whites as in *All God's Chillun Got Wings*, the dehumanization and exploitation of the working class by indifferent capitalists as in *The Hairy Ape*, the Faust-like nature of the American character, as O'Neill perceived it, as having sold its life and soul for material objects as the eleven-play projected Cycle was to illustrate. The apotheosis of O'Neill's crusade for universal brotherhood is found in *The Iceman Cometh*, which depicts a wide social spectrum: people from many walks of life and of different nationalities. Harry Hope's saloon symbolizes a universal melting pot where all men are equal and the word "brother" is used frequently. O'Neill sought in the play to capture, as he said, "the humor and friendship and human warmth and deep inner contentment of the characters." The greatest harm, as Hickey was to discover, is to break the link that binds. When all the diverse characters gather for Harry Hope's birthday party in a banquetlike setting, as we have here, Harry assures them: "Bejees, you know you're all as welcome here as the flowers in May."

O'Neill has identified this group of pitiful misfits in *The Iceman Cometh* as his "blood brothers," friends he had known during the period when he was a homeless misfit plunged in a personal shipwreck of alcoholic dissolution. Yet it was precisely through his association with these outcasts that O'Neill discovered truths about human nature and the human condition. Other world dramatists may excel O'Neill in lofty lyric power or philosophical discourse. None, however, surpasses him in the sheer magnitude of the men and women who people his plays. O'Neill understood the human psyche, its baseness and its greatness, as few other writers have.

One other tale, besides the friendship saga, obsessed O'Neill: his own tortured, convoluted life story. His relationship to his mother, father, brother, wives, and children is dramatized in endless variations in the canon. Because all human lives pivot around the same types of familial ties, O'Neill's work assumes universal dimensions. He speaks the common language of the heart, expressing the longings of all mankind to love and be loved, to belong, to determine the why of existence. Because this language is readily understood by people of all classes and races, O'Neill has become an international playwright, respected and produced in countries throughout the world.

O'Neill seems destined to continue to be honored for the legacy he has left us. As Pirandello states in *Six Characters in Search of an Author*: "He who was fortunate enough to be born a character" is immortal; "he cannot die." O'Neill has bequeathed us a vast gallery of immortal, unforgettable mythic figures: the bewildered Yank, crushed by an indifferent society, mourned only by whimpering monkeys; the pathetic Dion Anthony, forced to wear the mask of diabolic cynicism to protect his sensitive, ascetic, vulnerable face; the craggy-faced Ephraim Cabot, condemned at play's end to his life of loneliness, caught in the palm of the hand of his harsh Puritan God, made to his image; the iron-willed maiden Lavinia, turning her back on the world to immure herself in the Mannon home in self-afflicted punishment for her sin; O'Neill's prototype for all mother-as-betrayer figures, Mary Tyrone, in the play's final scene, perhaps the most memorable moment in modern drama, aimlessly adrift, forever lost to husband and sons in her selfish narcotic stupor; the vanishing figure of Jim Tyrone, leaving his safe refuge in the Hogan household, doomed to end his life in blindness and a straitjacket.

The Theatre for Today's World, as O'Neill has defined it, should be "a source of inspiration that lifts us to a plane beyond ourselves and drives us deep into the unknown within and behind ourselves. The theatre should reveal to us what we are." He adds: "Holding the mirror of a soul up to a nation; it is time we returned to this." The theatre, as O'Neill views it, has a twofold purpose: to act as a moral force, making us aware of our ignoble lives when they are lived on the lower plain of reality or revealing our true mystic natures in lives lived on a higher moral level, and to mirror the image of the state of its citizens, gauging the collective moral well-being of a nation. For example, the sickness of soul found in the four Tyrones in *Long Day's Journey into Night* is merely indicative of the sickness of the American character, the microcosm of the family reflecting the macrocosm of society.

As scholars or theatre practitioners, we must perpetuate for posterity the recorded history of twentieth-century man as portrayed in world drama and encourage our fellow citizens to read and see plays, like those of O'Neill, that depict the realities of life with all its complexities and tragedies and that reflect portraits of human beings, victims of a flawed inner self and fated by some behind-life force. There is no limit to what we can do here to keep the spirit of dedication to O'Neill alive.

While I was transcribing the restricted O'Neill material at Yale for publication, I found a short passage in O'Neill's handwriting from Nietzsche's *Thus Spake Zarathustra*, dated "November 15, 1927 Shanghai." It starts with the familiar lines of the poet saying to his heart that he is a wanderer and mountain-climber and concludes with the self-realization that the poet long has been abroad, scattered among things and accidents. The intriguing question is what experience during his visit to Shanghai inspired these thoughts. He had, as he said, come "to China seeking peace and quiet." The concept of the self long abroad and scattered could, on the creative level, refer to the profusion of his plays; on the personal level, it could mean the outpouring of his being, his thoughts and spirit. In another sense, O'Neill cannot be said to belong mentally solely to any one country but to the world. He had scattered his inquiring spirit afar, that part of him that ever sought truth and wisdom--turning for religious and philosophical inspiration to China and the East, to Lao Tzu, Confucius, and Buddha, as well as Vishnu and Mohammed; and to Europe, to Nietzsche, Freud, Schopenhauer, and Marx, and for theatrical inspiration to Strindberg, Chekhov, Ibsen, Kaiser, and Toller. We, too, during this Theatre Festival should scatter the self abroad, giving to each other in O'Neill's spirit of brotherhood the best that is in us and taking away from this conference the inspiration and determination to sow the germinal seeds of this centennial celebration, each in his own country, to reap renewed interest in O'Neill in the Theatre for Today's World.

Virginia Floyd

Introduction From the People's Republic of China

Haiping Liu

"It was fortunate that Eugene O'Neill was born in 1888."

Many of my friends, both at home and abroad, have made the same remark to me recently. It is true that, were the American dramatist born a year later, there could have been no such enthusiastic celebration of his centenary in China as was launched in Nanjing and Shanghai successively from June 6 to 14, 1988. The social and political upheaval in China in the spring of 1989 and the subsequent return to strained diplomatic and cultural ties between China and the West would have rendered the international conference *Eugene O'Neill: World Playwright*, jointly sponsored by Nanjing University and the Eugene O'Neill Society, and the accompanying Nanjing/Shanghai *O'Neill Theatre Festival* practically impossible. A number of Sino-West academic and art projects scheduled for the summer or fall of 1989 had to be canceled almost at the last moment. While deploring most sincerely the waste of time, energy, and resources on the part of those project organizers and other people involved, I could not help congratulating Eugene O'Neill, all the scholars and theatre practitioners who came from afar to participate in his centennial in China, my colleagues here in the English Department and myself, who together had spent nearly two years in the preparations, on our common better luck.

The statement, however, could also be interpreted from a different direction in time. That is, if O'Neill had been born, let us say, one or two decades earlier, could his centenary in any way have been celebrated in China? The answer would be, emphatically, "No!"

For some thirty years after 1949 when the People's Republic was founded amid the cold-war scorn and scoffing of the Western nations, the political and cultural atmosphere in China was hostile, by and large, to modern Western literature and the arts. Except for a few authors such as Jack London, Ethel Voynich, and Upton Sinclair, whose works were seen as bitter exposes of the "decadence" of the bourgeoisie and the capitalist system, or like Sean O'Casey, who came from a proletarian background and became a Communist later in his life, modern European and American writers were generally either snubbed or ridiculed. "Critical realism," a term favored by Soviet critics to categorize works exposing the evils of the old social order, was the yardstick against which the works of the nineteenth and twentieth-century foreign writers would have to be intemperately measured, just as "revolutionary realism" or "socialist realism" was a criterion strictly applied to the assessment of the writings by Chinese authors.

Eugene O'Neill as a playwright was seldom concerned with social criticism. He was also known for his restiveness and occasional blasphemies about realism. "Damn the word 'realism, ' " he once said. On other occasions, he described realism as "morbid" and "doomed." He experimented extensively with expressionistic techniques in many of his plays. It is understandable, in a sense, that he should have been rejected in China. While the successful productions of his late plays in the mid-1950s restored and enhanced his position in the West as a leading figure in twentieth-century world drama, O'Neill and his plays were virtually unheard of in the world's most populous nation during the three decades from 1949 to 1979.

Occasionally, his name did appear in books or journals, but more often than not merely as a target of revilement. Examples can be found in a book called *References to Foreign Literature*, edited by the Department of Chinese, Beijing Teachers' College. In this book containing essays translated from Russian critics, O'Neill was labeled "a corrupted element in the American literary circle," and his plays were described as "full of totally decadent ideas of life," "inhuman," and "one-hundred percent fascist." It may seem dumbfounding today that people would have chosen such stuff for translation and publication. But we should bear in mind that it was published in 1957, a year that is usually remembered by the Chinese in association with the hair-raising Anti-Rightist campaign, during which hundreds and thousands of intellectuals and cadres who held, or were believed to hold, dissident views were branded "counter-revolutionary rightists" and were forced out of public life or banished to hard labor in remote areas.

It was not until the end of the 1970s that a climate materialized in China favorable for the reception of O'Neill and other modern

Western writers. Many historical changes took place then. The United States liquidated its cold-war stance towards China, and diplomatic relations between the two nations were normalized. China undertook a long journey that called for massive reform and opening. The biased, narrow views on art and literature were repudiated; a more rational and tolerant, still Socialist-oriented but far less dogmatic policy to encourage initiative, creativity, and cultural exchanges with the outside world began to take shape.

Having been sealed off for so long, the Chinese were eager to know what had been going on elsewhere in the world and were enthusiastic about new and unfamiliar approaches to problems. The dramatists and theatre practitioners, who tried to touch upon deeper truth in life, felt uncomfortable with the orthodox "realistic" style in dramaturgy and stage production. They craved for new ideas and techniques to enrich their dramatic repertoire. It was only natural that they should have turned to O'Neill, who had written so unsparingly on his country and his own family and had so courageously and persistently experimented with the dramatic form. But the affinity between O'Neill and China, like that between other literatures or theatres, was not purely literary or theatrical. The practical and professional need to learn from O'Neill was compounded with and, to a certain extent, amplified by the mounting popular affection of the Chinese for American culture in general.

O'Neill's name and plays thus began to appear in Chinese media with increasing frequency. Apart from single plays that appeared scattered in periodicals and anthologies, at least four different works appeared that contained translations of O'Neill plays exclusively. A more ambitious four-volume collection of all O'Neill's published plays is avidly anticipated. It is quite common now for an O'Neill play to have two or three and sometimes even four different Chinese translations. In addition, three biographies and monographs on O'Neill have been rendered into Chinese. Croswell Bowen's *The Curse of the Misbegotten: A Tale of the House of O'Neill* was published in 1988, and the translation manuscripts of the other two (the unabridged *O'Neill*, by Arthur and Barbara Gelb, and Frederic I. Carpenter's *Eugene O'Neill*) were sitting on the desks of the publishers as of late 1989.

To Chinese scholars and critics, the American dramatist represented an unexplored mystery; his life and career, as well as his individual plays, all crammed and crowded with drama, seemed inexhaustible subjects for interpretation and reinterpretation. The knowledge that O'Neill attached great interest to Chinese history and culture and that Orientalism, especially Taoism, formed a distinctive aspect of his art further endeared him to Chinese readers and critics. As a result, the 1980s saw no fewer than one hundred-and-fifty articles on O'Neill and his plays carried in various kinds of literary and theatre magazines, not including those B.A. and M.A. theses not intended for publication. Also published were two book-length studies, Wang Yigun's *Eugene O'Neill's Career as a Dramatist* and Haiping Liu and Zhu Dongling's *Chinese-American Cultural Dialogue through Drama-- Eugene O'Neill and China,* and two collections of critical essays, one by Chinese authors and one translated from foreign scholars. A source book, *Eugene O'Neill's Ideas on Drama and Theatre,* will be published soon. It is not surprising, therefore, that in the past few years more has been written in China on O'Neill that on any other foreign dramatist, including even Shakespeare.

In terms of theatrical productions also, O'Neill has emerged quickly as the most-favored foreign dramatist in China. No less than ten of his dramas have been staged by professional theatres. Some of them enjoyed different productions by theatres in different cities. *Anna Christie,* for one, within three years had five productions in four cities, including the 1984 Beijing production directed by George White from the Eugene O'Neill Theatre Center of the United States. Most of these performances, such as *Desire under the Elms* in Shenyang, *Mourning Becomes Electra* and *Anna Christie* in Beijing, *Hughie, Marco Millions,* and *The Great God Brown* in Shanghai, and *The Emperor Jones, Beyond the Horizon,* and *Long Day's Journey into Night* in Nanjing, were considered major theatrical events and were therefore shown on television networks to an audience in the millions.

Another instance of Chinese enthusiasm for O'Neill was evidenced in the number of academic conferences held on the American playwright. Within less than two years, three nationwide symposia were convened, in addition to the international conference in Nanjing. The Central Academy of Drama in Beijing hosted the first in February 1987 and the more recent one in December 1988, both of which were directed by Professor Liao Kedui and attended by scholars, senior and young, from all over the country. The other symposium occurred in Tianjin in May 1988; the participants were graduate students majoring in American literature and theatre.

These facts and figures, dull as they may appear, should indicate the unique position O'Neill occupies in China today. However, it would be wrong to assume that his Chinese connection has a history of only ten years. In fact, it can be traced back to the early 1920s, when O'Neill had just established himself as a playwright of some importance in his own country.

The name Eugene O'Neill first appeared in China in an essay surveying the major contemporary American authors and their works in

Xiao-Shou-Yue-Bao (*Fiction Monthly*, Vol. 13, No. 5) in 1922. After some extensive discussion on Sinclair Lewis's *Main Street*, John Dos Passos' *The Three Soldiers*, and Sherwood Anderson's *The Triumph of the Egg*, the essay concludes with an inconspicuous, passing remark on O'Neill: "As far as drama is concerned, the young playwright Eugene O'Neill is very popular and might well be considered the foremost dramatist in the United States today." None of his plays was mentioned, however, and even the name of Eugene O'Neill was spelled out in English, not translated into Chinese.

Again in 1922, a play called *Zhoa, the King of Hell* was produced in Shanghai. It was a close, though concealed, imitation of *The Emperor Jones* in plot, characterization, and style. Hong Shen, who wrote and directed the play and also acted the leading role in it, had studied at Harvard and taken Professor George Pierce Baker's "English 47" course in playwriting. He had seen the American prototype performed on Broadway shortly before he returned to China to become one of its founders of modern theatre. His indebtedness to O'Neill in conceiving the play, however, was not acknowledged until he was challenged years after its publication.

The two odd occasions on which O'Neill made his literary and stage debut in China marked a characteristic beginning of his long and sometimes strained and even treacherous relationship with China. In fact, it took another eight years before any other of his plays was translated into Chinese.

As in the past decade, China was undergoing a most profound cultural and political change in the early decades of the twentieth century. The ancient civil examination system had been abolished. A large number of students were sent abroad, about 20,000 each year, mainly to Japan, the United States, and Europe. Western-style schools and colleges were opened in many Chinese towns and cities. The intellectuals, some of whom had returned from abroad with newly-acquired perspectives, were infuriated to find their motherland in an enervated state at the mercy of imperialist powers. They realized that China could only be reformed and revived through fundamental changes. A vigorous intellectual campaign, later known as "The May 4 Movement," broke out in 1919, challenging the basic values of the traditional culture.

An important aspect of the movement was the attack on the *wenyanwen*, or the classical written language, which had been largely created by about 200 b.c. and was still in use despite its sharp divergence from the everyday speech. Strongly advocated was the use of the *beihuawen*, or spoken language, as a written medium for all purposes of communication. Likewise, the traditional Chinese theatre, which was operatic in nature and whose content and language were far removed from modern life and plain speech, was also under heavy fire. The straight theatre, known as *Huaju* (spoken drama) in Chinese, was introduced from the West, through Japan at first, during the second decade of this century. It developed rapidly in the years that followed, for it was regarded by the activists of the cultural movement as an efficient means to awaken the "benumbed masses," whom they saw as "fast asleep inside an iron house without a window."

Newspapers and magazines devoted much of their space to the translation and discussion of modern European drama both as a "window" to the outside world and as an aid to maturing China's newborn modern theatre. Within seven years (1917-1924) over 170 foreign plays were translated, representing more than seventy European dramatists from seventeen different nations.

However, the intense drive to translate foreign plays began to subside around the mid-1920s, when China's own first generation of modern dramatists had come to the fore. By the end of the 1920s, China had become very selective in introducing foreign writers and their works. It was at about this time that O'Neill paid a visit incognito to China, which, ironically, helped spread his name.

According to an account in a literary magazine called *Xing Yue* (*New Crescent*, Vol. 1, No. 11) in 1929, O'Neill was interviewed several times at his residence in a hotel by a Chinese journalist during his one-month stay in Shanghai in late 1928. The magazine also carried a long article about O'Neill's life and career. This was followed by a number of essays in other journals, which also capitalized on the camouflaged visit to introduce his plays and American drama in general.

The next year, 1930, witnessed the first publication of his plays in Chinese. The book contained all seven one-act plays from the original collection *The Moon of the Caribbees and Six Other Plays of the Sea*. After that, more translations of O'Neill's dramas, including his extra long *Mourning Becomes Electra* and *Strange Interlude*, came out in quick succession.

It would be superficial, however, to assert that the growing Chinese interest in O'Neill was merely curiosity aroused by his mysterious visit. In fact, it had much more to do with the newly discovered relevance young American literature held for China. Commenting on the parallel between the emergence of an independent American literature and the New Culture Movement in China, an editorial in the influential magazine *Xiedai* (*Modern*, Vol. 5, No. 6, 1934) pointed out:

Of all the present-day literatures in the world, the American is the only one, besides that of the Soviet Union, which can be called "modern" in the true sense of the word. . . . Today's U.S. is an example of the possibility of establishing an independent national literature in the 20th century. What a great encouragement it is to our Movement which has cut off all its ties with the past tradition and is struggling to form a new and independent literature.

O'Neill's enthusiasm for the art theatre movement, his experience of transforming various influences into a style of his own rather than sticking to one particular mode or "ism" and his success in lifting American drama from almost nothingness to a level of serious literature with international recognition naturally became fresh sources of inspiration for his Chinese colleagues in their restless search for new directions.

By the end of the 1930s, O'Neill had already been exerting strong influence on Chinese drama and theatre. Beside Hong Shen's *Zhao, the King of Hell*, mentioned before, O'Neill also made his presence felt in such plays as Wang Duching's *Before the National Day* (1928) and Cao Yu's *The Thunderstorm* (1934) and *The Wilderness* (1937). Some O'Neill plays were taught in the classrooms of newly founded drama schools or university English departments. At least five of his plays, namely, *Ile, In the Zone, Before Breakfast, Beyond the Horizon* and *The Emperor Jones*, were mounted on Chinese stages from 1930 to 1936.

In retrospect, there is little doubt that if there had been peace in China from 1937 to 1945, instead of the drawn-out War of Resistance against Japanese aggression, O'Neill would have been even more widely translated, produced, and studied, especially after he won the Nobel Prize for Literature in 1936. But during the eight long years of the national crisis, when works of propaganda rather than of art were demanded, O'Neill and his plays were largely ignored.

However, in December 1941, with war still on the rampage, *Beyond the Horizon* was adapted and performed at Chongqing, the provisional war-time capital. Under its Chinese title *Yao Wang (Look Far into the Distance)*, the adaptation, though set now in a Chinese village, retained much of the original plot and characterization. Two young cousins, one a romantic poet and the other a practical farmer, fall in love with the same girl in the neighborhood. The triangle leads to the mismatch of the poet and the girl and mismanagement of the farm, on the one hand, and the self-imposed exile of the elder cousin, the practical farmer, on the other. The play ends in similar disillusionment in life for all three characters involved. The major alteration made in the Chinese version lies in what it is that lures mankind beyond the horizon. In *Yao Wang*, it is bravery and sacrifice in the distant battlefield, rather than the elusive beauty and meaning over the ocean in the original, that constitute the drama of the poet protagonist. It is also in the army and on the battlefront that the innocent practical farmer loses his simplicity and is corrupted.

Shortly after the war was over in 1945, serious attempts were made to reestablish fruitful ties between O'Neill and China. In spite of the Civil War (1946-1949) that closely ensued, a new translation of *Strange Interlude* was published in book form. The premier of *The Iceman Cometh* on Broadway in October 1946 was soon echoed in China by an article entitled "O'Neill and *The Iceman Cometh.*" The next two years, 1948 and 1949, saw the publication of two different Chinese translations of *Mourning Becomes Electra*, one by Zhu Maixi and one by Huang Wu. The latter is worth some special mention, for it was part of the twenty-volume American Literature Series, a project jointly sponsored by China's National Association of Art and Literature and the United States' Information Service, represented by the famous historian John K. Fairbank. The project, nevertheless, turned out to be ill-fated. No sooner had the series been published than Sino-United States diplomatic ties reached their lowest ebb and the books were left on shelves to gather dust. What was more, the people involved all would suffer greatly for it. Fairbank, it was said, was suspected of being sympathetic with the Chinese Communists and was under investigation in the cold and frenzied years of McCarthyism in the United States. Across the Pacific, the Chinese editors and translators in question were suspected of being "U.S. culture spies" and were interrogated and harassed in numerous political and ideological movements, especially during the years of the so-called Cultural Revolution (1966-1976).

This is to me the background, historical and otherwise, of the international conference *Eugene O'Neill: World Playwright*, which took place at Jinling Hotel in Nanjing on June 6-9, 1988, of the accompanying O'Neill theatre festival, which was extended to Shanghai for another four days, and of the international book exhibit on O'Neill and theatre in general held at the Nanjing University Library concurrent with the conference. Only in such a context, it seems, can we explain the recent outburst of zeal in China for O'Neill and understand the full significance of the centennial celebration in Nanjing, Shanghai, Beijing, and Tianjin.

We are indebted, indeed, to Eugene O'Neill for bringing the United States and the world closer to the Chinese people and the Chinese closer to the United States and the world. We trust it is a right trend, and a right trend will not be reversed. We believe that the days are gone, and gone forever, when people working for international cultural exchanges were suspected and persecuted. We can hope that tensions between China and the United States and other Western countries will not continue for long.

Nanjing University
Nanjing, China

Introduction From the United States

Lowell Swortzell

O'NEILL IN CHINA: A REPORT ON THE CENTENARY CELEBRATION

Visitors arriving in Nanjing on June 5, 1988, recognized at once that the entire city knew why they had come. Glaring at passersby from lampposts, store windows, and any flat surface large enough to hold a poster was the pen-and-ink portrait of a glum, singularly unhappy man. Even so, delegates to the international conference *Eugene O'Neill: World Playwright* were overjoyed to be frowned upon by that familiar (if seldom quite so unpleasant) face. Overhead, bright red banners strung across the wide streets also proclaimed the festival in both Chinese and English. O'Neill had no reason to look so sour because, as all of China and much of the world soon would learn (see *New York Times*, June 13, 1988), scholars and theatre practitioners had come to join their Chinese counterparts, some two hundred altogether, in celebrating the playwright's centenary. With the presence of representatives from Belgium, Great Britain, Japan, West Germany, the Soviet Union, Sweden, India, Hong Kong, and the United States, the next four days would be the most truly international tribute paid O'Neill since he won the Nobel Prize for literature in 1936.

Jointly sponsored by Nanjing University and the Eugene O'Neill Society, the conference consisted of presentations from thirty O'Neill scholars, panel discussions by directors, actors, and designers, performances of four O'Neill plays, and a large exhibition of books and production photographs depicting O'Neill's reception in China since the 1920s. Funding came from as many different places as the participants (who with the help of their respective universities paid their own ways to Nanjing), but with major support contributed by Nanjing

University, the China Fund, Occidental Petroleum, the Amity Foundation, the United Board for Christian Higher Education, Penguin Books, Ltd., Cambridge University Press, and the United States Embassy in Beijing. In every way, the conference was a worldwide cooperative effort.

Throughout his life O'Neill developed his interest in the East by reading about Chinese philosophy, history, and culture, learning which he put to greatest use of course, in *Marco Millions* (1928). He spent a month in Shanghai in 1928, absorbing city life, most particularly that of the local bars. Drunk much of the time and fighting off a nervous breakdown as well as efforts of his wife Carlotta to control him, O'Neill finally was hospitalized. However traumatic his stay (not to mention that of Carlotta, who moved to another hotel after being slapped with his full strength), the playwright's fascination with China remained firm. He later used his income from the Nobel Prize to build his beloved Tao House in California in what he and Carlotta considered the Chinese style; it was here, of course, that he wrote his last great plays.

China first discovered O'Neill in 1922 when novelist Mao Dun in a critical article introduced his early plays. *The Emperor Jones* particularly impressed theatregoers who had never before dealt with expressionism as a theatrical style. Its success paved the way for additional productions of O'Neill plays in the 1920s and 1930s. Prevented by war and later by the political upheaval that long suppressed Western influence in the arts, his plays did not return to Chinese stages until the 1980s. Now, according to Professor Haiping Liu who conceived and organized the conference and recently published a history of O'Neill's impact in China, most of his works have been translated and several have proved popular with theatregoers.

Certainly that was the case in Nanjing, judging from the applause that greeted *Beyond the Horizon, Long Day's Journey into Night,* and *The Emperor Jones,* performed in Chinese, and *Hughie,* played in English by an American company. Performances were held at local theatres before public audiences, eager and appreciative to listen even when there was no air-conditioning in temperatures over 100 degrees Farenheit. While the majority of theatregoers appeared to be of college age, the older generation was also well represented. Reactions to all four plays proved that nuances of humor and attention to detail of characters and situation were understood and fully appreciated, even if the plays were new to the audiences and in two cases quite different in performance from O'Neill's original vision of them.

The Emperor Jones had been given an experimental staging, according to its director Changnian Feng, because he wished in dance, music, and spectacle to reveal Jones' inner world through physical action. His stylized and heavily symbolic mime emphasized the Emperor's intensely frightened psychological state. Instead of the steady drumbeats O'Neill required to create this effect, Feng employed numerous musical variations to show Jones' changing moods as he moved closer and closer to self-destruction. Asked about the surprising amount of sexuality in the production when none is mentioned in the text, the director replied, "Jones is a man on his deathbed, reviewing his life. His sexuality should be seen as his fate, and not taken literally." Other symbols included a witch doctor who holds the secrets of life and death, a fire god standing for desire and power and a recurring image of Jones on a cross. This last was not intended as a Catholic symbol, the director insisted, nor Baptist either (which Jones at one point had been), but as a universal theme: "O'Neill wanted to explore big themes, not specific religious or racist ones." So did the director.

He achieved his desired universality in stark theatrical terms: rope ladders suggesting an impenetrable web from which Jones cannot escape, frequent images of blood, piercing jungle sounds, and a chorus who often changed identities from being O'Neill's "formless fears" to the director's trees, slaves, and torchbearers. Omitting the first and last scenes on the basis that they were too realistic for this production, he turned the play into a ritualistic frenzy which, when it found its primitive origins, thrilled the audience and strikingly fulfilled the director's desire to produce this play in a new way.

Beyond the Horizon, likewise more an adaptation than a translation, was no longer set in New England but transposed to a rural region of China. During rehearsals the company visited the countryside and copied actual hairstyles, dress, and local manners, even how a local farmwife wiped her nose on her sleeve (which in performance proved to be too real and got a loud unintended laugh). Colorful farming practices and household customs became part of the action. Director Guodong Xiong pointed out that his actors were intellectuals for whom playing rural roles was most difficult, especially for Jinming Shi as Robert Mayo, who had to cut off his hair to look like a young farmer. His poetic sensitivity to escape the drudgery for which he was physically and emotionally unsuited provided the production a tragic dimension that overcame the play's obvious, melodramatic view of fatalism. While we rarely felt compassion for his selfish wife or oafish family, we loyally supported Robert's futile dream of salvation, not just because the actor compelled our sympathy but also because we could see in his struggle O'Neill's own battles with responsibility, health (Robert suffers from tuberculosis just as the young playwright did), and the frustrations of being an artist in a hostile, ever-darkening world.

Surprisingly, this production ended on a happy note with a glowing sun rising as Robert dies. When asked if this violated O'Neill's intention, the director replied: "I followed the text. Perhaps there is a problem in translation; the last line is 'Yes, we--,' an unfinished sentence. 'A hopeless hope is finally a hope,' I kept telling the cast."

Such optimism was nowhere apparent in *Long Day's Journey into Night*, as produced by the Drama Theatre of the Nanjing Military Subarea of the People's Liberation Army. This marked the first production of the play in China. Translated but not adapted, the text was played without an intermission and lasted for more than three hours. Presented as a realistic period-piece, the traditional production closely followed O'Neill's demands, drawing strong performances from all four haunted Tyrones. For non-Chinese-speaking viewers familiar with the text, the great speeches emerged with as much fascination as ever, and the tragic power of the play clearly could be felt by everyone, including the Chinese critics who promptly heralded this as O'Neill's greatest work.

Hughie, presented by the Eugene O'Neill Theatre Festival based in California, also was new to China. Professor Liu translated it in 1982 as a dramatic text, putting Erie Smith's Times Square idiom into an appropriate Shanghai dialect he knew from childhood. But still he felt the Chinese would not like the play because it had no action, and he wondered if Americans really liked it either. Then at an O'Neill conference in Boston, he watched a tape of Jason Robards, Jr., as Erie and realized it could be played. And after seeing Stan Weston as Erie and Charles Bouvier as the Night Clerk, he said, "This was reconfirmed tonight. I thank you for bringing *Hughie* to China." Now it seems only a matter of time before a Chinese production follows.

The conference papers covered a wide range of interests from such literary investigations as O'Neill's place in modern tragedy by Yuan Henian and his use of dramatic languages in *The Iceman* and *Long Day's Journey* by Jean Chothia to such comparative studies as that of structures of forgiveness in the endings of *A Moon for the Misbegotten* and Ibsen's *Peer Gynt* by Rolf Fjelde and that of Strindberg's influence on O'Neill's circular structure by Albert E. Kalson and Lisa M. Schwerdt. Of special interest were the large number of papers by Chinese scholars. Yu Zhao explored the difficulties the Chinese have in understanding O'Neill's tragic purposes when his plays end without the problems having been resolved happily. "As Chinese tragedians are concerned about the happiness of man in the present world, all the problems they put forward usually are solved right within the plays," she writes. Obviously, this is not the case in most of O'Neill's work, which must be examined with a new and "unhappy" definition of tragedy. Jinglang, Zhu the director of the Shenyang Theatrical Company and a noted actress as well, spoke on her feelings in preparing *Desire under the Elms* for Chinese audiences. These papers prove that there is more than a problem in translation in introducing O'Neill to Chinese audiences; there are vast cultural differences that must be bridged and explained without losing the integrity of the original work. The concern of Chinese scholars and artists to meet such demands clearly explains the success of O'Neill's plays with Chinese audiences.

Other papers also looked at O'Neill in performance: Betty Jean Jones on directing *A Touch of the Poet* in North Carolina, Egil Tornqvist on Igmar Bergman's staging of *Long Day's Journey* in Stockholm, and Yoshiteru Kurokawa's mounting of *Mourning Becomes Electra* in Japan. My own paper on *The Emperor Jones* as a source of theatrical experimentation from the 1920s until the present examined manifestations of *Jones* in opera, film, and modern dance, as well as significant stage revivals. This was delivered just before we saw the Jiangsu Art Theatre production, which will require a chapter of its own in any future stage history.

The stated goals of the conference were to contribute to the exchange and understanding between Chinese scholars and artists and those from abroad, to enhance the friendship between people, to enliven the academic atmosphere in China, and to vitalize the Chinese theatre. By living and breathing Eugene O'Neill's life and art for four days (often in temperatures over 110 degrees Farenheit it was difficult to breathe at all!), we accomplished that and more. In acknowledging O'Neill's triumphs and failures, we recognized the importance in every country of the dramatist determined to advance the theatre of his age. Little wonder then that the Chinese made O'Neill look so serious on their posters: He symbolizes the hopes for the future of their theatre just as he has for ours, and as he continues to do in his second century.

New York University
New York, New York
United States of America

Brutus Jones, played by Cai Wei, lifted by the "Little Formless Fears" in the Jiangsu Art Theatre production of *The Emperor Jones*, performed as part of *Eugene O'Neill: World Playwright*, June 1988. The play was directed by Feng Changnian and choreographed by Su Shijin. (Courtesy Haiping Liu)

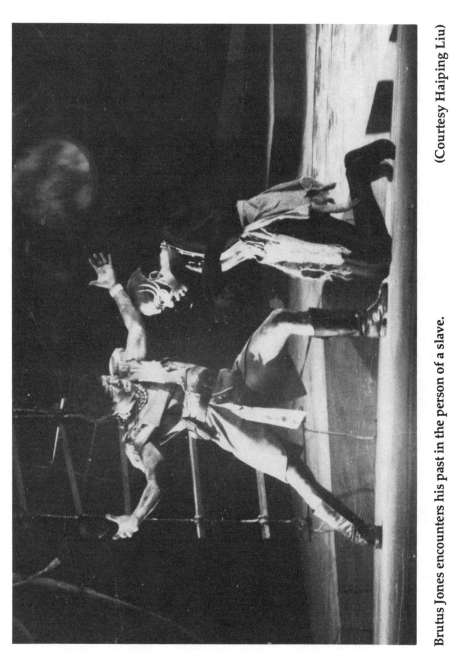

Brutus Jones encounters his past in the person of a slave.

Jones in his flight through the jungle is surrounded by moving trees. Costumes for this production were designed by Hu Fuhua. (Courtesy Haiping Liu)

Typical of the spectacular concept of *The Emperor Jones* is this scene when Jones is literally entrapped in the web of his conscience. Settings were designed by Wang Zhengyang.

(Courtesy Haiping Liu)

Jones stripped of his power nears the end of his flight. Mime for this stylized production was created by Xue Hong and Hu Fuhua. (Courtesy Haiping Liu)

Part One

O'Neill's Philosophic
and Religious Motifs

1

Eugene O'Neill's *Tao Te Ching*: The Spiritual Evolution of a Mystic

Virginia Floyd

"He who comes to understand the Tao at dawn can die peacefully at dusk." (1)

It was at the dawn of his life, in his early formative, most impressionable years, that Eugene O'Neill discovered Taoism. His youthful interest in Lao Tzu was strengthened in later years by reading the works of and about the Chinese sage, and his *Tao Te Ching*, "Tao" meaning the path or "the way of all life, *te*, the fit use of life by men, and *ching*, a text or classic." (2) Evidence shows that Lao Tzu's *Way of Life* influenced both the life and the plays of Eugene O'Neill.

Perhaps the most significant single factor in O'Neill's early life, in that it affected his development personally and dramaturgically, was his rejection at age fifteen of Catholicism, the religious faith he ardently believed in throughout his childhood, a rejection that would ever be linked in his mind and his work to his discovery at that age of his mother's shameful years as a drug addict. She refused to give up morphine despite his prayers to God, and mother betrayal came to be equated in his mind with God betrayal.

What an unhappy, doomed family! Guilt-ridden, the mother holds her husband James responsible, saying his miserliness led him at Eugene's birth to hire a cheap, unskilled doctor who first prescribed the drugs. Little wonder the playwright-son came to believe that family fate is rooted primarily in the past, in one's collective and individual heritage. James O'Neill had not always been wealthy as he was then, as a successful stage actor. While he had known bitter poverty in Ireland in the Great Famine and later as an Irish immigrant laborer in America, his stingy nature contributed to his family's tragedy.

James and Ella O'Neill, because of their Irish Catholic

heritage, sent their son Eugene at age seven away from them to live at a Catholic boarding school that had strict religious teachers. Little wonder Catholicism had pervaded his being by the time he later renounced his faith. He had, by that time, unconsciously absorbed two conflicting strains: first, from rigid religious teaching at Catholic schools came a Jansenistic Irish Puritanism, reinforced by the Calvinistic Puritanism of his New England environment; second, the more personal influence of his parents and their Irish heritage produced in him an Irish mysticism. In *Long Day's Journey into Night* O'Neill called himself a dark, or black, Irishman, defined as a unique person, "set apart from other Irish by his dark hair and eyes, and this mystic nature, which is supposed to put him in close touch with the stuff that dreams, poetry, and tragedy are made on." (3) The dramatist's natural mystical nature was nurtured in later years by his selective reading of and developing understanding of Taoism.

In some respects it was a providential act of fate that led to O'Neill's early rejection of his adolescent concept of Catholicism. For all the years following, subconsciously, he undertakes a spiritual odyssey in his life and work, seeking a substitute for his lost faith. In a number of the major plays, he pits Catholicism against a variety of psychological or spiritual forces, often denigrating his childhood faith, yet never fully relinquishing it for any other. The philosophical and religious stages chronicled in *Days Without End* for a novel's eighteen-year-old college student are identically those of O'Neill at that age when he attended Princeton. In his search to replace a lost faith, the student, like O'Neill, tried "the mysticism of the East. First it was China and Lao Tzu that fascinated him." (4)

It is understandable why O'Neill, like Walt Whitman and that other New England writer, Henry Thoreau, became one of the Chinese philosopher's disciples, attracted as he was particularly to Lao Tzu's creative quietism, which Bynner calls "the fundamental sense commonly inherent in mankind, a commonsense so profound in its simplicity that it has come to be called mysticism." (5) By the very fact he considered the origin of life, Lao Tzu "was a mystic as anyone must be who ventures either a positive or negative guess concerning what is," Bynner stresses, "beyond the mind of man to know." (6) O'Neill, too, used a similar term, one he coined for this concept that he discovered in August Strindberg's *The Ghost Sonata*, calling it a "behind-life force." (7) O'Neill states that to see life is:

to see the transfiguring nobility of tragedy in seemingly the, most ignoble debased lives. And just here is where I am a most confirmed mystic for I am always trying to interpret life in terms of lives, never just in terms of character. I am always acutely conscious of the force behind--fate, God, our biological past creating our present, whatever one calls it--Mystery certainly. (8)

Glimpses of O'Neill's Irish mysticism emerge even in his first one-acts. Rose, at the close of *The Web*, 1913, as she is led off to prison is made "aware of something in the room which none of the others can see--perhaps the personification of the ironic life force that has crushed her." In one of many others, the dying Yank in *Bound East for Cardiff*, 1914, has a vision of a mysterious "pretty lady dressed in Black." In the early full-length Puritan play, *Desire under the Elms*, 1924, the spirit of the dead mother of Eben Cabot, a self-portrait, haunts him and pervades the family farmhouse and is laid to rest only when her son has avenged wrongs done to her. Traditionally, the play is viewed merely as naturalistic with the characters simply pawns locked into physical traits derived from heredity and environment. O'Neill, however, aims for something more through the use of mysticism for a supernaturalism in his plays, enabling viewers to identify also the qualities of soul, of the inner being of characters, perceiving them so deeply on so many levels of meaning that they seem to take on universal and, at times, mythic dimensions.

In O'Neill's early apprenticeship period, 1913-1920, where he makes his first attempts to use mysticism to signify a "behind-life" force, personal happenings in his life, such as his sea experiences, become the focus of his one-acts. In the 1920s he looked beyond the self and responded to an inner impulse for social justice, focusing on two serious problems. First, he was outraged by the indifferent, cruel consequences of capitalism, the economic system that exploits, dehumanizes, and impoverishes the workers, and by those in government who ignored the needs of the poor. He expressed his indignation in a number of plays from *The Hairy Ape* to *Long Day's Journey into Night*. It is possible he compared this Capitalist system to the political doctrine of Taoists, which maintains that the duty of the ruler is to protect his people from experiencing material wants and to impose a minimum of government.

O'Neill believed ardently in the equality and brotherhood of man. He vehemently denounced the racial discrimination by whites against people of other races, against blacks particularly in the 1920s. He was distressed by his countrymen's total disregard of the humanity, dignity, and rights of those they considered inferior. In Taoism, in contrast, no laws govern correct behavior. "Men's conduct depends on instinct and conscience. [Their] own gentle kind way of life suggests to neighbors how natural, easy, and happy a condition it is for men to be members of one another." (9)

To expose and attack racism, O'Neill wrote three plays between 1918 and 1923 that have black characters (*The Dreamy Kid*, *The Emperor Jones*, and *All God's Chillun Got Wings*), and conceived a number of ideas in the 1920s for others. In 1929, two years after he sailed to Shanghai on the *Andre Lebon*, he noted an idea for a play called "Unchartered Sea," which would depict the romance between a beautiful young woman, apparently Chinese, of the East and an American poet from the West. They are viewed as pariahs by the prejudiced bourgeoisie. O'Neill writes of "the conflict of races on board, the trend of the races of the world struggle today, the essential characteristics, the awakening of the East to the West." After a shipwreck at sea, he notes the two are willingly "left behind--the extra boat--the island--regeneration and happiness--the ships go by and they never signal." (10) O'Neill had perhaps a personal as well as a social motivation for attacking any type of discrimination. He himself had been forced to endure prejudice, for his own Irish family suffered cruel ostracism because of their Celtic nationality and Irish Catholic religion and were disdained by wealthy Yankee New Englanders in his hometown of New London.

O'Neill was aware that the discrimination problem had broad ethnic dimensions, cutting across cultural, racial, religious, and geographical lines. Invariably, he depicts nonwhites, non-Christians, and non-Europeans as morally, spiritually, and/or physically superior. For example, one of O'Neill's ideas in his 1918-1920 notebook, entitled "Reincarnation," states: "Idea for long play--reincarnation--oldest civilization, China 1850 (?)--modern times during war--South Sea Island, 1975--same crises offering a definite choice of either material (i.e. worldly) success or a step toward higher spiritual plane--Failure in choice entails immediate reincarnation and eternal repetition in life on this plane until spiritual choice is made." (11)

Ethnic confrontation appears again in two historical dramas of the early 1920s. In *The Fountain*, 1921, among the Spanish about to sail with Columbus in 1492 is Juan Ponce de Leon, desiring "to conquer for Spain that immense realm of the Great Kaan which Marco saw." In the New World that's discovered, Juan is horrified when the Spanish "Knights of the True Cross" beat and enslave innocent Indians and monks torture the natives to convert them to Catholicism. Rather than riches, Juan seeks and finds the mysterious "Spring of Life," the "Fountain of Beauty," from which four religious figures spring, one of whom is the Chinese poet who originated the tale of the fountain's healing power. The four priests, representing all faiths, are equal, demonstrating that all dreams of God are but one dream. Juan experiences this ecumenical mystical experiencing, feeling unity with all creation only after undergoing suffering and a personal inner regeneration.

In a second historical play, *Marco Millions*, 1925, set in the thirteenth century, Marco Polo, an ignoble Old World representative of the Catholic Pope is sent to Cathay to the Great Kaan when no requested wise man can be found in the West. With his spiritual hump, Marco, who is perhaps the most amoral, insensitive character in O'Neill's vast gallery of materialists, symbolizes the rapacious American capitalist. O'Neill called Polo Brothers and Son "my American pillars of society."

In the 1923 scenarios, the Great Kaan, one of O'Neill's noblest and wisest creations and a man engaged in a relentless quest for a spiritual absolute, has, when the Polos arrive, "completed the conquests laid down for him--only the West remains--He is too weary and disillusioned with power, has become a disciple of Taoist mysticism." A second Tao reference found in the notes was also omitted. O'Neill described the fifth stage of the Polos' original journey to the East, stating: "Lao Tzu (China) Cambaluc." In the final version of the play Confucian, Taoist, Buddhist, and Moslem priests accompany the bier bearing the Kaan's beloved granddaughter. In early notes a Nestorian Christian rather than a Confucian priest is used. O'Neill's omission of the Confucian probably indicates he preferred the mystical ethics and values of Lao Tzu's Taoism "rather than the practical proprieties of Confucius." (12) The Kaan in the final version speaks: "Priest of Tao, will you conquer death by your mystic way?" The Priest replies: "Which is the greater evil, to possess or to be without? Death is." After urging all in his court to pray, the Kaan prays, too, saying, "rest in peace."

Observe O'Neill's threefold attack in *Marco Millions*. First, what is berated here is not a vague Christianity but a Catholicism that is corrupted and reduced to opportunism, hypocrisy, and exploitation against a superior Eastern religion. Second, the deeply flawed Marco is, to the Kaan, the living symbol of the arrested development of Western civilization. Third, in early notes the Kaan "sees the East as partially redeemed by its hard-won culture but the West seems to have no culture or to have destroyed it."

O'Neill claims to have used for his research the hero's actual account of his adventures, *The Travels of Marco Polo*. In a summer 1923 letter he states: "Am reading and taking millions of notes" from this book among others. The dramatist, however, found Marco's book to be "defective in Chinese manners and peculiarities. Associations in China were chiefly with foreigners."

Just as research and work on *The Fountain* probably provided inspiration for *Marco Millions*, the latter seems to have given O'Neill the idea for a drama on the "Career of Shih Huang Ti, Emperor of China, whose rule ended in 201 B.C." Both plays reveal O'Neill's interest in the merits of Taoism versus Confucianism and the rule of despots, men like Marco and Shih Huang Ti, as opposed to that of enlightened, benevolent Emperors like Kublai Kaan. (13)

In the period when O'Neill sought a replacement for his lost faith, he turned to and found a meaning for existence in Lao Tzu. The Chinese mystic and his *Way of Life* continued to influence the author in the early 1920s, while he was recording notes for plays made prior to the period of his early research in 1925 for the projected work on Shih Huang Ti. Recording new information on Taoism, O'Neill became fascinated by the female and male forces, the *yin* and *yang* principles, as they related to Taoism and by the way Lao Tzu "fused mysticism and pragmatism into a philosophy" through "which he believed all men could discover their lives to be peaceful, useful and happy." (14)

O'Neill planned to depict not only the public life of Shih Huang Ti but also his personal familial conflicts--"his identity of the past with his mother," who for autobiographical purposes is described as a "singing girl," musical as had been Ella O'Neill, for whom the Emperor has incestuous feelings. Formerly called Cheng, Shih Huang Ti, or "First Sovereign Lord," in a nine-year period concluding in 221 b.c. conquered the six independent states and unified China. Because the conquered Chous ruled by virtue of fire, the new rulers, the Ch'ins, "must from mystic necessity rule by virtue of water, the element that destroys fire." (15) The Emperor becomes obsessed by the desire to build and uses masses of chained convicts to construct 670 palaces and numerous roads; over 700,000 castrated convicts are doomed to spend their lives building the Emperor's mausoleum, a 22-square-mile tomb, guarded by the 550 life-sized terra-cotta warriors and horses archaeologists in Xian have already excavated.

Because of his heinous crimes, the Emperor was afraid to die. Early in his reign he had sent an expedition of 3,000 young boys and girls to search for the drug of immortality on the "mystic island of P'eng lai." Just before he dies, he asks his magicians again about "the wonder-island" (16) on the edge of the world where the plant of immortality grew. Years after the Emperor's death, Chang Tao-lin, an alchemist of the second century, was reputed to have discovered the drug of immortality after receiving magical power from Lao Tzu. Although O'Neill never completed a scenario for "The Play of Shih Huang Ti," he continued his exploration of Taoism, working sporadically on this material over a nine-year period, from 1925 to 1934.

Three years later, in 1937, O'Neill and his wife built a new home in California and called it Tao House, not only because of the special influence Lao Tzu and Taoism exerted on the author's work and because of the profound and lasting effect of Taoism on O'Neill's inner being but also, as he was in the late 1930s entering his last and greatest creative period, because of his hope to continue and deepen the mystical "Way of Life" conducive to the spirit of Lao Tzu. The O'Neills "placed four wrought-iron symbols from Chinese calligraphy that spelled Tao House" on the courtyard's doorway and had a brick wall built behind the house that "twisted and wound--in observance of the Chinese proverb that evil moves only in a straight line." (17)

Years later when the O'Neills moved east to New York, the dramatist's good friend, Hamilton Basso, visited their penthouse in the east eighties in 1948 and described it in a subsequent article: "It is furnished with things O'Neill has gathered all over the world. The dominant note is Chinese. A small, heavy, vaguely catlike stone animal, turned out by a Chinese sculptor a few centuries before Christ, greets visitors as they enter, and there are ancient Chinese prints on the walls of the living room." (18) These furnishings are merely trappings, that is true, but through them O'Neill may possibly have externalized the feelings of inner peace that Taoism gave him, the quietism that brought him patience, forbearance, and fortitude, particularly later in life in his last lonely suffering years.

Something magical seemed to happen to O'Neill when he moved into Tao House. In 1939 he put aside the massive eleven-play historical cycle and conceived his three greatest plays--all containing varying degrees of mysticism, all confessional dramas based entirely on his family and friends: *The Iceman Cometh, Long Day's Journey into Night,* and *A Moon for the Misbegotten,* O'Neill's memorable memory plays. By the time he reached this last creative period, from 1939 to 1943, physical and mental travails and his years of deep introspection and Taoist quietude had tempered his soul.

There is much of O'Neill in the old "foolosopher" of *The Iceman Cometh,* Larry Slade, who has a gaunt Irish face and "a mystic's meditative pale-blue eyes." His face has "the quality of a pitying but weary old priest." O'Neill identified strongly with Larry, saying his "favorite bit" in all his plays is Larry's third-act "let me live" speech. The play, which rivals *Long Day's Journey into Night* for the distinction of his greatest work, is O'Neill's loving tribute to many lifelong friends he made during his down-and-out drinking days in New York. The play abounds with meaningful religious connotations but is most memorable for the value it sets on the brotherhood of man, on the deep need of each for the other or, as Lao Tzu states, "how natural, easy and happy condition it is for men to be members of one another."

Long Day's Journey into Night tells the searing brutal tale of the four tormented Tyrones, who love but also hate and ruthlessly try to destroy each other. The two most alike, Mary and her younger son Edmund, have had mystical experiences, which they describe in the play. A drug addict the past twenty-four years, wretchedly injecting morphine into her body, Mary has discovered her own version of Lao Tzu's quietism and mystic contemplation. Yet at one time in the early spring of her life before disillusionment set in, she had a girlish dream of dedicating herself to a life of prayer as a nun. She recalls a vision she had while praying in Lourdes when the Virgin smiled and blessed her with consent. She remembers this in her last speech of the play when she has entered the long night in a narcotic trance, to the horror of the three Tyrone men. She reminds them of what she had once been and now knows, after these many years, how to torment them, implying by the very fact of her condition what each has contributed to her situation.

Edmund, in his most memorable mystic experience, had been bound for Buenos Aires on a Squarehead square-rigger: he became drunk on the beauty of the sea, lost in the rhythmic harmony of the flow of life and, perhaps for the only time in his life, he says, he belonged to something greater than his own life, perhaps even to God. Later he describes a veil being drawn back by an unseen hand that provides a vision of beatitude that allows him for a brief second to see the secret and its meaning.

Here stands the real Eugene O'Neill, sharing perhaps the great climactic mystic experience of his life. How feeble they seem in retrospect--those first faltering steps in the early plays as he sought for his characters the consolation of a benign "behind-life" mystic force in their lives. Only here in this scene in *Long Day's Journey into Night*, with these soaring profound words that are so obviously the author's own, is it at last possible to discover O'Neill's mystical spiritual evolution. Here in this play there is only confrontation of the self-- awareness and understanding. Yet it ends with each character locked in solitary aloneness and the despair of the soul's dark night; forgiveness does not come until it is painfully atoned for in *A Moon for the Misbegotten*.

There were times in 1943 when he was working on *A Moon for the Misbegotten* that O'Neill was so ill he could write only a page a day. He endured all the pain to complete this loving requiem for his brother Jamie, which is set in September 1923, two months before his death. The Irish Hogans, Phil and Josie, lend the play much of its broad Celtic humor, but it is mainly a tale of repentance and redemption.

Jamie, or Jim as he is called in this play, unfortunately betrayed his dead mother, desecrating her memory while accompanying her body home to New London on a long five-day train ride, fortified with a case of bourbon with a blond whore for company. Like his brother Eugene, he has gone to strict Catholic schools; he is now guilt-ridden and seeks to confess his sin against his mother and be forgiven by the symbolic Earth Mother figure, Josie Hogan. The entire play resembles a mystical meditation, for, after Jim's confession, the mother's spirit is felt in the moonlight, as Josie says, "I feel . . . her soul wrapped in it like a silver mantle and I know she understands and forgives." Jim does feel a blessed peace, "as if all my sins had been forgiven." O'Neill himself, vicariously, through Josie bestows a final absolution on his brother: "May you rest forever in forgiveness and peace."

Tragically, ten years later, days before his own death, O'Neill sought the consolation he bestowed on Jamie. He made a telephone call to a Catholic rectory, identified himself, and said, "I would like to see a priest." When the priest arrived, he, like the one who tried two days earlier to see O'Neill, was told by O'Neill's wife in a vicious act of cruelty, "There was a mistake." The final irony: he who had spent his creative years giving his gallery of characters a satisfying faith, in his words, "to find a meaning for life in, and to comfort the fears of death with," (19) was left to die without spiritual consolation.

What he had absorbed in his heart and soul in the noble life he had lived, harming no man, doing good for all, would comfort him in his last lucid moments, whether it was the simple "Our Father" he once put on the lips of the dying Dion Anthony and William Brown in *The Great God Brown* or whether it was the *Tao Te Ching*, Lao Tzu's mystic *Way of Life*. There was no fear in this soul's mystic meeting with the Absolute-- neither in life nor in death. "He who comes to understand the Tao at dawn can die peacefully at dusk."

NOTES

1. A. E. Grantham, *Hills of Blue* (London: Methuen and Co., Ltd., 1927), 6.

2. Lao Tzu, *The Way of Life*, translated by Witter Bynner (New York: G. P. Putnam's Sons, 1980), 9.

3. Hamilton Basso, "Profiles: The Tragic Sense--III," *New Yorker*, 13 March 1948: 37.

4. Eugene O'Neill, *Days Without End*, in his *The Plays of Eugene O'Neill* (New York: Modern Library, 1955), 3: 503.

5. Lao Tzu, 12.

6. Lao Tzu, 20.

7. Eugene O'Neill, "Strindberg and Our Theatre," used in a

Provincetown Playbill for *The Spook Sonata*, 3 January 1924, in *O'Neill and His Plays*, eds. Oscar Cargill, N. Bryllion Fagin, and William J. Fisher (New York: New York University Press, 1961), 108.

8. Eugene O'Neill, "A Letter to Arthur Hobson Quinn," in *O'Neill and His Plays* 125.

9. Lao Tzu, 8.

10. Virginia Floyd, *Eugene O'Neill at Work: Newly Released Ideas for Plays* (New York: Frederick Ungar Publishing Co., 1981), 210.

11. Floyd, *Eugene O'Neill at Work*, 32.

12. Lao Tzu, 11.

13. Virginia Floyd, *The Plays of Eugene O'Neill: A New Assessment* (New York: Frederick Ungar Publishing Co., 1985), 302.

14. Lao Tzu, 20.

15. Grantham, 46.

16. At the same time O'Neill was making extensive notes for the "Career of Shih Huang Ti" in May and July 1929, he was also working on *Mourning Becomes Electra*. Grantham's references to the "mystic island of P'eng lai" and the "wonder-islands" may have inspired O'Neill's description of the "blessed isles"--the elusive, desired refuge of all the Mannons in the New England trilogy.

17. Louis Sheaffer, *O'Neill: Son and Artist* (Boston: Little, Brown & Co., 1973), 472.

18. Basso, 42.

19. Barrett H. Clark, *Eugene O'Neill: The Man and His Plays* (New York: Dover, 1947), 120.

2

Eugene O'Neill and Puritanism

Marcus Konick

God and religion haunt the plays of Eugene O'Neill. This is no accident. Writing to George Jean Nathan, the playwright says that *Dynamo* "will dig at the roots of the sickness of today as I feel it--the death of the old God and failure of science and materialism to give any satisfactory new one for the surviving primitive religious instinct to find a meaning for life in, and to comfort its fears of death with. It seems to me that anyone trying to do big work nowadays must have this big subject behind all the little subjects of his plays or novels, or he is scribbling around the surface of things." (1)

But O'Neill's attitude toward God is ambivalent. It is expressed in the autobiographical role of Edmund in *Long Day's Journey* when he cites Nietzsche that God is dead. Later he says pantheistically that he was set free, dissolved in the sea, and became white sails and flying spray and that he belonged to something greater than his own life, to life itself, even to God. As Judith Barlow puts it, "From the earliest sea plays we find O'Neill's characters, by virtue of their humanness, out of rhythm with a world more suited--in Edmund's words--to seagulls and fish." (2)

No wonder that against that ecstatic vision the creeds of the religions O'Neill encountered seemed false, stilted, and deformed. The eyes of the church in *All God's Chillun Got Wings* are closed blindly against the prejudice that divides the black and white ghettos. Yank is ignored by the white churchgoers on Fifth Avenue in *The Hairy Ape* as if he did not exist.

Although O'Neill personally forsook his native Irish Catholicism at the age of fifteen, religion was seldom out of his consciousness, whether Catholicism, Puritanism, Protestantism, the Salvation Army, or Taoism. Moreover, his characters are invariably

14   Marcus Konick

measured against strict moral standards and punished in accordance with them. The origins of this code are to be found in ancient Greek drama, Catholicism, and Puritanism alike.

O'Neill expresses a wide range of attitudes toward Christianity. Catholicism comes off best, providing the only vital standard religious experiences in his works, despite such criticism as Melody's of Nora in *A Touch of the Poet*, when he damns her priests for talking about her sin, and the description of the three nobles in *The Fountain* as "cruel, courageous to recklessness, practically uneducated--knights of the true Cross, ignorant of and despising every first principle of Christianity."(III 383) Nevertheless, Mary yearns for the peace she feels only the Virgin can give her in *Long Day's Journey into Night*, and Tyrone reminds her that because she has flouted her faith in the Catholic Church she has suffered nothing but self-destruction. John Loving in *Days Without End* describes the parents in his novel thus: "They were both devout Catholics. . . . But not the ignorant, bigoted sort, please understand. No, their piety had a genuine, gentle, mystic quality to it. . . . And their God was One of Infinite Love--not a stern, self-righteous Being Who condemned sinners to torment, but a very human, lovable God Who became man for love of men and gave His life that they might be saved from themselves."(I 510) Loving's priestly uncle is the only sympathetic portrait of a clergyman in the entire O'Neill canon.

Protestantism on the other hand comes in for little but criticism. The "Sallies" of the Salvation Army are never treated with anything but contempt, as in *Anna Christie, All God's Chillun Got Wings,* and *The Hairy Ape*. In *The Iceman Cometh* Hickey says, "Ministers' sons are sons of guns," and Larry satirizes prayer for a few more moments of life. (I 709) In *The Hairy Ape* the Protestant minister is named Dr. Caiaphas, the priest who presided at the trial of Christ. St. John Ervine summarizes the attitude: "A man has only to mention that he is a Methodist minister to receive the entire contents of Mr. O'Neill's vast vials of wrath. The Rev. Hutchins Light, in an incoherent piece, *Dynamo*, catches it severely, and a minister's son, Theodore Hickman, the protagonist of *The Iceman Cometh*, rails against his father as if he were the original owner of horns and hooves." (3)

Puritanism is portrayed as critical, loveless, joyless, and eternally frigid. Ervine says, "Mr. O'Neill is as puritanical as Mr. Shaw, but his puritanism, unlike Mr. Shaw's, unlike Milton's, unlike Andrew Marvell's, has no grace or geniality. It is sour stuff and makes a Pilgrim Father, in comparison with Mr. O'Neill, seem a blood relative of Sir Toby Belch. Yet no one denounces puritans so frequently and so ferociously as Mr. O'Neill who spits and spews upon their tombs as if they had done him personal injury." (4)

Although this somewhat overstates the case, it has some truth. But the origins of asceticism and strict morality and intolerance can be found in both Catholicism and Puritanism. However, for purposes of this paper, we must distinguish between the two sources. The Catholic influence is associated with the crucifix, the Virgin Mary and the saints, confession and forgiveness, the procreational duty of woman, and love as the prime divine attribute. On the other hand, Puritanism is seen as dour, Bible-quoting, self-righteous, frigid, unforgiving, and joyless. This puritanical concept is expressed most clearly perhaps in *Desire under the Elms*:

CABOT.   (*Raising his arms to heaven with fury he can no longer control*) Lord God o' Hosts, smite the undutiful sons with Thy wust cuss!

EBEN.   (*Breaking in violently*) Yew 'n' yewr God! Allus cussin' folks--allus naggin' 'em!

CABOT.   (*Oblivious to him--summoningly*) God o' the old! God o' the lonesome!

EBEN.   (*mockingly*) Naggin' His sheep t'sin! T'hell with yewr God! (III 227)

and later:

CABOT.   God's hard, not easy! . . . I kin feel I be in the palm o' His hand, His fingers guidin' me. (III 236)

O'Neill recognizes, however, that such hardness is not the exclusive characteristic of Protestants. In *A Moon for the Misbegotten* he describes Mike Hogan thus: "He never forgets that he is a good Catholic, faithful to all the observances, and so is one of the elite of Almighty God in a world of damned sinners composed of Protestants and bad Catholics. In brief, Mike is a New England Irish Catholic Puritan, Grade B, and an extremely irritating youth to have around." (5) Hogan later describes his wife's family: "The rest of them was a pious lousy lot. They wouldn't dare put food in their mouths before they said grace for it. They was too busy preaching temperance to have time for a drink. They spent so much time confessing their sins, they had no time to do any sinning." (6) It is this broader definition of Puritanism, whether Catholic or Protestant, set in the New England environment, which we shall employ in this paper.

What is the source of this antipathy toward Puritans? Perhaps it can be found in O'Neill's youth in New London, Connecticut. Arthur and Barbara Gelb point out that the Yankee aristocracy of the town, such as the Chappells, considered "the O'Neills as something not far above riffraff. Their attitude was due to the unsavory combination of James's shanty Irish background, his career as a 'road' actor, and his unpretentious mode of living." (7) Mrs. E. Chappell Sheffield said, "we associated the Irish automatically with the servant class." (G 95) Ella's drug addiction made matters worse. Although she lived in New London for thirty years, the women never called upon her. Further, because of Eugene O'Neill's friends and relations with the "seamstresses" of the Bradley Street red-light district and his brother's drinking, one local girl was warned, "The O'Neill boys are terrible. They're drunk and dissolute."(G 92) This was reflected in *Ah, Wilderness!*, *Abortion*, and many other plays in which the protagonist is concerned lest his peccadillos make him unfit to associate with decent girls: "The insult rankled: otherwise O'Neill could not have written so virulently of--for example--Cornelius Melody's hatred for the Yankees who snubbed him." (G 92) The Chappells became the Chatfields in *Long Day's Journey into Night*; the Harknesses, whose estate, Waterford, he considered to represent "the power of Mammon," became the Harkers in *Long Day's Journey into Night*, Harder in *A Moon for the Misbegotten*, and Harford in *A Touch of the Poet*.(G 91-92) (8) In addition, "His austere view of New England owed something to the stories Robert Edmond Jones used to tell of his grim New Hampshire background." He described New England as "violent, passionate, sensual, sadistic, lifted, heated, frozen." (9)

Within O'Neill's own family, to adopt his broader definition of Puritanism, his spinster aunt, Lil Brennan, "often protested to Ella and James that Eugene's reading should be censored."(G 82) In *Ah, Wilderness!* Richard's parents are concerned about this. In *The First Man* O'Neill shows his relatives as "capable of judging others only by the standards of their own limited experience, and by petty pride and stultifying conventionality."(G 93)

Puritanical beliefs are matters of concern throughout O'Neill's plays. Basic is a belief in original sin, defined not theologically as the fall of Adam and Eve, but as procreation. Judith Barlow says, "O'Neill's plays demonstrate little faith in the power of God's grace to make the individual whole again, but the concept of original sin informs them all." (10) So the children are blamed for their mothers' problems, as Edmund is for his mother's drug addiction in *Long Day's Journey into Night*, initiated at his birth. Hogan, in *A Moon for the Misbegotten*, tells his son, "When I think your poor mother was killed bringing that crummy calf into life! (*Vindictively.*) I've never set foot in a church since, and never will." (11) The concept invades *Mourning Becomes Electra* when Lavinia recognizes her sins, she says, "It takes the Mannons to punish themselves for being born!"(II 178)

Suffering and self-sacrifice were virtues in the Puritan mind, born of this sense of original sin as well as the sin of the individual. The connection is made in *Strange Interlude,* when Nina says, "You must give his wife courage, Doctor. You must free her from her feeling of guilt!" and Darrell replies, "There can only be guilt when one deliberately neglects one's manifest duty to life." (III 86-87) He says of Nina, "She's got to find normal objects for her craving for sacrifice." (III 37) Ephraim in *Desire under the Elms* says, "Mebbe they's easy gold in the West but it hain't God's gold. It hain't fur me. I kin hear His voice warnin' me agen t'be hard an' stay on my farm." (I 268) The women in the poor Yankee families, like Ephraim's wife and like Con Melody's in *A Touch of the Poet* while Con seeks to imitate the Yankee grandees, consider it their duty to work themselves to death. It penetrates to even non-Puritans like Jim in *All God's Chillun Got Wings* who feels it is his duty to support the prejudiced wife who hates him.

Under such circumstances, joy is subject to suspicion. In *Mourning Becomes Electra* Christine tells Lavinia: "Puritan maidens shouldn't peer too inquisitively into Spring! Isn't beauty an abomination and love a vile thing?" (II 145) Joy is often considered pagan, and Dion in *The Great God Brown* says, "Be born! Awake! Dissolve into dew--into silence --into night--into earth--into space--into peace--into meaning--into joy --into God--into the Great God Pan!" (I 267) Caligula in *Lazarus Laughed* cries, "Pleasure is dirty and joyless! Or we who seek it are."(III 351) Hickey, son of a minister and false Messiah, seeks to destroy what little joy remains in their illusions for the besotted denizens of Hope's Bar in *The Iceman Cometh.* He brings only tension, disillusionment, and death.

According to this thinking, death is the goal of life. In *Mourning Becomes Electra*, Mannon says, "That's always been the Mannon way of thinking. They went to the white meeting-house on Sabbaths and meditated on death. Life was a dying. Being born was starting to die." (II 54) The Mannon house participates in this grim view, and Christine says, "Each time I come back after being away, it appears more like a sepulchre! The 'whited' one of the Bible--pagan temple stuck like a mask on Puritan gray ugliness."(II 17)

To survive in such an environment, one must be hard-bitten and stubborn. Such is Captain Bartlett in *Gold* and *Where the Cross Is Made.* He cries, "I be sailin' out as I planned I would in spite of all hell!" (II 691) Captain Keeney in *Ile* is of the same breed. Of Ephraim Cabot in

Desire under the Elms, Natanson writes, "This old Methodist farmer is tough, and he invests his egotism and ruthlessness with religious motives. . . . Protestant fanaticism--with his special flavor of the Old Testament--permeates even the love scenes." (12)

Despite protestations of humility, pride infects these Yankees. In ancient Greek, Catholic, and Protestant theology it is the root of all sins. In O'Neill it is rigorously punished. Dion in *The Great God Brown* says, "But pride is a sin--even in a memory of the long deceased! Blessed are the poor in spirit!" (I 287) In *Dynamo* Reuben becomes drunk on the power of electricity and on his own mission, seeing himself as "the new saviour who will bring happiness and peace to men!" (II 477) He dies before the machine he worships. John Loving, who in his pride has committed adultery out of self-love and self-hate, dies at the foot of the cross. Lavinia, in *Mourning Becomes Electra*, who has taken upon herself the right to cause murder in the name of justice, loses her mother, brother, and lover and is condemned to the convent of her Puritan mansion. Brutus Jones is destroyed by his usurpation of power. In *The Hairy Ape* Yank pridefully refuses to heed the warning whistle of the engineer to get back to work and threatens to kill him, only to find the white wraith of Mildred before him. As a kind of avenging "angel," she drives him to challenge an indifferent world and be strangled by a gorilla. In O'Neill pride indeed leads to destruction.

O'Neill attacks the puritans as sterile. Mrs. Harford, Emma in *Diff'rent*, the cloistering of Lavinia in *Mourning Becomes Electra*, and Nina's second, passionless marriage in *Strange Interlude* are examples. The Gelbs say that "O'Neill's interest in this type of woman was heightened and influenced by the Lizzie Borden case. Miss Borden, an allegedly extreme example of the repressed New England spinster, was charged with the hatchet murder of her father and stepmother." (*G* 437) O'Neill and his friends often discussed the case.

But lust also plays its role. The rivalry of Christine and Lavinia for Brant's love, the love of Cabot's third wife for his son, and the lust of Cabot himself and of Abraham Bentley in *The Rope* for their pretty young wives prove that the blood of Puritans can run hot. Eben Cabot defends his affair with the town's prostitute by saying, "By God A'mighty, she's purty, an' I don't give a damn how many sins she's sinned afore mine or who she's sinned 'em with, my sin's as purty as any one on 'em!" (III 311) Josie in *A Moon for the Misbegotten* is torn between virginity and profligacy. Laszlo, commenting on the reception of the plays, says, "Freudianism was welcome to the souls that had been withered by puritanism." (13)

Yankees are shown as money-grubbing. This is of course fused in

O'Neill's mind with memory of his miserly father. Ephraim Cabot is so viewed by his children, Captain Bartlett in *Gold* and *Where the Cross Is Made* is driven insane by desire for treasure, though his wife warns him against it. Joel, in *More Stately Mansions*, tells his money-hungry brother, "I want to warn you against the growing unscrupulousness with which you take advantage of others' misfortunes." (14) And Simon says, "Father had scruples. He disguised his greed with Sabbath potions of God-fearing unction at the First Congregationalist Church." (15) Captain Keeney's desire for *Ile* results in his wife's breakdown. In *A Touch of the Poet* Mrs. Harford gives her family history, telling how they made a large fortune out of privateering and the slave trade, which climaxed their long battle to escape enslavement by actually enslaving themselves. Thus even the Puritan struggle for freedom and democracy is tarnished. There are no other references in all of O'Neill's work to the indebtedness of America to the Puritans for their positive contributions.

However O'Neill attacked Puritanism, he still used its standards to measure and punish his characters. This has been amply illustrated. But it is worth noting that sometimes he even introduces characters solely or primarily to establish the Puritan ethic by which the others will be judged. Such is Mike Hogan who, after the caustic introduction previously cited, is never seen again. So also is Joel in *More Stately Mansions*, except for casting a leering glance at Sara.

Both Catholicism and Puritanism urge confession as a condition upon which any forgiveness is given. Anna Christie is forced to confess her prostitution but must be cloistered for a year, awaiting the return of her forgiving fiance and father. Hickey confesses the murder of his wife and goes to his trial. John Loving atones and is forgiven by Elsa. The confessions of Josie and Jim in *A Moon for the Misbegotten* result in peace, if not fulfillment. In *Strange Interlude* Nina exclaims: "I've wanted to run home and 'fess up, tell how bad I've been, and be punished! Oh, I've got to be punished, Charlie, out of mercy for me, so I can forgive myself." (III 44) Orin, in *Mourning Becomes Electra*, tells his sister, "Were you hoping you could escape retribution? You can't! Confess and atone to the full extent of the law! That's the only way to wash the guilt of our mother's blood from our souls!"(II 152)

O'Neill found the Puritan concept of pairs of contrasts congenial to him. (16) His characters are haunted by conflicts of long-suffering virtue and self-indulgent sin; of self-sacrificing humility and service to others as opposed to egotism and pride: of indulgence in sloth, sex, drink, drugs, and illusion as contrasted with strict ethical principles. In these conflicts the devil is always defeated. Men are driven to their knees by an avenging God; but to those who confess and atone for their sins, providing those sins are not mortal, he will grant purgatory and hope of eventual redemption. But the punishments will be strictly appropriate. These antitheses are played out against the greatest conflict of all, O'Neill's search for a loving God of joy, in combat with his puritanical Catholic obsession with a stern God of justice.

NOTES

1. Doris V. Falk, *Eugene O'Neill and the Tragic Tension* (New Brunswick, N.J.: Rutgers University Press, 1958), 128.

2. Judith E. Barlow, *Final Acts* (Athens, Georgia: University of Georgia Press, 1985), 106.

3. St. John Ervine, "Counsels of Despair," *Eugene O'Neill's Critics: Voices from Abroad*, eds. Horst Frenz and Susan Tuck (Carbondale and Edwardsville, Ill.: Southern Illinois Press, 1984), 80.

4. Ervine, 80.

5. Eugene O'Neill, *A Moon for the Misbegotten*, in *Best American Plays, Fourth Series, 1951-1957*, ed. John Gassner (New York: Crown Publishers, 1958), 135.

6. O'Neill, *Moon*, 139.

7. Arthur and Barbara Gelb, *O'Neill* (New York: Harper and Row, 1962), 94. (Subsequently cited in text as *G* with page number.)

8. Cf. Louis Sheaffer, *O'Neill: Son and Artist* (Boston: Little, Brown & Co., 1973).

9. Sheaffer, 130.

10. Barlow, 106.

11. O'Neill, *Moon*, 136.

12. Wojcieck Natanson, "O'Neill's Comeback," *Eugene O'Neill's Critics: Voices From Abroad*, 119.

13. B. Nagy Laszlo, "The O'Neill Legend," *Eugene O'Neill's Critics: Voices from Abroad*, 124.

14. Eugene O'Neill, *More Stately Mansions*, shortened from the author's partly revised script by Karl Ragner Gierow and edited by George Gallup (London: Jonathan Cape, 1960), 79.

15. O'Neill, *Mansions*, 105.

16. Laszlo, 124.

3

Iceman and *Journey, Yin* and *Yang*: Taoist Rhythm and O'Neill's Late Tragedies

James A. Robinson

In a 1932 letter to Frederic Carpenter, Eugene O'Neill indicated that years before, "the mysticism of Lao-Tse and Chuang-Tzu probably interested me more than any other Oriental writings." (1) O'Neill's attraction to these ancient Chinese philosophers had led him in the early 1920s to read the James Legge translation of their works, the *Tao Te Ching* and the *Chuang Tse*, while undertaking research for *Marco Millions*. In those sacred texts of Taoism, O'Neill not only found confirmation of his own mystical intuition that a dynamic universal force (called the *Tao* by Lao Tse) united man and the universe but also discovered an encouraging variant of his own dualistic tragic vision as well. For, as John Henry Raleigh first pointed out, O'Neill viewed reality dualistically, as a series of unreconciled polar conflicts --between land and sea, night and day, man and woman, past and present, life and death--conflicts that doomed man to perpetual, futile struggle. (2) But the early Taoist texts O'Neill read presented similar dualistic oppositions as ones of complementary polarity, in which the polar principles--called *yin* and *yang*--alternate and interpenetrate in the dynamic rhythm of the Tao. According to Taoism, the *yin* is dark, receptive, female, intuitive, and still; the *yang* is light, aggressive, male, rational and active. As one expands, the other diminishes, until the point is reached where the process is reversed--a cycle that continues throughout eternity. Moreover, *yin* and *yang* also contain the seeds of each other, so that these two apparent opposites actually intermingle as well. Thus unified by interpenetration as well as by involvement in the same eternal cycle, *yin* and *yang* represent the hidden unity of all phenomenal oppositions. Hence, it is hardly surprising that Taoism appealed to the tormented O'Neill, who longed to transcend his Western, dualistic world view and attain a vision of a larger, flowing unity that promised peace and harmony.

In my book *Eugene O'Neill and Oriental Thought*, I argued that O'Neill's interest in Eastern philosophy peaked in the 1920s, in such plays as *Marco Millions, The Great God Brown* and *Lazarus Laughed* and that the treatment of Larry Slade, Hickey, and Mary Tyrone in *The Iceman Cometh* and *Long Day's Journey into Night* represented the playwright's attempt to repudiate his earlier attraction to Oriental mystical systems. (3) Beneath that overt rejection, however, O'Neill's imagination continued to conceive reality in terms of dynamic polarity. Consequently, both *Iceman* and *Journey* struggle to harmonize their thematic oppositions between past and future, life and death, being and nonbeing in the same way the Tao reconciles *yin* and *yang*: by projecting the opposing terms as interpenetrating, or as rhythmically alternating, or as both. The pessimistic plots of both *Iceman* and *Journey* make tragically clear O'Neill's inability to attain thereby the serenity that Taoism offers; but his effort shows the persistence of the appeal of this aspect of Taoism to his vision.

In *The Iceman Cometh*, the Taoist dynamic operates most obviously in the relationships of two of the play's numerous couples. For Lewis and Wetjoen, and Harry Hope and Jimmy Tomorrow, form complementary pairs that resemble *yin* and *yang* in their dynamic. The relationship of Lewis and Wetjoen represents harmony in opposition. Possessing contrasting features--one is "lean" and "square-shouldered," the other "huge" and "slovenly" (4)--the two men fought on opposing sides in the Boer War. They are simultaneously united by their friendship, which originated in their mutual participation in an exhibition on the war. That which separates them paradoxically joins them, suggesting the principle of complementary opposition uniting *yin* and *yang*. The relationship of Harry Hope and Jimmy Tomorrow is more complex; for the focus on past and future they respectively symbolize takes us closer both to the pipe dreaming that is the thematic core of *Iceman* and to the Taoist manner in which O'Neill structures the play's thematic oppositions.

In a sentimental monologue halfway through act one, Harry Hope remembers the time he almost ran for alderman, and vows to renew his political involvement; moments later Jimmy Tomorrow, in counterpoint, dreams about regaining his former position in public relations. For both, however, pipe dreams for the future rest on self-deceit about the past. With no chance of winning twenty years ago, Harry used his wife's death as an excuse to withdraw from the race and the world; Jimmy conveniently forgets being fired for drunkenness. The close proximity of their speeches, however, allows Larry Slade to articulate their symbolic connection. Harry's maudlin reminiscences about Bessie (who actually "nagged the hell out of him") prompts Larry's remark, "Isn't a pipe dream of yesterday a touching thing?" And when Jimmy vows to spruce up his appearance for a future interview, Larry sardonically comments, "The tomorrow movement is a sad and beautiful thing, too." (603) While Hope focuses on illusions about the past and Jimmy leads the "tomorrow movement," they actually form another complementary couple who represent the interdependence of false memories and empty ambitions--the neurotic state of mind that afflicts virtually all the barroom derelicts. As Larry laughingly crows to Jimmy, "Worst is best here, and East is West, and tomorrow is yesterday. What more do you want?" (600) The identity of "yesterday" and "tomorrow," apparent opposites, again resembles that of *yin* and *yang*: past and future interpenetrate at Harry Hope's saloon.

Iceman also mingles another pair of opposites--life and death--in a similarly Taoist fashion. Hickey, the "iceman" of the title, is of course the clearest representative, and agent, of death in the play. But Hickey has been awaited as a bringer of life, and in act one the men recall happily the parties he has thrown. Moreover, after they dismiss his behavior as insane in act four, riotous life erupts in the bar. Nor is this interpenetration of life and death limited to Hickey, for it recurs in various contexts, involving both minor and major characters. Wetjoen and Lewis, for instance, engage in a "happy dispute over the brave days in South Africa when they tried to murder each other" (593); their current camaraderie results from deadly past encounters. References to Rosa Parritt betray a similar ambivalence. "She'll get life" in prison, Parritt states, knowing it will resemble death, for spiritually "she is dead and yet has to live." (584, 720) The equation of life and death also applies to the "End of the Line" saloon itself. "Dis dump is like a morgue wid all dese bums passed out" (574), Rocky observes in act one. But the setting simultaneously represents elemental life: adequate shelter and food, companionship, and sufficient drink to maintain illusions. When Hickey exposes their pipe dreams and "takes the life out" of their alcohol (as the derelicts repeatedly complain), the men shift toward death and only return to life after Hickey's departure. Even Larry Slade, who remains directed toward death at the finish, participates in the life/death interfusion. Larry sagely informs Parritt that the pipe dream "gives life" to everyone in the bar; his own pipe dreams, of course, include a supposed yearning for death.

Another, more metaphysical opposition--between being and nonbeing--also is portrayed by *Iceman* as resembling *yin* and *yang* not just in interpenetration but also in rhythm. Hickey's nihilist gospel

preaches killing pipe dreams and thus confronting the void at the center
of existence; Larry ultimately does so, associating both characters with
this fundamental Oriental tenet. But Taoism, while stressing the quiet
emptiness of the Tao, also insists upon its dynamism: motion and
stillness, being and nonbeing, engage in a cosmic rhythm within it.
"Decay and growth, fullness and emptiness, when they end, begin
again," said Chuang Tse. (5) A similar rhythm characterizes *Iceman*.
At the beginning, a totally silent stage finds all asleep but Larry and
Rocky. Even after various derelicts awake, converse, and pass out again,
Larry can point to the "beautiful calm in the atmosphere." (587) The
room thus approximates the stillness of nonbeing. But Parritt soon makes
Larry anxiously suspicious about Rosa's betrayal, and the agitation
becomes general after Hickey enters and soberly attacks everyone's pipe
dreams. The stillness gives way to motion and violence, to being, in acts
two and three, as friends turn on each other, and Harry bitterly
denounces the hangers-on during his birthday speech. After all have
lost their pipe dreams, however, the stillness returns, but with a
difference: it now suggests the men's dumb despair in facing the void. At
act four's commencement, "there is an atmosphere of oppressive
stagnation in the room, and a quality of insensibility" with the
derelicts "sunk in a numb stupor which is impervious to stimulation."
(696) Their stillness punctuates Hickey's confession, which contains four
intervals of dead silence. Only after Hickey pleads insanity does the
room gradually return to life, with singing, shouting, and laughter at
the conclusion. Illusion, the foundation of being, has returned, and
nonbeing recedes into the background. Only Larry, "oblivious to their
racket" (728), a solitary emblem of stillness, stares into the void Hickey
has bequeathed him.

In *Long Day's Journey into Night*, O'Neill's vision again aligns
itself with the Taoist polar dynamic. But again, instead of suggesting
harmony and reconciliation, the cycles contribute to a prevailing sense
of entrapment. In a 1940 letter to George Jean Nathan, O'Neill
articulated his awareness of the plight of James, Mary, Jamie, and
Edmund Tyrone: "At the final curtain there they still are, *trapped
within each other by the past*, each guilty and at the same time
innocent, scorning, loving, pitying each other, understanding and yet not
understanding at all, forgiving but still doomed never to be able to
forget." (6) O'Neill's words point up not just the source of the
entrapment--the inescapable past, with its incompatible lives, infant
deaths, addictions, and alcoholism--but in their oppositions of guilt and
innocence, understanding and not understanding, the words point also to
the alternating currents of love and hate, blame and forgiveness, that
provide the play's texture. Beneath those currents lie deeper ones, of

death and life, being and nonbeing, conceived in a *yin* and *yang* relationship; but O'Neill's intuition of this deeper harmony cannot set the Tyrones free.

As with *Iceman*'s Hickey, the chief character in *Journey*--Mary Tyrone, the play's emotional center in her devotion to the past--mingles life and death in her personality. As Mary bumps about the attic in act four searching for her wedding gown, Edmund observes that by this time she'll be nothing but a ghost haunting the past back before he was born. Mary's ghostly journey not only implies her death but allows her to obliterate Edmund's present identity, as well as Tyrone's. The past Mary visits is deceased because the innocence she seeks there has been destroyed by years of unhappy experiences. What Mary seeks is gone, so her mind's retreat to the past while her body continues in the present mingles life and death within her ghostly personality.

But the interpenetration of death and life is scarcely limited to Mary. The tubercular Edmund reveals his death wish when he describes his walk in the fog as a ghost belonging to the fog and the fog as a ghost of the sea. As a ghost within a ghost, Edmund resembles his mother; and though he does not pursue the dead past, it stalks him in the form of Jamie, the play's most explicit death-in-life figure. In his long speech warning Edmund, Jamie alludes three times to that part of him which is dead. Jamie's spiritual demise derives from his unrealized potential, and he looks back with sardonic regret rather than longing. "'Look in my face,'" he recites from Rossetti in the final act, "'My name is Might-Have-Been; /I am also called No More, Too Late, Farewell.'" (168) Pathetically resigned to his failure, Jamie speaks lines that reflect on his father. Tyrone harbors his own obsession with his squandered talent that resulted from endless performances as the Count of Monte Cristo. Like Jamie, he broods upon the "Might Have Been," incorporating a dead, even nonexistent, past into his present life.

To varying degrees, then, all four Tyrones mix life and death in their obsession with the past. Confronting the past leads O'Neill (as in *Iceman*) to face the void. As modern existentialism asserts, living in the past or future means an encounter with that which does not exist. But in *Journey*, that nothingness both penetrates and occasionally alternates with its opposite being, as with the *yin* and *yang* of the Tao. Nonbeing dwells in the silences that punctuate the action; the dead quiet when Mary is alone in the third act; the stillness that surrounds the sad, bewildered, broken Tyrone when Mary departs to inject herself with morphine at the act's conclusion; the cracking silence that follows her final, theatrical entrance toward the end; the motionlessness of all at the final curtain. As in Beckett or Pinter, these silences communicate the emptiness enveloping the characters. At the beginning of act two, scene two, moreover, these dead silences structure the action by alternating with the spoken lines. The pathos of the situation produces the stillness. As the three men fully comprehend Mary's return to morphine, her chattering provokes noncommittal replies or silence; and after the phone call from Dr. Hardy confirming Edmund's tuberculosis, two more dead moments ensue following Mary's angry tirade against doctors. After her departure, the conversational flow resumes. But the pauses in this scene--the play's turning point, and the last time the family appears together before the final curtain--give evidence of the manner in which O'Neill's rhythmic imagination corresponded to the cycles of the Tao. The characters and audience shift back and forth between sound and silence, plenitude and vacancy, resembling the rhythm of *yin* and *yang*. For the Western O'Neill, however, the complementary unity of being and nonbeing that this implies brings not peace but intensified despair.

That despair comes from the realization that there is no escape --not even through mystical visions of the unity of life such as Edmund recollects in his act four speech recalling the moment on the square-rigger when he dissolved in the sea and became part of the moonlight, the ship, the sea, and the sky. The epiphany is momentary: soon Edmund is alone and lost in the fog again, painfully aware, like Larry Slade at *Iceman*'s curtain, of his attachment to the people who have tormented him. Edmund's and Larry's inner conflict duplicates O'Neill's, of course, as he wrote *Iceman* and *Journey*: confronting his ghosts in order to escape them, he came to realize how inescapable they were. Equally inescapable was his dualistic tragic vision, whose personal sources are so apparent in the conflicts that riddle the "Tyrone" family, that is, the O'Neill family. Driven by the need to resolve the personal conflicts that resulted from his family life, O'Neill turned to Taoism, whose rhythmic conception of existence appears in both *Iceman* and *Journey*. Past and present, life and death, being and nonbeing alternate and interpenetrate like *yin* and *yang* as O'Neill strives to discover the dynamic unity behind life's oppositions that Taoism perceives. The continuing tyranny of his unhappy past, however, doomed his quest for unity to only intermittent fulfillment, as both plays make clear. No character in either play is liberated into serenity through union with the Tao. While abstinence from activity, the Taoist principle of *wu wei*, provides ample time to recognize the illusory nature of life, the truth sets no one free. For the primary mode of both plays is that of modern Western naturalism, which locates one's destiny in the determinism of history; and the promise of bliss implicit in both plays' Orientalism serves ultimately to highlight the prevailing sense of despair.

NOTES

1. Quoted in Frederic I. Carpenter, "Eugene O'Neill, the Orient and American Transcendentalism," in *Transcendentalism and Its Legacy*, eds. Myron Simon and T. H. Parsons (Ann Arbor: University of Michigan Press, 1966), 210.

2. John Henry Raleigh, *The Plays of Eugene O'Neill* (Carbondale and Edwardsville: Southern Illinois University Press, 1965).

3. James A. Robinson, *Eugene O'Neill and Oriental Thought: A Divided Vision* (Carbondale and Edwardsville: Southern Illinois University Press, 1982), chs. 1, 5 and 6 passim.

4. *The Plays of Eugene O'Neill* (New York: Random House, 1954), 3: 575-76. (All subsequent references will be documented in the text.)

5. *The Texts of Taoism*, trans. James Legge (1891; rpt. London: Oxford University Press, 1927), 383.

6. Letter to George Jean Nathan, 15 June 1940, in Jackson Bryer and Travis Bogard, eds., *Selected Letters of Eugene O'Neill* (New Haven: Yale University Press, 1988), 506-7.

4

Eugene O'Neill's *Marco Millions*: Desiring Marginality and the Dematerialization of the Orient

James S. Moy

During the late nineteenth century, American theatrical representations of the Orient in general and of the Chinese in particular usually offered characters consisting entirely of fetishized aspects of difference residing upon the American landscape, (1) as if to remind the viewer that the unique foreign qualities of the Orient could never be assimilated into the American geography. One need only look to New York City's recent Lincoln Center revival of Lindsay and Crouse's *Anything Goes* (1934) for a brief and embarrassingly comic reminder of how late nineteenth-century audiences viewed this Orient. Indeed, the fact that an institution that likes to regard itself as America's national theatre company sees fit to offer such a piece suggests that perhaps we have not much progressed in the past one hundred years.

Still, by the beginning of the twentieth century, perhaps realizing that the Chinese could not or would not be easily assimilated, the Chinese came to be portrayed in their exotic, foreign, homeland locales. These portrayals employed some subtle shifts, particularly among writers who would use the Chinese character for seriously intended projects. Clearly, Eugene O'Neill's *Marco Millions* must be counted among these. My aim in this essay is to examine O'Neill's treatment of this position.

Although some of the thematics behind the play can be traced through O'Neill's notebooks, it is clear that the piece was written between the summer of 1923 and January 1925, when the copyright was issued. At an intermediate stage in October 1924, O'Neill recorded that in *Marco Millions* he had written to his surprise "two good long plays of two and one-half hours each--at least." (2) Finally cut to a single evening length piece and published in April 1927, *Marco Millions* did not receive its first staging until January 9, 1928, at the Guild Theatre in New York. Brooks Atkinson's review of the opening night performance offers the following summary:

Ten scenes of *Marco Millions* record the journey of the merchant Polos through Persia and India to Cathay. Under a special dispensation from the Great Kaan, who is fascinated by Marco's lack of perception, the younger Marco goes through the kingdom, organizing furiously with the high spirits and the arrogant self-assurance of a bustling business man. In everything material he succeeds with a brilliance matched only by his cheap ethics. He fails only in awareness of the ancient culture of Cathay and in Princess Kukachin's despairing love. Acting under orders of the Great Kaan, he takes her out to Persia in a voyage two years long. Never once does her unselfish affection burn through the greedy, egotistical shell of his character. Mr. O'Neill chronicles all this in terms of emotional tragedy as well as satire. While Marco is swilling wine and costly viands at a banquet in Venice, and saluting his fat, stupid bride, boasting and gorging, the Great Kaan sits disconsolate in his throne room, eating out his heart for his home-sick, love-sick granddaughter, who could never speak her love. Marco's "spiritual hump" had been, strangely enough, their undoing. (3)

Clearly, in *Marco Millions* O'Neill sought to contrast the obsessive materialism of a Babbitt-like character with a positive representation of a romanticized historical China. Despite the clear comic intent of the piece, one could assume that the Chinese would at least receive a "positive," if not "realistic," portrayal within this framework. Indeed, after a superficial reading, this seems to be the case as O'Neill clearly offers the Polo family in a less than flattering light. Still, one is left troubled by a similar but unarticulated lack in the supposedly more appealing characterizations of the Oriental figures.

Both in visual appearance and in stage action, Marco and his uncles do not come off well. Costumes for Polo and company made the three appear almost buffoonish. Robert Coleman of the *New York Daily Mirror* described Marco as a "cheap, soulless, handshaking, baby-kissing politician." (4) Similarly, Alexander Woolcott of *The World* called Marco the "eternal portrait of the globe-trotting business man who takes notes on everything and sees nothing, who memorizes all he hears and learns nothing." (5)

If O'Neill was successful in his satirical portrayal of the Venetian trading family, his use of the Orient proves problematic. His characterizations of the Chinese are intended to show subtle differences:

Against the subtlety of Kublai, the Great Kaan of Cathay, and his poetic wisdom, Mr. O'Neill has set the crude, braggart character of Marco, greedy, expeditious, material-minded and obtuse. In all the gorgeous variety of scenes in the throne-room or on the extravagant ships bearing the love-sick Princess out to Persia, Mr. O'Neill has been specific by contrast rather than by statement. Yet the implications of his bizarre pageant are always articulate and forceful. (6)

Indeed, I take issue with Atkinson's assertion that all of the implications of O'Neill's "bizarre pageant are always articulate and forceful." For, while it seems obvious that O'Neill's portrayals of the Orient are intended to provide positive contrast to the blind materialism of the Western characters, the manner in which this Orient is constituted creates an internal tension that has the potential to ultimately subvert O'Neill's project.

It has been argued that through the use of recurring scenes in the middle part of the first act, O'Neill hoped to provide Marco's decline into callousness with a universal quality. (7) If this is true, an odd tension emerges between O'Neill's desire for the wisdom of the Orient and the Polo characters he sends East to carry out his project. To begin with, if the Orient is the site for the righteous ancient wisdom that O'Neill would have us accept, it is curious that as he progresses Eastward, Marco becomes more hardened, and the prostitutes more aggressive and cynical. Implicit here is the idea that the threat is both female and Asian. Marco's pattern of resistance to the active Oriental woman/prostitute is established. After the encounters with the prostitutes, Marco could not possibly be interested in anyone other than his bovine Venetian betrothed. Within this pattern, Kukachin is imprisoned. She is trapped within the broad array of that Western catalogue that lists the Orient as passive, weak, and feminine while the West is viewed as active, dominant, and male. For her to be anything other than passive and distant in her unrequited love for Marco would cause her to be grouped with the active Asian female prostitute.

The Oriental woman, thus neutralized, when coupled with the absence of any European female characters with whom the Asian men might prove sexual threat, served to render O'Neill's Orient a place devoid of even the potential for romantic involvement. This of course draws focus to the contrast between what could be called an oddly ironic sentimental Oriental love and Marco's very business-like "love" relationship with Donata.

Beyond this, there exists a disturbing sameness about the manner in which O'Neill articulates the Orient. Again, while scenes three and four of the first act were designed to provide a universal feeling,

O'Neill's efforts seem more successful at trivializing or denying differences between various Eastern cultures. It is suggested, for example, that Persia is little different from India. Save for variations in the religious architecture and the presence of the disdainful snake-charmer in India, O'Neill would have us believe that the frozen background characters--"Only their eyes move, staring fixedly but indifferently at the Polos" in both scenes--are somehow universal. In the first production of *Marco Millions*, this problem was aggravated by the need to eliminate a scene set in Mongolia that provided a transition between India and the Polos's arrival in China. The net effect is a conflation of every geographic setting from Persia to China into a single, awkwardly-defined, narrative space of "Other" called China where the main action of the play occurs. Within this place O'Neill seemed not to differentiate between Mongol and Chinese, as all seem to live and work together happily. Yet, Marco Polo's memoirs (O'Neill's notes claim a careful reading of this text), (8) suggest a significantly different situation:

And you should know that all the Cathayans detested the Great Kaan's rule because he set over them governors who were Tartars, or still more frequently Saracens, and these they could not endure for they were treated by them just like slaves. You see the Great Kaan had not succeeded to the dominion of Cathay by hereditary right, but held it by conquest; and thus having no confidence in the natives, he put all authority into the hands of Tartars, Saracens, or Christians who were attached to his household and devoted to his service, and were foreigners in Cathay. (9)

O'Neill's Marco travels to China to fill the Great Kaan's request for representatives of the wisdom of the West. In an amusingly self-reflexive fashion, this is also the place in which O'Neill hopes to locate a philosophy that can satisfy his personal quest for significance in life. Accordingly, the play speaks the desire of O'Neill's Asia through the language of the West. Kublai, realizing that his granddaughter has fallen hopelessly in love with Marco, declares, "Life is so stupid, it is mysterious," and later threatens to have Marco killed. (10) But his advisor Chu-Yin admonishes him in soothing tones and reminds the ruler: "The noble man ignores self. The wise man ignores action. His truth acts without deeds. His knowledge venerates the unknowable. To him birth is not the beginning nor is death the end. [Kublai's head bends in submission. Chu-Yin continues tenderly.] I feel there are tears in your eyes. The Great Kaan, Ruler of the World, may not weep. " (*MM* 97)

Similarly, Chu-Yin calms an angry Kukachin by suggesting that she have a "Little sleep, Princess, and you will be beautiful. The old dream passes. Sleep and awake in the new. Life is perhaps most wisely regarded as a bad dream between two awakenings, and everyday is a life in miniature." (*MM* 98)

Still, the Great Kaan is human, and he finds himself torn between the desire to act forcefully on his granddaughter's behalf and the supposed path of Eastern wisdom, passivity and avoidance:

She will die. Why is this? What purpose can it serve? My hideous suspicion is that God is only an infinite, insane energy which creates and destroys without other purpose than to pass eternity in avoiding thought. Then the stupid man becomes the Perfect Incarnation of Omnipotence and the Polos are the true children of God. . . . I begin to resent life as the insult of an ignoble inferior with whom it is a degradation to fight! (*MM* 134)

To his credit O'Neill did not resort to the use of pidgin English to provide his Asian characters with dialogue. Most of his predecessors in American playwriting had employed a curiously degraded English for great comic effect as Asians would seek to express themselves in their adopted foreign American tongue. O'Neill's use of English was entirely appropriate, as the ideas being expressed are uniquely his own American notion of what constituted Asia. It seems, however, that ultimately O'Neill found Oriental philosophy intriguing and novel but less than satisfactory, as he has Kukachin drowsily declare: "Your wisdom makes me sleepy." (*MM* 98) And, finally, even the Great Kaan attacks the wisdom of the Orient: "Your words are hollow echoes of the brain. Do not wound me with wisdom. Speak to my heart!" (*MM* 153)

While the materialistic West is shown to be "unromantic," O'Neill's Eastern detached "wisdom" proves impotent in the face of the Western desire for money and power. As Marco proclaimed: "I kept my nose to the grindstone every minute. (Proudly) And I got results. I don't mind telling you, Donata, I'm worth over two millions!" (*MM* 141-142) Given this ambiguous position, it becomes less clear what O'Neill sought to portray through *Marco Millions*. Clearly, the dominant materialistic Western position is not a utopian enterprise to be sought after. In contrast to this, O'Neill created what initially appears to be a privileged Imaginary Orient beyond the margins of the West. But, this too is finally dismissed by its dominant practitioners in the play, Kublai and Kukachin. The philosophical positions to which O'Neill gave free play are thus left floating and indeterminate.

In seeking to create a marginal utopian Orient beyond his realm of experience, O'Neill had fallen into a trap. Virginia Floyd observed that despite "Kukachin's passion and Kublai's heartbreak at her death, the play lacks warmth and emotional intensity. The numerous scenes and characters, the panoramic passing of time and peoples, seems to preclude a sensitive treatment." Indeed, of some significance here are the spectacular scenery and the almost Brechtian displacement of the viewer through a series of some ten episodes. While Percy Hammond of the New York *Herald Tribune* complained that the Guild Theatre performance was "warped a little by its eight intermissions," (11) Atkinson reported that the opening production "pours from the stage in rapturous beauty. . . . The telling of the story involves theatrical richness, a kaleidoscope of scenes. Costumes of surpassing patterns and colors, processionals, chorals, mobs, bells, gongs, bands, a fury of wild voices, dark brooding silhouettes against the sky, and brief passages of exalting discourse on grand themes." (12)

   It could be said that O'Neill offers China to his viewers in much the same way a tourist might describe the high points of his summer holiday, memories of a "heathen" place never experienced. (13) In the foreword to the published volume of *Marco Millions*, O'Neill decried the fact that Marco Polo of Venice "dictated the book of his travels but left the traveller out. He was no author. He stuck to a recital of what he considered facts." (*MM* 5) In his play, O'Neill inserts the viewer into the powerful position of the tourist before whom he parades the carefully selected "high points" of an imaginary philosophical excursion to China. Here, then, the discourse of the Orient, of the Other as articulated through the tourist culture's vision in O'Neill's *Marco Millions*, is in many ways typical. (14) The Orient is rarely given voice for, the moment the Other speaks, it becomes a threat. Like O'Neill's predecessors, the capturing/controlling gaze serves as the mechanism for manipulation, as the montage of fetishized traits typical of nineteenth-century American portrayals of the Orient is replaced by a rapid displacement of the viewer through a sequence of locales peopled by spectacular mannequins. (15) Through this process, the Orient is displaced into the space of representation, as white actors pretend to be Chinese, and almost immediately doubly displaced into the space of the void that emerges between the numerous episodes of the play. Thus, as Marco and family move from one setting to another, suitcases in hand, without substantive interaction, so the audience comes away with nothing.

   In designing his imaginary marginality called China, O'Neill fell into the trap of stereotyping the Orient, thereby displacing/erasing the reality while China disintegrated into representation. A mere representation, yes, but ultimately one based upon a difference within a structure that denied the need to act or to be taken seriously as even the fictional Marco Polo walks out puzzled in the play's epilogue. This

China, an "infantilized" and "perfect" but finally empty imaginary locale, was constructed merely for an exercise, (16) a space that served O'Neill's purpose while voiding the reality. Such a forced closure at the site of representation leaves open the possibility of rupture. This potential for rupture finally subverts and neutralizes O'Neill's project in *Marco Millions*.

NOTES

1. See my "Mark Twain and Bret Harte's *Ah Sin* Locating China in the Geography of the American West," paper presented at the 4th Hong Kong International Comparative Literature Conference, Chinese University of Hong Kong, 17-21 August 1987.

2. Arthur and Barbara Gelb, *O'Neill* (New York: Harper & Row, 1987), 563. For detailed treatments of the evolution of this play, see John H. Stroupe, "*Marco Millions* and O'Neill's 'Two Part Two-Play' Form," *Modern Drama* 13 (February 1971): 382-92, and Virginia Floyd, ed., *Eugene O'Neill at Work* (New York: Frederick Ungar, 1981), 57-67. The longer, uncut version of *Marco Millions* is available in Travis Bogard, ed., *The Unknown O'Neill* (New Haven: Yale University Press, 1988), 195-307.

3. *New York Times*, 10 January 1928: 28.

4. *New York Daily Mirror*, 11 January 1928: 27.

5. *The World* (New York), 10 January 1928: 28.

6. *New York Times*, 10 January 1928: 28.

7. An Min Hsia, "The Tao and Eugene O'Neill," diss., Indiana University, 1979, 71. Hsia's dissertation, along with a later piece, "Cycle of Return: O'Neill and the Tao," in Horst Frenz and Susan Tuck, eds., *Eugene O'Neill's Critics: Voices from Abroad* (Carbondale: Southern Illinois University Press, 1984), 169-73, provide interesting treatments of Taoist influences on this O'Neill play. Of note is the Taoist active/passive dichotomy, which clearly intrigued O'Neill.

8. Virginia Floyd, ed. *Eugene O'Neill at Work* (New York: Frederick Ungar, 1981), 57. Floyd reports that O'Neill's "large collection of 'millions of notes,' excerpts from *The Travels of Marco Polo*, the historical hero's actual account of his journey to the East and stay at the court of the Great Kaan" has survived and is available at Yale University's Beinecke Library.

9. Marco Polo, *The Book of Ser Marco Polo, The Venetian, Concerning the Kingdoms and Marvels of the East*, trans. Henry Yule, 2 vols. (New York: Charles Scribners' Sons, 1903), 1: 418.

10. Eugene O'Neill, *Marco Millions* (London: Jonathan Cape,

Ltd., 1927), 94. (Subsequently cited as *MM* with page number.)

11. *Herald Tribune*, (New York) 10 January 1928: 28.

12. *New York Times*, 10 January 1928: 28.

13. It is amusing to note that O'Neill's list of characters for *Marco Millions* catalogued all non-Western figures in the play under the general heading of "heathens." Ironically, in the fall of 1928 O'Neill would pay a visit to the Orient, touring through Ceylon, Saigon, Singapore, Hong Kong, and Shanghai. The Gelbs report that despite "his high hopes, O'Neill ultimately found no peace or satisfaction in the East" (p. 680). Later the Gelbs quote Mai-mai Sze, a close friend of the O'Neills, saying that "Gene and Carlotta traveled to the East like a pair of tourists." (686) See also Horst Frenz, "Eugene O'Neill and China," *Tamkang Review* 8 (Fall/Winter 1979): 5-16, for an interesting focussed study on this subject.

14. See Edward W. Said, *Orientalism* (New York: Random House, Inc., Vintage ed., 1979); Edward W. Said, "Orientalism Reconsidered" in *Literature, Politics & Theory: Papers from the Essex Conference 1976-84*, eds. Francis Barker, Peter Hulme, Margaret Iversen, Diana Loxley (London: Methuen, 1986), 210-29; and *Reflections on Orientalism: Edward Said, Roger Bresnahan, Surjit Dulai, Edward Graham, and Donald Lammers*, ed. Warren I. Cohen (East Lansing: Michigan State University, Asian Studies Center, 1983).

15. Indeed, this notion of the panoptic gaze is even more pronounced in the earlier uncut version of *Marco Millions* as cinematic displacements serve as bookend-like devices in act one, scene two, and act eight, scene one. See Travis Bogard, ed., *The Unknown O'Neill* (New Haven: Yale University Press, 1988), 196; 204-11; 296-301.

16. Paul Bruckner, *The Tears of the White Man: Compassion as Contempt*, trans. by William R. Beer (New York: Free Press, 1986), 37.

5

O'Neill's Understanding of Chinese Thought in *Marco Millions*

Gang Li

For more than seven hundred years *The Travels of Marco Polo* has greatly appealed to readers and scholars of East and West alike. This is partly because it is the earliest firsthand European account of Asia and partly because it is one of the first endeavors aimed at East/West understanding. It is not a book of adventures but one of sketches. Anyone who has read it must have been shocked by Marco Polo's reticence concerning personal matters, which is indeed a pity. However, this is also a blessing for those readers who are imaginative. The void Marco Polo has left "has been eagerly filled in by romantic hero-worshippers, who see him as a brilliant young courtier enamoring princesses and governing provinces: indeed, a Marco Polo myth has been current for centuries and has often provided a theme for novelists, film makers, or dramatists." (1)

Eugene O'Neill's *Marco Millions* (1927) is based on this myth. The title, O'Neill once explained, was his imitation of the Italian "Il Milione"--"tacked on mockingly to Marco Polo's name by the scoffing rabble in Venice, who thought his stories about the East such awful lies." He wanted "to render poetic justice to a man unjustly world-renowned as a liar"; he argued that Marco Polo was not a liar but a man of action and ambition. However, O'Neill believed he sold his soul for material wealth and blindly destroyed the poetic beauty in life. (2)

As usual with historical plays, *Marco Millions* serves as a mirror of O'Neill's time, around which the Western world saw the breakup of a civilization: All the traditional values and beliefs were challenged and in danger of being repudiated altogether. The disorientation of modern existential man seemed to be inevitable. Americans of the time were in a "dilemma of the split self, the materialist-businessman/idealist-poet dichotomy." (3) *Marco Millions* is concerned with this dilemma, which O'Neill tries to solve by introducing "the Eastern loveliness," especially the Taoist view of life, death, and dreams, to the Western audience.

The Taoist influence in *Marco Millions* has been studied by quite a few critics in both the East and the West. Owing to different points of departure, it is understandable that they hold opposing views on certain issues: Does the play end on an Eastern note or a Western one? However, they all seem to agree that the Taoist influence permeates almost every aspect of the play: theme, structure, characterization, dialogue, and setting. From the study of several critics, we know that Taoism is not the only Chinese influence in the play. The Confucian influence, though much less, is still there.

Professor James A. Robinson has done a thorough study of the Taoist influence in the play in his *Eugene O'Neill and Oriental Thought*, which we will not repeat here. (4) However, some additional points may be made about the Taoist influence on the structure of the play.

If we rule out the epilogue, which is not actually played on the stage, the play opens with the corpse of Kukachin (granddaughter of the Great Kaan, Kublai) on its way home and ends with its arrival. Kukachin appears more alive than dead in both scenes, which makes the play's structure a self-contained cycle of life and death. It pertains to our study that this is not a coincidence but a result of O'Neill's conscientious effort, for "the scene depicting the funeral service for Kukachin is placed first in the scenario but is later transposed intact to the end of the play." (5) Such an arrangement also makes the life experienced by the characters structurally conform to what Chu-yin, a Chinese sage in the play calls it: "a bad dream between two awakenings." (6) In the Taoist point of view, man awakes only when he is an ignorant child who covets nothing and when he is dead, having become fully aware of the vanity of life.

According to the Taoist teachings, to live is to live a simple and spontaneous life; to die is a thing neither to be feared nor to be desired. In fact, Chuang Tzu had a rather witty philosophy telling people how to survive and prolong their lives. However, what is embodied in the following song of Kukachin's appears contrary to this philosophy:

> If I were asleep in green water,
> No pang could be added to my sorrow,
> Old grief would be forgotten,
> I would know peace. (*NP* 274)

There is little doubt that Kukachin cherishes a death-wish.

As Robinson's study shows, O'Neill's understanding of the Chinese Tao is, on the whole, accurate and deep. From the study of a Chinese scholar we know that O'Neill's understanding of Confucianism in the play, though overshadowed by Taoism, is far from being shallow. In the last scene, the priest of Confucius is asked by the Kaan to answer if he is able to bring Kukachin back to life. He replies, "before we know life, how can we know death? Death is." (*NP* 300) In *Confucian Analects* we have the following dialogue:

Chi Lu, a student of Confucius, asked about serving the spirits of the dead. The Master said, "While you are not able to serve men, how can you serve their spirits?" Chi Lu added, "I venture to ask about death?" He was answered, "While you do not know life, how can you know about death?" (7)

The priest's answer is in agreement with the Confucian view of death. (8)

After discussing the Chinese influence in the play, it is time to bring to light the argument about whether the play ends on an Eastern note or a Western one. James A. Robinson's interpretation of the play, in his *Eugene O'Neill and Oriental Thought* is made on the whole in terms of monistic Taoism. However, he argues that, for all the Eastern messages it carries, "*Marco Millions* . . . does not end on this Eastern note" (*R* 117) and "the healing monism of the Tao fails to bridge the enormous gap between East and West." (*R* 7) This conclusion is derived from his analysis of the play's epilogue.

After the curtain falls, a man "dressed as a Venetian merchant of the later Thirteenth Century" is discovered among the audience; he is "none other than Marco Polo himself, looking a bit sleepy, a trifle puzzled." However, before long, "his face begins to clear of all disturbing memories of what had happened on stage," and the noise and the people of the outside world "recall him at once to himself." He gets into his luxurious limousine and "with a satisfied sigh at the sheer comfort of it all, resumes his life." (*NP* 304)

Since Robinson's analysis of this epilogue is not only fascinating but also carries the gist of the thesis of his book, it is worth quoting here at length:

The protagonist's obtuse complacency and materialism is thereby projected onto the Western audience, and juxtaposed one final time with the Oriental beauty and wisdom displayed in the previous scene. The juxtaposition reveals the divided vision of O'Neill. . . . O'Neill's Western side has the final word. The Eastern loveliness Marco (and the audience) has witnessed briefly baffles, then bores, him, and his incomprehension seems both inevitable and characteristic of Westerners. From this angle, East and West represent antagonistic approaches to life, and this antagonism does not simply govern the relations between Occident and Orient, but lies at the heart of the universe. However much O'Neill may satirize the Western greed and insensitivity of his protagonist, the playwright cannot divorce himself from the dualistic Western world view, since it constitutes the essence of his dramatic, tragic vision. (R 117)

The tone of this analysis seems rather pessimistic. Not only does the play end on a Western note, but Westerners are doomed for their inability to understand "the Eastern loveliness." However, Virginia Floyd's study, in her *Eugene O'Neill at Work*, makes us question this. Though Marco's stark insensitivity is projected onto the audience, at the same time the audience is also given an opportunity to make their own choice between "the serene spiritualism of the East and the destructive materialism of the West." (R 109) (9)

The 1923 scenario of *Marco Millions* had six parts, which in fact formed two "good long plays," as O'Neill said. Originally, there were two prison scenes, one set at the beginning, the other at the end, in which Marco was seen dictating his memoirs to a fellow prisoner. In 1925 O'Neill condensed the two long plays into one and eliminated the two prison scenes. The second prison scene was replaced by the present epilogue. (10) Floyd's explanation for this change throws light on our study:

as O'Neill's later plays--especially the nine-act *Strange Interlude*-- attest, mere length would not compel O'Neill to eliminate the two prison scenes. Nor was he motivated by theatrical considerations. Even in his bleakest early plays like *The Personal Equation* and *The Straw*, the dramatist leaves man with some faint glimmer of a hopeless hope that change is possible. As a last scene, however, the prison walls--like the four walls later in the Tyrone household--seemingly trap a character who has already become a captive of the past and doomed in the hopelessness of the present. (11)

O'Neill was attempting, as Floyd's study reveals, to include in the epilogue an idea he had a few years earlier: "contrasting the oldest civilization of China and that of modern times--same crises offering definite choice of either material (i.e., worldly) success or a step toward higher spiritual plane" (a late entry in O'Neill's 1918-1920 notebook). (12)

Indeed, for "all the Eastern messages" the play carries and for O'Neill's understanding of Chinese thought, which stresses unity and the spiritual rather than division and the material, O'Neill hoped that the audience would not follow Marco's wrong choice.

NOTES

1. Fosco Maraini, "Marco Polo," *Encyclopaedia Britannica*, 1985 ed., 572.

2. Arthur and Barbara Gelb, *O'Neill*, abr. ed. (New York: Dell Publishing Co., Inc., 1965), 304.

3. Virginia Floyd, ed., *Eugene O'Neill: A World View* (New York: Frederick Ungar Publishing Co., 1979), 31.

4. James A. Robinson, *Eugene O'Neill and Oriental Thought: A Divided Vision* (Carbondale and Edwardsville: Southern Illinois University Press, 1982), 108-17. (Subsequently cited as *R* with page number.)

5. Virginia Floyd, ed. and ann., *Eugene O'Neill at Work: Newly Released Ideas for Plays* (New York: Frederick Ungar Publishing Co., 1981), 62.

6. Eugene O'Neill, *Nine Plays* (New York: Random House, 1954), 62. (Subsequently cited as *NP* with page number.)

7. Confucius, *Confucian Analects* in *The Four Books*, trans. James Legge (Shanghai: The Chinese Book Company, 1930), 142.

8. Yaoxin Chang, "The Influence of Chinese Culture on American Literature," *Foreign Literature Studies* 1 (1985): 51.

9. Floyd, *Eugene O'Neill at Work*, 66.

10. Floyd, *Eugene O'Neill at Work*, 59-65.

11. Floyd, *Eugene O'Neill at Work*, 66.

12. Floyd, *Eugene O'Neill at Work*, 58.

6

The Uses of Pessimism: Some Random Thoughts about Eugene O'Neill

Zhiji Ren

From *Beyond the Horizon* to *The Iceman Cometh*, Eugene O'Neill experienced the reverse of a "pilgrim's progress." His path led him from hope, though a vain one, to complete despair, as though knowledge, apart from being an enlightenment, was a source of suffering. This regression approximately describes the course the playwright followed in his creative career and results in a tragic view of life that finds persistent expression in his later plays. It manifests itself roughly in two themes: dreams as opposed to reality and noncommunication as opposed to understanding.

This paper explores O'Neill's later plays along these two thematic lines and the art he employed for their fullest expression.

Eugene O'Neill never ceased to delve into the suffering that is caused by the conflict between dreams and reality. A conflict of this kind, however, does not necessarily evolve into a tragedy if the dreamer remains throughout in a "submerged" state of intoxication. But as soon as this intoxication begins to alternate with sobriety, then tragedy becomes inevitable, which is the case in almost all of O'Neill's plays on this theme. A dreamer suffers little unless he knows he is dreaming. Knowledge, instead of being a helper here, acts as an evil agent that hastens the destruction of the person in the know. All the dreamers in O'Neill's plays become tragic heroes because they have the knowledge that they are deceiving themselves in dreams. When, for instance, Melody in *A Touch of the Poet* is in one of his dreams, "he squares his shoulders defiantly. He stares into his eyes in the glass. . . ." (1) But when he is in one of his rare sober moments, especially when he is goaded by his insolent daughter Sara, "he crumbles, his soldierly erectness sags and his face falls. He looks sad and hopeless and bitter and old. . . ." (2) When Melody finally wakes up to the reality of his pretenses, he "leers into" the mirror and says, "Be Jasus, if it ain't the mirror the auld loon was always admirin' his mug in while he spouted Byron to pretend himself was a lord. . . ." (3) Could there be anything more tragic than looking into yourself and finding yourself to be a fake?

The impact of sobriety upon dreamers proves to be fatal in *The Iceman Cometh* when those patrons in the bar "rise up for air," only to become suffocated and sick by the decompression of reality. Dreams are water to these denizens of the deep. Without them, they die. "We are such stuff as dreams are made on," as James Tyrone quotes Shakespeare, "and our little life is rounded with a sleep." In *A Touch of the Poet*, the stubbornness of Melody in sticking to his pretenses would have succeeded in making him a Quixotic hero had he not been clubbed out of it by the Harford gang, which sends him instead reeling back into reality. He wakes up, yes, and here lies his tragedy, whereas Don Quixote is tragic only in the cosmic sense, never in a personal one. In the O'Neill plays, woe to the hero who wakes and knows. Byron expresses the phenomenon in these lines:

> Sorrow is knowledge, they who know the most
> Must mourn the deepest o'er the fatal truth,
> The tree of knowledge is not of life.

Therefore, it is by no means accidental that in *A Touch of the Poet* O'Neill makes Melody recite again and again from Byron's "Childe Harold." Perhaps O'Neill is obliquely criticizing himself through his criticism of Melody. Perhaps he was Byronic in some way, and knew it.

O'Neill's concern with noncommunication among homo sapiens reached disproportionate dimensions in his later life and found release through a spree of unrestrained confessions by all the members of the Tyrones in *Long Day's Journey into Night* and by Jim in *A Moon for the Misbegotten*. In both cases, there is a love-hate situation that, on the surface, seems to be the most unlikely soil for misunderstanding. In both cases the material grounds that breed disharmony among family members seem lacking. But throughout *Long Day's Journey*, audiences are flabbergasted by characters who recriminate one another even while they are conscious of the love that exists between them. What could have made them so relentlessly unforgiving? Before answering this question, let's examine their love-hate situation and see whether it is beyond human effort to mend.

Edmund, the youngest son, loves his mother dearly but thinks she hates him because his birth, so he was told, has ruined her health and caused her to be dependent on drugs. He feels he's not wanted and suffers from problems of identity. Hoping to become a poet he is fully aware of his inability to express himself poetically, except "to stammer." His poor constitution and guilt about his mother scarcely help the situation. While he blames his father for not having provided first-rate medical care for his mother, he can't help liking him.

Jamie, the eldest son, loves his mother so much that his love almost amounts to an Oedipal fixation. He is extremely jealous of his brother Edmund; and his mother's accusation that he is responsible for the death of Eugene, the brother who died of measles, traumatizes him, virtually reducing him to a ne'er-do-well and a cynic. He also blames his father for his mother's problems and, by the same token, holds his father accountable for his own failures, too.

Mary loves her husband and sons but longs for a house she could really call home. Her dream is gradually eroded by the itinerary of the stock company in which James stars and by her acceptance of his stinginess. Further, she is guilt-ridden by the deaths of her father and her second child Eugene, for which she also blames both Tyrone and Jamie. When she was in convent school, she wanted to become first a concert pianist and later a nun. She thinks her marriage to Tyrone came between her and her faith and led directly to her present predicament.

James, the head of the family, loves his wife and his sons but practices a kind of parsimony that incurs their resentment. His obsession with financial security estranges him and blows away his dream of reaching his true height as an actor. He tries to drown his frustration in drink and is resigned to the accusations of his wife and sons and to the hopeless situation he faces. His fear of ending up in a poorhouse, acquired when he was a boy, has grown so far out of proportion that neither love nor ambition could dislodge it from his mentality.

Just as the Tyrones have been condemned to a babel of endless noncommunication with only occasional releases, so has Jim in *A Moon for the Misbegotten*. The respite is but temporary relief, never meant as eternal absolution, which comes only with death. As Jim says of his dead mother, "She is now free from worry. From pain. From me." But for the living there is only straight suffering, with pauses scarcely long enough to render life bearable. The transient nature of such a respite is made quite evident by the title. It is only "a moon," not two, or more. "It was a damned soul," says Josie of Jim, "coming to me in the moonlight, to confess and be forgiven and find peace for *a night*." (4) (Emphasis is mine.) Yes, to find peace in confession, that's what Jim is seeking, and a temporary emotional relief is achieved. After Jim confesses his despicable behavior in relation to his mother, he falls asleep upon Josie's breast. When he awakes at dawn, he departs without so much as a hint whether he'll return. But the moon is real even if it's only for one night. That one night of release from the grip of reality is a blessing of a lifetime, a worthy bargain for one who is condemned for life.

In *Hughie* the two characters are engaged in lackadaisical dialogue that fails even in achieving an apology of communication. This total absence of give-and-take shocks the audience into realizing the utter futility of life. There are sightings, but never arrivals; the story is simple and uneventful.

Erie, a gambler, returns to the hotel drunk. He tries to start a conversation with the night clerk by the name of Hughes, the namesake of his predecessor Hughie, whom Erie had befriended and who recently has died. His death has plunged Erie into grief that started him "off on a bat." Erie tries to engage Hughes in conversation about the former night clerk, but Hughes is preoccupied with the boredom of his work. Try as he will, Erie never succeeds in making Hughes open up. Just as he is about to quit, the night clerk suddenly agrees to play a game of craps with him, which throws Erie into instant ecstasy and a flurry of renewed confidence.

From the beginning the two characters proceed along separate grooves of thought; their paths never cross. Even their agreement to play craps is by no means a connection. It's a near miss at best, for neither actually veers from his own track. While the night clerk plays to kill time, Erie uses it to "purge his soul of his grief" for Hughie and to boost his confidence. Their relationship is a musical counterpoint in which melodic themes, instead of weaving into each other for harmony, run along, as it were, in mathematical parallels. This creates a desperate situation that throws O'Neill's tragic view of life into strong relief. The despondency behind the scene is all the more poignant when we take note of the social status of the protagonists--both on the bottom rung of the social ladder, both losers. They are the very people who seem most likely to benefit from sympathy and mutual understanding, but O'Neill has placed a chasm between them. Will they ever see eye to eye? Will their separate parallel themes ever come together in harmony? The prospect is most unlikely. Then may we say that *Hughie* is a counterpoint devoid of harmony? Definitely not. It is almost a perfect counterpoint in that the tragic message of noncommunication is driven relentlessly home. For knowledge, though painful, enlightens, and illumines our way to further knowing.

NOTES

1. Eugene O'Neill, *A Touch of the Poet* (New Haven: Yale University Press, 1957), 43.

2. O'Neill, *Poet*, 116.

3. O'Neill, *Poet*, 176.

4. ----------. *A Moon for the Misbegotten* (London: Samuel French, Inc., 1950), 96.

Part Two

O'Neill in Comparison

7

Structures of Forgiveness: The Endings of *A Moon for the Misbegotten* and Ibsen's *Peer Gynt*

Rolf Fjelde

O'Neill's last play, *A Moon for the Misbegotten*, stands in the company of Sophocles' *Oedipus at Colonus*, Shakespeare's *The Tempest*, and Ibsen's *When We Dead Awaken* as its author's final decipherment of life. His three preceding companion dramas--*The Iceman Cometh, Long Day's Journey into Night*, and *Hughie*--might fairly be summarized by the lament of Antigone in the first of these forerunners, after she witnesses her long-suffering father's death: "Now the finish /Comes, and we know only /In all that we have seen and done /Bewildering mystery." (1) With this concluding work, however, as befits its change of setting into open air from the three previous plays' oppressive interiors, O'Neill opens a tentative redemptive pattern in the dramatic material. Instead of a foreground desolation ambiguously offset by ulterior traces of order, *A Moon for the Misbegotten* envelops and qualifies the individual desolation of James Tyrone, Jr. with an objective order and meaning that defines his situation, even though it cannot penetrate to his core of despair.

That order and meaning, which this inquiry seeks all too briefly to specify, are vital for discerning and accurately rendering the play's essential action. Primarily a function of its intrinsically Irish-American milieu (O'Neill went so far as to insist that no one not of Irish extraction be cast for it) and, as well, of its suffusion by deep and intimate family memories, the dominant order in the play derives from the intense Catholicism of his childhood. (2) His biographers Barbara and Arthur Gelb write, for example, that in his twelfth year, distraught over learning of his mother's drug addiction, he "fasted and confessed and made fervent acts of faith, hope, love and contrition, solemnly [accepting] the body and blood of Christ." (3) His final play marks his last and most artistically assimilated return to Catholic doctrine, if not as articles of personal belief, at least as sources of organizing structure.

At the same time, the final judgment that permeates *A Moon for the Misbegotten* gains additional resonance from a work that powerfully impressed itself on O'Neill's imagination early in his playwriting career, namely, Ibsen's *Peer Gynt*. During the winter of 1917-1918 he was recorded as reciting aloud enthusiastically from the verse of the play. (4) Travis Bogard has traced its recurrences in *The Emperor Jones*, (5) and Egil Torngvist its influence on *Marco Millions*. (6) It is not amiss to see *Peer Gynt* as resurfacing yet again in the design of this last drama, particularly in the fourth act, wherein Ibsen's motifs closely coincide with O'Neill's theatrical strategy. As we shall see, even the strict Catholicism surrounding Jim Tyrone's abortive quest for forgiveness finds, in the playwright's hands, more than usual accord with its Protestant analogy of Peer Gynt's repentance (*metanoia*, change or turning of mind) in heart's sorrow from a life that has missed the mark.

Within its single, minimally varied outdoor set, suggestive of a fixed, unalterable destiny--as Jim Tyrone says, "a plot I had to carry out"--the action of *A Moon for the Misbegotten* is built upon and unified by an interlocking series of mock deceptions and betrayals. Initiating the sequence, act one climaxes in the apparent betrayal of Phil Hogan by his farm landlord Jim Tyrone, who gloats that Hogan's hotheaded quarrel with his adjacent property owner, the millionaire T. Stedman Harder, has driven the asking price of the rundown farm sky high, turning its every boulder to gold. Act two then concentrates on Hogan and his daughter Josie's counter-betrayal, whereby she will drink the alcoholic Jim into her bed and a forced marriage that would secure the farm, as well as Tyrone's probated inheritance, permanently for the two of them.

Early in act three, both schemes are dispelled by Tyrone's confession that he had deceptively gone along with Harder's vengeful purchase bid, the better to punish him by a later rejection. Finally, in the conclusion of the play in act four, Josie accuses her father of betraying her in turn by pretending Jim's sellout, which Hogan knew to be counterfeit, was real. In this way, she charges, he aimed to have her exploit the appeal of her fictional virginity for Tyrone as marriage bait, ensuring, in the likely event of Jim's near-future death, the legacy exclusively for himself. For this offense, Josie threatens to leave home. In her father's eyes, this is yet another betrayal matching those of her three brothers, who abandoned the farm to make lives in the larger world (the last of them, Mike, departs at the opening of the play). Repeating the earlier pattern with Tyrone, both betrayals are rendered mock and void when Hogan confesses he had merely sought to force the reluctant lovers to drop their "damned pretending" and openly accept each other. Josie hears an unmistakable sincerity in her father's voice, trusts him, and agrees to remain on the farm.

These are the major deceptions and betrayals that spin this basically comedic plot, but they hardly exhaust the variations on the theme in the play. Jim's brief raffish anecdote about passing off the prostitute Dutch Maisie as his sister at the Catholic prep school is a cameo comic deception; and his anguished account of revenging himself on his dead mother, bound east by train for burial, night after night with the doll-faced whore carries the theme toward a tragic dimension. Both movements of the main plot, the first focused on Tyrone's deception, the second on Hogan's, takes the form of a betrayal generating a counter-betrayal, healed in due course by a confession, restoring emotional openness. The underlying tension has been identified by the psychologist Erik Erikson as the most fundamental of all the reiterative stages of the life-cycle, "for the solution of the nuclear conflict of basic trust versus basic mistrust in mere existence is the first task of the ego, and thus first of all a task for maternal care." In this light it is entirely fitting that the most memorable image at the core of O'Neill's drama is a *pieta* tableau: Jim's exhausted head cradled and, at the same time, dead to the world on Josie Hogan's Earth-Mother breasts.

Of all the works in O'Neill's repertory of known influences, it is Ibsen's *Peer Gynt* that conspicuously ends in a similar tableau. The defining situations are nearly the same: a wayward, life-weary, world-besotted traveler, having squandered himself on a succession of worthless, predatory women, comes back to the forgiving arms of one who, though not the biological mother, psychologically and spiritually fulfills that role. Peer's Solveig, in her final song, even prefigures the title of the other late Tyrone drama in her metaphor, thrice recurring, of the long life's-day journey. (7) For the four ill-fated Tyrones, that journey leads to the night of a common death-in-life, frozen in time, while for Peer it culminates in a long-postponed self-commitment illuminated by a sunrise of renewed hope.

The paths of both men converge on two humble, ramshackle cabins that hold for each what he most desperately needs to redeem his experience of the world as an amoral wilderness. For James Tyrone the name of that wilderness is Broadway, the rapacious fringe of the commercial theater, a hell hard as broken glass, populated by flint-eyed tarts who, as Josie understatedly observes, don't neglect their business. (8) Peer Gynt arrives out of a comparable Dantesque dark wood, without guideposts or landmarks, where he peels the centerless onion, and next from a burnt-out moor where subhuman trolls and one-hoofed devils move about, repossessing defective humans who have existed by no more than half measures and evasive compromises.

The scope of *Peer Gynt* is not confined to an immediate foreground of deception and betrayal; it expands to include the whole geography of the long life's-day journey home. The action of the play explores an adventure-prone locus of origin in Norway through the first three acts. Act four proceeds to trace a great arc across the North African desert from Morocco to Cairo, then returns for reckonings and judgments to Norway in act five. The full circuit thus duplicates the Great Boyg's spurious advice to Peer, always to go roundabout. By circumscribing the entire continent of Europe, moreover, the play implies that the Gyntish escape from accountability is a general malaise of modern Western man. Ibsen's action, in short, is world-historical and future-directed, whereas O'Neill's by contrast is intensely personal and past-imprisoned. Peer's predicament evokes the jeopardy of a civilization; the Tyrones' evokes the haunting anguish of one family in a way that touches families everywhere.

It is forgiveness for themselves, for the pain they endlessly inflict upon each other, that the various members of the Tyrone family seek; and none with more stricken ambivalence than the professedly cynical Jim from his secular Mother Confessor and blessed nonvirgin Josie Hogan. The classic literary exposition of what Catholic forgiveness entails is found in Canto IX of Dante's *Purgatorio*. Dante the pilgrim soul is conveyed, in a state of unconscious surrender, by St. Lucy, *Santa Lucia*, patroness of clear-sighted vision, to the very threshold of the purgatorial climb proper, where he sees, cut in everlasting stone, the three steps that every penitent must ascend to the upward path. In John Ciardi's verse translation:

> We came to the first step: White marble gleaming
> so polished and so smooth that in its mirror
> I saw my true reflection past all seeming.
> The second was stained darker than blue-black
> and of a rough-grained and a fire-flaked
>   stone,
> its length and breadth crisscrossed by many a
>   crack.
> The third and topmost was of porphyry,
> or so it seemed, but of a red as flaming
> as blood that spurts out of an artery. (9)

The first penitential step is *confession*: to admit one's grievous fault in the mirror of self-reflection. The second step is *contrition*: to feel it in true sorrow and repentance, the "broken and contrite heart" of Scripture. The third, the outpouring of the heart's blood, is *restitution*: "making good" above and beyond mere measure both to the injured party and to oneself. Only then is forgiveness merited and possible.

Jim Tyrone, however, is alcoholically muddled about the conditions of forgiveness. Confession is at the heart of his visit to the Hogans, father and daughter; he arrives motivated by physical desire, nostalgia, camaraderie, and the sharing of a bottle, but he stays until he can unburden himself of the bitter and complex memory of desecrating his mother's last journey home. No question that he has climbed the first stair.

Contrition is another matter, though. To be forgiven one must first forgive; and this he adamantly cannot do for his father. "He was a lousy tightwad bastard," he complains. "He knows I hated him, anyway--as much as he hated me. I'm glad he's dead. So is he. Or he ought to be." (10) With respect to his mother, for leaving him alone through her inconsiderate death, he wants revenge attained through debased variants of wine, women, and song: the case of booze aboard the train, the whore with the polar bear smile, and the sentimental vaudeville ballad he replays again and again in the phonograph groove of his brain, "baby's cries can't waken her/ in the baggage coach ahead." (11) The possibility, essential to restitution, of making good to anyone at all in his life, is wholly beyond Tyrone's terminal despair.

But as the comparison with and perhaps influence of *Peer Gynt* brings out, in this last of his late masterpieces, O'Neill is writing not just a parochially conceived family tragedy. With so many of his earlier plays, he was concerned to write American drama out of the national mainstream; and *A Moon for the Misbegotten*--the "only Irish need apply" casting notice notwithstanding--is far from an exception. Jim Tyrone damns himself beyond the pale not only by Catholic doctrine but also by Protestant denial of that grace accessible to the priesthood of all believers. In Ibsen's tradition, derived from the Danish theologian Kierkegaard, it is the leap of faith involved in the choice of one's true self, carrying one over death and destruction to a new plane of existence, that is the equivalent of being forgiven. By returning to what one once purely was, one recovers the potency of authentic becoming, of moving ahead into the creative possibility, once more, of freedom. "What was lost is given back." (12) It is, stated more elaborately than usual in evangelical Christianity, what is meant by being "born again." It is why, when for the first time in Ibsen's drama, Peer goes straight through to Solveig, the God-bearing image, not roundabout into compromise and the cheapening of life, he is reduced, or restored, to the condition of a little child, made new and possible once more, even as a weary, eighty-year-old man, in Solveig's cradling arms.

The core of Ibsen's final scene is poignantly paralleled in *A Moon for the Misbegotten*. O'Neill makes it unmistakably clear that Jim Tyrone is in no sense capable of being born again. His life is locked irretrievably in what once was--those painful memories; that unique yet generic family; those words spoken, never to be called back; those betrayals of responsibility and love (the two are the same) suspected, walked in upon unawares, understood only gradually. "There is no present or future," Tyrone tells Josie, "only the past happening over and over again--now." (13) This is the veritable Inferno of Dante, where the punishment is the transgression itself, experienced endlessly, without remission.

Against this merciless self-damnation Josie tries every wile and every appeal she knows. Against the stubborn ghosts of past betrayal, frozen hatred grounded in old unforgotten hurt, she practices every resource of forgiveness, which is healing grounded in love. And against her irrepressible compassion, unswayably, tragically, and one must say as well with regret, willfully, selfishly, indulgently, Jim Tyrone closes her out. He rejects the option of being born again. Like Ivan Karamazov, he wishes only to turn his ticket back. "It was my mistake," she tells her father. "I thought there was still hope. I didn't know he'd died already--that it was a damned soul coming to me in the moonlight, to confess and be forgiven and find peace for a night." (14)

At the end of Sophocles' last decipherment of life, the aged Oedipus, who has lived long and suffered much, is translated by the gods from the grove at Colonus to his rest, amid heavenly signs and wonders. Shakespeare's *The Tempest* concludes in a marvel of restorations and a prayer that will pierce to mercy itself and free all faults. In *When We Dead Awaken*, the artist Arnold Rubek and his model Irene, two of Ibsen's perennially aspiring transcenders of human limit, struggle upward toward the sunrise that gilds the Peak of Promise, and over their downfalls the black-habited nun utters the words, *"Pax vobiscum"* ("Peace be with you"). All these can be accounted variant structures of forgiveness and reconciliation.

The remarkable phenomenon of *A Moon for the Misbegotten* is that it is a play not of forgiveness, but of the failure of forgiveness. O'Neill tough-mindedly will not relieve his protagonist Jim Tyrone of accountability for his actions, and the structures of this judgment are anchored firmly in the provisos of the religious traditions dominant in his characters' lives. It is that very tough-mindedness that makes the futile generosity of Josie Hogan's spirit shine more brightly, even as the last act sunrise, reminiscent of Ibsen, glows more vividly in its enveloping growth. The playwright has ensured that hers is the dominant and final light of the play, the proof that grace is actual in certain singular spirits. In 1920 with *Beyond the Horizon*, at the beginning of his career, O'Neill gave the American theater a standard of seriousness from which it could never retreat. Twenty-five years later, at the close of his creative life, he presented it with something greater. With *A Moon for the Misbegotten*, in the creation of Josie Hogan, he gave it the imperishable bequest of a living soul.

NOTES

1. Sophocles, *Oedipus at Colonus*, trans. Robert Fitzgerald, *The Complete Greek Tragedies*, vol. 2, ed. David Grene and Richmond Lattimore (Chicago, Ill.: University of Chicago Press, 1959), 150-51.

2. Travis Bogard, *Contour in Time: The Plays of Eugene O'Neill* (New York: Oxford University Press, 1972), 448.

3. Arthur and Barbara Gelb, *O'Neill* (New York: Delta Books, 1962), 71.

4. Egil Tornqvist, "Ibsen and O'Neill: A Study in Influence," *Scandinavian Studies* 37 (3) (August 1965): 213.

5. Bogard, 136-37.

6. Torngvist, 224.

7. Henrik Ibsen, *Peer Gynt*, trans. Rolf Fjelde (Minneapolis, Minn.: University of Minnesota Press, 1980), 209.

8. Eugene O'Neill, *A Moon for the Misbegotten* (New York: Vintage Books, 1974), 97.

9. Dante Alighieri, *The Purgatorio*, trans. John Ciardi (New York: New American Library, 1961), 105.

10. O'Neill, 83.

11. O'Neill, 72, 98.

12. George Price, *The Narrow Pass: Kierkegaard's Concept of Man* (New York: McGraw Hill, 1963), 200.

13. O'Neill, 82-83.

14. O'Neill, 104.

8

Politics and a Proletarian Tragedy: A Comparative Analysis of the Reception of Eugene O'Neill's *The Hairy Ape* in Germany and the United States

Ward B. Lewis

In the fall of 1986 Peter Stein returned as guest director to the Theatre at Lehnin Square, Berlin, after a two-year absence from that theatre, where he had directed for more than a decade. (1) The forty-nine-year-old Stein, characterized by the critic Wolfgang Ignee as the highest cultural export of the nation--as once had been Max Reinhardt or Bertolt Brecht--brought with him the Italian scene designer Lucio Fanti for their production of *Der harrige Affe* (*The Hairy Ape*). Two flops earlier in the season raised the expectations of theatregoers.

The critics were struck by the employment of chorus--in group scenes with stokers, capitalists, police, prison inmates, union members, and finally apes--as well as by Fanti's staging. Fifth Avenue rose sharply as it receded into the background; stylized, black, pointed buildings in pale light formed a street canyon reminiscent of the effect of Dr. Caligari. The prison scene was blacker than night, and Yank's fellow inmates were identifiable only by their pale fingers gripping the cell bars. The ensemble appeared in furs in five cylindrical cages in the monkey house of the zoo.

Such scenery requires assembly and rebuilding with pauses as long as thirty minutes between the scenes with the lights on and considerable noise generated by the construction. An intermission of an hour was needed for the rebuilding of the ship in the first part to the Fifth Avenue scene in the second. Roland Schafer as Yank provided the only continuity, and the extended intervals put such a severe strain upon him that the staging overcame the action and the actors.

The director attempted to hark back to the leftist origins of the Theatre on the Bank of the Halle where he had first achieved renown. A glance through the program notes, an impressive volume of one hundred and seventy-five pages, including Stein's own translation of O'Neill, establishes this political intent. It includes lines by John Dos Passos descriptive of the financial empire of J. P. Morgan, the stock market, unemployment, and police brutality. Even more overtly political, however, are a photograph of a row of cell blocks in an Alabama prison, an account by Jack London of the beating and torture he endured in a California prison, and IWW posters, including one illustrating the Wobblies united as a fist. Also included are a story of the martyrdom of Joe Hill, which initiated what is described as "one of the greatest campaigns of protest in the history of the American and international workers movement," (2) a picture of the final zoo scene from a Moscow production of 1929, and text by Friedrich Engels on the development of the human hand from that of the ape.

The structure of class society was emphasized in the scenery in the first part of the drama. A gigantic ship rose three stories high before the eyes of the spectators. Far above on the upper deck, capitalists promenaded along the railing in the fashionable dress of the twenties. Mildred (Corinna Kirchhoff), pale, emaciated as a skeleton, narcissistic, and elegantly artificial in an expensive white cocktail dress, was accompanied by her aunt (Christine Oesterlein), heavily made up in a bright red dress.

The mid-deck area revealed the cramped living quarters of the stokers, containing narrow iron beds beneath a ceiling so low they could not stand erect--a twisted throng of half-naked bodies, of roaring, reeling ruffians.

The ship's horn and the sound of pounding engines accompanied the movement of steel plates that retracted to reveal the boiler room in the hold of the ship, a space broad, steep, and low. Coal dust hung like black fog in the air; a feeble light was provided by three bulbs. Half-naked stokers whose faces and chests were covered by soot and gleaming from sweat handled gigantic coal shovels before the furnaces to create a chiaroscuro effect. The choreography of ballet defined the simultaneous movement of fifteen shovels into the glowing red mouths of fifteen furnaces in a way to suggest that the human being is a machine.

The Berlin critic Klaus Nothnagel found his Marxism rewarded in Stein's interpretation of O'Neill. The old days of class struggle are recalled when Yank discovers there is no connecting link between poor swine and the higher forms of life ("hohe Tieren"). Mildred evokes a desire in him that can only find expression in class hatred. (3)

Thus spoke Berlin. The provincial critics and others, however, found the class struggle compromised in O'Neill/Stein. Michael Stone in the *Rheinischer Merkur* contended that the enormity of the stage effects defeated Stein's attempt to recall the leftist origins of the

Theatre on the Bank of the Halle. And the theatre journal *Die Deutsche Buhne* put it somewhat differently: scenery and breathtaking choreography so stupefied the spectator that he or she could only marvel at the illusionary effects the theatre was capable of. (4) For that reason or because of the drama itself it was unclear whether *Der harrige Affe* concerned a proletarian committed to class struggle or constituted a modern Everyman tragedy.

Urs Jenny, editor of the national news weekly *Der Spiegel*, found a source of the problem in the music by Peter Fischer and suggested thereby just how political this interpretation was not. A love motif heard when Yank is most antagonistically class conscious suggested that his desire for class struggle had its origins in eroticism. (5)

It is Yank himself who is most problematic. One reviewer observed that his encounter with the IWW revealed him as an egomaniac incapable of adopting a socially oriented perspective. (6) The reputed drama critic Georg Hensel recalled the characterization of Yank as "an orphan child of the world" ("*ein Waisenkind der Welt*") made by Alfred Kerr more than sixty years earlier; Hensel pointed out the obvious fact that Yank is an anarchist, not a socialist; he wants to destroy the world, not change it. (7)

Most negative was Gert Gliewe of the Munich *Abendzeitung*, who implied that *The Hairy Ape* was ill conceived: "It consists of a dose of anticapitalist criticism and a portion of socialist mythology warmed up with superficial existential doubt and served up by Stein as world theatre." (8) Urs Jenny, another dissenter, went so far as to state that the evening was marked by the curse of pseudo significance.

The last word, arguably, is that uttered by the prestigious weekly *Die Zeit*. Here Benjamin Henrichs observed that Peter Stein's comeback was overwhelming in its effect; both O'Neill's work and the public were overwhelmed. (9) Stein produced a miracle of the theatre, and it was all the same to him if *Der haarige Affe* spoke to contemporary political realities.

These differences of critical opinion were generated by what was perceived as the political nature of O'Neill's work. Quite aside, however, from the question of whether O'Neill/Stein was Socialist or Marxist was consideration of the work from another political perspective, one based in the German dramatic tradition of political theatre. Eugene O'Neill's *Der haarige Affe* is interpreted in the light of drama by Ernst Toller and Bertolt Brecht, as it had been for the sixty years since it first premiered in Berlin in 1924. Playing upon the title of Toller's most famous work *Masses and Man* (*Masse Mensch*, 1921) the leading national theatre journal, *Theater heute*, described Yank as "a modern man of Masses and Man" ("*ein moderner Mann der Masse*

Mensch"), and the newspaper *Die Zeit* noted how O'Neill successfully united two aspects of Toller's drama: the apparition of the animal-like horde and the ideal of the awakening proletarian. (10) Revealing the German penchant for literary history, Georg Hensel recalled how the eminent critic Herbert Ihering had recognized the qualities of Toller's writing in O'Neill's work six decades before.

The comparison with Brecht is made in the same breath. For Klaus Nothnagel *Der haarige Affe* recalled his countryman's revolutionary theatre. Benjamin Hennichs identified the play as the American cousin of Brecht's *Baal*, related by Expressionism. (11) Jurgen Beckemann in the title of his review suggested a comparison to Brecht's *In the Jungle of Cities*; the critic credits Stein for his feeling for tradition as he reaches back to the social critical beginnings of the original Theatre on the Bank of the Halle and at the same time projects beyond the present theatre with a didactic drama by O'Neill after the fashion of Brecht illustrating false, inadequate proletarian behavior and its tragicomic consequences. (12)

Analysis of the initial reception sixty years earlier of O'Neill's drama reveals the peculiar manner in which the work is regarded in German dramatic and literary tradition. On October 31, 1924, O'Neill's work first opened at the Tribune in Berlin, directed by Eugen Robert with Eugen Klopfer as Yank. The critics were unanimous in their perception of the political nature of the drama. Friedrich Dusel in the stolidly bourgeois journal *Westermanns Monatshefte* hailed *Affe* as the beginning of American social drama wherein O'Neill holds a warning before the eyes of his countrymen. (13) The two principal critics of the time occupied a position on the left of the political spectrum and welcomed the work warmly. Julius Bab, who just a few years later would be driven into exile during the Third Reich and find refuge in New York, referred to O'Neill's splendidly bitter proletarian tragedy ("*die groBartig herbe Proletariertragodie*"). (14) O'Neill presents the calamity of the proletarian being more deeply, movingly, significantly, and terribly than anywhere in world drama since Georg Buchner's *Woyzeck*. (15)

Alfred Kerr, like Bab a Social Democrat who would be forced into exile, was probably the most influential drama critic of his time. An American Germanist has written the following about him: "For almost forty years his reviews and criticism of the theatre in Berlin, during what was probably the liveliest period of that lively city's theatrical history, set the pace for and in large measure determined the taste of the German stage." (16) Kerr attributes to O'Neill's Irish background the fact that he is a champion of the oppressed. Familiar with New York theatre and the productions of The Provincetown

Players, Kerr purported to adopt O'Neill as his godson and extolled those characteristically American aspects manifested in *Affe*: images and effects that are not diffuse or uncertain but forceful, sure, and right on target. (17)

A feature of O'Neill's technique struck Kerr as a cliche in German drama. This was the use of contrasts such as boiler room with promenade deck, proletarian with millionaire, black figures with white ones. Nevertheless, O'Neill more than redeems himself: "He smashes holes in the rigid golden wall of the mountain of capital. The conscience of his day cries from him. Somehow he grips the audience by its heart, and it sees strength beyond the contrived." (18) Especially effective was the scene at the offices of the IWW, whom Kerr equated with the Social Democrats and who are represented in a hopelessly bureaucratic session, for which the translator Else von Hollander experimented with twenty dialects to find the corresponding Yankee tone, sporty and directly to the point. (19)

Kerr cites Robert Edmond Jones for the admitted influence of Ernst Toller's drama *Masses and Man* upon *The Hairy Ape*. Jones had seen a production by Jurgen Fehling in Berlin, which left its mark in the chain of stokers before the fiery furnaces, the rolling of the ship, and the sound of engines. (20)

The connection between Toller's work and that of O'Neill causes the two dramas to reinforce each other in the consciousness of the audience. *Masses and Man* was first performed publicly three years before O'Neill's work, at which time--although Alfred Kerr characterized it as excessively peaceful--it was prohibited in Bavaria as provocative of class hatred; it was denounced by some critics as a Communist mass, a celebration of Bolshevism. (21) Written against the backdrop of the November revolution of 1918, it deals with the subject of nonviolence and the degree to which the means employed influence the quality of the goal, here, the kind of socialism.

A strongly expressionistic work like O'Neill's, *Masses and Man* is subtitled "A Fragment of the Social Revolution of the Twentieth Century" and dedicated "To the Workers." (22)   What O'Neill subtitled in seeming contradiction "A Comedy of Ancient and Modern Life in Eight Scenes" constitutes a timeless statement about an individual's sense of his own worth and his perception of his relation to the world. Toller similarly presents a dialectic. He offers in seven short scenes a play about the relationship of a person to the masses of his fellow human beings and the price, individual and collective, to be paid for social progress in the twentieth century.

Scenes of Toller's work appearing alternatively as "visionary abstracts of reality" or as "dream pictures" achieve a surreal effect, which is reinforced by anonymous robot-like figures, especially those representing bankers and brokers speculating upon war. (23) These are not unlike the members of Mildred's class on Fifth Avenue, "a procession of gaudy marionettes, yet with something of the relentless horror of Frankensteins in their detached mechanical awareness." (24)

Central to *Masses and Man* are The Woman, representing the individual human and his or her feelings and conscience, and the Nameless One, who speaks for mankind and advocates the revolution. A dialectic is posed between the two, between man and the masses, between individual moral values and social impulses. This latter opposition exists as a tension in every person. The Woman reaches a conclusion:

If I took but one human life,
I should betray the Masses.
Who acts may only sacrifice himself.
Hear me: no man may kill men for a cause.
Unholy every cause that needs to kill. (151)

As an individual member of the masses, The Woman shared the guilt of this body for the bloodletting that ensued, and the work ends in tragedy as she is executed.

The production which Robert Jones saw opened at the People's Theatre on Bulow Square on September 29, 1921, directed by Jurgen Fehling. A theatre recognized as fully bourgeois attempted with his direction to distinguish itself as contemporary and political. (25) Mary Dietrich as The Woman contributed to an aggressive interpretation with flowing movement and fanatical language, accompanied by the music of Heinz Thiessen. What Jones saw and the effect it evoked are described in the words of Julius Bab:

Supported by the scenery of Strohbach, Fehling created a dramatic work of overpowering force: stairs built upon the stage towered into emptiness, and upon them masses huddled together like a single creature quivering and screaming. Shadows as tall as a tower wandered across the horizon menacing sinisterly. When the base of the stairs was suddenly illuminated figures hissed like demons from Hades. (26)

The dialectic posed by the self-consciousness of an individual standing in relationship to society about him is associated with another dramatist, with whom O'Neill's name forms a constellation. This is Bertolt Brecht, who provides additional grounds for comparison with O'Neill in that his dramatic figure Baal bears similarity to Yank.

In the lines of a song from a drama Brecht expresses perfectly the sentiments of Toller's Nameless One, the spokesman of mankind and voice of the revolution. "What base act would you not commit," he is asked, "in order to eradicate baseness?" (27)

The sacrifice of individual morality upon the altar of collective social progress is demanded in slightly different words when Brecht observes: "Those who have sympathy for the many are permitted none for the few." (28) No quarter is shown in the struggle to achieve the revolution; "in this battle there are only blood stained hands and those which have been hacked off," observes a character. (29)

Just as Yank represents to the other stokers "a self-expression, the very last word in what they are, their most highly developed individual"(40) so does a dramatic character of Brecht embody the epitome of individuality. This is Baal in the drama bearing that name, who like Yank defies society and suffers a miserable demise. In compulsive pursuit of the pleasures of the senses, the asocial Baal sings, drinks, and copulates, abandoning his female victims to suicide. In a drama that is a celebration of nihilism, Baal embodies an unbridled force--vital, procreative, and destructive--that is quietly extinguished in death like Yank.

The work was first played in Leipzig on December 8, 1923, and followed the performance of a drama by Toller that unleashed Nazi tumult in the theatre. (30) Brecht's play fared not much better and incited disruption in the audience, because the forces of the right objected to it as an immoral and disgusting insult to pure German art. After being revised, the drama was only slightly more tolerable to its political opponents when directed by Brecht at the German Theater in Berlin on February 14, 1926. Oskar Homolka as Baal was almost driven from the stage by whistling, yelling, and clapping. *Baal* has nevertheless survived and was filmed in 1969 by Volker Schlondorff with Rainer Werner Fassbinder interpreting Baal as a contemporary student intellectual who discloses the evils of capitalism.

If *Der harrige Affe* is interpreted in Germany within this political context, and indeed, has been so understood since its very first appearance in that country, *The Hairy Ape*, which opened March 9, 1922, in New York, was greeted by reviews which were not only "surprisingly tepid" (Gelb 498) but extraordinarily apolitical, and O'Neill himself denied his politics. (31) The fact that Yank comes to share Long's attitude toward the exploitation of "the damned Capitalist class"(44) and seeks to revenge himself upon it are largely overlooked. Alexander Woolcott of the *New York Times* detected not a trace of politics in his initial review, nor a month later in a second column when the play moved from the Provincetown Theatre on Macdougal Street to the Plymouth Theatre on Broadway. (32)

Authors of journal articles, granted more time than the newspaper drama critics for a thoughtful consideration of O'Neill's play, were no more inclined to political perceptions. The contributor to *Dial* was not, nor was the critic for *The Bookman*, who thought the drama was so poorly written that the audience could read into it anything it wished. (33) Stark Young, an editor of *The New Republic*, couldn't decide whether the play offered pessimistic social criticism or not, but Ludwig Lewisohn, an associate editor of *The Nation*, was clear. "Mr. O'Neill proclaims no tendency." (34)

It would be an oversimplification to say that politics in *The Hairy Ape* were totally ignored. J. Ranken Towse of *The Evening Post* characterized the work as "a tract in favor of the IWW"; and Heywood Broun in *The World* stated that O'Neill has "found a cause" and "become a propagandist." (35) It was, however, a trade publication that recognized the work for what it was. Writing in *Theatre Magazine* under the name "Mr. Hornblower," the critic hailed *The Hairy Ape* as the play of the year and his candidate for the Pulitzer Prize: "a study profound and moving in its picture of the futility of brute power in its sole opposition to the conventions of society and the overwhelming authority of capitalistic control." (36) The critic goes on to describe those such as the writer for the illustrated monthly magazine *The Century*, who felt threatened by O'Neill's play and asked why one should tolerate "such a menace to things as they are." (37) Hornblower observes: "They are the reactionaries who insist that reference to class prejudice should be ignored, and that there is no such thing as inequality." (38)

NOTES

1. It had been built to his design. In the late 1970s, when Stein threatened to leave the Theatre on the Bank of the Halle, the Berlin Senate agreed to renovate the Mendelssohn Building at Lehnin Square at a cost of millions of marks. The journal *Theater heute* describes what resulted as a gigantic structure that is a combination of exhibition hall and school auditorium; with expensive technology and gigantic mobile podia, it is a stage monstrosity possessing the charm of an airplane hanger. Michael Merschmeier, "Erste-Klasse-Leiche," *Theater heute* 12/86 (December 1986): 1.

2. Eugene O'Neill, *Der haarige Affe*, Theatre Program, Schaubuhne am Lehniner Platz, Premiere 9 November 1986, 31.

3. Klaus Nothnagel, "Absturzende Umbauten," *Die Tageszeitung*, 14 November 1986.

4. Michael Stone, "Brutal schoner Gewaltakt," *Rheinischer Merkur*, 14 November 1986. Rev. of *Der haarige Affe, Die Deutsche Buhne* 5 (May 1987): n.pag.

5. Urs Jenny, "King Kong trifft Fraulein Amerika," *Der Spiegel*, 40, 47 (17 November 1986): 272.

6. Monika Handschuch-Hammann, "Die Geschichte einer Seele oder die Herrschaft des Buhnenbildes," *Mitternachtszeitung* 11 (Winter 1986-1987): 29.

7. Georg Hansel, "Zur Holle mit euch, Jungs!" *Frankfurter Allgemeine Zeitung*, 11 November 1986.

8. Gert Gliewe, "Klassenkampfers Ende im Kafig des Gorillas," *Abendzeitung*, 11 November 1986: 7; Jenny, 272.

9. Benjamin Henrichs, "Gesang aus dem Feuerofen," *Die Zeit*, 41, 47 (21 November 1986): 15-16.

10. Merschmeier, 1. Henrichs, 15.

11. Henrichs, 15.

12. Jurgen Beckemann, "Im Dickicht der Stadte verloren," *Kolner Stadt Anzeiger*, 11 November 1986.

13. This does not mean that Dusel found the work adequate. Chagrined that American drama was so fashionable upon the German stage, he muttered that, if this was realistic social drama of the New World, God should preserve Germany against imports. Friedrich Dusel, rev. of *Der haarige Affe*, "Dramatische Rundschau," *Westermanns Monatscheft* 137 (1924-1924): 534.

14. "Die groBartig herbe Proletariertragodie," Julius Bab, *Schauspieler und Schauspielkunst* (Berlin: Oesterheld, 1926), 152.

15. Julius Bab, *Das Theater der Gegenwart* (Leipzig: J. J. Weber, 1928), 212.

16. Ian C. Loram, "Alfred Kerr's America," *Deutschlands literarisches Amerikabild*, ed. Alexander Ritter (Hildescheim and New York: Georg Ohms Verlag, 1977), 468.

17. Alfred Kerr, *Die Welt im Drama*, ed. Gerhard F. Hering (Koln, Berlin: Kiepenheuer and Witsch, 1964), 212.

18. "Ein Dichter schlagt hier Offnungen in die starr gewordene Mauer des Kapitalbergs. Das Zeitgewissen ruft aus ihm. Er faBt irgendwie dem Horer ans Herz--der uber Talmihaftes hin eine Kraft sieht." Alfred Kerr, *Newyork und London. Statten des Gerschicks. Zwanzig Kapitel nach dem Weltkrieg* (Berlin: S. Fischer, 1923), 77.

19. Alfred Kerr, rev. of *Der haarige Affe, Berliner Tageblatt*, 1 November 1924.

20. Kerr, *New York*, 78, credits Jones with the direction as well as staging, whereas Gelb, 494-95, indicates direction was by Arthur Hopkins and James Light, staging by Cleon Throckmorton as well as

Jones. Arthur and Barbara Gelb, *O'Neill* (New York: Harper and Row, 1974), 494-95.

21. This according to Toller as recorded in Rosemarie Altenhofer, *Masse Mensch*, ed. Jost Hermand, *Zu Ernst Toller: Drama und Engagement* (Stuttgart: Ernst Klett, 1981), 130.

22. For the extent of O'Neill's debt to the German expressionists, especially in *Ape*, see Mardi Valgemae, "O'Neill and German Expressionism," *Modern Drama* 10 (September 1967): 111-23.

23. Ernst Toller, *Masses and Man, Seven Plays*, trans. Vera Mendel (London: John Lane the Bodley Head, 1935), 113. (Subsequent references to this source will be indicated parenthetically with page numbers in the text.)

24. Eugene O'Neill, *The Hairy Ape*, in *Nine Plays* (New York: Modern Library, 1941), 69. (Subsequent references to this source will be indicated parenthetically with page numbers in the text.)

25. Gunther Ruhle, *Theater fur die Republik* (Frankfurt a. M.: S. Fischer, 1967), 321.

26. Fehling schuf "(mit Unterstutzung des Buhnenmalers Strohbach) ein Szenenwerk von hinreiBender Kraft: auf dem Stufenbau der Buhne, der gespenstisch ins Leere ragte, ballten sich Massen wie ein einziges zuckendes und schreiendes Lebewesen zusammen, uber den Horizont wanderten turmhohe Schatten mit unheimlicher Drohung, im plotzlich erhellten Sockel des Treppenbaus zischten Figuren wie unterweltliche Damonen." Bab, *Das Theater der Gegenwart*, 176.

27. "Welche Niedrigkeit begingest du nicht, um / Die Niedrigkeit auszutilgen?" From "Andere die Welt: Sie braucht es," Bertolt Brecht, *Die MaBnahme, Gesammelte Werke* 2 (Frankfurt a. M.: Suhrkamp, 1967), 652. Subsequent references to Brecht's *Gesammelte Werke* in the following two endnotes will be indicated as *GW* preceding the page number.

28. "Die mit vielen Mitleid haben durfen keines haben mit den wenigen." Brecht, "Zu *Mutter Courage und ihre Kinder*," *Schriften zum Theater* 3, GW 17, 1140.

29. "Ja, aber in diesem Kampt gibt es nur blutbeleckte Hande oder abgehauene Hande," says Langevin in Brecht, *Die Tage der Commune*, GW 5, 2174.

30. This was *Hinkemann* in the Altes Theater the evening before.

31. Gelbs, 498. In an interview from 1922 shortly after *Ape* was written, O'Neill recalls how he once was an active socialist but how he has now "come to feel so indifferent toward political and social movements of all kinds." O'Neill, "What the Theatre Means to Me," ed. Oscar Cargill et al., *O'Neill and His Plays: Four Decades of*

Criticism (New York: New York University Press, 1961), 107.

32. Alexander Woollcott, "The Play," rev. of *The Hairy Ape*, *New York Times*, 10 March, 1922: 18.

33. G. S., rev. of *The Hairy Ape*, "The Theatre," *Dial* 72 (May 1922): 548-49. Rev. of *The Hairy Ape*, *The Bookman* 55 (May 1922): 284.

34. Stark Young, "The Hairy Ape," *New Republic* 30 (22 March 1922): 112-13. Ludwig Lewisohn, "Drama. The Development of Eugene O'Neill," rev. of *The Hairy Ape*, *Nation* 114 (22 March 1922): 350.

35. Gelbs, 498.

36. "Mr. Hornblower Goes to the Play," rev. of *The Hairy Ape*, *Theatre Magazine* 35 (May 1922): 305. This constitutes an early statement of the position defined by Doris Alexander, who sees the drama as an expression of O'Neill's anarchism: "*The Hairy Ape*, then, presents a profoundly pessimistic social philosophy which rejects entirely the status quo, but sees no answer for man in a better society, and no hope for destroying the existing society." Doris Alexander, "Eugene O'Neill as Social Critic," Cargill, 396.

37. Rev. of *The Hairy Ape*, *The Century* 104 (September 1922): 749.

38. "Hornblower," 305.

9

Eternal Recurrence and the Shaping of O'Neill's Dramatic Structures

Albert E. Kalson and Lisa M. Schwerdt

In his Nobel Prize acceptance speech in 1936 Eugene O'Neill acknowledged to the people of Sweden what students and critics of his plays had already recognized, his enormous debt to one of their countrymen. "The greatest happiness this occasion affords . . . ," he declared, "is the opportunity it gives me to acknowledge, with gratitude and pride . . . the debt my work owes to that greatest genius of all modern dramatists, your August Strindberg. . . . [His] influence runs clearly through more than a few of my plays and is plain for everyone to see." (1)

For Egil Tornqvist, author of critical studies of both Strindberg and O'Neill, the American's homage to Sweden's foremost dramatist is hardly surprising: "Time and again he had acknowledged Strindberg's influence; and now when he was addressing the Swedish Academy and the Swedish people, it seemed an appropriate way of expressing his gratitude for being honored with the prize." (2) The critic cites as more revealing a passage near the conclusion of the speech in which O'Neill links Strindberg with the German philosopher Friedrich Nietzsche: "For me," O'Neill declared, "he remains, as Nietzsche remains, in his sphere, the master, still to this day more modern than any of us, still our leader." Tornqvist comments, "It seemed natural to mention him along with the Swede, for Nietzsche was the only other writer who had exercised an influence on him comparable to that of Strindberg."

O'Neill's public bonding of himself with the Swede and the German may hold even more significance than has heretofore been recognized. Although scholars have acknowledged the relationship between Strindberg and Nietzsche--who even engaged in a brief correspondence--and the influence of each of the two individually on

O'Neill, no one, not even Tornqvist, has explored fully the specific aspect of their work that points to an integral relationship among the three of them. In emphasizing the extent to which the philosopher influenced the *content* of the work of both dramatists--his views on tragedy, on women and marriage, on the role of the superman in the concept of the will to power--critics have neglected the manner in which another Nietzschean concept provides a *form* for their drama--the circularity of eternal recurrence. (3)

In the words of Walter A. Kaufmann, "Nietzsche's philosophy of power culminates in the dual vision of the superman and the eternal recurrence." (4)   Because the two concepts appear at times to be contradictory, many Nietzsche interpreters, considering recurrence of lesser importance, have disregarded it. According to Kaufmann, however, Nietzsche himself, who referred to eternal recurrence as "doctrine," looked upon it as the climax of his philosophy: "The man . . . who has organized the chaos of his passions and integrated every feature of his character, redeeming even the ugly by giving it a meaning in a beautiful totality--this *Ubermensch* would also realize how inextricably his own being was involved in the totality of the cosmos: and in affirming his own being, he would also affirm all that is, has been, or will be." (5) Eternal recurrence, which Nietzsche traced back to classical antiquity, to Heraclitus and Pythagoras, even to the myths of archaic peoples, had for him a scientific basis, or so the philosopher could believe as he read in Heinrich Heine, whom he admired, that "time is infinite, but the things in time, the concrete bodies, are finite. . . . Now, however long a time may pass, according to the eternal laws governing the combinations of this eternal play of repitition, all configurations which have previously existed on this earth must yet meet, attract, repulse, kiss, and corrupt each other again." (6) The *Ubermensch* consequently embraces life totally, accepting its pain along with its joy, as he lives fully in the moment and recognizes in it all time-- past, present, and future: "Nothing that is may be subtracted, nothing is dispensable. . . . My formula for the greatness of a man is *amor fati*: that one would not have anything different, not forward, not backward, not in all eternity." (7)

The concept of eternal recurrence, however, contains within itself a negative component. Like the absurdists who ignore the positive implications of existentialism, of man defining himself, to dramatize instead its negative aspect of man in the void, Strindberg and O'Neill too eventually turned from the joy and triumph inherent in Nietzsche's philosophy to the futility it holds for the man who recognizes himself as something less than the superman. For Strindberg, who for a time believed in the power of his will, recurrence led to passive acceptance and resignation; for O'Neill, who as a young man exalted in its promise of renewal, it finally meant despair.

This essay will attempt to indicate a new direction for those who, having taken their cue directly from O'Neill and scrutinized the influence of Strindberg and Nietzsche on his work, have focused perhaps too narrowly on only a part of that influence. An understanding of the O'Neill aesthetic calls not only for an exploration of form in the plays of Strindberg but also for attention to that specific aspect of Nietzsche's philosophy which led the American dramatist to an adaptation of Strindbergian structures.

O'Neill's life, as critics have noted, was as tortured as Strindberg's own. Like Strindberg, who also thought himself the unwanted child of parents of differing backgrounds, O'Neill was mired again and again in devastating love-hate relationships that became for him, as for Strindberg, the very basis of his work. Strindberg's simultaneous need for and revulsion against women is echoed in O'Neill's life and his work, as the Swede taught the American to see woman at one and the same time as sustaining angel and avenging devil, at once as mother, as wife, as whore. Aware of O'Neill's feelings of a personal kinship with Strindberg, Agnes Boulton, his second wife, paved the way for others:

Gene was very impressed by Strindberg's anguished personal life as it was shown in his novels (*The Son of a Servant* and others, all autobiographical); particularly of his tortured relationship with the women who always seemed to be taking advantage of him. . . . These novels Gene kept by him for many years, reading them even more frequently than the plays. . . . I imagine he had the same feeling of identification with the great tortured Swede up to the time of his own death. (8)

And critics like S. K. Winther followed: "O'Neill turned more to the autobiographical writings than he did to the plays, for it was Strindberg's conception of life that influenced O'Neill in his mature work, and not specific scenes from the plays." (9) Biographer Louis Sheaffer reinstated the plays as Strindberg's primary influence, citing *Welded* (1922) as O'Neill's own *Dance of Death* (1901), (10) and Arthur and Barbara Gelb, pointing out similarities between *All God's Chillun Got Wings* (1923) and the same Strindberg play, wrote, "Compare Jim's speech . . . 'I can't leave her. She can't leave me'--with Alice's speech about her husband in *The Dance of Death*: 'We have been trying to part every single day--but we are chained together and cannot break away.'" (11)

An even more striking borrowing from Strindberg sheds light on situation and theme in the works of O'Neill. In *The Father* (1887) after the Captain admits to his wife Laura how he was drawn to her because he felt incomplete in himself as an unwanted, will-less child, she responds, "I loved you as if you were my little boy. But didn't you see how, when your feelings changed and you came to me as a lover, I was ashamed? . . . The mother became the mistress--horrible! . . . The mother was your friend, you see, but the woman was your enemy. Sexual love is conflict." (12)   That same conflict is illustrated in *Desire under the Elms* (1924) when Eben, determined to hate the stepmother who has stolen into his home and taken his beloved mother's place, is drawn to her by an overwhelming sexual attraction. "Don't cry, Eben! I'll take yer Maw's place! . . . Let me kiss ye, Eben!," Abbie tells him in his mother's parlor, and adds, "Can't ye see it hain't enuf--lovin' ye like a Maw--can't ye see it's got t' be that an' more . . . fur me t' be happy--fur yew t' be happy?" (13)   Embracing Abbie as mother, as wife, as whore, Eben embraces his Strindbergian fate. Strindberg's abiding theme is O'Neill's as well. But *The Father* suggests yet another aspect of the Swede's plays that would have an effect on the American dramatist-- its incipient circular form. Strindberg's play concludes with its protagonist becoming a will-less child again.

Twelve years before the Nobel speech in an article he called "Strindberg and Our Theatre," printed in the program for the Provincetown Player's production of Strindberg's *Spook Sonata* in 1924, O'Neill had indicated that Strindberg's impact on the development of drama went beyond content alone to embrace form as well. He wrote:

Strindberg knew and suffered with our struggle years before many of us were born. He expressed it by intensifying the method of his time and by foreshadowing both in content *and form* [our italics] the methods to come. All that is enduring in what we loosely call "Expressionism"--all that is artistically valid and sound theatre--can be clearly traced back through Wedekind to Strindberg's *The Dream Play, There Are Crimes and Crimes, The Spook Sonata,* etc. (14)

That O'Neill was a pioneer in the expressionistic movement in America, a movement that owed much to Strindberg, is obvious in the style of a play such as *The Hairy Ape* (1921). But perhaps by "form" O'Neill meant more than an expressionistic style. The very structure of plays by Strindberg as diverse as the expressionistic *To Damascus* (1898-1901) and *Crime and Crime* (1899), a realistic play that approaches expressionism only in the symbolic elements of its settings, seems to have influenced the patterning of such diverse O'Neill plays as the expressionistic *The Emperor Jones* (1920) and the realistic *Beyond the Horizon* (1917) and *Long Day's Journey into Night* (1940). Plays by both Strindberg and

O'Neill share a cyclical pattern of a forward progression followed by a movement backward, a pattern evident in dramatic structure and underscored by scenic arrangement.

Strindberg's typical pattern is a movement from a narrow focus on personal relationships to a wider frame in which the relationships are universalized as the dramatist considers man in society, man in an historical setting. This is accomplished through a pattern of repitition and revisiting; setting remains the same while characters' perception or understanding changes. In its simplest form in *Miss Julie* (1888), Jean, the male servant, rises to power by debasing a single female aristocrat, only to revert to the lowest extreme of the social order at the sound of his master's bell. The most fully developed presentation of the pattern is to be found in the first part of *To Damascus*, an expressionistic trilogy that introduces a recurring Strindbergian ploy--the actual repetition of events.

To Damascus chronicles much of Strindberg's own life up to 1901, his marriages, travels, mental disturbances, attempted cures. *Part I* of the trilogy, written in 1898, opens with the Stranger setting out to find happiness, with each scene recording a different event on his journey. The seventeen scenes are carefully divided by scene nine at the convent/asylum, in which all the characters from the first eight scenes are brought together as the Stranger sees all those he has transgressed against in the past. Through the offices of the confessor he achieves self-recognition and comes to understand his sin of selfishness. After the scene, which functions as both thematic and structural turning point, the following eight scenes repeat earlier dialogue and take place at the same locales as those preceding scene nine, except that they occur exactly in reverse order with the play ending where it began. (15) There is the suggestion, however, that life has improved as the Stranger, again writing in the sand as he was doing in the opening scene, collects the letter he had earlier been afraid to confront and finds the money for which he had hoped.

In revisiting the earlier scenes of action, Strindberg dramatically conveys his notion of positive change in the midst of eternal stasis. Although historical events may repeat themselves, they can be made qualitatively better through the involvement of the aware individual. Although the Stranger visits the same places in the second half of the play as in the first, he now moves from mere comment upon the world to a consideration of its meaning; interest shifts from the self to others as the cause of the Stranger's unhappiness; his selfishness towards the rest, becomes clear to him. Although the trilogy moves progressively toward the suggestion that union with the beyond is the cure for life's pain, the drama is not one of conversion, but rather of struggle, suggesting hope, yet stopping short of certainty. In *To Damascus* Strindberg emphasizes human connection--that man does not exist in isolation, that the only break from recurring human despair comes with the recognition of one's own part in causing that despair. But before man acknowledges his culpability, he will repeat his mistakes over and over again.

Crime and Crime, written a year after the first part of *To Damascus*, this time in a realistic vein as Strindberg tried his hand at boulevard comedy, also demonstrates in its movement from crime to repentance a cyclical pattern with a return to the beginning. The play begins in the cemetary at Montparnasse, foreshadowing the doom that is to befall the characters. Strindberg originally planned to end the play as he had begun it, at the cemetary, but changed his mind in an attempt at a more positive ending to what is in fact an unusually pessimistic comedy. In its final form the play moves twice from a simple cafe, to a restaurant, to an outdoor scene. The first sequence (act one, scene two; act two, scene one; act two, scene two) takes the characters from the Cremerie, to the fancier Auberge des Adrets, to a luxurious outdoor restaurant in the Bois de Boulogne. The second sequence (act three, scene one; act three, scene two; act four, scene one) takes the characters back to the Cremerie, again to the Auberge des Adrets, but finally to the Luxembourg Gardens, an outdoor setting with--this time--no restaurant, no refreshment for the lovers whose relationship the play charts. The first sequence suggests the flowering of the love between Maurice and Henriette with their happiest moment coming in the restaurant in the Bois. But in the second sequence doubts enter the relationship, which founders at last in the Luxembourg Gardens where Maurice and Henriette, meeting in the shadow of a statue of Adam and Eve, accuse one another of serious crimes. As the first male and female were forced out of paradise, Maurice and Henriette, facing the reality of their bleak situation, are ordered to leave the gardens at closing time, and the scene reverts to the Cremerie.

In the second restaurant sequence Strindberg directs his audience to notice the repetition of events. Henriette says: "How everything repeats itself! Just the same situation and the same words as yesterday, when it was *you* who were expected." This time she is speaking to Adolphe about Maurice as earlier she had spoken to Maurice of Adolphe. Although the characters change, the situation remains constant. In the play's final scene (act four, scene two), yet another reversion of the Cremerie, Maurice echoes Henriette's words: "Everything repeats itself." (16) Even as Maurice learns by the end of the play that everyone in some way pays for his crime, that the crime itself holds its own punishment and the doer must repent, Maurice's friend Adolphe and Henriette also hint at crimes in their past that they too must pay for. (17)

That all the characters in fact go through a similar sequence of crime and repentance prefigures a repetition of actions in the later Strindberg play in whose American production O'Neill was involved, *The Spook Sonata*, or, as it is more frequently translated, *The Ghost Sonata* (1907). Here the student, recounting his father's fate, underscores the fact that what Hummel, seemingly the villain of the piece, has just done, stripping others bare because he can no longer stomach their hypocrisy, is the same action that the student's father had performed some years before, exactly the same crime the father was guilty of. Whereas Hummel's actions seem a crime to the student, the same course of events involving his own father seem to him the commendable action of a principled man. Good and evil are in the eye of the beholder.

Returning to his expressionistic mode, Strindberg intended to follow the pattern of *To Damascus, Part I* in another work employing a pilgrimage motif, *A Dream Play* (1902), which was to become in 1926 the second of his plays to be produced by O'Neill's Provincetown Players. In *A Dream Play* Indra's Daughter descends from heaven to earth to explore the plight of mankind, and, finding it too much to bear, leaves earth for heaven again as a castle, the symbol of life itself, is consumed in flames, giving way to a giant chrysanthemum. Evert Sprinchorn has demonstrated that the play follows the scenic pattern of *To Damascus* by, in its later scenes, reversing the order of the scenes of the earlier part. But the pattern is not as slavishly followed as before: instead of an exact scenic reversal, *A Dream Play* includes some settings to which there is no return, yet the play's basic movement is from castle to theatre corridor to cave to the Foulstrand-Fairhaven scenes, then back again to cave to theatre corridor to castle. Sprinchorn writes, "Strindberg has simply made subtler use of the cyclical structure." (18) That subtler use suggests that as Indra's Daughter prepares for her mortal death, her entire life on earth flashes before her as the places she has visited, the people she has met reappear in reverse and rapid order. The play's cyclical pattern is reinforced by the expanding use of stage properties as well as by revisited settings. As Sprinchorn further notes, "Strindberg has artfully made the stage properties remain the same throughout while serving different purposes. The linden tree becomes a hat tree and then a candelabrum; the doorkeeper's room becomes the Lawyer's desk and then a pulpit; while the mysterious door becomes the Lawyer's files and then the door to the church sacristy." (19)

The play's pattern of repetition, rather than demonstrating mere stasis, extends meaning into social reflection. Consideration moves from the one to the many, from Indra's Daughter's relationships with first the Officer, then the Lawyer, then the Poet--three personal relationships revealing that everyone causes the sufferings of the one he loves and suffers himself as a result; the play then offers a view of society at large in the Foulstrand-Fairhaven scenes in which whole classes enslave other classes as the rich exploit the workers who make their comforts possible. A similar expansion takes place in O'Neill's expressionistic *The Emperor Jones* as Brutus Jones, individual exploiter of a primitive island tribe, becomes as the play progresses a symbol of an entire race as he himself is exploited and victimized through the ages as the dramatist explores a collective unconscious. Yank in *The Hairy Ape* also learns as the play's scope widens that he is not merely the object of the singular Mildred's revulsion, but is an excrescence to the world at large, a world encompassing New York society at one end of the scale and at the other the Industrial Workers of the World.

Sprinchorn suggests that the cyclical structure of *A Dream Play* and other Strindberg works is dictated by the dramatist's theme: life is unbearable because its miseries, in varying forms, are endlessly repeated. That theme is further underscored within the overall cyclical structure of *A Dream Play* by a scene (not noted by Sprinchorn) involving the Officer in recurring events that itself serves as a pattern in later plays by O'Neill. The Officer, who earlier in the play grows old before the audience's eyes as he waits at the stage door for his beloved who never arrives, later finds himself in a schoolroom with young boys. He has regressed to his former youthful self, repeating the same mistakes, hearing again the lessons he never learned, never profited from. Driven to madness, the Captain in *The Father* (1887) also regresses to become a child again, allowing his old nurse to trap him in a straitjacket. So too does Ella in her madness regress to childhood in the last scene which recalls the opening scene of O'Neill's *All God's Chillun Got Wings*, and Mary Tyrone in a drug-induced state at the end of *Long Day's Journey into Night* speaks with longing of her innocent days at school before her fateful meeting with James Tyrone.

In *A Dream Play*, Strindberg, borrowing images from the Eastern religions that attracted him, has Indra's Daughter enter as a burning castle that is transformed into a chrysanthemum. In the period in which O'Neill too was influenced by Buddhism, Hinduism, and Taoism even as he explored Christian legend and myth, he makes use of almost identical images of man's oneness with the universe, of resignation, serenity, even rebirth through fire. In *The Fountain* (1921), Juan Ponce de Leon sees the materialization of a woman with the face of his beloved

Beatriz enveloped in a burning fountain *"until her figure is like the heart of its flame"* (*CP*, II, 225). Again in *Lazarus Laughed* (1925) death through fire leads to understanding and acceptance as Lazarus, who appears younger in each scene as the play progresses, is burned at the stake as his soul flies "back into the womb of Infinity." (*CP*, II, 628) (20).

O'Neill, however, does more than simply echo Strindbergian images in similar circular structures. His borrowing of technique points to an important difference in outlook as well. Whereas Strindberg in his later work offered his protagonists a solacing vision of a healing death, O'Neill more characteristically offered no hope for any alleviation of life's pain. The American's first tentative structural borrowing as well as his generally more pessimistic outlook can be seen in the realistic *Beyond the Horizon*, a circular journey reminiscent of *To Damascus*. The pattern of the settings of *Beyond the Horizon* is that of the Strindberg play but on a much reduced scale. The play moves from "The Road" to "The Farm House" to "The top of a hill on the farm overlooking the sea," then retraces its locales--back to "The Farm House," back to "The Road," ending where it began (*CP*, I, 572).

Robert's last words suggest a new beginning, fulfillment, transcendence in death: "I'm happy at last . . . free to wander on and on-- eternally! . . . It isn't the end. It's a free beginning--the start of my voyage! I've won . . . the right of release--beyond the horizon!" (*CP*, I, 652). Travis Bogard writes: "His death is close to a blessing, both a release from pain and a reunification with the element that is rightfully his." (21) But the play's final moment undercuts Robert's words, perhaps Bogard's reading as well. *A Dream Play's* closing vision is the flowering chrysanthemum, and *The Ghost Sonata* offers a romantic painting, Bocklin's "Isle of the Dead," suggesting a release into a beautiful afterlife for the spirit of the dying girl. *Beyond the Horizon*, on the other hand, offers only Robert's brother's empty words to Robert's wife Ruth: "I--you--we've both made a mess of things! We must try to help each other--and--in time--we'll come to know what's right. . . . And perhaps we--" O'Neill's intention is made clear with his insistent stage direction--*"desperately"*--before Andrew's last, unfinished phrase. More telling still is the direction that follows Andrew's unconvincing words: *"But RUTH, if she is aware of his words, gives no sign. She remains silent, gazing at him dully with the sad humility of exhaustion, her mind already sinking back into that spent calm beyond the further troubling of any hope"* (*CP*, I, 653). The play is over. There is nothing ahead for the dead or the living--only repetition, never change. O'Neill's is a static tableau in contrast to Strindberg's more comforting endings.

With the expressionistic *The Emperor Jones* O'Neill expands his horizon as the scenes in the play progress from the personal to the universal as Strindberg's plays do. In the beginning a particularized man confronts himself as Jones grapples with the Little Formless Fears. As the play progresses, Jones engages in social relationships, as active agent when he remembers the porter he has slain for cheating at dice, as passive agent when he recalls his beating at the hands of the chain gang guard. Eventually the character represents not merely the plight of Jones but also that of the black man in a white world and an alien environment. As Jones joins the witch doctor in chanting, he realizes that as an individual he is unimportant, that he must sacrifice himself. The play's movement comes full circle. The last scene returns to the setting of scene two and the reappearance of Smithers, dressed as he was in scene one. Smithers, drawing attention to the concept of escape and return, comments that if Jones "lost 'is bloody way in these stinkin' woods 'e'ed likely turn in a circle without 'is knowin' it. They all does." (22) That man's beginning contains his end is suggested as Smithers jeers at the natives: "I s'pose you think it's yer bleedin' charms and yer silly beatin' the drum that made 'im run in a circle when 'e'd lost 'imself, don't yer!" (23) O'Neill repeats the pattern in another expressionistic play in Yank's circular journey into the world in *The Hairy Ape*. The play moves from the firemen's forecastle--O'Neill writes: "*The effect sought after is a cramped space in the bowels of the ship, imprisoned by white steel. The lines of the bunks, the uprights supporting them, cross each other like the steel framework of a cage*" (*CP*, II, 121)--to a prison cell on Blackwells Island, and finally to the monkey house at the Zoo where Yank dies in the gorilla's cage.

A similar circular movement involving a progression from personal relationships to a more universal consideration, as in *A Dream Play*, occurs in the realistic *All God's Chillun Got Wings*. The black and white youngsters move from sharing their childhood games and dreams to taking up their places in the battle between the races. At first, Ella and Jim can imagine they can ignore their color and live together happily. Later, Ella can be kind to Jim and proclaim their equality as long as she is dominant by virtue of her education. As soon as that equality becomes a possibility, is in fact threatened with Ella becoming his inferior should Jim become a lawyer, Ella goes mad. O'Neill does not repeat the opening scene of Ella and Jim as children but evokes it by having Ella implore him to pretend with her that they are children again who see no real differences between themselves. The relationship of one boy and one girl has taken on the tragic implications and complexities of racial confrontation.

Long Day's Journey into Night utilizes the same structural pattern as the end becomes the beginning as a tale of one man's family becomes every family in which an overpowering love unleashes its own destructive seed. Mary Tyrone transports herself as well as her husband and sons back to a past that is at once the present and the future for them all. As she becomes a young woman again at the end of the play, she shifts abruptly between the present and past tense in her speech and remembers the spring "I fell in love with James Tyrone and was so happy for a time" (*CP*, III, 828). (24) Yank and Brutus Jones go full circle. Ella and Mary Tyrone return to the past.

Other plays demonstrate O'Neill's two methods of beginning again--plays actually closing in the same locale as their opening, and plays closing with a character speaking of a return to a beginning. The Prologue of *The Great God Brown* (1925) takes place on "The Pier of the Casino" where Margaret, Strindbergian woman, says: "And I'll be Mrs. Dion--Dion's wife--and he'll be my Dion--my own Dion--my little boy --my baby!" (*CP*, II, 479). The play's Epilogue, years later, takes place on "The Pier of the Casino" as Margaret urges her sons never to forget their father, then kisses the mask of Dion with the words, "My lover! My husband! My boy! You can never die till my heart dies! You will live forever" (*CP*, II, 535). (25) *Marco Millions* (1923) doubles the return to a beginning, but home for its major characters represents opposite sides of the world and opposing world views. Marco travels east, then goes home to the material West to marry Donata, his childhood sweetheart. Kukachin, loving Marco, for a time travels with him westward on a journey to her intended husband, Arghun Khan, only to return to her spiritual home in the East, where, as she dies, her grandfather Kublai, the Great Kaan, weeps, "You are a little girl again" (*CP*, II, 466).

Strange Interlude (1926) does not return to the setting of its opening scene in the Leeds' home, but a circle is about to be completed and is underscored as Nina, watching her son's plane in flight, says bitterly to Darrell. "He's leaving me without a backward look!" to which Darrell responds, "No! He's circling. He's coming back!" On Darrell's departure, she turns to Charles Marsden: "Sons are always their fathers. They pass through the mother to become their father again" (*CP*, II, 816-17). Nina, another Strindbergian woman who has played the roles of wife, mother, and whore, is about to return to her childhood home, to grow old by becoming a girl with Charlie taking the place of her father.

In play after play both Strindberg and O'Neill complete a cyclical structure with a return to a beginning. In Strindberg the pattern is frequently that of an initial movement in one direction with a second movement reversing that direction, actually repeating its scenes, as in *To Damascus, Part I*, and *A Dream Play*. The return in Strindberg suggests a movement toward betterment, alleviating a pessimistic gloom. The

Stranger gains self-knowledge; the castle, purified by flames, gives way to the flower. O'Neill follows the pattern on a reduced scale in *Beyond the Horizon* and ends *The Great God Brown* in the setting in which it begins. More characteristically, however, the American dramatist suggests the cycle beginning again without actually dramatizing repetitive scenes. Yet for both, life repeats itself. The difference in their circular patterns may perhaps be traced to their idiosyncratic understanding of Nietzsche's complex philosophic concept of eternal recurrence, to which the philosopher alluded again and again in *Thus Spake Zarathustra, The Will to Power, Ecce Homo*, and *Nachlass*, never fully defining it within a single work.

Nietzsche, the god of both Strindberg's and O'Neill's idolatries (26), used the terms "eternal return" and "eternal recurrence" interchangably, sometimes employing the German word "*Wiederkunft*" (return), sometimes the work "*Wiederkehr*" (recurrence). In *Nietzsche's Thought of Eternal Return*, Joan Stambaugh attempts a distinction which she admits the philosopher himself never made. She writes: "A recurrence is something which has *run through* its course and occurs again. A return implies a turning about and going back to an original place or state. . . . *Return* emphasizes a going back, a *completion* of movement. *Recurrence* emphasizes *another* occurrence or beginning of a movement." (27) One might simplistically conclude that Strindberg believes in return--his characters move out and then come back-- whereas O'Neill is a believer in recurrence--everything begins again. Yet *Strange Interlude* suggests that Nina must first *return* for events to *recur*.

Another distinction in Strindberg's and O'Neill's views of the Nietzschean concept may be more useful in understanding their similar but divergent patterns. Strindberg's repetitive closures, despite an overall pessimism in his works, are more positive than O'Neill's. The Swedish author seems to have tempered Nietzsche's views with his own lifelong study of Eastern religions as he attempted to find solace in his own suffering. Strindberg needed a belief in the soul or spirit living on, a belief in death as the gateway to new life. Yet Nietzsche, his intellectual master, was unconcerned with Eastern thought in his most productive years. Nietzsche denied the transmigration of the soul; nor does his concept of eternal return coincide with the *samsara*, the cycle of birth and death of Buddhism that offers rebirth through karma--one's deeds or actions. (28) If Nietzsche's eternal recurrence may be negatively interpreted to impy its existence without meaning and without purpose, at one and the same time, it positively affirms the self-attainment of the Same--*das Gleiche*---in every moment: "I come again, with this sun, with this earth, with this eagle, with this serpent--*not* to a new life or a better life or a similar life: I come back eternally to this same, selfsame life, in what is greatest as in what is smallest, to teach again the eternal recurrence of all things." (29) In Stambaugh's words, "Nietzsche calls upon man to use his creative power in the shaping of his own fate." (30)

Adrift in a Nietzschean sea of "ill will against time and its 'is was'" (*TSZ*, p. 140), O'Neill's characters reflect his own despair in failing to reach the liberation that comes of having willed their present. O'Neill, a sometimes Taoist but ever the reluctant Roman Catholic for whom the ultimate movement is a linear one toward heaven or hell, was drawn to Nietzsche, who, like his creation Zarathustra, was "advocate of the circle" (*TSZ*, p. 216). Walter Kaufmann comments on the most significant of Nietzsche's many works that deal with eternal recurrence: "What we find again and again in *Zarathustra* are the typical emotions with which a boy tries to compensate himself" (*TSZ*, "Translator's Preface," p. xvi). Whereas Nietzsche, approaching madness, became again the arrogant, willful child, O'Neill, the despairing child, found in the philosopher's work a chance to begin anew. Yet, paradoxically, he turned from its positive aspects to embrace the negative credo of eternal return, the soothsayer's words that Zarathustra repeats: "'All is the same, nothing is worth while, knowledge chokes'" (*TSZ*, p. 219). O'Neill's content owes much to what was personally meaningful to him in Nietzsche's philosophy, but it was Strindberg who eventually looked beyond Nietzsche, who offered O'Neill the cyclical form that both dramatists found necessary for an exploration and expression of that philosophy in dramatic terms.

NOTES

1. Eugene O'Neill, Nobel Prize acceptance speech, quoted by Arthur and Barbara Gelb, *O'Neill*, rev. ed. (New York: Harper and Row, 1973), 814.

2. Egil Tornqvist, "Nietzsche and O'Neill: A Study in Affinity," *Orbis Litterarum*, 23 (1968): 97. The entire article, pp. 97-126, underscores the importance of the O'Neill-Nietzsche relationship and includes a brief discussion of the possible effect of eternal recurrence on the content of *Anna Christie* and *The First Man* (p. 106).

3. Tornqvist, *A Drama of Souls* (New Haven and London: Yale U. Press, 1969), in a section he heads "Parallel Situations," pp. 241-52, writes: "More common in O'Neill's plays than . . . narrative parallels is the parallel situation which in stage action shows the characters in the same circumstances in which they themselves or their forebears have

earlier found themselves" (p. 246). Citing Cyrus Day, "*Amor Fati*: O'Neill's Lazarus as Superman and Savior," *Modern Drama*, 3 (1960): 297-305, Tornqvist mentions Nietzsche in this section only in reference to "Lazarus' gospel that there is no death, that there is only change--his version of Nietzsche's 'eternal recurrence'" (p. 252). His one reference to Strindberg in this section is a note in regard to O'Neill's stage direction concerning the glaring sun at both the beginning and end of *Thirst*: "The prime example in modern drama of a circular recurrence technique is Strindberg's *To Damascus*" (p. 249, n. 9). Timo Tiusanen, *O'Neill's Scenic Images* (Princeton: Princeton U. Press, 1968), states: "The idea of eternal recurrence . . . not only provided the consoling solution in a few of his plays; it also gave him the prototype of play structure, the circle" (p. 35). Scattered allusions to circles of time and the seasons appear throughout the book without reference to the influence of Nietzsche or Strindberg on form in O'Neill's plays despite Tiusanen's frequent mention of the German and the Swede. Laurin Porter throughout *The Banished Prince: Time, Memory, and Ritual in the Late Plays of Eugene O'Neill* (Ann Arbor and London: UMI Research Press, 1988) attempts distinctions between Nietzsche's eternal recurrence, the mythic return of archaic man as explored by Mircea Eliade in *The Myth of the Eternal Return*, trans. Willard R. Trask (New York: Pantheon Books, 1954), and "the paradigm of the classical historian who perceives history as a series of repetitive cycles" (p. 24). Porter is on surer ground with the following statement: "Whatever the source of O'Neill's vision, whether he draws upon his reading of Nietzsche or dips back unconsciously into the Catholicism of his youth, it seems clear that on some level, as he reaches a critical junction in the action of these late plays, he entertains the possibility of an eternal return, whcih breaks through the limitations of now and then, of present and past " (p. 10). No mention of Strindberg is made in her study.

4. Walter A. Kaufmann, *Nietzsche: Philosopher, Psychologist, Antichrist* (Princeton: Princeton U. Press, 1950), 270.

5. Ibid., 281.

6. Heinrich Heine, quoted by Kaufmann, 280. Kaufmann notes the confusion among scholars as to the work by Heine in which that passage first appears but adds that at least one of the books in question was in Nietzsche's library (pp. 279-80, n. 9).

7. Friedrich Nietzsche, quoted by Kaufmann, 212. The passage is actually a conflation of two sections of *Ecce Homo* ("The Birth of Tragedy").

8. Agnes Boulton, *Part of a Long Story* (London: Peter Davies, 1958), 71.

9. S. K. Winther, "Strindberg and O'Neill: A Study of

Influence," *Scandinavian Studies*, 31 (1959): 105.

10. Louis Sheaffer, *O'Neill: Son and Artist* (Boston: Little, Brown, 1973), 100.

11. Gelb, 233-34.

12. August Strindberg, *Six Plays of Strindberg*, trans. Elizabeth Sprigge (Garden City, New York: Doubleday, 1955), 41-42.

13. O'Neill, *Complete Plays 1913-1920*, ed. Travis Bogard (New York: The Library of America, 1988), 2: 354. Subsequent references drawn from this edition are cited parenthetically in the text as *CP*. The first year of the approximate date of composition, as in "Appendix I," *O'Neill and His Plays*, ed. Oscar Cargill, N. Bryllion Fagin, and William J. Fisher (New York, New York U. Press, 1961), 480-82, appears parenthetically in the text after the first mention of each O'Neill play.

14. O'Neill, quoted by Sheaffer, 124.

15. Gunnar Brandell, *Strindberg in Inferno*, trans. Barry Jacobs (Cambridge, Massachusetts: Harvard U. Press, 1974), cites a letter to Gustaf af Geijerstam, 17 March 1898, in which Strindberg comments on *To Damascus*: "The art lies in the composition, which symbolizes the repetition that Kierkegaard speaks of" (pp. 269-70). The letter makes no further reference to the Danish philosopher. Brandell writes: "Strindberg's idea of return or recurrence has nothing at all to do with Kierkegaard's 'repetition,' which happens to be one of the most obscure of all his ideas. For Kierkegaard, 'repetition' was the most difficult and the most desirable of all experiences.... For Strindberg, repetitions were partly a torture, partly a moral duty."

16. Strindberg, *Five Plays of Strindberg*, trans. Elizabeth Sprigge (Garden City, New York: Doubleday, 1960), 100, 117.

17. Just as he had intended to use Mendelssohn's "Funeral March" as a recurrent accompaniment to *To Damascus*, Strindberg hoped to underscore the repetitive action of *Crime and Crime* with music. In connection with the play's French translation he wrote his friend Leopold Littmanson on 21 June 1899: "Please mention Beethoven's D-minor Sonata parenthetically. The finale and particularly bars 96 to 107 should be given special attention. These strains always bore their way into my conscience [sic] like a bit. It has to sound as if the musician were practicing these bars over and over, that is, repeating, repeating, with pauses in between. And then, again and again" (quoted by Martin Lamm in *August Strindberg*, trans. and ed. G. Carlson [New York: Benjamin Blom, 1971], 323). A less sophisticated but more insistent sound effect, the tom-tom in O'Neill's *The Emperor Jones*, in much the same way bores its way into the consciousness of Brutus Jones as well as the audience. Clara Blackburn, in "Continental Influences on Eugene O'Neill's Expressionistic Dramas," *American Literature*, 13 (1941), 113,

extends Strindberg's use of rhythm and musical effects to include "his practice of arranging the dialogue for emotional effect by picking up phrases and repeating them as in a musical composition." She sees this as further evidence of Strindberg's influence on O'Neill. Strindberg's repetition of a lyrical passage, such as the one that opens and closes the final scene of *The Ghost Sonata*, does seem to be echoed by the repeated lyrical phrases in O'Neill's *Lazarus Laughed* and *The Fountain*.

18. Evert Sprinchorn, "The Logic of *A Dream Play*," *Modern Drama*, 5 (1962): 354. Freddie Rokem, "The Camera and the Aesthetics of Repetition: Strindberg's Use of Space and Scenography in *Miss Julie, A Dream Play*, and *The Ghost Sonata*," in *Strindberg's Dramaturgy*, ed. Goran Stockenstrom (Minneapolis: U. of Minnesota Press, 1988), observes: "Instead of visually repeating the scenic images from part I in reverse order in part II, Strindberg often repeats on the level of dialogue and appearence of representative characters. These repetitions become in effect reminders of the scenes that are missing" (p. 118); Rokem offers a valid conclusion: "The principle of repetition was an attempt to artistically concretize something beyond the particular fate of the individual and to reach a dramatic formulation of a universal human condition" (p. 123). He applies Strindberg's comment on Kierkegaard (see n. 15, above) to *A Dream Play*: "The central lesson Indra learns about humankind is that everything in life is repetitious" (p. 121). Although Strindberg seems to have made no specific mentions of Nietzsche's concept of the eternal recurrence, he would have found that idea given greater emphasis in the works of the German philosopher with whom he corresponded in 1888-89 (see n. 26, below).

19. Sprinchorn, 357.

20. James A. Robinson, in *Eugene O'Neill and Oriental Thought: A Divided Vision* (Carbondale and Edwardsville: Southern Illinois U. Press, 1982), 106, makes a convincing case for the elements of Eastern religions that he finds in three O'Neill plays and discusses the various circles within the structure of *The Fountain* by alluding to the *yin/yang* dynamic. Aware of Strindberg's influence on O'Neill, he nevertheless fails to note the similarities of the images at the end of these plays to Strindberg's endings for *A Dream Play* and *The Ghost Sonata*.

21. Bogard, *Contour in Time: The Plays of Eugene O'Neill*, rev. ed. (New York: Oxford U. Press, 1988), 130.

22. O'Neill, *The Emperor Jones, Anna Christie, The Hairy Ape* (New York: Vintage Books, 1972), 51-52.

23. Ibid., 53. Blackburn notes "a similarity in the arrangement of the scenes in *To Damascus* and *The Emperor Jones*." She writes: "The former begins as a certain street corner, proceeds through a series of scenes, and ends at the same street corner. In O'Neill's play there is no

repetition of setting, but the action ends at the same place at which it started" (p. 116).

24. *Long Day's Journey into Night* evokes Tiusanen's most penetrating observation on O'Neills structural circles: "'The past is the present, isn't it? It's the future, too. We all try to lie out of that but life won't let us' ... Mary complains. ... If the first sentence could be taken as the motto for O'Neill's technique, the second reveals the core of his tragic vision. ... This is a statement in which O'Neill's method of constructing his play and his vision meet one another. ... We see how deeply ... [the circle] was rooted in his personal attitude of life. Fate is in the circles, in the inescapable repetitions, in the power of the past over the present and over the future" (p. 301).

25. Bogard, in *Contour in Time*, observes that "*The Great God Brown* begins and ends in a courtroom. In the prologue and epilogue set on a wharf, the benches form a rectangular space reminiscent of a court of law--an effect that is repeated by the arrangement of furniture in later scenes in the play" (pp. 270-71). This is similar to Strindberg's use of furniture and props in shifting scenes that Sprinchorn points out in "The Logic of *A Dream Play*," p. 357.

26. Brita M. E. Mortensen and Brian W. Downs, *Strindberg: An Introduction to His Life and Work* (Cambridge: Cambridge U. Press, 1949), comment on the Strindberg-Nietzsche relationship: "He never read *Zarathustra*, apparently, and probably knew little of his writing at first hand" (p. 41n); on the other hand, Michael Meyer, *Strindberg* (New York: Random House, 1985), states that "a letter he wrote to [Dr. Anders] Eliasson on 15 July [1895] ... suggests that he read with him, surprisingly for the first time, Nietzsche's *Thus Spake Zarathustra*" (p. 323); in a letter to Nietzsche, 4 December 1888, Strindberg wrote: "You have given to mankind the most profound book that it possesses. ... I end all my letters to my friends: read Nietzsche!" Meyer makes it clear that the letter was written shortly after Nietzsche sent Strindberg a copy of *Twilight of the Gods* (p. 205); V. J. McGill, *August Strindberg: The Bedeviled Viking* (New York: Russell and Russell, 1965), 287, however, quotes the same line, inserting "(*Thus Spake Zarathustra*)." In a letter to Verner von Heidenstam, 17 May 1888, Strindberg wrote: "Buy yourself a modern German philosopher by the name of *Nietzsche*. ... *There you can read everything*") quoted by Lamm, p. 259). O'Neill made no secret of his admiration for *Zarathustra*; in a letter to Benjamin De Casseras, 22 June 1927, he wrote: "*Zarathustra* ... has influenced me more than any book I've ever read. I ran into it ... when I was eighteen and I've always possessed a copy since then and every year or so I reread it and am never disappointed" (*Selected Letters of Eugene O'Neill*, ed. Travis Bogard and Jackson Bryer [New Haven and London: Yale U. Press,

1988], 245-46); Boulton writes of *Zarathustra*: "It was a sort of Bible to him, and he kept it by his bedside in later years as others might that sacred book. In those early days in the Village he spoke often of *Zarathustra* and other books of Friedrich Nietzsche, who at that time moved his emotion rather than his mind. He had read the magnificent prose of this great and exciting man over and over again, so that at times it seemed an expression of himself" (p. 57).

27. Joan Stambaugh, *Nietzsche's Thought of Eternal Return* (Baltimore and London: Johns Hopkins U. Press, 1972), 30.

28. Robinson stresses the influence of Nietzsche's *The Birth of Tragedy* and *Thus Spake Zarathustra* on *The Great God Brown* and *Zarathustra* on *Lazarus Laughed*, but suggests parallels between the doctrine of eternal recurrence and the samsara that Nietzsche probably did not intend (pp. 126-27). As Robinson himself points out, "many Western thinkers (particulary modern ones) are surprisingly 'Eastern' in their concepts and values. . . . Differences between East and West almost invariably involve emphasis, not absolute opposition. We should not be surprised, then, that many notions associated with the mysterious East . . . appear frequently in Western philosophies" (p. 33). Robinson further suggests "that O'Neill absorbed Eastern ideas from thinkers like Christ, Plato, Emerson and Schopenhauer, as well as from Nietzsche and Jung." That O'Neill was more concerned with the relationship of man to his personal god than with the tenets of any one religion is demonstrated by the procession in scene ten of *The Fountain*: "*One by one, within the fountain, solemn figures materialize. First the Chinese poet, now robed as a Buddhist priest; then the Moorish minstrel, dressed as a priest of Islam; and then the Medicine Man. . . . lastly, Luis, the Dominican monk of the present. Each one of them carries the symbol of his religion before him.*" Juan stares as they fade from sight and speaks: "All faiths--they vanish--are one and equal. . . . God! Are all dreams of you but the one dream?" (*CP*, II, 224-25). In *Marco Millions* four holy men--a priest of Tao, a priest of Confucius, a Buddhist priest, and a priest of Islam--offer an identical message: "Death is" (*CP*, II, 463).

29. Nietzsche, *Thus Spake Zarathustra*, trans. Walter Kaufmann (Harmondsworth: Penguin, 1978), 221. Subsequent references drawn from this edition are cited parenthetically in the text as *TSZ*. Part of this passage in Alexander Tille's translation (1896) is quoted in "Nietzsche and O'Neill" by Tornqvist, p. 106, who states as well: "A testimony to his concern with *Zarathustra* are the copious excerpts he made from this work; out of the eighty chapters which make up the book he took down passages from some fifty on nine large pages" (p. 100).

30. Stanbaugh, 54.

10

Leo Tolstoy's *The Power of Darkness* and Eugene O'Neill's *Desire under the Elms*: A Road to Redemption

Maya Koreneva

In his introduction to an English-language collection of Russian plays, the editor G. R. Noyes remarked in connection with Leo Tolstoy's *The Power of Darkness* that the scene in which the protagonist, Nikita, kills the newborn baby he had by his lover, "ranks with the sleep-walking scene in *Macbeth*." (1) The comparison made here is obviously based on the way the two plays affect the audience. Yet it seems to me that it would be more appropriate and more illuminating to compare the Russian play with Eugene O'Neill's *Desire under the Elms*."

There exist numerous similarities among the plot, subject-matter, and structure of these plays. The similarities are striking indeed. Both *The Power of Darkness* and *Desire Under the Elms* have at their center the struggle over the farm and over the land. Though they are deeply involved in the conflict, the characters find themselves also entangled in a web of greed and lust, love and hate, vengeance and deceit, incestuous desires and infanticide.

Moreover, religion--Russian Orthodox and American Puritanism --plays a most prominent part in both *The Power of Darkness* and *Desire under the Elms*. It serves as the ideological context of the action, as well as one of its driving forces, in the two plays. The opening scene of the O'Neill drama introduces us directly into the situation. Simeon, Peter, and Eben, sons of Ephraim Cabot, work like slaves on the farm of their callous and tyrannous father, who, though old enough, will not release his hold on the farm. The elder sons, Simeon and Peter, believe that two-thirds of the farm belong to them, for they earned their shares, in Peter's words, "by our sweat." (2) But they do not dare to say that openly to their father because they are "scared 'f him." (144) The younger son, Eben, claims that the farm is his by right as it had been his mother's before Ephraim stole it from her.

Then they receive news that their father "got himself hitched to a female." (146) Simeon and Peter, deeming the situation hopeless for them, decide to go to California. To ensure his rights on the farm, Eben offers them three hundred dollars each for their shares of it. He has taken the money from a hiding-place where the father keeps it. Yet again Eben claims that the money belonged to his mother, and now it belongs to him.

Abbie, who comes to the farm as Ephraim's third wife, does not conceal her motives. In Eben's words, she was "bought" by Ephraim "like a harlot." (160) She has done it, Abbie explains, because "I'd most give up hope o' ever doin' my own wuk in my own hum." (160) Now she delights in the sheer sound of the words to which she can add the word "my": "This be my farm--this be my hum--this be my kitchen--!" (161) Cold-heartedly she starts her affair with Eben to have a child by him, having got Ephraim first to promise that he would "will the farm" to her. (170) She obviously uses her sensuality as a means of ensuring her future. Though less materialistic, Eben also has another motive than love at the beginning. For Eben, it is his mother's "vengeance" on Ephraim. (179)

What we have, then, at the heart of the play is the classic triangle, marked with incestuous motif, with Abbie trying to use the mother image to bring Eben closer to her: "I'll kiss ye, self-righteously, pure, Eben," she says seductively, "same 's if I was a Maw t' ye--an' ye kin kiss me back 's if yew was my son--my boy--sayin' good-night t' me!" (178)

What both of them fail to take into account is their own human nature, which brings to ruin their plans at the very moment when they seem closest to realization. Abbie and Eben enter the contest sure of themselves, without any trace of "romantic" illusions on either side, making their lust instrumental to the achievement of their aims.

But they misjudge themselves. Their alienation from humanity, from human values, is far from complete. The action takes a turn that is both ironic and tragic. Their neglected humanity takes revenge on them: Abbie and Eben fall in love with each other. What they have regarded as a means now becomes the main object of their cravings. Yet, they are no longer free as they were at the start and cannot enjoy their love as they wish because it is poisoned by the knowledge of their original motives. When their baby is born, Ephraim believes it to be his own and, keeping his word, makes Abbie the owner of the farm. But this immediately endangers her relationship with Eben. As soon as Eben comes to know of the new situation with the farm, her love, in his eyes, is again nothing but a deliberate deceit.

"Ye've been on'y playin' yer sneakin', stealin' game all along," he cries self-righteously,"--gittin' me t' lie with ye so's ye'd hev a son he'd think was his'n, an' makin' him promise he'd give ye the farm and let me eat dust, if ye did git him a son!" (193) Eben threatens to tell the truth to Ephraim and leave for California, like his brothers.

This precipitates disaster. In a desperate attempt to prove that her love for Eben is now free of self-interest, Abbie kills her baby who, she believes, has come between her and her lover.

We find a similar classic triangle at the beginning of *The Power of Darkness*. It is presented by the owner of the house and the family plot, and also the head of the family, Petr, and his young wife, Anisya, and Anisya's lover, Nikita. Although the latter is just a "hired help" [once Abbie calls Eben "a hired help" (175)], and not a blood relation of any of them, he can be regarded, more or less, as a member of the family, a sort of a substitute son in a household of women. Beside Anisya, there are also Petr's daughter by a previous marriage, Akulina, and Anisya's and Petr's daughter Annie. Through this triangle, the motif of incest is introduced.

When Anisya approaches Nikita to discuss openly the prospects of their marriage after her present husband's death, saying to him that he would be then "the master of the house," the young fellow characteristically answers, "No use guessing. What do I care? I do the work as if it was for my own self. The master likes me, and his wife-- well, she's in love with me. And if women love me, I'm not to blame." (553)

Nikita's words show a both certain affection--one may say, a filial affection--for his master and rival, for whom he harbors no hostility and surprisingly little care for his lover Anisya. This is important for the development of the plot. Throughout the play Nikita's role remains predominantly passive; he is moved to act as chessmen on the chessboard are moved, rather than to act himself. Those who surround him push him in different directions: into the realm of sensuality (Anisya), toward material success (his mother, Matrena), toward spiritual purification (his father, Akim), the contrast of his parents' positions prefiguring his inner conflict at the end of the play.

Though Nikita is almost indifferent to material gain, his mother is not. For her it is the focus of activity. Under Matrena's influence Anisya decides to do away with her ailing husband, whom she considers to be the main obstacle to her marriage to Nikita. She feels it necessary to act promptly because she is afraid of losing her lover, whom his father, Akim, has decided to marry to an orphan girl Nikita had seduced. Anisya puts poisonous powder Matrena gave her into her husband's tea. Meanwhile Matrena talks Akim out of getting their son married to the seduced girl, envisioning a better future for him. If Nikita marries Anisya, he will get Petr's house and money, together with his wife.

Obsessed with money, she persuades Anisya of its primary importance: "Eh, darling, if he [the husband] gives the money to some one without your knowing it, you'll weep forever. They'll turn you out of the house empty-handed. You've worn yourself out, my precious, worn yourself out all your life with a man you don't love, and when you're a widow you'll have to go begging. . . . Just remember, girlie: if you slip up once, you'll never get straight again." (567) The slip she has in mind is by no means a moral one, as is made explicit by her subsequent speech: "If you make a slip now, you'll repent of it forever. He'll give the money to his sister." (570) To persuade her son Matrena says to him, "You get hold of the money, then the woman will be in your hands." (577)

Matrena's activity is not limited to persuasion and advice. She helps Anisya search her dying husband, and they do find the money he has hidden. So the stealing-of-the-money motif is as prominent in Tolstoy's play as in *Desire under the Elms*, the difference between them being that, unlike Eben, Tolstoy's characters do not even pretend they have a rightful claim to the money. But the happy future Matrena has envisioned for her son does not materialize. After their marriage Nikita feels estranged from Anisya--not in the last place because of her cruelty to her late husband--and in a short while he has a new lover. This time it is his stepdaughter, Akulina. Thus, the incest motif is reduplicated. Lust and corruption, which used to lie low, now break loose.

When the baby is born the ever-scheming Matrena negotiates, to avoid scandal, the possibility of marrying off the girl, promising to add a solid sum to her dowry. It is also Matrena who makes her son kill the baby. This is accomplished in a very cruel way. She stands like a fury over the reluctant Nikita while he crushes the baby under a board by sitting down upon it.

This is the turning point of the plot. Unable to silence the baby's wailing, which he keeps hearing and which is, most certainly, the voice of his conscience, Nikita first intends to commit suicide, but later on decides to repent. This decision is the only thing in the whole play that can be positively regarded as an action on his part. The play ends with a great repentance scene. During the wedding of Akulina, his last lover and the mother of the baby, Nikita publicly acknowledges his sin and asks everybody to forgive him "for Christ's sake." (622)

Akim had strongly disapproved of his son's lecherous ways and so refused to take needed money from Nikita or even to talk to him because, he said, "there's no decency in you." (589) He now sees in what is happening a sign of God. "God will forgive you, my beloved child! (Embraces him.) You have not spared yourself. He will spare you. God! God! This is His Work!" (622)

When Nikita is arrested and is to be taken away for questioning, Akulina volunteers suddenly to do her bit. "I'll tell the truth. Question me too," she says. (623) Her action, to a certain extent, is parallel to Eben's reconciliation with Abbie after he told the sheriff of the crime she had committed.

The Power of Darkness was written in 1886. It is Tolstoy's first play after his spiritual crisis and religious conversion in the 1870s. His picture of peasant life and characterization in it reflect his own ideological and moral quest. The "darkness" in the title of the play is primarily spiritual darkness, the moral nonbeing of the soul dominated by sin.

One of the best interpretations of the play belongs to Mikhail Bakhtin, who argued:

The Power of Darkness, as Tolstoy understands it, is, of course, least of all the power of ignorance caused by economic and political oppression, the power which is a product of history and thus, can be transcended by history. No, what Tolstoy bears in mind is the eternal power of evil over the individual soul, which has sinned once and one sin leads inevitably to another--"If a claw is caught, the whole bird is lost." And this darkness can be overcome only by the light of the individual conscience. So his drama is in its concept a miracle play, and that is why the socio-economic framework as well as the ordinary peasant life and the splendid, profoundly individualized peasant language represent only a frozen, unchanging background of and the dramatically dead cover over the working of the inner souls of his characters. (3)

I think, though, that Bakhtin's view of the socioeconomic aspects of *The Power of Darkness* should be accepted with reserve. Though they may seem permanent, many of those aspects, operative in the play's action, were brought into peasant life after the abolition of serfdom when Russian peasantry started to move, however hesitantly and timidly, along the capitalist ways of development.

The village life Tolstoy presents in his play has nothing to do with the ideal of patriarchal peasant life he cherished and advocated. There is no trace of communal ways made sacred by tradition in his picture. They are replaced by shameless money-grabbing that Tolstoy regards as the main cause of moral degradation. This is made clear by a long discussion of the bank system between Akim and Mitrich in act three, scene five. Tolstoy disapproves of the new developments in peasant life, of the destruction of the traditional ways and values, and makes Akim his spokesman: "Eh, I see, it's hard not to have money, y'see; and it's twice as hard if you have it, y'see. Anyhow God bids us toil. But you, y'see, just put your money in the bank and go to sleep; and the money, y'see, will feed you while you lie idle. That's nasty work, you know; 't ain't lawful." (586)

The very aggressiveness of the acquisitive instinct and the role the money motif plays in the action of the play show a great affinity between the life processes behind both Tolstoy's and O'Neill's dramas. From this common ground the two authors move, however, in different, if not the opposite, directions. Both present life at a crucial moment when their protagonists go through personal and economic, emotional, and psychological crisis. The old system of values on which the life of former generations was based has crumpled up. They are in search of the new system.

Tolstoy's characters find what they look for in the return to traditional Russian Orthodox Christianity. For Tolstoy the only possible solution to the man's tragic dilemma is the acceptance of God. Nikita finds not only consolation in God but also the power that enables him to face himself, his sinful nature. The way of Tolstoy's protagonist is that of spiritual illumination, which, however, leads him away from his fellow sinners, away from humanity. From then on the matter is settled for Nikita directly between God and himself. The play, characteristically, ends with his remark: "No use questioning. I did it all by myself. I planned it and I did it. Lead me wherever you want to. I shall say nothing more." (623)

This kind of solution was unacceptable to O'Neill. Rejection of traditional Puritan ideology and its ethical legacy is part of his play's message. The protagonists of *Desire under the Elms* fight fiercely against the "Angry God" of the Puritans. Their fight has to be so fierce precisely because they are still enslaved by the past, by the dead, though, if they feel it, they do not articulate their feelings.

While the actions of the protagonists of *The Power of Darkness* and *Desire under the Elms* look similar, the point of reference used by the authors to evaluate them is different. The basic category for Tolstoy is "sin." O'Neill qualifies the same actions in terms of "crime," though for one of his protagonists, Ephraim, the category of "sin" retains some validity. Tolstoy presents faith as a liberating force, as the source of ultimate truth. For O'Neill Puritanism does not represent the truth, nor does it have any liberating effect on his characters. On the contrary, his protagonists free themselves through rejection of repressive Puritanism. In this way Abbie and Eben come to recover their human nature and human values from which they were alienated by their obsession with material wealth, which, from the playwright's point of view, is not an individual trait but one of the most active social factors.

In *Desire under the Elms* the crime is treated in double perspective. Monstrous as Abbie's act is, it is also an act of purification. Killing the baby, she also kills the greed nesting in her heart. In Tolstoy's play the similar act is the crowning point of the accumulation of "sin," having no redemptive power in itself. On Abbie's part her crime is at the same time an act of love meant to prove that her love for Eben is at last free from base scheming.

Accordingly, the authors' strategy in these plays is different. The presentation of the crime scene corresponds with the specific aims Tolstoy and O'Neill had when they wrote their plays. Both Nikita and Abbie feel desperate when they commit their crimes, but in one case despair is marked by disgust, in the other it is marked by horror. The baby's wailing, the cracking of its bones mentioned earlier, amplify the nauseating effect the author strove for in *The Power of Darkness*.

In contrast the scene is ominously silent in *Desire under the Elms*. O'Neill's treatment of it focuses on the terrible struggle going on in Abbie's heart. She is torn between her love for the baby and her love for Eben, which at that moment seem to her tragically incompatible. In the end her love for Eben wins. But it is its very triumph that causes her downfall. Abbie sacrifices her newborn baby by bringing it onto the altar of the dark god of desire. Yet her offer is made in the name of love and because of her love her crime becomes ambivalent. Cruel and horrendous, her act contains in it at the same time, by the saving grace of sacrifice, a certain regenerative power. While Nikita's crime is caused by his moral blindness, Abbie is not deaf to the call of her conscience. It is the terrible choice between things that seem to her mutually exclusive that makes her go against it. Yet, having succumbed to evil, Abbie is aware that she has transgressed one of the fundamental laws of humanity.

In contrast to Nikita's repentance *Desire under the Elms* ends with the recognition of their personal responsibilities for their actions on the part of Abbie and especially Eben. By their self-judgment the moral order is restored in the play. They recover their humanity. All of them have to touch the bottom before their redemption is possible, but when they do, in the end, Abbie and Eben move again in the direction opposite to the one taken by Tolstoy's protagonist--not away from humanity to God, as Nikita did, but toward humanity. Of course, they move only toward each other. It is but the first step on their way to the brotherhood of men. Yet, to be able to take it, Eben and Abbie have had to undergo a spiritual illumination in its nature not unlike that of Tolstoy's protagonists.

NOTES

1. George Rapall Noyes, ed., introduction, *Masterpieces of the Russian Drama* (New York, London: D. Appelton and Co., 1933), 13. (All subsequent quotations from *The Power of Darkness* are from this edition; the page number is given in the text in parenthesis.)

2. Eugene O'Neill, *Nine Plays* (New York: Random House, 1954), 139. (All further quotations from the play are from this edition; the page number is given in the text in parenthesis.)

3. Leo Tolstoy, *Polnoe sobranie khudojestvennykh proizvedeniy* (Moscow and Leningrad, 1929), vol. 11, viii.

Part Three

O'Neill as Playwright

11

Eugene O'Neill, World Playwright: The Beginnings

Paul Voelker

When Eugene O'Neill began his playwriting career in 1913, he concentrated on plays with American settings. Six of his first nine scripts are set in the United States, five of the six in New York and Connecticut, the region where he grew up. The other three are "sea plays," set somewhere in the Atlantic Ocean. It was not until he wrote his tenth play, a one-act entitled *The Movie Man* (completed in mid-1914), that O'Neill turned his attention to a play with a foreign setting, Northern Mexico. Three plays later, O'Neill again turned his attention to foreign affairs, with another one-act, *The Sniper* (completed 1915), for which the locale is Belgium at the outbreak of World War I. With these two plays, O'Neill demonstrated that his artistic vision embraced the affairs of the world; but what specifically motivated his attention, in each instance, was the outbreak of war--civil war (the Mexican Revolution) in the first instance and, in the second, international armed conflict.

The Movie Man had a short period of gestation. The Mexican Revolution, of course, which provides the background for the play, was underway before 1914; but the particular event at the center of the play, Pancho Villa's contract with the Mutual Film Corporation of New York, did not become public knowledge until January of 1914. (1)

That the central situation in *The Movie Man* has a historical basis in fact has only come to light in recent years. As a result, this factual basis does not inform the extant criticism of the play or any of the major biographical accounts of O'Neill's life. But it is crucial to a proper perception of O'Neill's first comedy.

Proper perception of *The Movie Man* has been further clouded by the tradition of aligning it with O'Neill's protest poem, "Fratricide," with which it is contemporary, and placing all this against a context of O'Neill's later involvement with John Reed, the premier American correspondent of the Mexican Revolution, with whom O'Neill became intimately involved in the first years of the Provincetown Players. Reed's articles and accounts were appearing in the American press throughout the first half of 1914; but if O'Neill read them, he was not persuaded by Reed's enthusiasm for Villa.

The relationship between O'Neill's poem and the play is admittedly problematic. "Fratricide" was clearly inspired by a specific event in the spring of 1914. It was on April 21, that Admiral Frank T. Fletcher landed a force of United States Marines at Vera Cruz, Mexico, to interdict a shipment of German arms, because the Mexican president, Victoriano Huerta, would not apologize for detaining some American officials and would not salute the American flag. (2) The Admiral's action smacked of the worst sort of American imperialism, and so aroused O'Neill's radical ire that he fired off his nineteen stanza poem in protest. "Fratricide" was published less than a month after the landing, in a Socialist newspaper, the New York *Call* (May 17, 1914). (3) That O'Neill's stance in this poem is in some sense "radical" and that the poem is contemporaneous with *The Movie Man* has made it even easier to bring up Reed's name in the same breath, (4) but O'Neill's poem does not reflect Reed's stance either. O'Neill's radicalism was of a different stripe from Reed's, as Reed recognized when he met O'Neill. (5) "Fratricide," as the title indicates, is a poem about brother killing brother; what had incensed O'Neill most about the occupation of Vera Cruz was that soldiers had died in the process. The poem is not a glorification of Pancho Villa or any of the other leaders of the Mexican Revolution; O'Neill's sympathy lay with the peons and the poor American soldiers, who were dying to advance the cause of American economic interests. The villains in O'Neill's poem are "The plutocrats who cause the woe." In this attitude, O'Neill would have found agreement with Reed, but O'Neill's poem has no heroes, only victims, the American soldiers, whom he saw as "The poor! The poor who must obey/The poor who only live to die." This is the audience the poem is addressed to; men, in his view, who were playing "the skulking butcher's role. /For every peon that you shoot A brother's death/Will stain your soul." It is for this reason that the poem ends with the pacifist cry: "'All workers on the earth/Are brothers and WE WILL NOT FIGHT!'" (6)

Far from contradicting the position O'Neill takes in the poem (as one commentator has suggested), (7) *The Movie Man* is perfectly consistent in theme. O'Neill's satire of Mexican military leaders in general and of Villa in particular is wholly consistent with his championing of the poor in the poem. In O'Neill's view, the peons were just as much victims of the self-aggrandizing Mexican generals as were the American soldiers, who were asked to "bleed and groan--for Guggenheim! /and give [their] lives--for Standard Oil!" What has been consistently overlooked in *The Movie Man* is the moral perspective supplied by the only character besides the protagonist to remain on stage throughout the play, the Sentry, a "Mexican peon." (169)(8) He is the one character to most clearly reflect O'Neill's opinion of the two American filmmakers and the events of the play generally, in his two-word line, which is twice spoken and which frames the play--"Muy loco! [very crazy]." (171, 184)

Fundamentally, then, "Fratricide" and *The Movie Man* are grounded in the same political perspective, but where the poem is a sincere expression of dissent, overtly persuasive in its design, *The Movie Man* is only covertly persuasive. It is a work of satire, taking potshots at all the principal male characters, and like so much other satire, it is ultimately aimed at human greed and selfishness. *The Movie Man* is a piece of outrageous topical satire, an exercise in fun-filled iconoclasm that takes no prisoners. To suggest as much, of course, is to accept the fact that *The Movie Man* is not a milestone in the history of dramatic literature; but to acknowledge the obvious is not at the same time to assume that O'Neill's first comic play is a failure. It is a piece of ephemera, which would have had its greatest effectiveness in a production at the time it was written. Like so much topical satire, it quickly went out of date. To observe, as some commentators have, that *The Movie Man* is a "crude farce" or a "would-be comedy" is to miss the point of what O'Neill was up to. (9)

The playwright's primary job in such instances is to create a vehicle for performance. His responsibility is to place enough features in the script to make the situation and the butt of the satire recognizable. In this regard, O'Neill is eminently successful. The basic situation of a Mexican general named Pancho being involved with American filmmakers would have been immediately recognized by an audience of the day as a situation right off the front page of the paper. Beyond that, O'Neill includes a number of topical details and references that would have been spotted with pleasure by those who were properly informed. For example, in the first line of the set description, O'Neill indicates that the locale is "the suburb of a large town in northern Mexico" (169); the stronghold of Villa, of course, was the very same region. Another nice touch appears in the set decorations; O'Neill indicates that in "the left-hand corner several Mauser carbines are stacked." (169) It was well known that the Germans supplied the Mexican weapons.

Beyond such brief references, O'Neill also captures the underlying reality of the situation in Mexico in his basic plot complication. The man who is to be executed at sunrise, Anita Fernandez's father, is obviously a wealthy man. Fernandez, we are told, "Went to school in the States--Cornell or some place." (173) He has also been able to send Anita to convent school in New York City, and he lives in a "hacienda." (184) Consequently, there is little doubt that Fernandez is a rich man who, realistically, would not be inclined to support strongly Pancho's peon-centered agrarian revolution. As a consequence, the revolutionaries are extorting money from Fernandez to finance their cause. In fact, Fernandez is going to be killed partly "because they can't get any more coin out of him." (173)

The most recognizable feature of O'Neill's play, outside of the two film makers, is his portrait of Pancho Gomez. While Pancho Villa was not the alcoholic Gomez is (Villa did not drink or smoke), he was, to put it mildly, a notorious ladies' man; thus Gomez's treatment of Anita would also seem recognizable to an audience of the day. (10) What is more, O'Neill's Gomez has two traits that are true to Villa's character. The first appears when Gomez and Rogers are bargaining over Gomez's desire to stage a night attack, something expressly forbidden by the movie contract (a fact duly reported in the papers). (11) When Rogers first pulls out the contract, Gomez reacts "(With a defiant snarl) And if I say to hell, you! Then what you do, eh?" (182) In response, Rogers lists the extent of the Army's dependence on the Earth Motion Picture Company. Gomez reacts "(Softly--fingering his revolver) *Bueno*; but I can also have you shot, *hombre*." Then Rogers plays his trump card. "Nix on that rough stuff! You wouldn't dare. You've got to keep on the right side of the U.S.A. or your revolution isn't worth the powder to blow it to--Mexico." (182) Here again is a recognizable feature of the historical situation. The United States and President Wilson were officially opposed to President Huerta's remaining in office. This opposition to Huerta was not accompanied by official support of Villa, but it nevertheless indirectly aided his cause. (12) Tying this real detail of American policy to the interests of Earth Motion Pictures is a hyperbolic satiric jab of O'Neill's, and it does the trick with Gomez, who insightfully concludes that Rogers wants to make a deal, which he does--"the life of Ernesto Fernandez" (183) in exchange for a night battle. Gomez hesitates, only "for a moment" and then says, "*Bueno*, my friend, I accept your terms." (183) His hesitation is brief.

By this means, O'Neill portrays one of Villa's features that most struck John Reed, Villa's decisiveness, his ability to cut through the complexities and take meaningful action. (13) The other recognizable feature of Villa is in Gomez's regard for his men; Gomez's parting line is: "Should anyone wish me, *senor*, tell them that een the hour of battle Pancho Gomez, like the immortal Juarez, will ever be found at the head of his brave soldiers, *Adios!*." (183)(14)

Admittedly, O'Neill's portraits of Gomez and his general, Virella, are not flattering, but they are exactly what is to be expected in a satiric sketch. The two filmmakers fare no better; in fact, they fare much worse. Their racist remarks and their perception that military attacks and executions are only recalcitrant subject matter for the camera are not designed to elevate their characters in the eyes of the audience.

But *The Movie Man* is concerned with more than satiric characterizations. The major action of the sketch is the "love" story involving Anita and Rogers. The most important feature of this story is the effect Anita has on Rogers.

When, early in the play, Devlin, Roger's associate, asks Rogers to intervene in Fernandez' execution, Rogers has three good reasons not to: "Nix. Virella has a grudge against him and Gomez needs Virella. Anyway, I've got no license to butt in on their little scraps. Besides, it'll make a great picture." (173) But after Anita explains why she has come to Gomez' headquarters, Rogers changes his mind completely. The point at which Rogers makes his commitment is significant; it occurs when he realizes just how far Anita is willing to go to save her father:

ANITA.   I must see Gomez.
ROGERS.   (*Deliberately--looking steadily into her eyes*) Don't you know what Gomez will want--the price he will make you pay if he finds you here?
ANITA.   (*Closing her eyes and swaying weakly on her feet*) For the life--of my fathair--(*She sobs softly*)
ROGERS.   (*Looking at her in admiration*) God!
ANITA.   (*Fiercely*) I would keel myself to save him!
ROGERS.   But even if he said he'd free your father you couldn't believe him. What is Gomez' word worth? No, you must let me fix this for you.
ANITA.   (*Doubtfully*) But you--Gomez ees veree powerful, *senor* --ees it possible for you to do?
ROGERS.   (*Decisively*) I'll save your old man if I have to start a revolution of my own to do it. (178)

It is an even question whether Rogers is more moved by the extent of Anita's commitment or by his own vision of the beautiful Anita yielding her body to Gomez. One thing seems certain, Anita would not have fared so well if she were ugly.

It would not be much of an exaggeration to suggest that O'Neill wrote the entire play for the sake of Rogers' decisive assertion, "I'll save your old man if I have to start a revolution of my own to do it." On the surface, the line calls attention to Rogers' complete lack of sympathy and understanding with the events going on around him, but on a deeper level it suggests a theme capsulized in his final choice of a title, *The Personal Equation*. The idea, which O'Neill would treat seriously in less than year, is that all reformers and revolutionaries are suspect because they are really in it for their own personal ends. The "cause" is just a smoke screen for the deeper needs and objectives of the individual.

The idea is not presented in *The Movie Man* as tellingly as it is in *The Personal Equation*, but O'Neill is definitely trying it out, and it is a feature of all the principal characters. Rogers pushes aside the contract to do a favor for Anita and for himself; Virella uses the brutality of the revolution to get rid of Fernandez because he has a personal "grudge against him" (173); Gomez knuckles under to Rogers' demands because, among other things, Earth Motion Pictures "has promised to help [him] become President" (182); all of them have made a "personal equation" between their own self-interest and some larger cause. In the context of O'Neill's satire, the theme becomes simply another version of personal greed; but it is a foreshadowing of things to come.

Like *The Movie Man*, though in a serious vein, *The Sniper* was inspired by current events which aroused O'Neill's deepest emotions; and like his poem "Fratricide," *The Sniper* is finally an antiwar protest. (15)   The immediate event that inspired O'Neill's play, Germany's invasion of Belgium, began on August 4, 1914; (16) and by November 8, O'Neill had finished both a detailed scenario and a dialogue draft. (17)

The Sniper, then, is as topical a serious play as O'Neill ever wrote; and like *The Movie Man*, the play reflects in its content recognizable features of the news of the day, not only in its Belgian locale, but also in its reflection of the actual horror of shooting civilians caught with arms. But *The Sniper* is most interesting as a piece of discourse in the American political climate of the fall of 1914, when President Wilson was still arguing for the neutrality of the United States. (18) In this context, *The Sniper* does not appear as pro-neutral. In its emotional depiction of the consequences of neutral Belgium's invasion by the Germans, the play actually could have served, if produced, to stimulate "war fever." At bottom, however, *The Sniper* is truly an antiwar play, but it is also much more, it is a protest against warmongering human nature and the God who created it. (19) The play is also distinctly antichurch and antireligion.

In *The Sniper*, though some commentators have seen only the play's political implications, (20) the equally important metaphysical, or religious, implications are present from the beginning and fully integrated with the characters and the events. (21)

Subsequent to Rougon's entrance, carrying on his back the body of his dead son, Charles, the dialogue begins with the entrance of the Village Priest, as follows:

PRIEST.   Rougon!
ROUGON.   (*Not hearing him*) God, oh God!
PRIEST.   (*Laying a thin white hand compassionately on
             Rougon's broad back*) There, there, my son! It is the
             will of God.
ROUGON.   (*Startled by the sound of a voice, he jumps from his
             chair*) Eh? (*He stares at the priest with dazed eyes*)
PRIEST.   (*With a sad smile*) Oh, come now, it isn't possible that
             you've forgotten me.
ROUGON.   (*Snatching off his cap respectfully*) Pardon, Father. I
             was--I didn't know--you see--all this--. (190-191)

Not only is the central issue in the play, God's will, announced in the third line, but also O'Neill is able to capitalize on the conventional symbolism of the Priest as God's representative to foreshadow the progress of the play. The Priest's question of whether Rougon has forgotten him images Rougon's outcome; he will have forgotten his God, and worse, at the end of the play. Thus, in *The Sniper*, man's relation to God and religion is present as a thematic concern, both visually and verbally, from the beginning, just as much as the theme of war.

At this early point, however, Rougon is willing to accept a secular explanation of his suffering. Rougon asserts that it is all the fault of "those cursed Prussians!" (192) It is the Priest who introduces the concept of God's will, which Rougon refuses to accept. "His will? Ha! No, the good God would not punish me so--I, who have harmed no one." (191)

The first phase of *The Sniper* ends when Rougon and the Priest kneel down to pray for the repose of the soul of Rougon's dead son, Charles. The turning point in Rougon's development occurs during the prayer; in the stage directions, O'Neill makes evident his attitude toward religion and the Christian God. His views are manifest in the words "futile prayer" and in the connotations of "mumble," "sing-song," and "droning." It is also important to note, however, how Rougon's speech which interrupts the prayer: "Charles, Charles, my little one!" echoes Rougon's very first speech, "Charles! My little one!" (190)

Despite all of the Priest's efforts throughout the first scene, nothing has changed. Though the Priest reiterates, "God's will be done!" (199), Rougon is unimpressed, as the dialogue that follows the prayer demonstrates:

PRIEST.   Come, come, it is hard, I know, but you must bear it like a man. God's will be done! He, too, had a son who died for others. Pray to Him, and He will comfort you in your affliction.

ROUGON.   (*Placing his hand gently on his son's face*) Cold! Cold! He who was alive and smiling only this morning. (199)

As Rougon's response indicates, it is his son's dead body that defines his sense of reality, not the vision of a "good God." Rougon finds no consolation in his religion and, though he is not fully conscious of it, his attitude toward God has changed. He makes no further references to "the good God."

The climax in Rougon's development in relation to his God occurs at the end of the play. After he learns that both his wife and Charles's fiancee, Louise, have also been killed, Rougon becomes a sniper, bent on revenge. As the Captain prepares for the subsequent execution, he says, "If you have a prayer to say, be quick!" The dialogue continues as follows:

ROUGON.   (*With angry scorn*) I want no prayers!

PRIEST.   Rougon!

ROUGON.   (*Furiously*) To hell with your prayers!

PRIEST.   (*Supplicatingly*) Make peace with your God, my son!

ROUGON.   (*Spitting on the floor, fiercely*) That for your God who allows such things to happen! (207)

The Priest's next line, "May God have mercy on--"is interrupted by the command of the German Captain, "*Feuer!*" "There is a crashing report," and "Rougon pitches forward on his face" (207) and dies. Rougon has died with a curse on his lips; he has died hating his God. In the context of Catholic orthodoxy, Rougon has lost not only his life but also his salvation. His soul must be consigned to Hell.

When Rougon's final line, "That for your God who allows such things to happen," is compared with his earlier remark, "the good God would not punish me so--I, who have harmed no one," it is clear just how much his attitude changes during the course of the play. In conventional Christian terms the outcome must be considered tragic. Yet, the full significance of this tragedy only becomes clear when we recognize the causes of Rougon's damnation. The two most important factors, besides the external events of the war, are Rougon's own human nature and the Priest. Initially, Rougon's anger is aimed solely at "those cursed Prussians"; it is the Priest who introduces the concept of God's will. Initially, Rougon is in a mood to take immediate revenge; but the Priest urges him to postpone it. In the Priest's attempts to bring Rougon under control, he uses various arguments. He uses belief in a good God to assure Rougon that his wife is safe in Brussels and that he must be careful "for her sake, if nothing else." (192) To this motive for living, the Priest adds duty to country. "Your country has need of you. . . . You must live and help and bear your part of her burden as best you can. It is your duty." (197) When Rougon begins to object, the Priest attempts a compromise; by staying alive Rougon will not only "best serve" his country, but also "revenge" his "personal wrongs." (198) Throughout the first phase of the play, the Priest does everything he can to keep Rougon from endangering his own life, but as a consequence of his efforts and with the aid of events ostensibly ordained by God, Rougon has lost much more than his life. He has lost his soul. Ironically, however, at the end of the play, the Priest has no awareness of the impact of his efforts on the ultimate destination of Rougon's soul, nor is the Priest aware that the turning point in Rougon's development was the prayer for the repose of Charles's soul. But to O'Neill the ironies were obvious; all we need do is consider in the light of Rougon's outcome, his earlier description for the Priest of his immediate reaction to the devastation of his farm: "this finger itched to press the trigger and send at least one to hell for payment." (195)

Despite our considerable sympathy for Rougon and his plight, we must admit that Rougon himself is also a factor in his tragedy; and it is from this fact that the deepest and most pessimistic of the play's metaphysical implications arise. Rougon is a choleric man, quickly moved to anger. Rougon's nature is dramatized in the play's second major scene through his treatment of the traumatized "half-witted" (202) boy, Jean. The treatment is rough and brutal, characterized by brusque interruptions, a condescending attitude, and threats of violence.

Jean is only a messenger, and not very conscious of his role at that. He is full of intense fear, and when Rougon threatens him, he is only, as the Priest points out, "frightening [the boy]" (202) further. Rougon's effect on Jean is the same as that of the soldiers; all of them frighten the boy. By this identification, O'Neill indicates his own views on the ultimate causes of war and its unavoidability; war is a product of human nature and its attendant weakness. Rougon's bad temper is an innate characteristic, and it is just such a temperment that leads to war rather than peace, to revenge rather than forgiveness. Thus, although Rougon is victimized by forces beyond his control, he is also a victimizer. The guilt is universal, and that is the ultimate tragedy.

At bottom, *The Sniper* contains an orthodox pessimism about the nature of humanity; man's heart is evil and sinful. It is Rougon's emotions that gain control and drive him to revenge. Even more tragic is the image of a world without God to ameliorate this situation. Rougon's repudiation of his God leaves him alone in a world where other men dispense revenge by execution in the guise of justice.

The Sniper, then, is an antiwar play in the deepest sense of the term. It is not a protest against just a particular war, but a protest of all war. More tellingly, it is a protest against the ultimate causes of war, the nature of God (if He exists) and the nature of Man. As a result of the ironic portrayal of the Priest and the strength of Rougon's invective, the antichurch, anti-God attitudes that O'Neill suggested in his description of the Priest's prayer, are concretized in the dramatic action as well as in the setting. It is the communication of these attitudes that is the ultimate justification for the play. At bottom, the play embodies a pessimism that seems to make any political action beside the point.

In this respect, *The Movie Man* and *The Sniper* share a common vision, a vision that is ultimately political and pessimistic. Politically, both plays reveal O'Neill's underlying sympathy, at this time, for the peasant class, as its members are victimized by the military, the state, and the church. While *The Movie Man* is a piece of ephemeral, hyperbolic satire and *The Sniper* is a realistic tragedy with profound religious implications, both plays are also discourses of social criticism that reveal O'Neill's growing disbelief in the possibility of true social and political progress, a disbelief that would not be fully voiced by O'Neill on the American stage until some thirty years later, in *The Iceman Cometh*, by which time he had already become a world playwright.

NOTES

1. Louis Sheaffer, "Correcting Some Errors in the Annals of O'Neill (Part II)," *Eugene O'Neill Newsletter* 8.1 (1984): 16-17. Sheaffer's source is Terry Ramsaye, *A Million and One Nights: A History of the Motion Picture* (1926; New York: Simon & Schuster, 1964). The *New York Times* covered the whole affair in detail, beginning on January 7, 1914 (1.8), with follow-ups on January 8 (2.1), January 9 (2.1), January 10 (8.5), February 11 (2.2), and March 11 (2.6).

2. Samuel Eliot Morison, *The Oxford History of the American People*, 3 vols. (New York: New American Library, 1972), vol. 3, *1869 to*

the Death of John F. Kennedy 1963, 171.

3. Louis Sheaffer, *O'Neill: Son and Playwright* (Boston: Little, Brown, 1968), 278.

4. Cf. Sheaffer, *O'Neill*, 278; Travis Bogard, *Contour in Time: The Plays of Eugene O'Neill* (New York: Oxford University Press, 1972), 25.

5. Robert A. Rosenstone, *Romantic Revolutionary: A Biography of John Reed* (New York: Vintage, 1975), 252.

6. Eugene O'Neill, *Poems 1912-1914*, ed. Donald Gallup (New York: Ticknor & Fields, 1980), 43-46.

7. Bogard, 25.

8. All parenthetical page references are to the texts of *The Movie Man* and *The Sniper* in Eugene O'Neill, *Ten "Lost" Plays* (New York: Random House, 1984).

9. Timo Tiusanen, *O'Neill's Scenic Images* (Princeton: Princeton University Press, 1968), 63; John Mason Brown, "Finders Keepers, Losers Weepers," *Saturday Review*, 17 June 1950: 30.

10. Rosenstone, 157; Morison, 171.

11. Sheaffer, "Correcting," 16.

12. Morison, 171.

13. Rosenstone, 156.

14. Cf. Rosenstone, 165.

15. Sheaffer, *O'Neill*, 402; Lawrence Gellert, ed., *Lost Plays of Eugene O'Neill* (New York: The Citadel Press, 1950), 9; Doris M. Alexander, "Eugene O'Neill, 'The Hound of Heaven,' and the 'Hell Hole,'" *Modern Language Quarterly* 20 (1959): 199.

16. Irving S. Kull and Nell M. Kull, *An Encyclopedia of American History*, rev. Stanley H. Friedelbaum (New York: Popular Library, 1965), 330.

17. Eugene O'Neill, letter to Beatrice Ashe, c. 8 November 1914, Berg Collection of American Literature, New York Public Library.

18. Henry F. May, *The End of American Innocence: A Study of the First Years of Our Own Time, 1912-1917* (New York: Oxford U. Press, 1979), 362; Morison, *The Oxford History*, 175-76; cf. Sheaffer, 302.

19. Cf. Virginia Floyd, *The Plays of Eugene O'Neill: A New Assessment* (New York: Ungar, 1985), 86.

20. Sheaffer, *O'Neill*, 302; Doris M. Alexander, *The Tempering of Eugene O'Neill* (New York: Harcourt, Brace & World, 1962), 199; Gellert, ed., *Lost Plays*, 9; Tiusanen 49; Arthur and Barbara Gelb, *O'Neill*, enlg. ed. (New York: Harper & Bros., 1973), 272-73; Bogard, 52-53; John Henry Raleigh, *The Plays of Eugene O'Neill* (Carbondale: Southern Illinois University Press, 1965), 57.

21. Cf. Floyd, 86.

12

Three O'Neill Women: An Emergent Pattern

Jean Anne Waterstradt

One of the most revealing anecdotes about Eugene O'Neill's view of self is recounted by Louis Sheaffer in *O'Neill: Son and Playwright* (1) and repeated by Travis Bogard in *Contour in Time*. (2) It concerns the playwright's habit of continually looking at himself in mirrors. His Provincetown associate and friend George Cram (Jig) Cook accused him of being "the most conceited man I've ever known[;] you're always looking at yourself." O'Neill replied, "No, I just want to be sure I'm here." O'Neill's response foreshadowed his lifelong search for identity, for his place in the world. His landmark plays, beginning in the 1920s, all concern themselves in some way with such a search: his most memorable characters are propelled by the longing to find and establish themselves.

Three O'Neill dramas--one a lengthy novel-like experiment, one a trilogy utilizing myth, one a realistic modern drama touched by lyricism and suggesting the symbolic (3)--deal with the lives of three women as they seek their place, as they try to establish an ultimate identity.

O'Neill is not noted for either sympathy toward women or understanding their unique difficulties and virtues. Sheaffer refers to "O'Neill's feeling that a woman should devote herself to her man to the point of utter selflessness." The dramatist's myopia is further emphasized in his comment that "When a woman loves a man, she should be prepared even to give her life for him." (4) Sheaffer reminds us that "O'Neill created in the majority of his female characters either bitches and other agents of misfortune or impossibly noble souls. He could praise Woman only in exaggerated, unrealistic terms." (5)

Despite the dramatist's warped understanding of women, which is illustrated in these observations, it is possible to trace in the portraits of Nina Leeds of *Strange Interlude* (1927), Lavinia Mannon of *Mourning Becomes Electra* (1931), and Josie Hogan of *A Moon for the Misbegotten* (1943) something that might be termed O'Neill's developing attitude. If we leave aside the biographical connections and other sources of these plays, we should be able to view the three women individually and examine the extent to which they establish their own identities and find a home in the world. There is a great psychological and moral distance between Nina and Josie. Although O'Neill labeled *Strange Interlude* "my woman play," (6) *A Moon for the Misbegotten* is more clearly his real "woman play" because it defines and celebrates in woman the qualities of empathy, compassion, and courage. Josie, despite her earlier pretense, knows who she is. In her heartbreak over Jim Tyrone she will nevertheless go on living in the world. The attitudes and actions of both Nina and Lavinia contrast sharply with the course Josie takes: Nina is a perennial manipulator and escapist, and Lavinia turns to her dead, closing the Mannon house against light and life.

Each of these O'Neill women does face herself, does find a place for herself; but only Josie, after far less adventure and "worldly" experience than Nina and Lavinia undergo, emerges from the anguish of her loss still committed to life. Not surprisingly, O'Neill defines all three women mainly through their relationships to the men in their worlds, their fathers and lovers. They suffer in those relationships and, of course, respond in different ways to that suffering. In each play, the greatest problem consists of dealing with loss, of facing the reality of death.

Nina Leeds is sometimes described as the precursor of the heroines of modern soap operas. She has also been called "at once one of the author's most fascinating and least credible women" (7) and has been identified with the "Strindbergian destroyer." (8) She is the daughter of a professor immersed in the past. O'Neill describes the atmosphere of Henry Leeds' library as "that of a cozy, cultured retreat, sedulously built as a sanctuary where, secure with the culture of the past at his back, a fugitive from reality can view the present safely from a distance, as a superior with condescending disdain, pity, and even amusement." (9)

At the beginning of *Strange Interlude*, Nina's mother has been dead for six years, and as Charles Marsden describes her as "so aggressively [the professor's] wife" (*NP* 487), we can assume that she dominated the family. Thus Nina, without a mother from the age of fourteen, has lived through the turbulent adolescent years as the "boss" (*NP* 487) of her "temperamentally timid" (*NP* 488) father, who has "a natural tendency toward a prim provincialism where practical present-day considerations are concerned." (*NP* 489)

Nina's early years have also been influenced by her father's former student and devoted family friend, Marsden, who, although a man of "quiet charm" with an "appealing, inquisitive friendliness" (*NP* 486), is remarkably like her father. If he does not live in the past, at least he lives on the periphery of the present as an observer of life rather than a participant.

Juxtaposed against these two fatherly figures are, first, the dead Gordon Shaw, then the obtuse, decent Sam Evans, and, finally, the cynical, vital Ned Darrell.

Gordon, killed two days before the armistice that ended World War I, is first idealized and then beatified, not just by Nina but by everyone who knew him, except Professor Leeds. Competing with Gordon for Nina, her father wins initially by appealing to Gordon's fairness and honor but loses when Gordon's plane is shot down. *He* has hated Gordon, and now Nina hates *him*. Her plan to atone for what she describes as her "cowardly treachery to Gordon" (*NP* 500) involves leaving her father's house to give herself to other men, specifically wounded soldiers. She vows that she will "give and give until I can make that gift of myself for a man's happiness without scruple, without fear, without joy in his joy!" (*NP* 500) The attitude expressed in this promise is an early foreshadowing of her withdrawal from the world.

Nina's life at the hospital, among wounded soldiers, ends with her father's death, which is soon followed by her marriage to Sam, a "splendid chap, clean and boyish" (*NP* 528), who loves her but is too naive to understand her. Nina marries him because he seems to need her and she feels the need to have children (she never loves him). But in one of the main ironies of the play she aborts his child because of his mother's warning that the Evans blood carries the taint of insanity. Sam's boyishness and vigor wane and all but disappear as he struggles futilely for success; Nina now both despises and pities him. And, of course, he lives always in the shadow of the legendary Gordon Shaw.

Nina turns next to Dr. Ned Darrell, a college friend of Sam's whom she met at the hospital. In a cool, businesslike manner, she decides to "[pick] out a healthy male" (*NP* 567) for whom she feels no emotion and have a child by him that Sam would believe to be his own. Predictably, she and Ned fall in love and sustain a passionate relationship over many years. With the birth of Nina's son, who is named for Gordon Shaw, Sam's life changes. He grows prosperous and self-assured, having "a decided look of solidity about him, of determination moving towards ends it is confident it can achieve. He has matured, found his place in the world." (*NP* 592) In the single most famous speech in *Strange Interlude*, Nina, with all the important males in her life under one roof, says "triumphantly" in an interior monologue:

My three men! . . . I feel their desires converge in me! . . . to form one complete beautiful male desire which I absorb . . . and am whole . . . they dissolve in me, their life is my life. . . . I am pregnant with the three! . . . husband! . . . lover! . . . father! and the fourth man! . . . little man! . . . little Gordon! . . . he is mine too! . . . that makes it perfect! (*NP* 616, ellipses in the original)

She has everything she wants and appears in complete control of her world.

Eventually Nina loses her son to a young woman at the same time she loses her husband to death. Burnt out, she now has no reason or desire to marry Ned. Marsden's metaphoric explanation is appropriate: "[S]he is in love with evening" (*NP* 678). Nina is only forty-five years old at the end of the play when she decides that she is "so contentedly weary with life" (*NP* 682) and turns to "Father" Charlie for comfort and peace. This woman, whom the Gelbs call a "fascinating monster, embodying what O'Neill regarded as all that is both purest and blackest in Woman," quits the world to live in twilight. (10)

Lavinia Mannon is the daughter of a powerful family whose way of thinking has always centered on death. In act three of *Homecoming*, Ezra Mannon, her father, newly home from the Civil War, describes the quintessential Mannon view: "Life was a dying. Being born was starting to die. Death was being born." (*NP* 738) Now, however, the death with which as a soldier he constantly lived has caused him to think of life, to value it as he has never done before, and to try to make a new beginning of his marriage to Christine, who has long since found what she wants in another man, Adam Brant.

Like her father, Lavinia, with her feelings severely governed, yearns to embrace life. She wants to be loved, especially by her father, but the emotional gulf between them cannot be bridged, and he needs the support and love of a wife more than the adoration of a daughter. O'Neill's initial description of Lavinia's appearance and manner emphasizes the repression that grips her:

She is twenty-three but looks considerably older. . . . her body is thin, flat-breasted and angular, and its unattractiveness is accentuated by her plain black dress. Her movements are stiff and she carries herself with a wooden, square-shouldered, military bearing. She has a flat dry voice and a habit of snapping out her words like an officer giving orders. (*NP* 692)

As she watches her mother strolling in the garden, "Her eyes are bleak and hard with an intense, bitter enmity." (*NP* 692) She is alienated from both parents, from her father because of the emotional distance that cannot be closed and from her mother because of her hatred for Christine's infidelity.

Lavinia's association with Adam Brant has been promoted by Christine; it has never been intended to have any permanent meaning. But it does give Lavinia a glimpse of a way of life remote from her New England home. Brant, a sailor, knows the freedom and beauty of the sea and of the "Blessed Isles."

Lavinia also has a relationship with Peter Niles, a fitful one. The essential goodness and innocence of Peter and Hazel, his sister, contrast sharply with the guilt-laden, life-denying force that shapes the Mannons. Frederic E. Carpenter finds the brother and sister "so innocent as to be unreal." He also comments that "They woodenly persist in their love for the Mannons, despite repeated rejections, insults, and desertions." (11) That persistence, however, may indicate a quality in Lavinia and her brother, Orin, not readily apparent to those who are not so pure of heart. There is nothing prearranged about the Peter-Lavinia affair; it has come about as a natural result of friendship. Finally, even though it is more prolonged than the Adam-Lavinia relationship, it is no more successful. Lavinia's part in the murder of Adam Brant, in the suicide of her mother and brother, and in the drastic change in Peter's relationship with his family all work against her determination to marry Peter. She herself realizes the futility of her plans with, "And I couldn't bear to watch your eyes grow bitter and hidden from me and wounded in their trust of life! I love you too much!" (*NP* 864) She also tells the shocked Peter, "I can't marry you. . . . Go home. Make it up with your mother and Hazel. Marry someone else. . . . Love isn't permitted me. The dead are too strong!" (*NP* 865)

Only once does Lavinia break out of the restrictions that bind her as a Mannon. In her long trip to the Islands with Orin, she evidently experienced the freedom and wonder often associated with love. She returns from the journey looking like her mother. O'Neill says, "She seems a mature woman, sure of her feminine attractiveness" (*NP* 815), but the change in her is transitory.

Whether "the dead are too strong" or Lavinia merely ceases to fight against her inheritance, she gives herself to celibacy and isolation, to self-punishment. Michael Manheim points out, "[Lavinia's] reason has led her . . . from the simple idea that 'the past can be ignored' to the equally simple idea that 'the past cannot be ignored'; and that latter idea is to be the sum and substance of her personal Hell. She will live out her life only with the past and with no illusions about the past." (12)

Unlike Nina, Lavinia shows strength and determination. She does not succumb to dependency: no Charlie Marsden waits to make her decisions; she will live in her father's house with no father figure to comfort and protect her. Like Nina, however, Lavinia has resigned from the world.

Josie Hogan is the least attractive of the three women. In fact, O'Neill's description renders her more grotesque than feminine: "She is so oversize for a woman that she is almost a freak . . . [weighing] around one hundred and eighty." He also notes her broad shoulders and wide waist, which is "slender by contrast with her hips and thighs." She has "immensely strong" arms and legs. "But," he insists, "there is no mannish quality about her. She is all Woman." She has a distinctly Irish face, not a pretty one, O'Neill says; "but her large dark-blue eyes give it a note of beauty, and her smile, revealing even white teeth, gives it charm." (13) Even so, her physical appearance cannot compete with Nina's "striking" face, her "long, beautifully developed legs," her "extraordinarily large" and "deep greenish blue eyes." (*NP* 494-95) Nor does Josie have any of Lavinia Mannon's physical attractiveness. Even when Lavinia's initial woodenness is described, we are made aware of her resemblance to her handsome mother with the "same peculiar shade of copper-gold hair, the same . . . dark violet-blue eyes." (*NP* 692)

Josie is also the least privileged of the three women. Nina is the pampered daughter of a college professor, and Lavinia belongs to an aristocratic New England family. Josie, on the other hand, is the daughter of a poverty-stricken Connecticut farmer scratching out a living on inhospitable land. The Hogans live with a minimum of creature comforts. Neither Nina nor Lavinia has ever been required to work for a living, but Josie has toiled on the farm all her life. In fact, Phil Hogan depends on his daughter as he has never been able to depend on his sons.

All three woman have been deprived of maternal guidance and affection, Nina and Josie by their mothers' death, Lavinia by the emotional breach between her and Christine. O'Neill's treatment of this deprivation naturally varies with each play. The death of Mrs. Leeds is mentioned only by Marsden (*NP* 487), but the hostility between Lavinia and Christine permeates *Mourning Becomes Electra* until Christine's suicide. Josie's mother, dead for twenty years, is mentioned by both husband and daughter. "With a surprising sad gentleness" Phil speaks of her as "[a] sweet woman." And Josie remembers "[w]ith a teasing smile which is half sad" that her mother could put Phil "in [his] place when [he'd] come home drunk and want to tear down the house for the fun of it." Phil admits "[w]ith admiring appreciation" that "Yes, she could do it, God bless her." (*LP* 311) Thus it is clear that Josie's mother had a relationship with daughter and husband different from that of Mrs. Leeds in her family and vastly different from that of Christine Mannon in her family. Even the limited references to Mrs. Hogan underline that she is held in cherished memory.

The relationship of the mother to the daughter, the wife to the husband, is not, of course, the crucial relationship in these plays, but it at least implies something fundamental about the family. Far more significant in identifying these women, in helping them determine who they are, is their relationship to their fathers and lovers. Nina's father, devoted to the past and to the comfort in which he likes to explore the past, has interfered in his daughter's life and caused a loss that she can never forgive. Lavinia's father is incapable of the emotional warmth for which his adoring daughter yearns. They stand psychologically apart from each other and then are forever separated by his murder. The Hogans, however, work side by side to earn their meager living, and this physical proximity emphasizes, perhaps promotes, their emotional proximity, their commitment to each other. When Mike, as he prepares to leave home, calls his father "an old hog," Josie strikes him hard and advises him to "keep [his] tongue off Phil." She adds, "He's my father too, and I like him, if you don't." (*LP* 302) Although Josie and Phil hurl insults at each other, the exchange is really a kind of game, and they conclude by trading compliments: "If you ain't the damnedest daughter in Connecticut, who is?" "And if you ain't the damnedest father in Connecticut, who is?" (*LP* 309) It should be remembered that the name "Phil" means love. Josie's father is rightly named; he never falters in his love for his daughter.

However, it is in their relationships, especially in the outcome of those relationships, with the other men in their lives, their lovers, that these O'Neill women most clearly show their sense of self, their success or failure at making a place for themselves. Nina Leeds, after youthful promiscuity, after a loveless marriage, after prolonged adultery, at last in her widowhood turns to "dear old Charlie," who will return her to her father's house and to her daughter's role in that house. She resigns from life; she wants to "rot away in peace" (*NP* 679), to leave all decisions to Marsden, now her "father," to retreat into dependency. Lavinia Mannon, after Adam Brant, Peter Niles, and her island native, also resigns from life and determinedly gives herself to her dead.

Josie Hogan has loved only one man. Her feigned wantonness has never fooled her father, although out of deference to her pride, he pretends to believe her stories of conquest. Nor has it deceived Jim

Tyrone, who believes that he knows Josie better than her father does (*LP* 376). Josie has loved only Jim, but it is a love fated never to come to fruition. Out of self-loathing and profound world-weariness, Jim is slowly committing suicide through alcohol. There is only one night for Josie and Jim, and it is not a lovers' night. Under the moon she becomes not Jim's lover but an agent for his redemption: she listens to the terrible story of his transcontinental train ride with his mother's corpse; she comforts him; she cradles his head on her breast and lets him sleep the night away. In the morning she prays as he walks down the road away from her, "May you have your wish and die in your sleep soon, Jim darling. May you rest forever in forgiveness and peace." (*LP* 409) With the loss of Jim, Josie does not give up the world, as Nina and Lavinia have done. She accepts what she cannot alter and even consoles Phil: "Don't be sad, Father. I'm all right--and I'm well content here with you." Then she rallies her Irish sense of humor: "Sure, living with you has spoilt me for any other man, anyway. There'd never be the same fun or excitement." (*LP* 409)

Josie will go on living in her father's house, but unlike Nina and Lavinia, she will have a father to love her. Though she is deprived of worldly goods, she has an amply furnished soul that enables her to face down her tragedy and commit herself to life. Manheim analyzes her greatness as:

[residing] in her ability (1) to take and to return in kind all that the interior horrors of those who love her may prompt them to throw at her, (2) to maintain her individuality at all times, (3) to love in dimensions comparable to her physical size, and (4) to love deeply only someone as strong as herself. (14)

The chronological distance from the composition of *Strange Interlude* to that of *A Moon for the Misbegotten* is sixteen years, but the moral distance between Nina Leeds and Josie Hogan is the distance between a deceitful, destructive female devoid of values except her own self-fulfillment and a strong, humorous, loving woman who learns how to sustain and forgive frail human beings, even herself. Because of the different times and varying circumstances of the composition of *Strange Interlude, Mourning Becomes Electra,* and *A Moon for the Misbegotten,* it is clear that O'Neill did not consciously demonstrate that his concept of woman had changed as his art developed. However, it is also clear from an examination of these three major plays that there is a kind of progression in the view of women he presents. Nina Leeds, Lavinia Mannon, and Josie Hogan all search for their identities; they all attempt to find where and how they belong. In the end, Nina gives up control of her life to another person; Lavinia, out of conviction and strength, assumes the sins of all the Mannons and turns to their ghosts; but Josie, the last to be created, in the last play that O'Neill completed, grasps present reality and promises to endure.

NOTES

1. Louis Sheaffer, *O'Neill: Son and Playwright* (Boston: Little, Brown, & Co., 1968), 240.

2. Travis Bogard, *Contour in Time: The Plays of Eugene O'Neill*, rev. ed. (New York: Oxford University Press, 1988), xii.

3. Travis Bogard, introduction to *The Later Plays of Eugene O'Neill* (New York: Modern Library, 1967), xxv-vi.

4. Louis Sheaffer, *O'Neill: Son and Artist* (Boston: Little, Brown, & Co., 1973), 450.

5. Sheaffer, 500.

6. Arthur and Barbara Gelb, *O'Neill* (New York: Harper & Row, 1973), 289.

7. Sheaffer, 240.

8. Bogard, 305.

9. Eugene O'Neill, *Nine Plays* (New York: The Modern Library, 1941), 485. (The texts of *Mourning Becomes Electra* and *Strange Interlude* quoted from this edition are subsequently cited as *NP* with page number.)

10. Gelb, 628.

11. Frederic I. Carpenter, *Eugene O'Neill* (New Haven, Conn.: College and University Press, 1964), 132.

12. Michael Manheim, *Eugene O'Neill's New Language of Kinship* (Syracuse, NY: Syracuse University Press, 1982), 84-85.

13. Travis Bogard, ed., *The Late Plays of Eugene O'Neill* (New York: Modern Library, 1941), 301. (The texts of *A Moon for the Misbegotten* quoted from this edition are subsequently cited as *LP* with page number.)

14. Manheim, 197.

13

Author, Actor, Audience: The Metatheatrical Elements in the Late Plays of Eugene O'Neill

Mariko Hori

The word "metatheatre" reminds us of Lionel Abel who wrote the very influential book *Metatheatre* a few decades ago. (1) Since this innovative work was published, "metatheatre," "metadrama," or in other words, the "meta" view of drama has become popular among scholars. But the word "metatheatre" itself is difficult to define. Abel tried to define "metatheatre" as one of the genres, comparable to tragedy, but his attempt seems to have failed. Quite recently Richard Hornby wrote a stimulating work entitled *Drama, Metadrama, and Perception* in which Hornby treats "metadrama" as a cultural phenomenon by classifying major Western drama into six categories. (2) As far as Hornby's treatment is concerned, "metadrama" or "metatheatre" can be discovered in any play as an element in drama.

From a technical point of view, "metatheatre" demands the audience's consciousness "of being in a theatre watching a play." (3) Although O'Neill's plays do not demand such a strong metatheatrical consciousness of the audience, the playwright seems to have written them with a great awareness of their impact on the audience. I would like to apply one of Hornby's six categories, "role playing within the role," to the characters of O'Neill's late plays, in relation with their impact on the audience.

In spite of his ideal of connecting the playscript and its performance, Hornby neither really connects them nor gives any evidence by quoting the playscripts. I will discuss what Hornby missed in his analysis of O'Neill's role-playing characters. I will also place the author somewhere between the characters and the audience, in the last part of my analysis.

"Role playing within the role is a device for exploring the concerns of the individual in relation to his society," says Hornby. (4) Although this emphasis on the individual has been recognized since the Renaissance, the identity crisis becomes evident in modern times. When identity is lost, the only way to live in this world is to wear a mask--not an actual one--or to play a role. This sense of the necessity of role playing has become stronger and stronger, and in the absurd drama, the lost feeling of identity is destroyed and playing roles becomes the main action and behavior of human existence. The extreme absurdist critic of O'Neill, C. W. E. Bigsby, concludes that the characters at the end of *Hughie* are "mere role-players." (5) They are trying to retrieve their identity by putting themselves into some roles, however meaningless they know them to be. O'Neill's characters in his late plays are more or less shattered by their feeling of loss, but they try to be confident by putting themselves in some positive roles even if the roles are illusory. When the feeling of loss disappears from the characters, as in the end of *Hughie*, it resembles strongly an absurd drama. (6)

Other critics also refer to the characters in O'Neill's late plays as "role players." Citing Travis Bogard's comment on O'Neill's role playing characters who "present themselves as actors," (7) Judith Barlow agrees that Con Melody and James Tyrone are role players and adds Hickey and Erie Smith and Jim Tyrone in *A Moon for the Misbegotten* to that list. (8) Most of O'Neill's characters in his late plays are certainly "role players." But how are such role-playing characters described in each play? What kind of "roles" are they playing? What is the playwright's purpose in creating such "roles" for the characters? Do they help to create a "metatheatre"?

Words such as "role," "act," "actor," and "actress" are mentioned here and there in O'Neill's late plays. They are not simply metaphors but give the audience a metatheatrical experience during the performance.

When those metaphors are spoken on stage, they sometimes produce irony. Con Melody in *A Touch of the Poet*, for example, in spite of his voluntary isolation from others present on the stage, fears that nobody listens to his words. O'Neill in the stage directions confirms that he has no audience and, consequently, stares defeated with a real trace of tragedy in his handsome face. When Con and Deborah in *More Stately Mansions* deplore their having no audience present on the stage, there exists another audience outside the stage, which sees them on the stage and watches the play.

Let me cite another example from *More Stately Mansions*. Simon Harford asks his mother Deborah, "Are you still as accomplished an actress as you used to be? . . . What role do you play nowadays, Mother?" (*Mansions* 12) Deborah, who seems to Simon to have somehow lost her quality of an "actress," is on the real stage performed by an actress. Simon's question is followed by Deborah's "You forget I have no audience now." (*Mansions* 13) Again there is the audience who watches the performance before the stage. These metaphors are not only the exposure of the characters' fear of isolation and loneliness but also the expression of loss of identity.

When characters such as Con Melody and James Tyrone and Hickey tell their stories in a dignified manner, on the contrary, they are evidently self-confident, because they have acquired an "audience" --other characters who listen to their stories--even if the listener on the stage is only one person like Edmund Tyrone listening to his father's story. The sense of existence of others on the stage temporarily saves their fear of lost selves.

Con, Deborah, Hickey, James, and Mary have the strong consciousness of an "actor" or an "actress." Even when it is not mentioned, their behaviors are akin to those of actors or actresses. *A Touch of the Poet* is an interesting example in which to analyze the role-playing characters. The main role-playing character is Con. Sara is another, particularly when she is haunted by her feverish love for Simon. But Deborah, who appears less onstage in this play than in *More Stately Mansions*, is almost exaggeratedly shown as a role-playing character whose behavior and dialogue are very artificial and typical of a poseur. When she says that she flatters herself to have preserved a philosophic poise or pose, she is satisfied with her "pose," not with her "poise." "Pose" is what she makes, and it is not a natural behavior. She is a born role player. Con, in spite of himself being a role player, repeatedly blames Deborah's insult as only an "act." Deborah hides her true nature and "acts" unnaturally. She is putting on an actress-like air.

This kind of role playing is a device O'Neill often uses in his late plays to convey the identity crisis of the modern world to his audience. The role-playing characters feign self-confidence by covering their shattered lost selves in reality. Erie Smith in *Hughie* speaks a long monologue to an unknown Night Clerk, trying to gain his self-confidence. Erie says, "But now I got a lousy hunch when I lost Hughie I lost my luck--I mean, I've lost the old confidence. He used to give me confidence." (*Hughie* 35) To Erie, "luck" is the guts to live in the harsh reality. His old friend Hughie could give him "luck," which is, as Erie says, "confidence."

Those role-playing characters make themselves "heroic" persons even in their projected stories based on their illusion of the past.

In act four of *Long Day's Journey into Night*, all four Tyrones express their experiences in the past, but the experiences are chosen or modified because they are the most dramatic activities, and they often sound more dramatic than what actually seems to have happened.

The same is true of Con Melody in *A Touch of the Poet*. He lives in his heroic past, and every act of his is a "pretense," which is the key word in the play. He pretends to be an aristocrat and despises his peasant-like wife Nora and the peasant-like behavior and language his daughter Sara shows intentionally. He is a "hero" in the play. Being away from the other characters on the stage, he rejects the one-to-one equal communication with them and makes them just an "audience." Con in the third act sits at a table separated from his despised peasants and tells his heroic exploits in the Talavera War only to Jamie Cregan, who can share his experience in the war. He ignores other people on the stage and even treats his own daughter Sara like a waitress. But after he is humiliated by the Harford family at the end of the play, Con acknowledges his true self--that he is no longer an aristocrat. He shoots his mare, the symbol of the blood of an aristocrat, and in this way kills his role as an aristocrat. He denies his former self by saying that he is not "play-actin'," which was the Major's game. He finally identifies himself as one of the peasants he has been disparaging. He retreats from the role of a "hero." He now looks like a "grinning clown." He is "leering" and "jeering," which is a servile air--the privilege of a peasant or a base person like a "fool."

"Fools of farce can overcome the tragedy of helplessness and separation," says Katherine Burkman. (9) Although Burkman applies this measure to the absurdist's drama, the same idea can be found in O'Neill's plays. The first act of *A Moon for the Misbegotten* reveals an excellent comic farce among Phil, Josie, and Jim. Even after the shattered experience of Josie, who has found her love for Jim will not be fulfilled, she overcomes her tragic fate by reviving a witty comic dialogue with her father, and the same is true of Con Melody at the end of *A Touch of the Poet*. He overcomes his tragic fate by laughing at his miserable self, calling himself a "clown." To be a fool is a new way of living, a new role-playing status some of the characters in O'Neill's late plays have reached.

Larry Slade at the end of *The Iceman Cometh* calls himself a fool "with pity" (*Iceman* 222), too. Although he is shattered and in despair, like Con at the end of *A Touch of the Poet*, he is still isolated, sitting at a table separated from others. He neither "acts" nor forgets "death" brought by Hickey and Don Parritt. Larry does not boast of his glorious past, either. He might have experienced a dramatic past, but he does not tell much of it. His past is conveyed mostly by Don Parritt.

In spite of his being a deep philosopher, Larry is not the heroic character who stands in the center of the stage, while a fake philosopher Hickey stands on the stage and plays a heroic character in the play. Larry chooses the passive role, but he is the most important character in the play; and as he understands Hickey, the audience understands Hickey. Jean Chothia indicates Larry's peculiarity in relation with the audience as follows: "it (the fact that Larry is revealed so fully) does place Larry in a special relationship to the audience and makes his role a vital one in their perception of the action." (10)

A character similar to Larry is Edmund Tyrone in *Long Day's Journey into Night*. Both Edmund and Larry are on the stage as main characters of the play but somehow retreat or try to retreat from the main action of the play. They accept their roles as a "listener," an "observer," or a "spectator." When they listen to the other characters' talk, the audience outside the stage will feel that they are listening to the story through these listeners. In that sense, they are "mediators" between other characters on the stage and the audience. Their functions are "to listen and learn--basically passive, undramatic activities" as Barlow describes it. (11)

Josie Hogan in *A Moon for the Misbegotten* also plays the role of a "listener" to Jim Tyrone. At first she is forced to become a "temptress" by her father's "trick" of getting her married to Jim. But she finds herself being unwittingly pulled into the role of a "listener" and at the same time a "comforter" for Jim. When she listens to his confession, the audience listens to Jim's story through her. Josie functions as do Larry and Edmund, for "the play's central dramatic action occurs in the growth we witness in Josie's understanding of Jim, herself, and the world." (12) The Night Clerk in *Hughie*, from the beginning, accepts the role of a fake "listener." He pretends to listen to Erie Smith, but his professional habit prevents him from listening and responding to the guests. He is a role player in a true sense. But also in this play, the audience listens to Erie's story along with the Night Clerk.

Those listeners in the list above are weak as stage characters because of their lack of strong "role playing," but sometimes they are deep philosophers like Larry. Though Edmund is a weak character, we find O'Neill's voice in him, the playwright's assertion of his art and philosophy. Even the Night Clerk has deep philosophical thoughts in his mind, though I am afraid they are conveyed only through the stage directions in the script. They are playing the passive roles of a "listener" but also the important roles of a "mission" of the author. O'Neill seems to have a tendency to give his role to one of the passive characters. In the most autobiographical play, *Long Day's Journey into*

Night, it is evident that Edmund is the author himself, however fictional the play may be. In *The Iceman Cometh*, Larry is the nearest character to the author. He is "another alter ego of the author" and "one of O'Neill-like characters." (13) In *A Moon for the Misbegotten*, Josie Hogan is the character who "represents the author's viewpoint." (14) Then what of the Cycle plays? Martha Bower describes Simon in *A Touch of the Poet* as "the withdrawn, artistic, anti-social sickly O'Neill figure." (15) In this play, Simon is only mentioned by the characters present on the stage and is totally absent himself. O'Neill, by putting Simon out of the play, has kept the play from becoming a too-philosophical piece. Three main characters alternately shift from listener to nonlistener, but there is no special character comparable to Larry and Edmund and Josie. In *More Stately Mansions*, Simon is an irresolute character. In act two, scene three, where the audible thinking becomes the main dialogue of the scene, Simon is left out of the game of the two female characters. He wants to get either Deborah's or Sara's love, but neither is possible. He is weak and passive, but still very important. Without him, there is no love-hate relationship, no tension between the characters. Just like Larry, he gets involved in other characters' schemes and affairs and finally has to choose between Deborah's artificial summerhouse or Sara's motherly care. In the published script, Simon at the end of the play is almost insane, just like his mother, but after spending a year in an asylum he will find happiness with Sara, in O'Neill's scheme. (16) These passive near-author characters have a power to live in the future. They still can face the reality by objectifying it with the eyes of an author. It is an author's job to observe things going on around him.

　　　　Thus in O'Neill's late plays, the audience sees a "theatre" in which "listener-observer" figures sometimes play the role of a "fool" and convey the author's view, while they listen to other characters who play the roles of "heroic" actors or actresses. This dramatic device makes the plays of O'Neill resemble a "metatheatre." They are metatheatrical in the description of characters and their relationship with the audience, but they also are written with the playwright's metatheatrical sense that life itself is a theatre.

NOTES

O'Neill's texts used in this paper are as follows:
　　　　Eugene O'Neill, *The Iceman Cometh* (London: Jonathan Cape, 1947).
　　　　------, *Long Day's Journey into Night* (New Haven: Yale

University Press, 1955).

------, *A Moon for the Misbegotten* (New York: Vintage Books, 1974).

------, *A Touch of the Poet* (New Haven: Yale University Press, 1957).

------, *More Stately Mansions* (New Haven: Yale University Press, 1964).

------, *Hughie* (New Haven: Yale University Press, 1959).
Title and page abbreviations in parentheses after each of the quotations are all references to the preceding.

1. Lionel Abel, *Metatheatre: A View of Dramatic Form* (Clinton: The Colonial Press, 1963).

2. Richard Hornby, *Drama, Metadrama, and Perception* (Lewisburg: Bucknell University Press, 1986).

3. Thomas P. Adler, *Mirror on the Stage: The Pulitzer Plays as an Approach to American Drama* (West Lafayette, Indiana: Purdue University Press, 1987), 142.

4. Hornby, 85.

5. C. W. E. Bigsby, *A Critical Introduction to Twentieth-Century American Drama*, vol. 1, 1900-1940 (Cambridge: Cambridge University Press, 1982), 119.

6. Michael Manheim, *Eugene O'Neill's New Language of Kinship* (Syracuse: Syracuse University Press, 1982), 162.

7. Travis Bogard, *Contour in Time: The Plays of Eugene O'Neill* (New York: Oxford University Press, 1972), xviii.

8. Judith E. Barlow, *Final Acts: The Creation of Three Late O'Neill Plays* (Athens: The University of Georgia Press, 1985), 92.

9. Katherine H. Burkman, *The Arrival of Godot: Ritual Patterns in Modern Drama* (London: Associated University Presses, 1986), 64.

10. Jean Chothia, *Forging a Language: A Study of the Plays of Eugene O'Neill* (Cambridge: Cambridge University Press, 1979), 138.

11. Barlow, 111.

12. Stephen A. Black, "Letting the Dead Be Dead: A Reinterpretation of *A Moon for the Misbegotten*," *Modern Drama*, 29 (December, 1986): 544.

13. Virginia Floyd, *The Plays of Eugene O'Neill: A New Assessment* (New York: Frederick Ungar Publishing Co., 1985), 500.

14. Black, 544.

15. Martha Bower, "The Making of Eugene O'Neill's Cycle Plays: An Analysis of O'Neill's Writing Process and Gender Role Reversal," diss., University of New Hampshire, 1985 (Ann Arbor, Michigan: UMI Dissertation Information Service, 1987), 36.

16. Bower, 168-171. The epilogue is completely omitted from the published script of *More Stately Mansions*.

14

Eugene O'Neill's *Dynamo* and the Expressionist Canon

William R. Elwood

Students of acting, in their attempts to act characters in an O'Neill play, have always confronted early the process of dealing with that dark center of emotion inherent in his characters and in the ideas represented in his works. (1) The dark centers appear to represent a reflection of reality, an inability to cope with life as the playwright saw it.

The German Expressionist movement was clearly reflecting a similar view of life, although some would contend that the base of reaction from expressionism was ultimately an exhortation for return to positive values. It is safe to say that expressionism is centered upon an internal dramatization of ideas, not always dark, although mostly that is the case. If darkness or lack of many comedies in his canon is an indication, O'Neill indeed qualifies for comparison.

O'Neill is not unlike many German expressionist playwrights of the first quarter of the twentieth century in his search for a spiritual or aesthetic center to life. Although the Germans had begun perhaps a little earlier, he, writing at roughly the same time, was engaging in the study of individuals in search of that center. *The Emperor Jones* (1920) and *The Hairy Ape* (1922) show clear influences and parallels to works like Hasenclever's *Die Menschen* (1918) and Kaiser's *Von Morgens bis Mitternachts* (1916) or Toller's *Masse Mensch* (1921) or Kokoschka's *Morder, Hoffnung der Frauen* (1907).

The critical perspective of this paper is to cite the influence of the constituents of German expressionism in an O'Neill play that shows the clearest line of that influence. No digressions will be made to talk about the obvious influences in *The Hairy Ape*, with such scenes as the one on Fifth Avenue in which the rich people wear masks, or the obvious internal quality of *Strange Interlude*, with its inner dialogue.

That is to say, there are many manifestations of expressionism in the works of O'Neill. It is in *Dynamo* (1929) that two important things occur: the greatest concentration of expressionist elements and the transformation by O'Neill of those elements into a unique American form.

German expressionism is dated roughly from 1907 to 1925, from that time frame before World War I into the period of the Weimar Republic and prior to World War II. It was a period in Germany's history when there was a glorification of a *Weltanschauung* encouraged by victory in the Franco-Prussian war and by its admission to the community of nations. Germany was already beginning its expansion around the world in a fashion similar to that of England. Had it not misfired in two consecutive wars, Germany would have built an empire as impressive as Britain's. Losses in 1918 notwithstanding, Germany, with the help of Bismarck, had established firmly a mind set that was deeply materialistic and, some would say, rigid to the point of ossification.

It was within such an ambience that the young men and women of the time were beginning to question the Wilhelminian system. Where the expressionist poets, painters, and playwrights were concerned, the questioning seemed to center around perspective rather than subject matter, although it is generally known that there were two orientations, the mystical and the social in playwrighting at the time. That is to say, what Bismarck and Wilhelm had wrought was intact and in order where an external perspective of human values was concerned. The German expressionists began a search for what they called the *ich* or the soul of the human condition. They felt that the proper approach to playwrighting was from the soul and not from the rational and externally oriented faculty of logic.

To them the *ich* brought society closer to the truth. They wrote plays seen from an internal view. For example, if an individual trapped in a hostile environment attempts to *express* how he feels, he might see the walls of the room as slanting menacingly toward him. Burdened with a prescribed life-style in which the individual was bound to honor a rigorous code of behavior, the expressionist playwright sought to break the bonds of such imprisonment and articulate more truthfully what his *Seele* was really all about. Kurt Pinthus, in an anthology of expressionist poetry appropriately entitled *Menschheitsdammerung*, refers to the movement as one of iconoclasm. (2) Another aesthetician, Hermann Bahr, is eloquent as he describes the time in which the movement flourished:

Never was a time so shattered by horror, by fear of death. Never was the world so silent as a grave. Never was man so small. Never was he so timid. Never was peace so distant and freedom so absent. There arose a single shriek of distress. Art cried art also. In the deepest darkness it shrieked for help, for the spirit: that is expressionism. [translation mine] (3)

The movement, of course, is parallel to the kind of work Freud and Jung were doing. That is to say, they were beginning to explore the internal worlds of patients who were suffering from nervous disorders. They were pioneering in the world of the psyche. Terms such as id, ego, superego, anima, collective unconsciousness, and archetype were used to classify what the expressionist playwright called the *ich*. "As Freud and Jung were cartographers of the subconscious, the expressionists were its expeditionary force." (4)

German expressionism may be defined as follows: "The attempt to create the essence rather than the appearance of reality through the use of non-related realistic symbols." (5) The style has eight distinct constituents, but only three that apply specifically to O'Neill's *Dynamo*. They are the *ich*, as mentioned above, *unio-mystica*, and *Einfuhlung*, or empathy as articulated by Wilhelm Worringer. (6)

The word *ich* is the first person singular pronoun in German, meaning I, but it has another meaning, the closest definition of which is "the soul." In fact, in the scholarship of the period there is a subcategory called *ich-Stucke*. The constituent means simply that the play is written from an internal perspective, as can be seen from the previous "slanting walls" example.

Unio-mystica is a term used frequently by the expressionist playwright and is defined literally: a mystical oneness. In the plays characters, individuals and even collectives were often found searching for a form of union with something outside self (or collective self). Stemming from an observable human need to identify and merge with something greater than self, the term is obviously organically related to the *ich*. That is, once the internal self is identified, there is often a need to merge that self with another.

Einfuhlung or empathy (unlike the psychological term) is the projection of human-felt qualities into an object or person outside oneself. The German verb form *sich etwas einfuhlen* shows what is intended. It means to feel something onto something else. An example is to project human qualities into a nonhuman form, as in "a brutal winter." Winter has no soul or mind and therefore cannot be brutal. It is our projection of the imapct of the cold that we call brutal. Clearly, Reuben in *Dynamo* is projecting a deific life-force into an electrical machine.

Even if one assesses the influence of German expressionism in terms of these three constituents, it is easy to see how it found some roots in the American theatre. One need only to look at the following works to see some influence: *Roger Bloomer* (1923) and *Processional* (1925) by John Howard Lawson; *The Adding Machine* (1922) and *The Subway* (1929) by Elmer Rice; *Machinal* (1925) by Sophie Treadwell; *Singing Jailbirds* (1924) by Upton Sinclair; *Beggar on Horseback* (1924) by Kaufman and Connelly; and *The Great God Brown* (1926), *Strange Interlude* (1928), *Dynamo* (1929), and *The Hairy Ape* (1922) by O'Neill.

Interestingly enough, psychological realism finally prevailed, if indeed it is not the case that it still predominates. In Germany, expressionism was followed by a style called *Die Neue Sachlichkeit,* which could be translated as neorealism. What one makes of such a parallel is that expressionsim, like its cousins surrealism, futurism, and the like, can be seen as raw data for inclusion into a larger, can we say stable, style. Perhaps the same could be said for the deconstructionist tendencies of the late twentieth century. In any case expressionism provided here and in Germany a strong and compelling need to reassess conventional modes of drama and production. Naturalism and realism could no longer reign supreme as the dominant mode of writing and production.

Dynamo is a prime example because of the greatest or most intensive influence of the German movement. The constituents are there in force, the *ich, unio-mystica,* and *Einfuhlung* practically informing the piece rather than being components of it. Indeed we see all the characters from their *ichs,* their souls or psyches. In addition, O'Neill shows us how Ada, Reuben, and Mrs. Fife attempt such a communion. Certainly the dynamo receives heavy dosages of projection from almost all the characters, with Reuben representing the most and his father showing the least.

Where the influence of expressionism leaves off, however, is in the way in which O'Neill has Americanized the problem and conflict in the play. Several elements make the piece American: (1) the relative newness of the families to the community; the way they are trying to carve out something in the community, either by preaching against progress or exalting it; (2) the materialistic orientation to the conflict; the way in which natural forces (lighting) are perceived of as divine or natural; (3) the deification of things man-made, the dynamo; and (4) the idea that the center for spiritual or aesthetic sustenance can be found *anywhere* but in ourselves. As Americans, we still think that the channel is found through the genius of what man has made, the machine. O'Neill would be surprised (or maybe he wouldn't) to see our country still infatuated with technology, even if we haven't deified computers (or have we?). No, it is an American play.

What is *Dynamo* about? What is the core of meaning of this play, and how specifically does German expressionism manifest itself in the work? The play is about the misguided search for meaning and definition of self. It begins on an argument about the existence of God and the nature of commitment through love, punctuated literally by bolts of lightning, and ends on a false resolution, a tragic and fatal misdefinition of self.

The Light family is a God-fearing family, highly suspicious of progress, represented by the Fife family, the father of which works at the electrical plant, home of the dynamo. The two children from the families are attracted to each other and are thwarted by both fathers' bigotry. Reuben Light loves Ada and has in mind nothing more than falling in love with her. He knows that his father is opposed to a union with Ada, but he pursues his goals, confident that his Christian upbringing will stand him in good stead. Ada, on the other hand, is concerned about false values such as machismo (she is disgusted because he seems cowardly) but is still attracted to him.

The two fathers get involved in vicious arguments and forget the welfare of their respective offspring. When Mr. Fife tricks Reverend Light about a phony story concerning his "past," the children suffer. Reverend Light, aided by his wife, who is jealous of Ada's attraction to her son, attempts physical punishment. Both parents, however, betray Reuben, who rejects their religion and value system and leaves them. He says at the conclusion of act one: "There is no God! No God but Electricity! I'll never be scared again! I'm through with the lot of you." Ada, seeing too late that she loves Reuben, resents the prank and rejects her father.

When Reuben returns after fifteen months, hardened and cynical, Ada tries unsuccessfully to win him back. He, however, has replaced one misguided religion with another. He now worships the God Electricity as he says to his father upon his return: "Don't be a fool! Your Satan is dead. We electrocuted him along with your God. Electricity is God now. And we've got to learn to know God, haven't we? Well, that's what I'm after! Did you ever watch dynamos? Come down to the plant and I'll convert you."

He cruelly takes advantage of Ada by having sex with her and rejecting the idea that the act is one of love: "What we did was just plain sex--an act of nature--and that's all there is to it!" In the third act of the play, he has become absolutely subsumed into the dynamo as Goddess, praying before it and confusing Ada's love for him with betrayal to the dynamo. He murders Ada and attempts a *unio-mystica* with the dynamo by grabbing the carbon brushes of the machine and electrocuting himself.

In *The Hairy Ape* there is another treatment of the idea of misplaced value systems. Yank feels that he has no meaning and, instead of searching for it internal to himself, attempts a *unio-mystica* with primal forces in the other. It is primal in one play and manmade energy in the other.

Certainly O'Neill did not write morality plays *per se*, but there is much to examine in the play as a manifestation of the fated American penchant for machine as savior.

The constituents of expressionism manifest themselves as follows: the *ich* is most obvious by O'Neill's use of inner dialogue. Throughout the play the internal and external selves are exposed for the audience to see. Indeed, Reuben's final "conversion" (I say, perversion), is manifested through inner dialogue, the manifestation of the *ich par excellence*:

(He springs to his feet, and shielding his face with one hand from the sight of her, runs down the stairs to the lower oil switch gallery. He stops there, looking around him distractedly as if he didn't know where to hide, his thoughts hounded by remorse.) Mother! . . . have mercy on me! . . . I hate her now! . . . as much as you hate her! . . . give me one more chance! . . . What can I do to get you to forgive me! . . . and I can come to you? (A terrible look of murder comes on his face. He starts for the stairs, his hands outstretched as if he were already strangling her--then stops.) No . . . not with my hands. . . . Never touch her flesh again . . . how? . . . I see. . . . Switchboard room . . . in the desk.

The constituent *unio-mystica* operates on two levels in the play: the level on which Reuben and Ada feel for each other in the beginning of the play and, more importantly, the "conversion" of Reuben to the dynamo. Throughout the second and third acts it is clear that Reuben has become attracted more and more to the force of electricity as the answer to his problems and prayers. In act three, scene one, Reuben is kneeling before the dynamo, his arms outstretched in supplication. He says, "Mother! Don't you hear me? Can't you give me some sign? O Dynamo, who gives life to things, hear my prayer. Grant me the miracle of your love!" The stage directions read: "(He waits, his body strained with suspense, listening as if he expected the dynamo to answer him.)"

It is important to remember that *unio-mystica*, by definition, is that need to identify and bond with another human being or group of human beings; it is not a perversion. O'Neill says that it can be perverted, and in this case it is.

Finally, empathy is most obvious by the way Reuben projects life into a machine that generates electricity. This constituent is related closely to the *ich* and *unio-mystica*, but it functions differently. It is not necessary for the other two to be present in clear form for us (as audience members) to invest an object with a life force. In a Walt Disney movie, trees become people, to use an elementary example. What is occurring in this play, though, is an organic progression from *ich* (nurtured by desire for *unio-mystica*) to investiture of meaning outside oneself (as the characters in the play all lack a substantive value system). Mrs. Light is only afraid she will lose her son, while the Reverend is caught up in a rigid interpretation of the divinity. Mr. Fife is resentful that he doesn't have an engineering degree; Mrs. Fife is dotty; and Ada is shallow. Reuben, though possessed of the potential for depth, projects meaning into a likely candidate, a powerful machine whose use is inherently good for progress, for civilization.

It would be easy for us to see this play as quaint or historically interesting. However, *Dynamo* is perhaps more intriguing now, thirty-five years after O'Neill's death, than when it was written. What is relevant today in the play is the curious and frightening way in which our culture still looks for meaning in the wrong places. People still believe that the real source of strength and definition of self can be found in manmade "things." O'Neill's message in this and many other of his plays is simple: Things can destroy us and not give us what we think we will receive. The proper balance between "thing" and self has always been our greatest worry.

NOTES

1. When I was working on my master's degree in acting at the State University of Iowa, we used to talk a lot about those dark pools of emotion which seem so everpresent in the works of O'Neill. This was two or three years before I began a serious study of German expressionism, and certainly there is more to that movement than something (though useful) so imprecise as a dark pool of emotion. Still, it is not an inaccurate framework with which to begin a study of either O'Neill or German expressionsim.

2. Kurt Pinthus, *Menschheitsdammerung* (Hamburg: Rowohlt Verlag, 1964).

3. Hermann Bahr, *Expressionismus* (Munchen: Delphin Verlag, 1919), 111.

4. William Elwood, "Reinhard Goering's *Seeschlacht* and the Expressionist Vision," *To Hold a Mirror to Nature. Comparative Drama Conference Papers* 1 (1982): 40.

5. William Elwood, "Early Manifestations of German

Expressionism in New York Productions of American Drama," diss., University of Oregon, 1966.

6. Wilhelm Worringer, *Abstraction and Empathy*, trans. Michael Bullock (New York: International Universities Press, 1953).

15

The Black World of Eugene O'Neill

Thomas D. Pawley

Eugene O'Neill's black world is centered in two geographical areas, the Caribbean archipelago and the United States. It is a racially segregated world. Two one-acts, *Thirst* and *The Moon of the Caribbees*, together with *The Emperor Jones* are set in the Caribbean, while the one-act *The Dreamy Kid, All God's Chillun Got Wings*, and *The Iceman Cometh* are placed in the black enclaves of Manhattan and the Lower East Side of New York City. This paper will examine the Caribbean world.

The black characters in these plays are Afro-Caribbean and Afro-American, a distinction that is important because, although they have a common ethnic background, the racial experience of the two groups was not identical. Neither are all of the so-called black characters full-blooded Africans, a facet which O'Neill makes clear by designating their pigmentation in the stage directions. Both groups contain at least one mulatto character. This in itself may be a subtle commentary by the playwright, as, in the segregated world of this period miscegenation was taboo. There was in fact a monumental barrier between the two races in the first half of the twentieth century. In the Caribbean this barrier was not so manifest as in the United States, where it was omnipresent, continuously producing racial conflict and animosity.

O'Neill's utilization of black characters was by conscious design. One student of his work, Van Wyck Brooks, states, "The Negro was to reappear in *The Emperor Jones* and other plays,--for O'Neill was deeply concerned with the fate of this race." (1) Correspondence recently discovered by historian Dr. Samuel Hay in the Moorland-Spingarn Collection of Howard University reveals that O'Neill was supportive of the efforts of W. E. DuBois and Alain Locke to develop a

Negro drama. (2) While he was certainly sympathetic to the cause of Afro-Americans, O'Neill projects the stark reality of the worlds in which they lived, and it is not a pretty picture.

Thirst, written circa 1913, one of the "lost" plays, was first produced by the Provincetown Playhouse in 1916, with O'Neill himself playing the role of the mulatto sailor. It is a gruesome one-act melodrama about three nameless castaways, a gentleman, a dancer, and a West Indian mulatto sailor, drifting aimlessly on a raft and desperately in need of water. The raft is constantly being encircled by sharks. The Dancer goes mad and dies. Now the impassive Sailor suggests to the Gentleman that the two of them can survive. Horrified by this suggestion of cannibalism, the Gentleman throws the Dancer's body overboard where it is immediately devoured by the omnipresent sharks. A struggle ensues between the two men. Both fall into the sea, ending the play.

The Sailor, unlike the black characters in *The Moon of the Caribbees* and *The Emperor Jones* is apparently an educated man. His speech is not pidgin English or dialectal, as the Gentleman observes early in the play, saying, "he speaks good English. It cannot be that he does not understand us." (3)

His taciturn nature masks a perceptive mind. He has determined that the one possibility for his survival is for either the Dancer or the Gentleman to die; the only question is which one. This means that he has been contemplating murder, a prospect that is eliminated by the sudden death of the Dancer. But this in turn creates another impasse since cannibalism is abhorrent to the Gentleman.

Caribbean blacks are thus made to appear less civilized or more apt to revert to uncivilized behavior than whites. In moments of crisis the veneer of civilization disappears. O'Neill exploits this atavistic impulse again in *The Emperor Jones* in the ultimate scene when Brutus Jones grovels before an imaginary witch doctor.

Another recurrent theme regarding Caribbean blacks is their belief in charms of various sorts, one of which is music. Throughout the play the Sailor hums a mournful dirge. Finally in exasperation the Dancer asks him for an explanation:

DANCER.   Sailor! Will you tell me what it means--that song you are singing?
SAILOR.   (*Pointing to the shark fins*) I am singing to them. It is a charm. I have been told it is very strong. If I sing long enough they will not eat us. (*LP* 7)

Charms are sometimes objects, frequently jewelry or trinkets, for which blacks have a predisposition according to the Gentleman, who tells the

Dancer, "You might buy it (water) from him with that necklace of yours. I have heard his people are very fond of such things." (*LP* 22) However, when the Sailor spurns the offer, the Gentleman shouts, "The pig! The pig! The black dog!" (*LP* 25) excommunicating him from the human species.

The attitude of white males toward black men even under the extraordinary circumstances that the survivors face hints at a continuing confrontation between the two groups, particularly as it relates to white women. The first evidence of this attitude comes early in the play after the Dancer scolds the Gentleman and he reluctantly says, "Well, I will say no more then. You may talk to him if you wish. (He points to the Sailor with a sneer.)" (*LP* 5) But later, after apparently accepting him as an equal and calling him "our companion in misfortune," (*LP* 9) under the increasing stress of thirst, he refers to him in a derogatory manner and asks, "How do you account for your being on the raft alone with this nigger?" (*LP* 16) This introduces the perennial plaint of political demagogues of that era in the United States, that white women must be protected from black men. It is implicit in the Gentleman's thinking in the following: "You said someone kissed you. . . . Surely I did not, and it could hardly have been that sailor." (*LP* 16) The theme of interracial social relationships explodes in *All God's Chillun Got Wings*, becoming the centerpiece of the drama. However, early in his career O'Neill indicates he is conscious of its dramatic potential.

Near the end of the play the Dancer, obsessed with the belief that the sailor is hoarding water, tries desperately to seduce him, believing that in this way he will share it with her. She succeeds momentarily in shaking his resolve. (This scene is undoubtedly one reason why O'Neill played the part himself rather than running the risk involved in the casting of a black actor.) However, the Sailor controls his desires and rejects the Dancer's advances, causing a hysterical response from the woman: "Have I humbled myself before this black animal only to be spurned like a wench in the streets? It is too much! You lie, you dirty slave! You have water. . . . "(*LP* 28) Under emotional pressure and approaching madness, all of her sophisticated behavior has disappeared. At this point both white characters have revealed their subconscious if not their real attitudes toward blacks. Their surface civility is thus shown to be only a mask.

Melodramatic action as we have suggested is at the core of *Thirst*. In *The Moon of the Caribbees* the plot (what little there is) is insignificant. It is the characters, and more important, the mood of boredom that suffuses the play that occupy the playwright's attention.

According to Frederick Carpenter, "O'Neill considered [it] the best of his one-act plays . . . because it broke with the tradition of the commercial theatre by dispensing with formal action in order to develop more effectively mood, emotion, and character." (4)

Like *Thirst*, this one-act is a play of the sea. The principal characters are all seamen, a cross-section of European ethnic types whose lonely existence is momentarily broken by a drunken escapade and sexual encounter with a group of women described as "West Indian Negresses" and "distinct Negro types," perhaps to emphasize the intensity of the desires of the sex-starved sailors.

As in *Thirst*, music is utilized to accentuate the mood. The stage directions read: "A melancholy Negro chant, faint and far off, drifts crooning over the water." (5) Similarly the reaction to it is not unlike that to the humming of the sailor in the earlier play:

DRISCOLL.   Will ye listen to them naygurs? I wonder now, do they
              call that keenin' a song?
SMITTY.   It doesn't make a chap feel very cheerful, does
              it? (*He sighs.*) (*PO* 456)

The chanting on the shore is used to punctuate the dramatic action, reinforcing the mood and occasionally motivating the dialogue as in the following:

SMITTY.   (*listening to it [the music] for a moment*) Damn
              that song of theirs. (*He takes another big drink*)
              What do you say, Donk?
DONKEYMAN.   (*quietly*) Seems nice and sleep-like,
              Smitty. (*with a hard laugh*) Sleepy! If I
              listened to it long--sober--I'd never go to sleep.
DONKEYMAN.   'Tain't sich bad music, is it? Sounds kinder
              pretty to me--low an mournful--same as
              listening to the organ outside a church of a
              Sunday.
SMITTY.   I didn't mean it was bad music. It isn't. It's
              the beastly memories the damn thing brings
              up. (*PO* 466-67)

The singing also serves as the motivation for introducing two major ideas, which are also present in *Thirst*, that Caribbean blacks are little more than animals and that they are predisposed toward cannibalism, as the following dialogue suggests:

BIG FRANK.   They bury somebody--py chimminy Christmas, I tink
              so, from way it sound.
YANK.   What d'yuh mean, bury? They don't plant 'em down
              here, Dutchy. They eat 'em to save fun'ral expenses. I

	guess this guy went down the wrong way an' they got indigestion.
COCKY.	Indigestion! Ho yus, not' arf! Down't yer know as 'em blacks 'as two stomachs like a bleedin' camel? (*PO* 456)

It is hard to believe that the men are serious, but even to joke in these terms is indicative of their attitudes toward the local natives. It becomes clear in subsequent dialogue that Cocky's statement is an erroneous generalization about the Caribbean people, when in fact the basis for his generalization was an experience he had had in New Guinea. This causes Yank to retort: "Don't you know this is the West Indies, yuh crazy nut? There ain't no cannibals here. They're only common niggers." (*PO* 457) This is a less demeaning view than that in *Thirst* because apparently Yank was only joking when he first made the suggestion. Nevertheless, the statement probably resulted from a commonly held perception among the sailors, because it crops up again when Driscoll drunkenly addresses Bella during the dance scene as "me cannibal quane."

That the sailors do not generally hold black females in high regard is patently apparent. But this attitude is not so ingrained that it constitutes a barrier to social relationships with them. In fact their coming is eagerly awaited. When Driscoll reports their arrival the announcement "is received with great enthusiasm by all hands." The only negative response comes from Cocky after he glimpses the leader, Bella, whom he calls "Mrs. Old Black Joe;" he says:

I 'opes all the gels ain't as blooming ugly as 'er. Looked like a bloody organ-grinder's monkey, she did. (*PO* 461)

Although his squeamishness is ridiculed by Paddy, Cocky's complaint is not without justification, for Driscoll subsequently reports that the more desirable females among the group, "two swate little slips av things, near as white as you an' me" (*PO* 463), will remain with the officers.

The entire action of the play is built around the anticipation over the coming of the women, their arrival with its riotous consequences, and the aftermath to their departure. Clearly they are prostitutes bent upon exploiting the sailors through whiskey and sex and not to be revered and admired as models of decorum. Although he personally is not averse to associating with them, Cocky expresses disdain for the Captain's taking the same course of action, saying: "An' 'ere e' is making up to a bleedin' nigger! There's a captain for yer!" (*PO* 463)

For the seamen the women represent an infrequent opportunity that they know they must pay for, as Bella informs them in no uncertain terms when asked:

DRISCOLL.   Listen, Bella, I've something to ask ye for my little
             friend here who's bashful. Ut has to do wid the ladies
             so I'd best be whisperin' ut to ye myself to kape them
             from blushin'. (*He leans over and asks her a question.*)
BELLA.   (*firmly*) Four shillin's.
DRISCOLL.   (*laughing*) D'you hear that, all av ye? Four shillin's ut is.
             (*PO* 464-65)

And what is the women's attitude toward the sailors? They
have absolutely no inhibitions about proffering themselves. In fact one
of them, Pearl, aggressively pursues Smitty in much the same manner as
the Dancer in *Thirst* attempted to seduce the Sailor, now a black woman
attempting to seduce a white sailor. Smitty's rejection of her sexual
overtures prompts an outburst from Pearl, which is not unlike that of the
Dancer when she shouts, "You swine! You can go to hell!" causing the
Donkeyman to respond, "There's love for you. They're all the same--
white brown, yellow 'n black." (*PO* 470)

His comment may well sum up O'Neill's attitude toward the
female of the species. The Afro-Caribbean women in this play, like the
women in other O'Neill plays who frequent the bars and waterfront
dives, cater to the libido of sex-starved seamen. Ethnic differences are
of no consequence.

It is in *The Emperor Jones*, in which an Afro-American is placed
in a Caribbean setting, that the clash of the two cultures is best
illustrated. The Caribbean has remained closer to the African tradition
with its pantheon of Gods and myths and the physical proximity of the
jungle. Thrust into this world, O'Neill postulates that the Afro-
American will relive certain aspects of his racial heritage.

Brutus Jones, self proclaimed Emperor of a Caribbean island and
escapee from a prison in the United States, is suddenly confronted with
the fact that the natives whom he has been exploiting have finally
rebelled. He immediately proceeds to execute a previously conceived
plan of escape. Unfortunately for him he becomes lost in the jungle,
overwhelmed with fear and beseiged by visions of past events, real and
imaginary. Finally, exhausted and having used up his ammunition and
a self-protecting "magic" bullet, he is killed by his erstwhile subjects
near the spot where he entered the jungle the previous evening.
Although the physical setting is the Emperor's palace and the
surrounding jungle, most of the action takes place in Jones' mind. The
technique is expressionistic.

For an Afro-American, the Emperor's given name, Brutus, is
probably symbolic, perhaps even a play on words. It is certainly

reminiscent of the practice of nineteenth century American playwrights who gave black characters Roman names such as Caesar and Cato as comic devices, thus making them appear outlandish.

The throne room of the palace with its brilliant scarlet throne and orange cushions, a garish combination, introduces another facet of certain of O'Neill's black characters, a penchant for bright colors. This characteristic dominates the initial description of Jones: "He wears a light blue uniform coat sprayed with brass buttons, heavy gold chevrons . . . gold braid on the collar, cuffs etc. His pants are bright red with a light blue stripe. Patent leather boots with brass spurs and a belt with a long barreled pearl handled revolver complete his make up." (6) Even the dinner bell placed near the throne and used to summon his subjects is painted a bright scarlet. In the same scene Jones "pulls out an expensive Panama hat with a bright multicolored band and sets it jauntily on his head." O'Neill first used this device in *The Dreamy Kid* when Irene appears wearing a brightly colored dress.

The physical description of Jones recalls that of the women in *The Moon of the Caribbees*, "He is a tall, powerfully built, full blooded negro of middle age. His features are typically negroid." (*NP* 5) Jones is not a mulatto like the Sailor in *Thirst*. He is full-blooded African. As a mulatto he might have been less likely to respond to primitive, atavistic drives. In each of these plays O'Neill has taken pains to describe the physical characteristics of his black characters. They fall into two groups: light-skinned mulattoes (*Thirst* and *Moon*) and Negro types (*Moon* and *Emperor*).

Jones' speech is the same self-deprecatory urban Negro dialect that O'Neill uses in *The Dreamy Kid*. Unlike the Sailor's, his speech is characterized by omissions, substitutions, additions, and distortions of standard English phonemes and the repeated use of the word "nigger" for "Negro." This was one of the reasons that Afro-American critics rejected the play. Jones is much more articulate than the other Caribbean characters even if his language is less refined. On the other hand the speech of the Native Chief, Lem, is pidgin English, reminiscent of the language of African slaves, for whom English was a second language. The confrontation between whites and blacks which was subtly presented in *Thirst* reappears here in the opening scene in the verbal duels between Smithers, the Cockney trader, and Jones. Smithers expresses much the same disdain for blacks as the white characters in the previous plays as well as some of the conventional attitudes of American whites that O'Neill presents in *All God' Chillun Got Wings*:

SMITHERS.   Serve 'im right! Puttin on airs, the stinkin' nigger; 'Is Majesty! (*NP* 5)

His resentment of Jones stems from the Emperor's arrogance, "mighty airs," and lack of humility, an attitude shared by many American whites in the southern United States toward educated and well-to-do blacks, forcing them to live unpretentiously for fear of recrimination by the white community.

While the antagonism here is between an Englishman and an expatriate Afro-American, the racial attitudes of Jones have their genesis in the black experience in the United States. From the beginning he is contemptuous of Smithers. The model for his behavior is the "white quality" whom he has served on Pullman cars. They would undoubtedly regard Smithers as "trash," a derogatory term used by southern aristocrats for poor whites. Therefore, the play is in one sense a commentary on white middle-class attitudes as well as on white American standards of success. Smithers reenforces this assumption by attributing Jones' ability to convince the natives to believe in his magic bullet to "Yankee bluff." (NP 8)

At the height of his flight through the jungle Jones also sounds a note of antagonism heard in black protest plays of the 1960s in the United States, that the white man is a devil. He says, "I kills you you white debil, if it's de last thing I evah does! Ghost or debil, I kill you again." (NP 25)

Thus O'Neill has capsulized in these two characters some aspects of the racial conflict that was rampant in the United States and to a lesser degree in the Caribbean.

Much of Jones antagonism toward whites is directly traceable to events in the Afro-American experience to which O'Neill alludes. Early in the first scene Smithers' projects the spector of lynching:

SMITHERS.   And from what I've 'eard, it ain't 'ealthy for a black to kill a white man in the States. They burns 'em in oil, don't they?
JONES.   (*with cool deadliness*) You mean lynchin'd scare me? (NP 11)

Another source of Jones' antagonism is the brutal penal system in the southern United States. Scene four dramatizes this phenomenon. Convicts shackled with leg irons and under the watchful eye of armed guards were placed into "chain" gangs and forced to do backbreaking labor on roads and highways. The brutality of prison guards was legendary, and the hatred and fear they engendered was very, very real. Finally there was the "peculiar institution," slavery, shared by both Caribbean and American blacks. The bitterness created by the auctioning of men, women, and children and the agony of the despicable "middle passage," both of which are vividly portrayed in scenes five and six, left a legacy of hatred, fear, distrust, and envy among the descendants of the slaves. All of these are very much a part of Jones' nature and influence his behavior and attitudes.

In *Thirst* the Afro-Caribbean's penchant for charms was alluded to. In this play, belief in charms, ghosts, and the supernatural characterize the black characters. Born and raised in the United States, Jones exploits the natives' belief in magic as a means of self-protection. He convinces them that only a magic silver bullet that he alone possesses can effect his demise. So convinced are the natives of its power that they spend an entire evening molding a magic bullet with which to execute him. Their attitude is expressed by Lem, described as "a heavy-set, ape faced old savage of the extreme African type, dressed only in a loin cloth:"

LEM.   My men's dey got um silver bullets. Lead bullet no kill him. He got um strong charm.   I cookum money, make um silver bullet, make um strong charm too. (*NP* 34)

Jones also exhibits the same predisposition in referring to the silver bullet when he says, "I ain't lowin nary body to touch this baby. She's my rabbits foot." To which Smithers responds, "A bloomin charm wot?" (*NP* 10)   Jones' belief in and fear of the supernatural ("ha'nt" is the word he uses) is emphasized when he "sees" the apparition of Jeff, the Pullman porter whom he has killed. This mythical fear of apparitions was exploited in the American movies of the 1920s, 1930s and 1940s in scenes in which comic black actors would tremble violently at the mere mention of ghosts. One of these, Mantan Moreland, was noted for "rolling and bucking" his eyes. O'Neill has Jones do the same thing when he sees the apparition of Jeff: "Jones' eyes begin to roll wildly. He stutters." (*NP* 22) Thus one aspect of a comic stereotype is utilized in a serious character portrayal. It should be noted, however, that O'Neill makes his black protagonist recognize the contradiction and has him attempt to rationalize his behavior:

JONES.   H'ant! You fool nigger, dey aint no such things: Don't be Baptist parson tell you dat many times? Is you civilized, or is you like dese ign'rent black niggers heah?" (*NP* 24)

Thus conflicting impulses, the civilized and the primitive, are placed within the same individual.

Two other facets of the stereotyped portrayal of blacks in nineteenth-century American plays appear in this "new treatment" of the Afro-American: crap shooting and razor toting. A fixture of minstrelsy in the nineteenth and twentieth centuries, they occasionally carried over into serious drama, as in this instance. We learn in scene two that it is an "argument wid razors ovah a crap game" that sent Jones to prison. Later Jones imagines that he hears "an odd clickety sound ... like some nigger shootin' crap." (*NP* 11) The stereotype also included watermelon eating and chicken stealing, which the playwright eschews. Although O'Neill has treated these remnants of the nineteenth century seriously rather than comically, their presence was another reason for the negative reaction of many Afro-Americans to the production of the play during the 1920s and 1930s. These traits were linked to minstrelsy, in which both white and black performers in blackface grotesquely burlesqued the behavior of American blacks.

Finally, we must address directly the question of Jones' character. Is he a murderer? A primitive voodoo cultist? A carbon copy of an opportunistic white American businessman? All of these have been suggested as the basis of his character. Edwin Engel says, "Had Dreamy [reached] middle age he might have passed for Brutus Jones. . . . he would have had to remain unregenerate . . . in order to become more cynical, crafty, and unscrupulous." (7) Frederick Carpenter suggests, "*The Emperor Jones* is unique among O'Neill's plays also for its lack of any autobiographical background. It was created *de novo* from a mixture of folktale and imagination." (8) The scholar Walter Daniel offers still another explanation: "Brutus Jones ... O'Neill said [once] was patterned after Adam Scott, a Negro deacon on Sunday and a bartender during the week, whom he had known ... as a newspaper reporter in New London, Connecticut. The plot reflects some historical outlines of the story of Henri Christophe, the Negro slave, who made himself king of a section of Haiti in 1811 and ruled despotically until ... fearing for his life, shot himself in the head before he could be killed by his subjects." (9)

That Jones has killed two men is clear. But these homicides were unpremeditated, impetuous, emotional acts performed in the heat of anger. They were primitive responses to a perceived danger. The instruments of death were a razor (a stereotypical act) and a shovel, hardly the tools of premeditated murder. This is in keeping with O'Neill's acceptance of the belief during this period in the primitive nature of the Afro-American and of atavism as a controlling influence in the behavior of people. Edwin Engel postulates, "What made *The Emperor Jones* good theatre ... are [sic] its exploitation of the general preconception of the essentially primitive nature of the Negro. ... The madness of the fear-obsessed Jones demonstrates that man is the sum not only of his own past experience but also those of his race, a notion that is based upon the assumption of a psychical as well as a physical continuity between ancestor and descendent." (10) Jones then does what any primitive man would do. He strikes out wildly at a perceived danger. But this is not murder. Had he wished to, it would have been very easy in his all-powerful position as Emperor to eliminate those who opposed him. Instead he choose to "abdicate."

Jones is also a religious person, nominally a Christian. His beliefs are the product both of fundamental Protestant Christianity and paganism, vestiges of which continue to exist within him both consciously (ghosts) and subconsciously (the witch doctor). But his faith is tempered by opportunism modeled after the white businessmen he has observed so astutely. As he himself exclaims:

Doesn't you know dey's got to do wid a man was a member in good standin' 'o de Baptist Church? Sho' I was dat when I was a porter on de Pullman's befo' I gits into my little trouble. Let dem try deir heathen tricks. De Baptist Church done pertect me and land dem all in hell. . . . [But] It don't git me nothin to do missionary work for de Baptist Church. I'se after de coin, an I lays my Jesus on de shelf for de time bein. (*NP* 15)

Like the Dreamy Kid, the Emperor is not a dedicated Christian.

In summary, Jones is revealed as a ruthless but intelligent primitive. He has aped the behavior of those he served. But the culture he has acquired is only a veneer, as he has had little if any formal education, which is insufficient to harness his primitive impulses. Neither is he a man of great religious faith--his Christianity is only surface deep--except when he is terrified. The supernatural is very much a part of his subconscious, a heritage from the African past. His character has been shaped by his own experience and that of his race, the middle passage, slavery, the penal system, and, above all, American standards of success. Faced with an extreme emotional crisis, he is no longer able to cope with reality and becomes a panic stricken animal floundering in the jungle. This is the story that O'Neill tells so vividly.

Elemental forces of nature--the sea, sharks, the jungle--are a pervasive force in this Caribbean world and often pitted against man. Those who challenge these forces are destroyed by them. Those who do not are overwhelmed with ennui and sustain themselves through the universal and time-worn palliatives of drunkenness and sex. This is the image that evolves in these plays of the Caribbean, a world in which the black man is a central figure.

NOTES

1. Van Wyck Brooks, *The Confident Years, 1885-1915* (New York: E. P. Dutton and Co., 1952), 540.

2. Samuel Hay, "African American Theatre, a Critical History," unpublished manuscript.

3. Eugene O'Neill, *Thirst*, in *Ten "Lost" Plays* (New York: Random House, 1964), 9. (Subsequently cited as *LP* with page number.)

4. Frederick I. Carpenter, *Eugene O'Neill* (Boston: Twayne Publishing Co., 1964), 84.

5. Eugene O'Neill, *The Moon of the Caribbees*, in *The Plays of Eugene O'Neill* (New York: Random House, 1934), 455. (Subsequently cited as *PO* with page number.)

6. Eugene O'Neill, *The Emperor Jones*, in *Nine Plays by Eugene O'Neill* (New York: Modern Library, 1941), 5-6. (Subsequently cited as *NP* with page number.)

7. Edwin Engel, *The Haunted Heroes of Eugene O'Neill* (Cambridge, Mass.: Harvard University Press, 1953), 48.

8. Carpenter, 90.

9. Walter Daniel, *"De Lawd" Richard Berry Harrison and Green Pastures* (Westport, Conn.: Greenwood Press, 1986), 11-12.

10. Engel, 52-53.

16

Building Characters: Eugene O'Neill's Composition Process

Judith E. Barlow

George Pierce Baker, Eugene O'Neill's playwriting teacher at Harvard, once wrote: "The permanent value of a play . . . rests on its characterization." (1) O'Neill disagreed with many of his teacher's precepts, but he seems to have been in accord with this one. In large measure the greatness of O'Neill's drama arises from the emotional power that is rooted in his characters, characters who (at least in the case of the men) are wonderfully complex, richly ambiguous, and capable of evoking from audiences both sympathy and empathy.

Baker further observes in his book *Dramatic Technique* that dramatists should not rely on lengthy character descriptions and stage directions, either in play programs or in reading texts. Here, clearly, teacher and pupil part company. It is not just lack of sufficient trust in director or reader that leads O'Neill to provide extensive character descriptions at the beginnings of his plays, to reveal to us such particular information as the odor given off by Simeon and Peter in *Desire under the Elms* (they smell of earth), the color and fabric of Erie's socks in *Hughie* (white silk), the size of Sara Melody's feet in *A Touch of the Poet* (large), or the timbre of James Tyrone's voice in *Long Day's Journey into Night* (resonant). O'Neill conceives his characters so fully, knows them so well, that to him no detail is trivial; he wants us to see, hear, and even smell them as completely as their creator does.

In fact, O'Neill's character descriptions are usually far more copious in the early stages of writing; the descriptions that ultimately appear in the printed text are only what remain after he has carefully honed and pruned. Before they emerge in final form, O'Neill's plays progress through a number of incarnations--a scenario (full outline), one or more holograph manuscripts, and one or more typescripts--that often feature remarkably detailed character notes. For example, the scenario for *Mourning Becomes Electra* begins with a dozen pages of character description in O'Neill's minuscule handwriting. The entire opening section of the scenario of *A Moon for the Misbegotten* consists of similar portrayals; in that instance he did not even bother to sketch in the plot of act one. From the very first stages of composition, O'Neill felt that getting a grasp on a play meant getting a grasp on the characters who would inhabit it.

A brief look at O'Neill's creation of two of his most famous characters, Theodore Hickman (Hickey) and Larry Slade, protagonist and antagonist respectively in *The Iceman Cometh*, is revealing. In this barroom drama, O'Neill shows what happens when the fragile peace in Harry Hope's saloon, a peace balanced on dreams and drink, is temporarily shattered by the arrival of Hickey and his newfound gospel of honesty. The care O'Neill put into the exact shaping of Hickey and Larry is testimony to the meticulousness with which he created his plays, and his method of developing them suggests his general method of character building, particularly in his last creative years. (2)

O'Neill based many of his characters on friends and family members, and Larry Slade is no exception. The inspiration for Larry was O'Neill's mentor and drinking companion Terry Carlin. More than thirty years O'Neill's senior, Carlin was an anarchist, humanist, and philosopher (and alcoholic). The basis was so substantial that O'Neill used the name "Terry" in an early character list and in the scenario. The name "Terry" once even crept into the manuscript.

The origins of Hickey are more elusive. Critics have identified everyone from a newspaper executive who shot his sleeping wife to a collector for a laundry chain as models for the salesman. (3) Perhaps to confuse future scholars, O'Neill even contradicted himself: he once suggested to a friend that the basis for Hickey was "a periodical drunk salesman" (4) he knew, yet a little while later told another friend "No. I never knew [Hickey]. He's the most imaginary character in the play." (5) Arthur and Barbara Gelb are probably close to the truth when they cite O'Neill's older brother, Jamie, as an inspiration. (6) Not only is there a good deal of his style in Hickey's exaggerated bonhomie, but Jamie was actually a traveling salesman for a brief period and also spent two summers acting in a comedy entitled *The Traveling Salesman.* He played one of the title figure's colleagues.

Unquestionably another model for the characters is the playwright himself: there is a strong autobiographical strain in both members of this pair. In an article in the *New York Times*, O'Neill biographer Louis Sheaffer argues for the link between Hickey and the playwright, particularly in Hickey's attitude toward Evelyn. The combination of dependence and desire for freedom, of love, hatred, and guilt, which Hickey feels for his wife--a volatile mixture that finally explodes into murder--Sheaffer traces to O'Neill's ambivalence toward his mother. (7) It must be added that this ominous ambivalence also marked O'Neill's relationship with Carlotta Monterey, to whom the playwright had been married for a decade when he began *Iceman*. Although not as tragic in outcome as the Hickey-Evelyn union, O'Neill's third marriage was marked by emotional and even occasionally physical violence (in this case on both sides). Perhaps of all O'Neill's plays *Iceman* shows the darkest side of his view of women, his fear and hatred of those who are too caring and protective (Evelyn) and of those who are not caring and protective enough (Rosa). Much of this dark side is expressed through Hickey.

On the other hand, as numerous critics have pointed out, there are many similarities between O'Neill and Larry Slade. Larry's confession about being afraid to live but more afraid to die was, the playwright told a friend, one of his "favorite" speeches. After listening to a recording of himself reading the passage, O'Neill declared, "It wasn't Larry, it was my ghost talking to me, or I to my ghost." (8) Neither the short, rotund Hickey nor the aging, lice-infested Larry resembles the "classic" O'Neill autobiographical figure, the brooding, sensitive young man with dark eyes and hair; but there is a good deal of O'Neill in both these characters. Interestingly, Hickey "is about *fifty*"; O'Neill was fifty when he began work on *Iceman*. (9)

But if the origins of these characters lie in literature, biography, and autobiography, O'Neill's process of composition involved shaping this raw material into fictional form: he was writing dramatic literature rather than personal history. Just as the name of the play's antagonist changed from "Terry" to "Larry," so extraneous biographical traits were erased in the interest of dramatic goals. What began in life was transmuted into art; O'Neill's allegiance was to the play at hand, not to his sources.

A second movement of equal importance was the growing complexity of the characters as O'Neill's development of the play progressed, a movement perhaps most evident in the case of Hickey. Hickey as O'Neill first created him was a man who had murdered his wife and then come to the saloon not to help his friends nor seek their vindication for his deed but simply to tell them his story. Here is Hickey's announcement of his wife's death in the published text: "You see, I don't feel any grief. . . . I've got to feel glad, for her sake. Because she's at peace. She's rid of me at last." (p. 151) The tragedy of Hickey, like that of all O'Neill's mismatched married characters from the Mayos in *Beyond the Horizon* to the Tyrones in *Long Day's Journey into*

Night, is that he both hated and loved Evelyn. He acknowledges that love but cannot admit, to himself or anyone else, the anger and resentment that accompany it. The Hickey of the scenario, however, is not trapped in this tragic paradox; he is just a man who got rid of an unwanted spouse. Compare the speech above with the scenario version of the same announcement: "Her death was good riddance--I mean for her, to be rid of me--I feel no grief--I mean, for her sake--it was inevitable-- she was much too good for this world--too good for me--and now she's dead, thank God--I mean, thank God for her sake." (II, p. 7) Hickey's antipathy to Evelyn is so blatant in the scenario it is scarcely credible that he himself is not aware of it, and his expressions of concern for her ring hollow. The scenario leaves us puzzled rather than troubled: we wonder why Hickey killed his wife yesterday instead of simply leaving her twenty years earlier. The murder seems gratuitous.

Moreover, the revelation in the scenario that Hickey hated his wife may possibly shock the audience member (or reader), but it does not surprise either Hickey's friends or Hickey himself. Near the conclusion of the salesman's "confession" in the scenario, it is bar-owner Harry Hope, not Hickey himself, who at the climactic moment calls Evelyn a "God damn bitch." Apparently both unmoved and unsurprised, Hickey tacitly agrees with this characterization of his late wife. In the final version, Hickey accidently blurts out the condemnation of Evelyn. This startling revelation (akin to Lavinia's Freudian slip at the end of *Mourning Becomes Electra*) shocks the salesman as well as the audience, creating a stunning dramatic moment and forging a bond, however discomforting, between Hickey and us. We are equally horrified by the depth of his suppressed resentment against his apparently saintly spouse.

In a similar way, O'Neill also removed the early versions' strong suggestion that Hickey may be a madman. Word by word and line by line, O'Neill chipped away at dialogue references to "madness," "insanity," being "bughouse," and being "nuts," and he experimented with no fewer than five different versions of Hickey's final words and exit to prevent audiences from believing that Hickey has been insane since his arrival at the saloon. Hope's gang may be able to regain their peace at the conclusion of *Iceman* by convincing themselves that they have spent a day and a half entertaining a candidate for the state mental institution. Through his revisions, however, O'Neill denies the audience a similar solace. He prevents us from dismissing as mad ravings the painful truths Hickey reveals: that forgiveness can be more devastating than recrimination, that love can destroy, that hatred and love are often closely allied, and that the truth is too strong a light for most men's eyes to bear.

"A travelling salesman is the character around which the play develops, but there is no 'lead' in the usual sense." (10) With these words O'Neill touches on one of the most crucial aspects of *Iceman*. Protagonist and antagonist, purveyor of truth and advocate of "the wrong kind of pity," voluble evangelist and suffering priest, Hickey and Larry form an opposed pair who fight each other for the souls of the men in the bar. Because it is an O'Neill work, both men win and both men lose.

In his earliest conception of the play, O'Neill seems to have toyed with the idea of a cynically demonic Larry Slade. Stage directions throughout the manuscript and typescript refer to Larry's "mockingly diabolical irony" or his "strange diabolical grin." It is at least possible that these are biographical notes, apt descriptions of Terry Carlin rather than Larry Slade. Whatever the case, for all his professed cynicism, Larry is, as Jimmy Tomorrow says, "the kindest man among us." (p. 44) Accordingly, such notes disappeared as O'Neill edited the play.

As the portraits of Hickey and Larry underwent revision, so too did the relationship between them. O'Neill knew that drama resides not only within character but between characters, in the tangled, shifting interplay between two figures whose contrasting viewpoints cannot fully mask underlying affinities. Whether or not O'Neill first conceived Larry, Hickey, and the others as individual characters with separate stories to tell, the process of composition involved choreographing the dance that juxtaposes them all.

Part of their relationship is indeed antagonistic. Gradually O'Neill emphasized Larry's role as the "protector" of Hope's gang, adding instances in which he defends the men against Hickey's relentless insistence that they bury their pipe dreams. Surely Larry is trying to defend *himself* from Hickey's truth campaign, but he is also trying to save the others from Hickey's deadly elixir of honesty. Ironically, however, at the same time O'Neill was clarifying and sharpening the terms of the antagonism between Hickey and Larry, he was also emphasizing the similarities between them. O'Neill characters inevitably find--as Orin Mannon did in the Civil War--that the "other" they are confronting is actually a variation of the self. O'Neill's revisions of *The Iceman Cometh* underline this theme.

In the *Iceman* scenario, Larry's motives for condemning Don Parritt are primarily political: he and his anarchist friend Hugo Kalmar pass sentence on the traitor. Very different is the printed text, where a distraught and reluctant Larry, finally yielding to Parritt's begging to be let out of his misery, sends the young man off to the death he seeks. The relationships between Hickey and Evelyn on the one hand

and Larry and Parritt on the other are surely very different. But was Hickey's murder of his wife not an act of love and pity as well as an act of hatred and revenge? Was there not a touch of anger as well as compassion in Larry's condemnation of the young boy? Is it coincidental that Hickey understands Larry so well that he accurately predicts how Parritt will evict him from his seat in life's grandstand, or that Larry senses, long before the others do, the aura of death surrounding Hickey's newfound peace? Are Hickey and Larry not in many ways the dark and light images of the same figure? Through his composition process O'Neill took his raw material and gradually molded it into characters of great complexity. In the ambiguity of their motives and actions, these figures echo each other--and us.

NOTES

1. George Pierce Baker, *Dramatic Technique* (Boston: Houghton Mifflin, 1919), 234.

2. All unpublished materials referred to in this paper are in the Eugene O'Neill Collection, Collection of American Literature, Beinecke Library, Yale University. For a full description of the notes, scenario, manuscript, and typescripts of *The Iceman Cometh*, see Judith E. Barlow, *Final Acts: The Creation of Three Late O'Neill Plays* (Athens, Ga.: University of Georgia Press, 1985), 8-62, from which parts of this discussion are derived.

3. Louis Sheaffer, *O'Neill: Son and Artist* (Boston: Little, Brown, 1973), 493-94; Arthur and Barbara Gelb, *O'Neill*, enlarged ed. (New York: Harper & Row, 1973), 285.

4. Letter to George Jean Nathan, 8 February 1940. *"As Ever, Gene": The Letters of Eugene O'Neill to George Jean Nathan*, transcribed and ed. with introductory essays by Nancy L. and Arthur W. Roberts (Rutherford, N.J.: Fairleigh Dickinson University Press, 1987), 198.

5. Letter to Kenneth Macgowan, 30 December 1940. *"The Theatre We Worked For": The Letters of Eugene O'Neill to Kenneth Macgowan*, ed. Jackson R. Bryer, with introductory essays by Travis Bogard (New Haven: Yale University Press, 1982), 258.

6. Gelb, 285.

7. Louis Sheaffer, "Is O'Neill a Character in *Iceman?*" *New York Times*, 9 December 1973, sec. 2: 5. Sheaffer emphasizes O'Neill's negative feelings toward his mother.

8. Letter to Lawrence Langner, 13 May 1944. Theatre Guild Collection, Beinecke Library, Yale University.

9. Eugene O'Neill, *The Iceman Cometh* (New York: Random

House, 1946), 76. (Subsequent references are to this edition and will be given in the text.)

    10. Letter to Nathan, 2 August 1940, in Roberts and Roberts, 205.

17

Register and Idiolect in
The Iceman Cometh and
Long Day's Journey into Night

Jean Chothia

Words written to be read in private either as narrative or as first-person utterance in a lyric poem have a notably different function from dramatic language, which is words written to be heard spoken, as if they were the spontaneous utterances not of the author but of the invented characters.

Ezra Pound observed in the *ABC of Reading* that "Poetry is words" but drama is "people moving about on a stage and using words." (1) This mobility and use make all the difference.

O'Neill's dialogue, which works so well on the stage and creates such problems for literary critics, who usually work from the printed text, is a crucial case in point. Literary critical methods have been developed primarily in relation to poetry and prose fiction, which has led to misconceptions about the quality and control of particular dramatic texts. In the case of O'Neill, the evidence of performance, the test of audience, has repeatedly demonstrated that here we have plays whose language has been conceived for performance by speaking voices on a stage.

Stage language must quicken the *listening* imagination of the audience. It is thoroughly duplicitous. It must be much more shaped, meaningful, and economic than conversation ever is but must give the impression that it is conversation. Although preconceived, it must give the illusion of spontaneity; invented by a single consciousness, it must command belief that it originates from numerous different consciousnesses (the characters). The author must be elided, a new first person singular created with each new speaker. Performed in the continuing present and in a single highly artificial location, dramatic dialogue must command belief that it is uttered in a present different from the present in which the audience knows itself to exist and in a place in which the audience rationally knows it is not. It helps establish contexts of time, place and relationship for its successive speakers.

Much of our speech is phatic; we use it not to give factual information but to convey feeling: warmth, hostility, anger. What we find in effective stage dialogue is a mimesis not of the details of conversation as if transcribed from a tape recorder, but of its interactive structure--its give and take, its movement, the mutual assumptions it registers between participants. If our imaginations are to be fully engaged by the play, the dramatist must make us believe in the characters, in their separate identities and in the relationship between them. I want to look at a few of the many ways in which O'Neill does this.

In *The Iceman Cometh*, O'Neill differentiates the seventeen characters in Hope's Bar linguistically. Each has his (or her) own idiolect. This in itself is a remarkable tour de force. Nor is it only the lexis, the words, that each uses that are distinct. The social class and educational level of each are signalled in the sophistication or otherwise of their speech structure, in their capacity or inability to use complex syntactical transformations. Origin is indicated, in the grammatical solecisms of the foreigners, in the correctness of the Englishman Lewis, in the bartenders and whores who use the harsh slang of New York City that is characterized by an undertone of abuse and cynicism--a man is a "dope," a "poor sap," a "boob from de sticks," a "sucker," a "louse." The argot of each character's abandoned occupation colors his speech (The gambler: "play craps," "my stake"; the policeman: "fine pickings," "sugar galore"; the one-time journalist uses sentimental cliche: "bitter sorrows," "losing the woman one loves by the hand of death"; the anarchist falls into sloganeering). Besides informing us about the past, the recurrence of these echoes also demonstrates the degree to which each has atrophied, become fixed. It is a subtler and more complex version of the polyphony and group action of the early sea plays and *The Hairy Ape*. Even when the stage is physically torpid, it is always linguistically alive.

Each of the Tyrones in *Long Day's Journey* uses a General American idiom, but each also has access to alternative registers, to speech modes that derive from their reading or life-style. This brings color to the dialogue without the limitations or stereotyping apparent when a character speaks only a low colloquial form of the language, lively as that is in many of the early plays. Mary, under the influence of the drug, uses a gushing girlish register ("her eyes look right into your heart," "I was so mad at myself"); Tyrone quotes Shakespeare sententiously; Jamie parodies his father with distorted readings of Shakespeare and devastatingly apposite stage directions, quotes melancholic *fin-de-siecle* poetry or, more harshly, falls into coarse Broadway slang, while Edmund echoes the others' quotation, uses parodic versions of his brother's slang, and occasionally, budding poet, attempts to express his mystic experience in rhythmic poetic prose, which is always self-consciously placed by him ("I couldn't touch what I tried to tell you just now"). Such elements allow O'Neill to vary the surface of the play while creating a dense texture of implication and believably distinct characters.

More than that, the shifts between the alternative speech modes and the characters' consciousness of the idiosyncrasies of the others' speech patterns result in some of the most poignant moments, as when the hurt inflicted by Edmund's parody of Jamie's slang: "They never come back! Everything is in the bag! It's all a frame-up! We're all fall guys and suckers and we can't beat the game! . . . Christ, if I felt the way you do--," is measured in Jamie's simple reply, "I thought you did."

In *Long Day's Journey into Night* the impression of personal isolation is acutely rendered in the pattern of reaching towards confidence and collapse into recrimination. Although the fictional time span of the play is limited to a day and a night, it is expanded to include the recent and distant past of the characters because they search their memories for moments when they had optimistic belief in the future, for the disappointments and catastrophes that have diminished them, or for the never-to-be-located point where things went wrong and because, as they do this, their idiosyncratic language patterns are intensified.

What I am arguing is that, intuitively, because he has a remarkable ear, O'Neill has created speech characteristics that linguists have only recently begun to identify. Each character's language is distinct from each other's (this is idiolect) notably in *The Iceman Cometh*. In *Long Day's Journey*, each character has access to a range of registers, that is, uses different kinds of language, according to situation. The variant idiolects and registers contribute to our sense of individual reality but O'Neill also uses language to show relationship. We share areas of language, too; in linguistic terms, we are all members of a variety of speech communities. This perception is incorporated into the texture of language of the plays.

The people in Hope's Bar are a speech community. They have language and recurrent areas of discourse in common. The simulacrum of meaningful human interaction in which they all collude at the outset of the play enables them to live with themselves. We soon respond to their mutually echoic speech: they share slang words for whisky ("the Booze," "rot-gut") and for each other ("the old wise guy," "the gang," "the bums") and, importantly, they all share the rhythms of deception, they "smoke the same hop." Parritt, the outsider, calls them "tanks" not "bums," responds to none of the evidently habitual requests that he buy drinks, and instead of listening tolerantly to the others' pipe dreams, as is the custom, cries, "What a bunch of cuckoos."

Audience belief in the relationship among the four fictional Tyrones in *Long Day's Journey* is rooted in their shared "family rhythm." They address each other familiarly, teasing about personal matters--snoring, slimming, digesting. They laugh at the same jokes, and the laughter is deflected in evidently habitual reproach. Quarrels flare out of nothing and as quickly subside; allegiances shift, and each character interjects his or her word in a way possible only among people with a history of such interactions. Certain references (to Shakespeare, to music, to the Virgin Mary, to the dead baby, to cheap doctors) recur, establishing a sort of family mythology--O'Neill's version of the recurrent key words that characterize Ibsen's mature writing (the vine leaves in the hair in *Hedda Gabler*, the white horses of *Rosmersholm*). We are sensitized to areas of reticence between the characters through recurrent euphemisms they all use (the "summer cold," "the poison," "her curse") and by their sudden lapses into embarrassed silence (as at the opening of act four: "Tyrone: 'Your dirty Zola. And your Dante Gabriel Rosetti who was a dope fiend'--he starts and looks guilty").

We catch echoes of one character's speech in that of another. And this is always used expressively. Edmund, for example, engaging in reverie, adopts words habitual to his mother's drug-influenced speech: "fog," "alone," "lost," "hide," "ghost"; and Jamie, shortly afterwards, comments drunkenly on his own quotation of Wilde's "The Harlot's House": "not strictly accurate. If my love was with me I didn't notice it. She must have been a ghost." Without making anything explicit, O'Neill allows the audience to perceive the unconscious irony of Jamie's words and to recognize the part his relationship with his mother has played in warping his life.

From his earliest writing O'Neill used the doubling sense that the cold, the fog, even occasionally the sun, can be "outside and in" (to use Strindberg's phrase). This is intently and potently worked in this play. The early shared joke about Tyrone's foghorn snore is emphasized because elaborated by one of Jamie's disrespectful Shakespearean quotations, "The Moor, I know his trumpet." References to the fog accumulate so that, in context, Mary's lines that the fog "hides you from the world and the world from you, You feel that everything has changed and nothing is what it seemed to be," are highly charged and leave a trace that informs our response when Edmund begins his monologue, "I loved the fog, it was what I needed. . . . the fog was where I wanted to be." Because O'Neill has caught an accurate note of drunken hyperbole we laugh at Jamie's echo of this ("Front steps tried to trample on me. Took advantage of fog to waylay me. Ought to be a lighthouse out there. Dark in here too."). But we also catch the resonance of the verbal echo.

As this demonstrates, good dramatic language must function on several levels simultaneously. As well as marking out a speech community, the examples I've used evidently play an important part in creating the emotional texture of the action. O'Neill can raise the dramatic tension by contradicting the pattern: Mary appears with her hair hanging loose, a character fills the silence or a taboo is broken, as when Edmund says, "It's pretty hard to take at times, having a dope fiend for a mother."

O'Neill compounds the effect of such a word or gesture by using the shock, by incorporating response or failure to respond into the texture of action. As critics, we have to isolate examples to be able to analyze at all; but there is a risk that we will belie the interactive quality of good dramatic dialogue and the fact that the action at any given moment is not static: it is in process. As members of an audience, we hear not an individual line but a sequential piece of dialogue within the continuing action of the play.

Take the instance of Edmund's angry outburst, "It's pretty hard to take at times having a dope fiend for a mother." We too have been frustrated when Edmund has tried to tell Mary, "I've got to go to a sanatorium," and again, "you won't even listen when I try to tell you how sick. . . ." We have seen that, unlike us, Mary fails to respond to her son's appeal for comfort, O'Neill elaborates until we too want to punish Mary, but our hostility to the unfeeling mother breaks with Edmund's anguished cry and his naming of her as a dope fiend. As Edmund stammers his miserable apology, O'Neill asks for a pause. We expect Mary to respond to Edmund's appeal, we want the broken taboo to result in a new mutual confidence, but this is not Hollywood; instead, we have to endure Mary's moving slowly to the window, looking out into the fog and speaking with a "blank, far-off voice": "Just listen to that awful foghorn. And the bells. Why is it fog makes everything sound so sad and lost, I wonder?" After Edmund has stumbled miserably away, we are totally disarmed by the bare recognition evident in Mary's sudden cry, "Oh, James, I'm so frightened. I know he's going to die." Nor of course does the dialogue come to a standstill there, but at least such an extended excerpt enables us to see why O'Neill's dramatic dialogue can create such an intense listening response in the audience. He is composing with extended dramatic paragraphs as well as with individual sentences, and we have to take his rhythms.

We gradually come to know from such tormenting exchanges that timing is crucial in relationship and that in these relationships, the time will never be ripe, opportunities will always be missed, precisely because the cruellest denials are summoned by the most heartfelt attempts at mutual confidence.

The effect of the ending of *Long Day's Journey* could only be achieved in the dramatic form, where the verbal and the visual combine in scenic images; where we can hear one character while watching others who listen silently, tormented by the words, and where a word, a gesture, even a position on the stage, can create echoes, to activate our memory of other moments that have prepared and can now extend the immediate image: a chandelier turned full on, regardless of the electric company; a Chopin waltz played by the woman who might have been a concert pianist; the continually neatened hair hanging loose now; the wedding dress, retrieved from the old trunk in the attic, over her arm. Things that through repeated naming and gesture have become emblems of this family are now present on the stage. The first verbal act of the final sequence, Jamie's "The Mad Scene. Enter Ophelia," which combines witty quotation and broken taboo, is devastating. The various speech resources of the characters, quotation from Shakespeare, from *fin-de-siecle* poetry, Mary's gushing schoolgirl register, the men's anguished pleading, are potently interwrought throughout this sequence, when the characters are, at last, all together and all apart in the night of the title, to which the whole play has been inexorably moving, when Mary will have fully succumbed to the drug.

In the course of each of these late plays, attention is continually shifted from facts and events to their emotional significance. As the audience slowly becomes attuned to the texture of the dialogue, it is able to leap the gaps and to understand the shared assumptions, because O'Neill has confronted us with our own familiar patterns of conversation, has created a remarkable mimesis of speech through which to explore those themes of alienation, inarticulacy and dispossession that had occupied him since his early sea plays.

Shakespeare, whose work must provide the touchstone in the English language, includes frequent speech-markers within the intensely metaphoric texture of his iambic pentameter. Although scarcely investigated by critics, this is what ties his language to real speech and makes the human interactions in his plays believable despite all their linguistic artifice. O'Neill creates, for his own time, a highly artificial language that carries conviction as speech while being much more shaped, meaningful, and compact than any real speech is. O'Neill's sense of the way the phatic elements of conversation suggest relationship between speakers, his responsiveness to the patterns of actual conversation, and his capacity to transform these elements into dramatic dialogue, to create words in action, is fundamental to his drama and helps establish his claim as one of the major world dramatists.

NOTE

1. Ezra Pound, *ABC of Reading* (New York: New Directions, 1960), 46.

18

Mirrors of Consciousness: Narrative Patterns in O'Neill's *The Iceman Cometh*

Marc Maufort

Eugene O'Neill's late masterpiece *The Iceman Cometh* clearly belies Thomas Mann's definition of the drama as an art of the silhouette, focusing merely on the contours of reality. (1) In his 1939 play, the American dramatist borrows from the narrative techniques of the novel in an attempt to present us the deeper recesses of his characters' consciousness. Indeed, *The Iceman Cometh*, critics have noted, contains a large proportion of novelistic interior monologues, which differ markedly from the conventional Shakespearian soliloquy. (2) These scholars have nonetheless neglected to examine in detail the narrative or novelistic essence of O'Neill's asides. In this essay, I shall seek to assess the nature of the playwright's monologues and shall therefore concentrate on the structural patterns they generate throughout the drama. *The Iceman Cometh* will appear as a symphony of interior monologues alternating with dialogue in a mosaic design, evoking musical counterpoint. My analysis will, I hope, shed further light on the complex architectural underpinnings of one of O'Neill's most fascinating compositions.

My definition of the phrase "interior monologue," as applied to drama, is derived from the works of Peter Egri. He helps us understand how O'Neill adapts the novelistic interior monologue to the specificity of his plays. Like novelistic inner monologues, O'Neill's asides are characterized by their narrative free-associational mode. In other words, they are disguised as conversation but constantly remain centered on the protagonist's ego. (3)

In addition, I shall resort to Dorrit Cohn's study *Transparent Minds* for terms that distinguish various forms of novelistic inner monologues: the quoted, the self-narrated, the memory, and the autonomous monologues. (4)

The quoted monologue, generally detectable in pre-Joycean novels, emerges in third-person texts when the writer reports his character's inner speech directly, by using both the present tense and quotation marks. In first-person texts, if the character himself renders his own thoughts, that type of soliloquy can be identified as a self quoted monologue. In my study, these inner speeches will refer to a character's spontaneous unveiling of his reflections in the present tense. Because O'Neill transposes them in a dramatic context, I shall call them "modified quoted monologues."

The second designated novelistic soliloquy, the self-narrated monologue, appears in first-person texts. It constitutes a narrated quotation of a thought that occurred to the character at an earlier moment. The protagonist transforms himself as an author towards his own past but renounces any cognitive privilege. He relives, as it were, an existential crisis not yet solved.

Further, Cohn effects a distinction between the memory monologue, in which the mind is trained full-time on the past in an a chronological sequence, and the autonomous monologue, which records psychological events taking place at the same time as they are rendered through the character's mind. From that viewpoint, this second monologic form, marked by the use of the present tense, corresponds to what critics have termed the stream-of-consciousness method. I shall resort to the terms "memory" and "autonomous" to describe Hickey's long monologue in act four. Indeed, that soliloquy simultaneously reveals the character's obsession with the past and, in its present tense passages, the stream-of-consciousness quality of his reflections. These four categories of monologues can be found in varying degrees in *The Iceman Cometh*.

In this analysis, I wish to concentrate on the first and fourth acts of *The Iceman Cometh*. In these two parts of the play one finds the most representative instances of O'Neill's use of monologues. Moreover, the arrangement of soliloquies in these two acts sets the basic rhythm for the monologic patterns of the entire work.

O'Neill's drama is divided not only into four acts but also into a series of scenic units, corresponding to rhythmical modifications in the thematic and structural economy of the play. The first such scenic unit of act one contains dialogues and self-narrated monologues in equal proportions. Particularly interesting in this expository scene is O'Neill's unveiling of Parritt's and Larry Slade's consciousness. These revelatory moments establish the hidden bond existing between these two tormented creatures and offer us instances of self-narrated monologues. Indeed, in an apparent conversation with Larry, Parritt tells of his childhood. In doing so, he relives his previous state of mind and thus adopts the stance of a narrator towards his past experiences. He has not yet completely solved the existential crisis generated by the absence of his father whom, one senses, Larry now replaces. The interiority of Parritt's words, on the surface spoken to Larry, is indicated by the stage directions, according to which Parritt is "looking away":

I've never forgotten you, Larry. You were the only friend of Mother's who ever paid attention to me, or knew I was alive . . . and I had no Old Man. You used to take me on your knee and tell me stories and crack jokes and make me laugh. You'd ask me questions and take what I said seriously. I guess I got to feel in the years you lived with us that you'd taken the place of my Old Man. (5)

Conversely, Larry subsequently voices his attitude towards the Movement, O'Neill's symbol for anarchist associations, through a similar self-narrated monologue: "For myself, I was forced to admit, at the end of thirty years' devotion to the Cause, that I was never made for it. I was born condemned to be one of those who has to see all sides of a question. . . ." (30) This self-narrated monologue, characteristically written in the past tense, introduces a contrast with Larry's earlier modified quoted monologue: "It's the No Chance Saloon. It's Bedrock Bar, the End of the Line Cafe, the Bottom of the Sea Rathskeller! Don't you notice the beautiful calm in the atmosphere? That's because it's the last harbor." (25) In this present tense soliloquy, Larry expresses his philosophical interpretation of the bar in which Hope's habitues indulge in the comfort of illusions. The opposition between a modified quoted monologue and two self-narrated monologues, with its concomitant time shift, sets the basic rhythm of the monologic structure of the play, i.e., the alternation between past and present states of mind.

Towards the end of the initial act, another scenic unit records Hickey's entrance into the bar, one of the most crucial moments in the drama. That protagonist's reflections on what he calls pipe dreams, i.e., our false expectations, are significantly formulated in the self-narrated monologue mode. Explaining how he developed his present philosophy, Hickey, a salesman, identifies with his former state of mind, while performing the role of a narrator towards his own past. By telling of his experience, he urges his friends to destroy their own pipe dreams: "I finally had the guts to face myself and throw overboard the damned lying pipe dream that'd been making me miserable, and do what I had to do for the happiness of all concerned--and then all at once I found I was at peace with myself and I didn't need booze any more." (79) A few moments later, Hickey's thoughts take the shape of a modified quoted monologue, in which he describes the benefits derived from abandoning one's pipe dreams. O'Neill's notation, "his eyes close," clearly indicates the interior nature of Hickey's confession: "You can let go of yourself at last. Let yourself sink down to the bottom of the sea. Rest in peace. There's no farther you have to go. No single damned hope or dream left to nag you." (86) This sharp contrast between two types of soliloquies duplicates the pattern of alternation between present and past states of mind detected in the first scenic unit of the play.

The interior monologues that O'Neill introduces in this part of his drama confer unity upon the entire structure of the initial act. Indeed, as I have shown, the majority of such inner speeches are placed at the two extremes of the act, thus providing it with a unifying framework.

However, the most striking and innovative instances of O'Neill's use of monologic techniques can be found in the famous fourth act of *The Iceman Cometh*. Its central scenic unit constitutes perhaps the most original feature of the entire play, as it is almost completely based on Hickey's inner speech (225-245). In view of the unusual length of such soliloquy, one can indeed speak of a near-memory monologue, as most of its various divisions reveal Hickey's obsession with the past. The scene could even be regarded as a near-autonomous monologue, as its present-tense passages suggest. It would perhaps be more reasonable to say that, in this scenic unit, O'Neill moves towards the memory or autonomous monologue, as described by Cohn. This critic considers that such types of inner monologue must encompass the totality of the work in order to deserve that label. (6) But because Hickey's long monologue is so much free-associational, so close to the stream-of-consciousness method, one is indeed tempted to think of it as a memory or autonomous monologue. Moreover, like most stream-of-consciousness episodes, this long soliloquy records the character's oscillating thoughts with extreme precision, as the constant alternation between moments marked by the modified quoted monologue or by the self-narrated monologue indicates. In order to show the complexity of O'Neill's depiction of the oscillating process of Hickey's consciousness, it is necessary to explain in detail each division of this long aside.

In the first part of his reflections, Hickey is surprised that his friends have not been convinced by his theories. He voices his disappointment at the fact that the now disillusioned bums feel depressed in a modified quoted monologue, expectedly characterized by the use of the present tense: "Can't you appreciate what you've got, for God's sake? Don't you know you're free now to be yourselves, without having to feel remorse or guilt, or lie to yourselves about reforming tomorrow?" (225) From pages 226 to 231, Hickey tells of his attitude towards his wife. He explains how his alcoholism destroyed their relationship. Again, he confesses his thoughts in a speech [of which O'Neill stresses the interiority through his "As if he hadn't heard. . . ." (226)]: "You see, Evelyn loved me. And I loved her. That was the trouble. It would have been easy to find a way out if she hadn't loved me so much. Or if I hadn't loved her. But, as it was, there was only one possible way." (227) Thus, one of the most poignant moments of the play is conveyed through a self-narrated monologue. In a third part of the long monologue (231-236), Hickey deals with a more distant past, that of his childhood, again in a self-narrated monologue: "You see, even as a kid I was always restless. I had to keep on the go. You've heard the old saying, 'Ministers' sons are sons of guns.' Well, that was me, and then some." (231-232) This soliloquy is introduced by O'Neill's description of Hickey as "becoming musingly reminiscent." (231). A fourth division can be detected on pages 236-242, in which Hickey's thoughts concentrate on a less remote past. The hero now evokes the pain Evelyn inflicted upon him by systematically forgiving his inability to prove a worthy husband. Once more, O'Neill records Hickey's reflections through a self-narrated monologue: "Christ, I loved her so, but I began to hate the pipe dream! I began to be afraid I was going bughouse, because sometimes I couldn't forgive her for forgiving me. I even caught myself hating her for making me hate myself so much. . . . You have to begin blaming someone else, too." (239) The last and fifth part of Hickey's monologue introduces an abrupt change of rhythm. Hickey's thoughts are now rendered in the present tense only, through modified quoted monologues. Moreover, the latter represent the hero's own realization that the first parts of his long monologue rely on an absurd vision of life (242-245). The hero now proves unable to bear the implications of his confession that he murdered Evelyn out of hate and not because he wanted to free her from the pipe dream of marital happiness. Accordingly, he seeks escape into madness: "So I killed her. . . . I heard myself speaking to her. . . . 'Well, you know what you can do with your pipe dream now, you damned bitch!' No! That's a lie! I never said--! Good God, I couldn't have said that! If I did, I'd gone insane! Why, I loved Evelyn better than anything in life!" (242) This aside can be seen as a blend of the modified quoted and the self-narrated monologues, as it reflects simultaneously Hichey's present and past thoughts, i.e., respectively his judgment on his former deed and his reliving of his love for Evelyn. Thus, three characteristics should be emphasized about Hickey's long stream-of-consciousness monologue: First is its emphasis on time shifts, opposing the present time to the near or distant past. This device naturally corresponds to Hickey's oscillating thoughts: his present state of madness, his love for Evelyn, and his childhood. Second is the myriad of shorter divisions of which the monologue, itself a division within the fourth act, is composed. In other words, it takes the shape of a mosaic design.   Third, within Hickey's long monologue, two anticlimaxes of the entire drama can be located, Hickey's confession of his murder and his subsequent plea for madness. This convergence of climaxes and inner monologues indicates O'Neill's intent on revealing the psychological import of the main events of his play.

The situation of this fourth act is rendered even more complex through the fact that Hickey's reflections are counterpointed by those, of a shorter range, emanating from Parritt's mind. That hero voices his remorse at having betrayed his mother in two powerful self-narrated monologues, verging towards the modified quoted monologue: "Wouldn't I deserve the chair, too, if I'd--It's worse if you kill someone and they have to go on living. I'd be glad of the Chair! It'd wipe it out--It'd square me with myself!" (227) A few moments later, in a same type of soliloquy, he confesses the true motive of his betrayal: "I may as well confess, Larry. There's no use lying any more. You know, anyway. I didn't give a damn about the money. It was because I hated her." (241) Thus, Parritt's avowal of hate coincides exactly to that of Hickey (241-242), to the latter's confession of having called Evelyn a "damned bitch." I have shown elsewhere that this pattern of counterpointing monologues can be found in *Hughie*, written in 1941 and of which critics have repeatedly indicated that it contained a number of similarities to *The Iceman Cometh*. (7) This points to O'Neill's sense of continuity in his use of dramatic technique.

A comparable alternation of inner monologues can be observed in the very last scenic unit of act four, in which O'Neill focuses on the fate of both Larry and Parritt (246-260). The latter completes his confession in the form of a modified quoted monologue: "You know what I did is a much worse murder. Because she is dead and yet she has to live. For a while. But she can't live long in jail. She loves freedom too much. And I can't kid myself like Hickey, that she's at peace". (247) Shortly after this confession, Larry obliquely invites Parritt to commit suicide. A second inner monologue follows when Larry expresses his gloomy view of life. This metaphysical climax is expressed--as are most of the climactic scenes in this drama--in the monologic form, i.e., that of a modified quoted monologue. It takes place immediately after Parritt's suicide: "Be God, there's no hope! I'll never be a success in the grandstand--or anywhere else! Life is too much for me! I'll be a weak fool looking with pity at the two sides of everything till the day I die! . . . May that day come soon! . . . Be God, I'm the only real convert to death Hickey made here. From the bottom of my coward's heart I mean that now!" (258) This scene functions as a coda to Hickey's intensely monologic confession.

I hope to have made clear, in this short essay, that O'Neill's treatment of narrative, indeed novelistic, inner monologues in *The Iceman Cometh* reveals a high degree of complexity and craftsmanship. In addition, an analysis of the monologic nature of *The Iceman Cometh* helps clarify its composition pattern, indeed, its musical form. Throughout his career, O'Neill felt attracted by musical structures. In the 1931-1938 Notebooks, transcribed by Virginia Floyd, the August 1931 entry records the playwright's project to write a "Symphony Form Play." In his notes, the artist comments on his own view of the relationship between music and drama:

A play form--return of my old idea of using structure of symphony or sonata--justification (of) my unconscious use of musical structure in nearly all of my plays--impulsion and chief interest always an attempt to do what music does (to express an essentially poetic viewpoint of life) using rhythm or recurrent themes . . . (study authoritative books on structure of symphony, sonata etc . . . and let's see!). (8)

As O'Neill himself intimates, and as Stephen Black has demonstrated in a recent article, his reliance on musical patterns resides primarily in his special treatment of themes. (9) I would argue, however, that it is possible to see a musical analogy in the way he devises the very structure of *The Iceman Cometh*, as the alternation and counterpoint rhythms marking his use of monologues clearly evidence. Further, the monologic structure of *The Iceman Cometh* shows points of convergence not only with the symphony or sonata but also with the more vocal genre of opera. Focusing on the minds of essentially three characters, Hickey, Larry, and Parritt, O'Neill's interior monologues can be described as the arias of three solo singers against the choral background formed by Hope's habitues. Whether symphonic or operatic, the musical affinities of *The Iceman Cometh* can hardly be denied.

My examination of O'Neill's soliloquies offers a second key to the understanding of his concept of dramatic form. For among the various types of novelistic inner monologues delineated by Dorritt Cohn, O'Neill consistently resorts to those labeled as "figural," in opposition to those termed "authorial." (10) The first of these terms designates inner speeches in which the writer describes reality from the limited perspective of the character, whereas the second category refers to those inner monologues in which the author adopts an omniscient viewpoint. All the different types of soliloquies found in *The Iceman Cometh* are those depicted by Cohn as belonging to the figural genre.

Particularly, the self-narrated monologue corresponds to the novelistic "Style Indirect Libre," i.e., to a vision of the universe betraying the restricted viewpoint of the hero. But the authorial, omniscient method of the monologic form termed psycho-narration, in which the writer pretends to be aware of the tiniest details of his character's soul and chooses to interpret them, is definitely foreign to O'Neill or to his characters/narrators. (11) In all of O'Neill's monologues, his creatures relive for themselves the crisis they went through at an earlier time while the author remains absent. However, the absence of psycho-narration prevents O'Neill from fully rendering the unconscious side of his protagonists' mind. As Cohn demonstrated, only psycho-narration can image the hidden parts of the psyche, to which the hero himself has no access. Through a modified quoted monologue or a self-narrated, a memory, or an autonomous monologue, we see only what the character himself knows about the workings of his mind. In other words, the contents of the playwright's soliloquies focus not on the characters' unconscious, which by definition being a state of post- or preverbal nature cannot be articulated, but on their inner discourse. Viewed in that perspective, O'Neill's aside, with its rational structure, exhibits a number of analogies with pre-Joycean novels, namely with those of an early practitioner of the inner monologue, Henry James.

In summation, the intricate use of the monologic genre in this long epic masterpiece is clearly a challenge for theatre practitioners, who will need to devise appropriate methods for translating the artist's elaborate narrative patterns into an effective stage language.

NOTES

1. Quoted in Dorritt Cohn, *Transparent Minds. Narrative Modes for Presenting Consciousness in Fiction* (Princeton: Princeton University Press, 1978), 5.

2. See for instance Travis Bogard, *Contour in Time. The Plays of Eugene O'Neill* (New York: Oxford University Press, 1972), 79.

3. Peter Egri, "'Belonging' Lost: Alienation and Dramatic Form in Eugene O'Neill's *The Hairy Ape*," in *Critical Essays on Eugene O'Neill*, ed. James J. Martine (Boston: G.K. Hall, 1984), 77-111; see, in particular, pages 96-97. Egri calls O'Neill's soliloquy a "modified interior monologue." Unlike a conventional Shakespearian monologue, it is defined, Egri noted, by four characteristics: (1) a center of gravity lying on the ego revealed; (2) a tendency to project a free-associational stream of consciousness with an emphasis on oscillating emotions and thoughts; (3) potential as trigger of action, which it helps advance

through contrast and tension; and (4) a self-contained quality. While it is apparently addressed to another person, it remains centered on the protagonist's thoughts. It represents an utterance spoken in spite of another character.

4. See Dorritt Cohn, *Transparent Minds,* note 1. She discusses the quoted monologue on pages 59-98, the self-narrated monologue on pages 166-72, the memory monologue on page 247, and the autonomous monologue on pages 229-56. Cohn also expands on the concepts of "Vision avec" and "Style Indirect Libre" on pages 166-72.

5. Eugene O'Neill, *The Iceman Cometh* (New York: Vintage Books, 1957), 26. (All subsequent quotations are indicated in parentheses.)

6. Dorritt Cohn, 229-35.

7. Marc Maufort, "O'Neill's Variations on an Obituary Motif in *Bound East for Cardiff* and *Hughie,*" *Revue Belge de Philologie et d'Histoire,* 66 (3) (1988): 602-12.

8. Virginia Floyd, *Eugene O'Neill at Work. Newly Released Ideas for Plays* (New York: Frederick Ungar Publishing Co., 1981), 228-29.

9. Stephen A. Black, "O'Neill's Dramatic Process," *American Literature,* 59 (1987): 58-70.

10. Dorritt Cohn, 103-43.

11. Dorritt Cohn, 11-57; 143-61.

Part Four

O'Neill on Stage

19

Eugene O'Neill and the Provincetown Players: Watershed in American Theatre

Robert K. Sarlos

A great deal of myth surrounds much of the life and work of Eugene O'Neill, and appropriately so. After all, the playwright was a master mythmaker who wove greater and lesser elements of his life into the myths embodied in his scripts. Because he defied social and artistic norms on the one hand, yet simultaneously pursued recognition and success on the other, and because he played a pivotal role in American theatre and drama, admirers and detractors alike have worked at raising his career and his contribution to mythic levels.

The very first production of an O'Neill play on any stage, *Bound East for Cardiff*, naturally has figured prominently in the mythology, with early Boston newspaper accounts raising great expectations that seemed disproportionate to the event. But when the myths are cleared away, the facts of O'Neill's debut--in July 1916 on a Provincetown wharf, recently converted to a theatre in this sleepy Cape Cod fishing village that was turning into bohemian summer refuge--and of his continuing collaboration with the group that gave him this premiere are still impressive. They also contain seeds of dramatic tension.

The cast, made up mostly of Greenwich Village intellectuals and artists (the author spoke two lines), was rounded out by a couple of local residents; two professional actors, one of whom played the important role of Driscoll, got involved almost by accident. George Cram Cook, the group's *spiritus rector*, known to all as "Jig," created Yank, the central character. The tiny makeshift stage was crowded, as was the ramshackle auditorium. Emboldened by positive response to the evening, which was the second program of the summer and included two other one-acts, the group presented further "bills" of plays before formally organizing itself as "the Provincetown Players," in order to continue its anarchist venture that fall in the center of commercial theatre, Manhattan.

The artists, writers, and political activists whose collective and creative discontent had motivated them to write and stage plays the summer before were theatrical amateurs, rebels against Broadway, seeking an alternative to the prevailing industrial system of producing theatre; by contrast, O'Neill was hell-bent for a career on Broadway, attempting to open it up for his new dramatic vision. It is ironic that this would-be professional embraced, and was embraced by, a collection of stubborn amateurs, that a long-sought-for first performance of one of his plays grew from a distinctive group effort that he, a determined individualist, joined purely out of professional ambition. O'Neill immediately became the focus both of attention and of the Players' hope for the future.

The original devotion of the Players to the collective creative spirit of a group and the democratic procedures by means of which they hoped to liberate it stood in opposition to their chief playwright's rigorous (some would say, ruthless) pursuit of individual artistic integrity, to which everybody and everything was to be subordinated. Among the cardinal principles of the Provincetown Players' founding documents was a precariously wrought compromise between the opposing doctrines of collective and individual creation: namely, the idea that all members would rotate all functions but that the playwright whose script was being produced was to have complete authority over the process. The only outspoken holdout against the group's fundamental belief in democratically organized collective creativity from the outset, O'Neill paradoxically remained the Players' strongest pillar, not only on account of the quality and quantity of his plays but also because of his unparalleled drive. Jig Cook, the most enthusiastic advocate of spontaneous group creativity, became at once O'Neill's most fervent supporter and his opposite pole. On the one hand, the dramatist's achievement was seen both as proof of the theory of group creativity and its continuing inspiration: on the other, the Provincetown Players' principles and immediate goals were repeatedly subordinated to, or undermined by, his professional ambitions.

The group did, in fact, open "The Playwright's Theatre" (so named at O'Neill's insistence) in Macdougal Street, where on a shoe-string budget it led a precarious and stormy, but productive, existence for six seasons. During that time the Players put on another fourteen scripts by O'Neill and over eighty by other authors, including John Reed and Susan Glaspell, Djuna Barnes and Wallace Stevens, Michael Gold and Edna St. Vincent Millay, Evelyn Scott and Theodore Dreiser, before exploding in spontaneous combustion and yielding the playhouse and part of its name to the Experimental Theatre, Inc. (1)

Nothing shows the significance of the combined accomplishment of O'Neill and the Provincetown Players more poignantly than the popular claim that American drama *began* with O'Neill (as American scene design with Robert Edmond Jones, an artist present at the birth of the group, who repeatedly returned to it). Understandable as an attempt to glorify and capitalize on the Nobel laureate, such oversimplification in the long run diminishes rather than enhances O'Neill's stature. For the hyperbole of attributing *creation* of American drama to a single agent is too absurd to need refutation, whereas the assertion that the playwright was a key player in the *transformation* of American theatre can be demonstrated. Moreover, the latter claim also acknowledges the social and artistic context, the physical and psychological venue provided by the Provincetown Players during his initial years of experimentation with the stage. For no matter how much of a loner a playwright may be temperamentally, artistically he cannot function without a platform on which his works are mounted, without fellow artists providing the flesh and blood, the lath and canvas, the space and time that render scripts into live theatrical events.

Only by analyzing the *changes* in American theatre and drama that O'Neill and the Provinctown Players advocated in principle, practiced intermittently, and promoted both by direct example and through members who continued working in other theatres does an appropriate assessment of their radical function become possible. The Players' alliance with O'Neill went beyond a common fight for the centrality of the playwright's artistic visions and the creation of distinctly American forms of theatre and drama; it helped reshape American theatre in a way that made it more receptive to continued experimentation. For his part, O'Neill challenged some fundamental notions of the playwright's "trade"--the primacy of box-office considerations over artistic ones, the necessity of heroic leading characters in victorious action, and plot-centered, blueprint-oriented dramatic structure. Similarly, the Provincetown Players attacked fundamental assumptions of the theatrical "business" as it had evolved over two centuries from the English model in America--the star system with its implication of brand-name selling and the production company with its emphasis on mass production. Together, O'Neill and the Players were as surely attacking Anglo-American traditions of theatrical modus operandi as they honored the theatre's ancient roots of collective ecstasy and civic regeneration.

O'Neill's early plays were sometimes derided by the poets among the Players as being of the kitchen-sink school. Yet even in such plotless slice-of-life scripts as *Bound East for Cardiff* and *Moon of the Caribbees*, the dramatist clearly reached beyond naturalism for a poetic vision not primarily verbal, one that would exercise a hypnotic spell over spectators. Nor was his search for significant new form unrelated to indigenous new content: O'Neill was in pursuit of fundamentally American myths, American heroes, and American rites of passage. Ultimately, using the grand passions and sensation scenes from the heritage of melodrama, he turned to victims, rather than victors, for his mythic heroes. It is O'Neill's systematic exploration of the antihero--the poor, the failed, the forgiven--that best justifies the adjective "American" in his drama, even though, superficially viewed, this approach seems to fly in the face of the cherished "American Dream."

Yet, in his exploration of failure as the core of human experience in America, O'Neill's intuition parallels that of Eric Hoffer, the salty waterfront philosopher not unlike a character in the dramatist's seaplays, whose essays in *The Ordeal of Change* (2) and other books explained human progress, and especially the expansion of the American Frontier, as the creation not of an elite, but of the undesirables of society. With scripts that the socialist novelist Floyd Dell once described as "superb and beautiful romanticizations and glorifications and justifications of Failure," (3) O'Neill also prepared the American mind for acceptance of such latter-day dramatic heroes as Arthur Miller's Willy Loman, Tennessee Williams' Blanche Dubois, and Edward Albee's George and Martha.

The American theatre in which O'Neill grew up, as the youngest son of a leading Shakespearean actor who, not unlike Richard Burton more recently, had sold out to commercialism, was not primarily Art but Industry. With a double focus on stars and spectacles, it assembled its products in such centers as New York, Chicago, Philadelphia, and Los Angeles, distributing them for mass consumption along a vast network of circuits organized around the railroads crisscrossing the nation. In order to allow American artists to find autochthonous expression, which O'Neill exemplified in drama, they had to be liberated from an inferiority complex built into the structures and standards inherited from Europe. In theatrical terms that meant reinventing the "independent theatre movement" of Europe (as exemplified by Antoine's Theatre Libre, Strindberg's Intimate Theatre, and especially the Abbey) for American conditions and sensitivities. That reinvention, known as the Little Theatre Movement, culminated in the Provincetown Players, who were not only the sole group to produce American plays exclusively but also the most determined to break all aesthetic and organizational rules of traditional theatrical operation.

Believing, with the fearless editor of the *Little Review*, Margaret Anderson, that "art and anarchism exist for exactly the same kind of reason," (4) they were intent on reinventing the theatrical process itself, unwilling or unable to realize that in ignoring or abolishing old rules and conventions, they perforce were creating new ones. This is what distinguished the bulk of Players from O'Neill, who was neither ignorant of traditional aesthetic conventions nor afraid to replace them with new ones. For him, joining the avant-garde was not an end, but a means toward entering the mainstream. Even before the success of *The Emperor Jones*, he continued his direct attempts to penetrate Broadway, and with the Pulitzer Prize winning *Beyond the Horizon*, he did. But well before 1920, when both those breakthroughs occurred, O'Neill's more conventional script *In the Zone* was done by the Washington Square Players, a little theatre group genuinely seeking to enter the mainstream against which the Provincetowners determinedly had turned their backs. Surely, it was no accident that the postwar uptown reincarnation of the Washington Square Players, the Theatre Guild, became O'Neill's regular producing organization in his newly acquired respectability. By that time the Provincetown Players had ceased to exist but, with O'Neill, they had pioneered in a convulsive transformation of American theatre and drama.

Leading to the Federal Theatre Project, to the post-World War II institutionalization of Off-Broadway, and to the establishment of a regional theatre network in the sixties and seventies, that transformation: (1) recognized the international respectability of indigenous American artistic expression in the theatre, (2) made possible the financing of theatre through subscription as well as through private, community, corporate, and governmental subsidy, and (3) allowed, even demanded, ever-increasing artistic and political freedom for both playwrights and theatre companies.   It is this transformation, not the creation of American theatre and drama for which Eugene O'Neill and the Provincetown Players deserve credit; together they represent a watershed between two distinct eras of cultural history.

NOTES

1. For a detailed history and analysis of the players, see my *Jig Cook and the Provincetown Players* (Amherst: University of Massachusetts, 1982).

2. Eric Hoffer, *The Ordeal of Change* (New York: Harper & Row, 1963).

3. *Homecoming, An Autobiography* (New York: Farrar & Rinehart, 1933), 263- 64.

4. "Art and Anarchism," *Little Review*, March 1916: 3.

20

Dramatic Tension Between Expressionistic Design and Naturalistic Acting in *The Emperor Jones*

Felicia Hardison Londre

For the Provincetown Players to seek out a black actor to play the title role in Eugene O'Neill's *The Emperor Jones* in its 1920 premiere took an uncompromisingly strong commitment to realism. The American theatre was not then integrated. Although a black actor might play an occasional black walk-on role in a white play, it was standard practice to use white actors in blackface for Negro characters in speaking roles. Thus it was a bold step for the still-struggling company to cast Charles Gilpin in what was virtually a six-scene monologue, prefaced by some dialogue with a white actor who functioned as a kind of lackey to him. The public shock waves are clearly registered in published reviews of the production. The company had auditioned a number of white actors for the role but felt that none could read the lines convincingly. The dominant concern then was for the naturalistic quality of the performance.

When O'Neill wrote the play, however, he had been reading the German expressionist dramatists, and his conception of the play accorded with the tenets of dramatic expressionism: the reality that is communicated to the theatre audience is a subjective one, a distortion of objective reality as it is filtered through the perceptions of the central character. Twice in his stage directions O'Neill uses the word "unreal," and twice he specifies that the apparitions move like "automatons." He also calls for "marionettish" movements and "mechanical gestures," favorite devices of the machine-conscious German expressionists. His desire to stress the unreality of the forces acting upon Jones is further evident in his later comment that not only the Witch Doctor but "all the figures in Jones's flight through the forest should be masked. Masks would dramatically stress their phantasmal quality, as contrasted with the unmasked Jones, intensify the supernatural menace of the tom-tom. . . . " (1)

The juxtaposition of psychologically based realistic acting with highly stylized sound and visual design is both a challenge and a strength of *The Emperor Jones*. O'Neill was breaking new ground in the American theatre by featuring a black protagonist, by eschewing any love interest, by offering a "full-length" drama without intermission, and by putting most of the action in the form of a monologue. (2) At the same time, he differed from the European expressionists in his protagonist's fullness of characterization. (3) According to an essay on acting he wrote in 1925, O'Neill saw no incongruity in the "sensitive, truthful, trickless acting" of "plays of arresting imagination." (4) This paper will examine in several different productions the charting of what Travis Bogard calls "a difficult course between expressionism and realism" (5) in *The Emperor Jones*.

Charles Gilpin, who created the role of Brutus Jones at the tiny Provincetown Playhouse in November 1920, was "the first Negro ever cast by a white American company for a major role." (6) Like the character he portrayed, Gilpin had once been a Pullman car porter, but his considerable work with two black theatre companies made him the most experienced member of *The Emperor Jones* cast. Reviewers unanimously praised the "rich musical voice" (7) and "ease and naturalness of gesture" (8) that contributed to his "remarkably convincing," (9) "amazing and unforgettable performance." (10) In Gilpin's portrayal, wrote one reviewer, "the devastating terror of Jones is made gripping and real." (11) Another wrote of the 1924 revival: "*The Emperor Jones* gained a great deal of realism from Gilpin's performance." (12)

Reactions to the staging were more equivocal. The setting was historically important in that it marked the first American use of a plaster sky dome, which allowed some stunning lighting effects. Designer Cleon Throckmorton devised "some lightweight hanging silhouettes" (13) to allow faster scene changes than could have been accomplished with standing scenes. Nevertheless, some reviewers, like Alexander Woolcott, found the play "clumsily produced" in that "its presentation consists largely of long, unventilated intermissions interspersed with fragmentary scenes." (14) Another reported that "the production suffered from lack of smoothness in detail. One longed to see the eight scenes run through in quick succession with the house in continuous darkness and the beating of the drum uninterrupted; the stage floor covered sufficiently to kill the sound of the boards; the scene shifts made quickly, silently, and invisibly behind a non-transparent curtain."

Yet this same reviewer stated that "the settings were beautiful and the play of lights against the new dome a joy to behold." (15)

If the scenery appears crude by today's standards, we must remember that *The Emperor Jones* premiered in an ill-equipped, "microscopic theatre in Macdougal Street," a non-commercial enterprise where "orthodox theatregoers" rarely ventured. (16) Certainly, the black and white photographs upon which we must rely for visual evidence cannot convey a sense of the expressive fluidity of the lighting. The very simplicity and naivete of the visual elements apparently worked to enhance by contrast the subtlety and range of Gilpin's acting. Such mutual reinforcement of scenic effect and individual performance is suggested in one reviewer's recollection of Jones's prayer at the beginning of scene five: "Much can be said for Mr. Gilpin's beautiful voice, for the deep sky and the dark twisted trees against which the naked torso of the fleeing emperor was reared, to account for the heartbreaking beauty of this scene." (17) Another described it thus: "The moment when he raises his naked body against the moonlit sky beyond the edge of the jungle and prays is such a dark lyric of the flesh, such a cry of the primitive being, as I have never seen in the theatre." (18)

Even in that original production, however, with O'Neill present for consultation, some theatregoers missed the point of the expressionistic approach. This is evident in several reviewers' dissatisfaction with the ending of the play, a problem that was to plague a number of other important productions. Heywood Broun commented, for example, that O'Neill "has almost completely missed the opportunities of his last scene, which should blaze with a vast tinder spark of irony. Instead, he rounds it off with a snap of the fingers, a little O. Henry dido. We cannot understand just why he has allowed the Emperor to die to the sound of offstage shots. It is our idea that he should come crawling to the very spot where he meets his death and that the natives should be molding silver bullets there and waiting without so much as stretching out a finger for him." (19) It is my contention that the problem lies not in O'Neill's writing, but in the scene designer's lack of stylistic differentiation between the last scene and the jungle scenes that have preceded it. As long as Jones is on stage, then the jungle that we see must be the one that he sees, a hallucinatory projection of his fear-crazed mind. The illusion would shatter, the convention would be negated, if Jones were brought alive into the final scene with the flesh-and-blood natives. It is then the designer's responsibility to contrast the expressionistic jungle of scenes two through seven with a more objective reality for scenes one and eight. In this manner, scene eight would properly function as a mere coda, as the play's crisis and climax occur in scene seven, when Jones summons the inner resources to overcome a hypnotic compulsion to sacrifice himself to the pagan crocodile god. In fact, when Jones fires his last silver bullet against the "forces of evil," (20) we might say that he is metaphorically shooting the demon in himself. Thus, Jones really "dies" in scene seven, and scene eight must clearly represent a different plane of reality, a mundane one. Without the powerful presence of Jones in the final scene, it is imperative that the scenery reflect his absence by the absence of expressionistic elements. This change of focus within the production points up the importance of maintaining the tension between naturalistic acting and expressionistic design in the main body of the play. The problem with the Provincetown Playhouse's original production seems to have been that the plaster sky dome functioned as the dominant scenic element, unifying all the scenes and homogenizing the levels of reality in the play.

Although Charles Gilpin continued to appear in touring company revivals of *The Emperor Jones*, a promising young black actor named Paul Robeson was cast in the Provincetown Players' 1924 revival of the play in the theatre on Macdougal Street, and it was Robeson who toured the play to London and also performed in the 1933 film version. Critical comparisons of Gilpin and Robeson are abundant. Robeson had a natural advantage in his enormous, handsome physique and magnificent, rich voice. In terms of interpretation, however, we may cite O'Neill, who said in 1946: "As I look back now on all my work, I can honestly say there was only one actor who carried out every notion of a character I had in mind. That actor was Charles Gilpin." (21) Richard Watts, Jr., succinctly summarized the difference between the two portrayals: "[Robeson] is, of course, a magnificent figure throughout the drama. He is, as I have always thought, less effective in the role than was the late Charles Gilpin, chiefly because there is about Robeson a certain quality of spirit and intellect which makes you feel that he would never quite break under the strain of his visions." (22)

It is difficult to draw inferences about Robeson's performance in the context of a stage setting, as he revived the work so many times with different designers. The references to his rich, resonant voice and powerful presence persist whether the settings were "simple and to the point" as at the Westchester Summer Theatre in 1939, (23) or in "a reasonably real stage jungle," as in the North Shore Players' 1941 production, (24) or achieving a "completeness of stylized illusion" in the hallucination scenes as at the Deutsches Kunstlertheater of Berlin in 1930. (25) One of the more precise analyses of the relationship between the performer and his scenic space was for a 1940 production at the Westport Country Playhouse:

Mr. Robeson, of course, has played the fear-stricken emperor so many times, through the length and breadth of this and other lands, that it would seem that some day his performance would become perfunctory and mechanical. It is somewhat surprising, therefore, to witness again the reality of his braggadocio, the gradual breakdown of confidence, the descent and reversion to superstitious terror and the final magnificent collapse and never for a moment to feel that it is merely play-acting. Yet he accomplishes just that thing--largely through that great, mellow, fibre-shaking voice of his, for as you know, the entire play is done in semidarkness and the effect is upon the ear rather than the eye. . . . The first scene is a rather ordinary, conventional set showing the emperor's throne room. It is when this unnamed designer begins playing with the forest that he demonstrates originality. His trees, I presume, are constructed of hanging cloth, but above them, in a tangle of vines, branches, palm fronds and other outlines of jungle plant life, the whole mystic horror of the forest can be read. . . . In the fantasy of the ghostly convicts and again in the slave market, the characters, in rhythm with Mr McPhee's music, operate in slow motion, increasing the tension and heightening the suspense and terror. (26)

It is clear that this latter production stressed the unreality of the jungle scenes, and it is also significant that the reviewer referred to "reality" and "never merely play-acting" in Robeson's performance.

The 1933 film version was Robeson's first screen appearance. Although his acting showed as much of his "immense talent and conviction" (27) as ever, the film was only marginally successful. It has been criticized for the expansion of the story by screenwriter Du Bose Heyward to show episodes from Jones's life before his arrival on the tropical island where he makes himself Emperor. Thus the film's first hour is a realistic vision of black America from a sleepy South Carolina town to Harlem to the chain gang experience that precipitates his flight to a West Indian island palace. The jungle sequences are far less effective on film than in the theatre partly because the natural-looking foliage fails to create "the mood of mounting terror which is the drama's great quality." (28) According to Richard Watts, Jr., the jungle scenes "could have been made less monotonous than they are, by more effective lighting and a more striking manner of presenting the visions that haunted the fleeing Emperor. Double exposure is not the best way of making phantoms terrifying." (29) As a gesture toward expressionistic design, the use of double-exposed ghosts in the second half of the film is stylistically jarring after the realism of the first half. Thus we see that without the dramatic tension between realistic acting and expressionistic design "the ending loses considerable of its power through the loss of the proper building up of the climax." (30)

O'Neill's material underwent another media transfer when the Metropolitan Opera House of New York produced an operatic version of *The Emperor Jones* by Louis Gruenberg in 1933. Various artistic choices conspired to undermine what little tension there may have been between Jo Mielziner's grandiose, stylized stage settings and Laurence Tibbett's dedicated performance. Paul Rosenfeld felt that the music merely served "to accentuate what was already given by O'Neill; to work theatrically on the spectator while leaving the playwright to perform the real labor and touch the emotions." Describing the score as "a sort of superior bogey-music which plays wholly on the nerves," Rosenfeld felt that "it really reinforces the work of the stage-machinist more thoroughly than that of the dramatist." (31) The orchestra then took away from the scenery the expressionistic function of evoking the protagonist's emotional state, and it also undercut the effect of the famous tom-tom device, by which a steady drumbeat "starts at a rate exactly corresponding to normal pulse beat--72 to the minute--and continues at a gradually accelerating rate" (32) uninterruptedly until Jones's death. According to Rosenfeld, "the drumbeat was more organic and necessary than the music." (33)

The opera began with a prologue: "a pit-dark jungle, with grotesque figures at the side outlined in shining light, and swarthy faces peering through tall grasses," with an "invisible chorus of Negroes proclaiming vengeance upon Emperor Jones." (34) Those rumblings of "horrors to come" may have backfired by beginning too early a tension that was then interrupted by the "sultry," (35) slow-paced throne room scene (scene one of O'Neill's play). In the forest scenes, both the acting and the decor were disappointing to Stark Young, who commented that all Tibbett could do "in scene after scene, was to run around in circles and fall down in the middle of the stage, in the same spot scene after scene." Those settings, he said, were "only made worse by a device for choral effects where, amid green leaves on either side of the stage, we saw raised arms and clawing hands." (36)

Gruenberg's most serious tampering with O'Neill's work was his omission of the play's final scene. Instead of employing the aesthetic irony of a return to daylight and reality after Jones's death, the opera ended with the scene in which he confronts the witch doctor and the crocodile god, here portrayed as real beings instead of phantasms. As they no longer functioned as "the last horror" proceeding from Jones's mind, "all the cumulative drama was lost. And," writes Young, "--nobody will believe this--the witch doctor, instead of appearing among the shadows of the stage wood, as the terror of the superstition crept from the shadows of the Negro mind, came up out of the footlights, somewhere near the prompter's box, in the middle of the stage, a silly dancer figure, brightly rigged out like a ballet fantasy!" (37) In this version, Jones then shot himself. "A full chorus rushed in, opera style, and carried off the dead hero's body on their shoulders, after a certain amount of ballet prancing and the cheapest of crescendo efforts," (38) "orgiastically stamping and intoning a fierce paean." (39) The setting for this scene was judged by Stark Young "beyond words foolish and ugly." (40)

The first foreign production of *The Emperor Jones*, in Paris in 1923, was director Firmin Gemier's initial offering in an altruistically conceived plan to present one American play each season at the state-subsidized Odeon. The play's poor reception by French audiences so squelched his enthusiasm that he cancelled *The Hairy Ape*, which had been announced for the following season. The problem did not lie in the performance, for Habib Benglia, "a French colonial negro of great talent," (41) was described as "magnificent in his truculent utterances and in the art of mimicry with which he depicts real life." (42) The realization of the expressionistic forest scenes was decidedly flawed. The "dark cardboard silhouettes" that represented rocks and the "cloth strips" used for trees were "disappointing," (43) as was the lighting "which made the apparitions less suggestive than they should have been." (44) Director Gemier also undermined the required hallucinatory effect of Jones's flight by "sending detachments of natives across in front of the curtain, groping on hands and knees, as a reminder that the pursuit continued; sometimes the Emperor himself would cross and recross, or the cockney Smithers would shamble out and utter his cynical laugh. All this in darkened pantomime" (45) betrayed O'Neill's intention of having "the beat of the drums suffice to draw Brutus Jones into the arms of the natives who simply wait for him at the edge of the forest." (46)

One aspect of Walter Rene Fuerst's scenic design elicited raves from the French critics. That was the setting for the throne room in scene one: "a bare white room with an opening on each side, a red wooden throne in the centre, and to relieve the blank walls two strips of hieroglyphs that might have been Bengalese or merely a symbol for expressionism. It was an entirely satisfactory setting, well imagined and simple." (47) It is not surprising that, except for the addition of the "hieroglyphs," the foregoing description from the *New York Transcript* review corresponds closely to O'Neill's own specifications in his stage directions. That French setting, complete with hieroglyphs, spawned imitations as far away as Tokyo in a 1932 production, (48) and a 1956 community theatre production in Washington. (49)

The Emperor Jones was revived in Paris in 1950 by a young company called the Argonates under the direction of Sylvain D'Homme.

The title role was played by Habib Benglia, who was again praised for his "expressive face, calculated movements and tremendous presence." (50) This time, however, Benglia had excellent support from designer Jacques Noel's "workable, suggestive decor." (51) Reviewers were most ecstatic about the Segg Troupe of West African voodoo dancers who supplied "an eerie, ear-shattering tom-tom crescendo to counterpoint the proceedings." (52) The role of the witch doctor was "danced and shouted" by Diouta Seck, whose performance was for Frank Dorsey the "high point" of the play. He also praised the liveliness of the last scene when the stage was "filled with the picturesque dancers of the Segg troupe, with Alioune Diakita giving a trance-like performance as their chief." (53)

Casting a white actor as Jones negates the possibility of naturalistic performance from the start, as exemplified by the play's failure in Berlin in 1924 despite Oscar Homolka's sincere approach to the title role. The production suffered also because German audiences were apparently looking for political meaning. According to the *New York Times* correspondent, the *Deutsches Zeitung* described the play as "an American search for sensations and wild stage effects which tries to deride Kaiserdom." (54) It failed also in Vienna in 1926 despite Max Reinhardt's elaborate staging; there audiences, unfamiliar with black American history and culture, were puzzled by the play, and critics condemned it as "melodramatic rot." (55)

A 1927 Dublin production was found disappointing in that Irish actor Rutherford Mayne, "a man of big stature and . . . an unusually fine voice," displayed only a superficial understanding of the black ethos:

All through his performance Mayne was the white man beneath the dark make-up. . . . [In the forest scenes] Mayne became more and more restrained. . . . As the peril increased, the more subdued he became. He scarcely moved at all, but ever alert, ever listening, he seemed to weigh his every thought. Gradually he yielded to physical weariness until, at last, lying on the ground exhausted, he prayed softly to his Creator for aid. His Brutus Jones was a thinker . . . and his defeat proceeded from external rather than from internal causes. (56)

Again, we see that the play's success depends upon acceptance of a reality projected through the frenzied vision of the focal character, that is, upon a mutually reinforcing naturalism in performance and expressionism in design.

An apparently successful portrayal of Jones, not widely reviewed, was seen at Philadelphia's Hedgerow Theatre in 1929. Jasper Deeter, director of the theatre, had created the role of Smithers in 1920 and now revived it opposite Wayland Rudd. According to

Gwendolyn Bennett:

There was something fearful and contemptible about the Brutus Jones of Charles Gilpin; there was something almost childlike about the rollicking Emperor of Paul Robeson; Wayland Rudd did something that was a combination of both of these with a dash of something so poignant that it wrung your heart as you lived through the part with him. He seemed to give a larger futility to the role. He didn't seem so much a senseless bully caught in the toils of his own folly as a human being crushed by an insurmountable fate. (57)

Deeter revived the play again at the Hedgerow in 1945, playing Smithers opposite Arthur Rich, who gave a "workmanlike" performance on a "bare stage." (58)

For a 1964 Boston Arts Festival production starring James Earl Jones, director Ben Shaktman came up with:

a highly imaginative production concept that didn't work. . . . He used no scenery, only a big bare stage with a few platforms and backing flats; the emperor's physical surroundings were represented by a dozen almost-nude modern dancers--choreography by Daniel Nagrin-- who also, with no changes of costume, impersonated the phantoms that breed in Jones' frightened mind as he flees through the jungle. It sounds exciting . . . [but] a dozen dancers on a big bare stage simply did not, probably could not, conjure up a steamy, dense, close, paranoic jungle, brimming with dim shapes and murky terrors. (59)

The dancers, who functioned as palace pillars, stones, trees, and so on, according to Allan Hughes, were "as nude as they can be without risking arrest." (60) This underscoring of their humanness deprived the forces acting upon Jones's imagination of their terrifying mystery. It also brought confusion when they portrayed the witch doctor, chain-gang, and slave-auction apparitions, all of whose identities must be established by their costumes because they have no lines to speak. (61) The burden of communicating meaning in this production then rested even more heavily than usual upon the actor in the title role: "In barren light or teeming shadow, crowing or cringing [James Earl] Jones offered his audience an impressive piece of acting." (62) According to critic Julius Novick:

Mr. Jones' Jones was sustained from beginning to end on the grand scale: magnificent bluster, magnificent swagger, and now and then magnificent from-the-gut laughter. . . . The play is a struggle, an agon, between Jones and the jungle and the fears it breeds in him; Mr Jones reacted with conviction and power, but it was difficult to believe in what he was reacting against, and therefore difficult to become emotionally involved in his reaction. (63)

Although Novick declared himself generally receptive to such "adventurous experiment," he was forced to view "O'Neill as an old pro who knew better than the fancy-minded whippersnappers who try to improve upon him." He concluded that the script "seems to demand exactly the sort of scrim-and-drum production that the author envisioned." (64)

A 1977 Off-Off Broadway revival garnered mildly favorable reviews for both the performance by Rodney Hudson and the minimalist production. Hudson exuded "arrogant vitality" as the Emperor and was technically proficient at the growling, stammering, whining, and crying of the man surrendering to panic, (65) but both Mel Gussow and Holly Hill found him more convincing on the throne than in the jungle. (66) Again, this perception may have something to do with the halfhearted approach to expressionistic design. The island jungle was suggested with "stringy muslin webs and *papier-mache* masks on the walls" and red, blue, gold, and white lighting effects created with pinpoint accuracy. (67) Those elements were reinforced by "masked African-type rites; slow motion movements; identical acting groups on either side of the stage framing the action; chilling music that sounds like an electrified harpsichord." (68)

The historical evidence of past productions of *The Emperor Jones* testifies to the importance of remaining true to O'Neill's intentions, which clearly included a juxtaposition of naturalistic acting and expressionistic design. When John Ezell, set designer for Missouri Repertory Theatre's production of *The Emperor Jones*, researched the play's production history, he was most impressed by the approach of Donald Oenslager for the 1931 Yale University production. Those designs bespeak a rare sensitivity to the needs of the play as articulated in O'Neill's stage directions. According to Oenslager, the settings:

must seem to be the visible and tangible shapes which [Jones's] own inner deep, dark terror and fears conjure up. I have attempted to treat the background of the forest as an active participant in the play, as a changing background, to Jones a constantly living and antagonizing force, from which he tries continually to escape. . . . The forest that Jones first enters is a forest of realistic darkening shadows of immense tree trunks and branches. . . . Gradually in Jones's mind the realistic tree forms of the jungle become the imagined habitations of dark brooding spirits of ancient worship. From scene to scene these tree forms appear to become more and more the embodiment of primitive negro sculpture. . . . In the convict scene the trees are resolved into towering barriers of rudely hewn, solemn posts, set about like prison bars. In the scene of the slave market these same posts assume more expressive shapes of primitive carving. They are modeled totemistic shafts. . . . In the scene of the slave ship, the shafts of the previous scene are merged into monstrous negro fetishes, gigantic but with the squat contours of pygmies, that cradle, yet stare impassively down upon, two long rows of ebony bodies which rise up and fall away into darkness. Two spotlights from below highlight the polish of their bodies and cast their distorted rhythmic images over the background of fetishes to make an inseparable union of magic shapes and shadows. Into this animistic chaos Jones hurls his frenzied body. (69)

John Ezell's designs for the Missouri Repertory Theatre's production, which opened August 19, 1988, build upon some of the elements that worked especially well in the Yale production. Planning for the play, Ezell distinguished three stylistic levels of reality in the play. The first, scene one's throne room, was to be a shallow setting at the front of the stage, a white wall with a long red tongue of carpet projecting forward from the throne and draping down off the front of the stage like a stream of blood. Ezell thought that, as Jones once worked as a shoe-shine boy, Jones's conception of a throne might resemble an elevated shoe-shine stand. When the Emperor leaves the throne room to begin his flight through the jungle, natives will enter, look around, and torch the place. A portrait of Jones will go up in flames, as the white wall is flown out and the audience enters a second level of reality. Scene two, at the edge of the jungle, at twilight, is a transitional scene between the realism of the palace and the full-blown expressionism of the engulfing jungle. In scene two, Jones has not yet succumbed to hysteria. The Little Formless Fears merely trigger certain reflexes, which will grow into panic only after darkness descends. The Formless Fears, one for each of Jones's subsequent hallucinations, were to be played by small dancers in sacklike costumes that cover the entire body and constantly change shape. Scene eight, the final scene of the play, which occurs in full daylight, must be on the same level of absolute realism as scene one; however, it will be tied thematically to scene two, since it takes place in the spot where Jones both enters the jungle and is carried out of it as a corpse.

The third level of reality is one that exists only in Jones's mind, images of his actual past and his primordial race memory, which he projects onto the jungle that encircles him. Scenes three to seven then were to use phantasmagorical lighting effects projected onto Ezell's ingeniously conceived setting composed of hundreds of black elastic strips about three inches wide and about three inches apart, strung vertically on floor-to-pipe batten frames. Behind these rows of vertical strips, various patterns would be projected onto a sky eye. The plantation people wear unreal, masklike, white-faced makeup, and the black bodies were to be rubbed with glycerin to make them shine. For the slave-ship scene, an overhead patterned template would descend over the mound where the rows of slaves sit and remain suspended just above their head level. Scene seven was to feature voodoo idols, eighteen to twenty feet high, rolled on from the wings. The crocodile god was to be played by a dancer holding a stylized, oversize African crocodile mask, as it was thought that any attempt to depict a real crocodile might cause the audience to release their nervous tension through laughter.

The production and design concepts for Missouri Rep's *Emperor Jones* were somewhat fluid at this writing. When the show opened, it took into account the lessons of history. The acting was as naturalistic as for a play by Ibsen, and the scenery evoked expressionistically the state of mind of a strong personality going crazy with fear. This is what O'Neill wanted. The only mystery is why theatres do not follow his directions more often.

NOTES

1. Louis Sheaffer, *O'Neill: Son and Artist* (Boston: Little, Brown and Co., 1973), 81.

2. Sheaffer, 30.

3. Timo Tiusanen, *O'Neill's Scenic Images* (Princeton: Princeton University Press, 1968), 110.

4. Eugene O'Neill, "Are the Actors to Blame?" *O'Neill and His Plays: Four Decades of Criticism*, eds. Oscar Cargill, N. Bryllion Fagin, and William J. Fisher (New York: New York University Press, 1961), 113.

5. Travis Bogard, *Contour in Time: The Plays of Eugene O'Neill* (New York: Oxford University Press, 1988), 135.

6. Sheaffer, 32.

7. "Provincetown Players Stage Remarkable Play," *Brooklyn Eagle* (9 November 1920).

8. Clipping dated 24 November 1924, Lincoln Center Theatre Library, New York.

9. "Not as Others Are, But Still Worth While," *The Outlook*, 22 December 1920: 711.

10. Alexander Woollcott, *New York Times*, 28 December 1920, 9.

11. "A Pullman Porter Emperor," clipping dated 7 November

1920, Lincoln Center Theatre Library, New York.

12. Clipping dated 24 November 1924, Lincoln Center Theatre Library, New York.

13. Sheaffer, 33.

14. Alexander Woollcott, *New York Times*, 7 November 1920, 1.

15. *The Quill*, November 1920, 24.

16. Alexander Woollcott, *New York Times*, 28 December 1920, 9.

17. Clipping dated 8 November 1920, Lincoln Center Theatre Library, New York.

18. Clipping from *New York Telegram*, 23 October 1920, Lincoln Center Theatre Library, New York.

19. Heywood Broun, "*The Emperor Jones*," *New York Herald Tribune*, 4 November 1920, in Cargill, Fagin, and Fisher, 146.

20. Eugene O'Neill, *Nine Plays* (New York: Modern Library, 1954), 32.

21. Sheaffer, 37.

22. Richard Watts, Jr., *New York Herald Tribune*, 24 September 1933.

23. L. N., "Robeson in *Emperor Jones*," *New York Times*, 20 June 1939, 25.

24. Elliot Norton, "General Custer Brought Home the Bacon Again," *Boston Post*, 20 July 1941.

25. C. Hooper Trask, *New York Times*, 25 May 1930, 1.

26. Sidney B. Whipple, "Summer Theater," *New York World-Telegram*, 6 August 1940.

27. Norman Kagan, "Black Experience in the Cinema," *The Village Voice*, 24 June 1971, 69.

28. Watts, Jr.

29. Watts, Jr.

30. Watts, Jr.

31. Paul Rosenfeld, "O'Neill into Opera," *The New Republic*, 74 (22 February 1933): 48.

32. O'Neill, 14.

33. Rosenfeld, 48.

34. "*Emperor Jones* in a Raucous Operatic Triumph," *The Literary Digest* (21 January 1933), 15.

35. Arthur Mendel, "The Emperor Jones," *The Nation*, 15 March 1933, 297.

36. Stark Young, *The New Republic* 75 (24 May 1933): 47.

37. Young, 47.

38. Young, 47.

39. Rosenfeld, 47.

40. Young, 47.

41. M. A. B., *New York Times*, 18 November 1932, 2.

42. "*Emperor Jones* in Paris," *Literary Digest* 79 (29 December 1923): 24.

43. "Eugene O'Neill in Paris."

44. M. A. B., 2.

45. M. A. B., 2.

46. Horst Frenz, "Eugene O'Neill in France," *Books Abroad* 18 (1944): 140.

47. "Eugene O'Neill in Paris."

48. Scrapbook, Lincoln Center Theatre Collection, New York City.

49. Cover photograph, *Players Magazine*, February 1956.

50. Mosk., "*Emperor Jones*, Paris, March 5," *Variety*, 22 March 1950.

51. Mosk.

52. Mosk.

53. Frank Dorsey, "Paris Does *Emperor Jones* with African Voodoo Troupe," *New York Herald Tribune*, 5 March 1950, 3.

54. "*Emperor Jones* in Berlin," *New York Times*, 10 January 1924, 18.

55. "The Puzzling *Emperor Jones*," unidentified clipping dated 19 May 1926, Lincoln Center Theatre Collection, New York City. See also "'Emperor Jones' Puzzles Vienna," *New York Times*, 18 May 1926, 28.

56. J. J. Hayes, "An Irish *Emperor Jones*," *New York Times*, 13 February 1927, 4.

57. Gwendolyn Bennett, "The Emperor Jones," *Opportunity*, September 1930, 271.

58. Lewis Nichols, "The Play," *New York Times*, 17 January 1945, 18.

59. Julius Novick, "Theatre Afield: Jones as Jones," *The Village Voice*, 20 August 1964, 10.

60. Allen Hughes, "Theater: Boston Festival," *New York Times*, 6 August 1964, 20.

61. Allan Hughes, "Dancers Are Scenery in *Emperor Jones*," *New York Times*, 18 August 1964, 5.

62. Godfrey John, "*Emperor Jones*--new depths sounded," *Christian Science Monitor*, 11 August 1964.

63. Novick, 10.

64. Novick, 10.

65. Holly Hill, "*The Emperor Jones*," *New York Theatre Review*, December 1977, 40.

66. Mel Gussow, "Classics Today, Visions Tomorrow," *New York*

Times, 23 September 1977, C-5.

67. Hill, 40.

68. Mel Gordon, "Eugene O'Neill's Jungle Movie Tragedy," *Villager*, 22 September 1977.

69. Donald Oenslager, *Scenery Then and Now* (New York: W.W. Norton, 1936), 252-54.

21

The Emperor Jones as a Source of Theatrical Experimentation, 1920s-1980s

Lowell Swortzell

The play was not yet twenty-four hours old before someone began experimenting with it. Heywood Broun's enthusiastic review appeared in the *New York Tribune* on November 4, 1920, saluting the work as "so unusual in its technique that it might wait in vain for a production anywhere except in so adventurous a playhouse as the Provincetown Theatre." (1) For all his praise for the play and its author, he added this note: "We cannot understand just why he [O'Neill] has allowed the Emperor to die to the sound of off-stage shots. It is our idea that he should come crawling to the very spot where he meets his death and that the natives should be molding silver bullets there and waiting without so much as stretching out a finger for him." (2) Indeed, this new ending is worth considering, for Broun is not alone in thinking that Jones' offstage death diminishes the tragic heights to which the play is headed. But before he further rewrote the play, the critic checked himself: "Of course, all this goes to show that *The Emperor Jones* is truly a fine play. It is only such which tempts the spectator to leap in himself as a collaborator." (3)

And leap they have, from the 1920s through the 1980s, making *Jones* O'Neill's most adapted play and a major source of inspiration for experimentation among other writers, directors, designers, composers, and choreographers. Here we will examine some of the major and more unusual manifestations the play has been given by these eager collaborators.

We have long known the original production was an experiment itself, as had been O'Neill's earlier one-act plays. *The Moon of the Caribbees* played on the psychology of the audience to reinforce a sense of isolation and loneliness through native songs that drifted out over the waters. *Bound East for Cardiff* further underscored these feelings through a foghorn moaning its dirge for the dying Yank. *Where the Cross Is Made*, more experimental still, had endeavored to make the audience question its sanity with the appearance of three sailor-ghosts who were seen only by the hallucinating hero and the playgoers. Now with *Jones*, O'Neill wanted to discover how much experimentation the ticket-buyers could take, and from the earliest moments of Jones' self-doubt, he called forth a parade of apparitions and the ceaseless sound of a tom-tom that compelled the spectator to actively enter into the psyche of the Emperor and accompany him to his regressive destiny. "There was an idea and an experiment," O'Neill said, speaking of the drum, beginning as a pulse beat and slowly becoming intensified, "until the heart-beat of every one present corresponds to the frenzied beat of the drum." (4)

In directing the production, Jig Cook experimented with his famous dome, which was covered in white plaster so that when lighted it gave illusions of depth and spectacle new not only to the Provincetown stage but also to the American theatre in general. Likewise, the casting of a black actor in the title role was an innovative risk for a small, company but one that paid off at once as serious theatregoers eagerly paid to see Charles S. Gilpin give what was hailed as an outstanding performance. When the play transferred to Broadway, it was supported for an initial run of 204 performances, which fostered revivals throughout the 1920s and two years on the road.

THE EMPEROR JONES AS OPERA

In 1933, when the play reemerged as an opera at the Metropolitan Opera House, it starred a favorite white baritone of the time, Lawrence Tibbet, in utterly unconvincing blackface and wig. His performance, however, overcame his minstrel-show appearance; Olin Downes in the *New York Times* insisted, "his impersonation . . . in all its details, is a proud possession of the American stage." (5) But the opera itself, as it turned out, was not long to be a "proud possession" of the musical stage, lasting only eleven performances in New York and being seen only briefly in Los Angeles and San Francisco. Louis Gruenberg, the composer, had seized on the musical ideas inherent in the play, particularly the persistent beating of the drum, and remained faithful to O'Neill's text. Where he proved most original was in his use of the enormous chorus, which appears in photographs to number more than a hundred strong; composed of both dancers and singers, it served several functions, as protagonist, commentator, native population, and the victims of Jones' brutality. At first, the singers were heard from offstage, their voices protesting Jones' oppressive treatment; but as the action developed, they gradually became visible first in small groups and later as a powerful mass.

Jones and Smithers often were given accompanied recitative, which the critics found awkward but no more so than the spoken dialogue sprinkled throughout the opera. In general, the music, according to the critic of the *New York Herald Tribune*, "is skillful, discreet, ingeniously adapted to the action and the discourse, sympathetically reflective of mood and of emotional growth." But, he thought, it did not heighten or intensify the play but often appeared intrusive and superfluous. (6)

Besides Tibbet's effectiveness, the scenery most pleased critics and audiences. The general manager of the Metropolitan, who had engaged Broadway designer Jo Mielziner, was at first shocked by his drawings, stating that neither he nor any member of his staff "had ever in their lives seen leaves of the size and shape you have shown in your jungle designs." (7) Even so, they told him to continue with the settings, which indeed revealed a stylized forest of skyscraping tree trunks, vines, and massive leaves that completely swamped the huge stage. Peering through them were faces, sometimes full, sometimes only the eyes, that evoked what Mielziner called "Jungle Terror." For the Voodoo Dance, an enormous mask looked down from the rear while the trees turned into extended shapes resembling elongated carved African figures, actual examples of which the designer had studied for this production. "If one wanted to pay a just tribute to the genuinely creative contribution of Mr. Mielziner," a critic wrote, "one might describe the work revealed to us yesterday as *The Emperor Jones*, a play by Eugene O'Neill, set to scenery by Jo Mielziner." (8)

O'Neill had approved the operatic treatment, which changed the ending to show the Emperor's death on stage. But one critic noted that the author, "that lonely and inimitable genius was nowhere to be seen." (9) There is no indication that he ever saw the opera.

THE EMPEROR JONES AS A FILM

United Artists released the motion picture version in 1933, directed by Dudley Murphy with a screenplay by Du Bose Heyward, whose play *Porgy* had made a favorable impression on Broadway in 1927. But with the exception of Paul Robeson, who recreated his stage performance and for whom the film essentially seems to have been made, no one apparently cared much about the material. The result is a primitive product filled with typical Hollywood anachronisms and paradoxes. When Jones arrives on the tropical island, we see natives wearing sombreros while Smithers appears in an African safari helmet and the then-current dictator wears a formal silk tophat a la Fred Astaire. Later, Jones sports a broad-brimmed Panama hat, but this is soon discarded for a safari helmet to show that he has attained equal status with Smithers. Once Jones declares himself Emperor, his palace attendants wear busbies, those tall fur hats designed for the guards outside Buckingham Palace. The universality of the story clearly has been defined in its millinery. Although the slave-auction and all references to it have been eliminated, presumably to avoid offending audiences, a reception scene has been added at which the Duke and Duchess of Manhattan and Lord and Lady Baltimore are presented as vulgarly dressed, ostentatious minstrel-show characters.

It is more than twenty-five minutes into the film before O'Neill's play begins. In the meantime, we see a series of short scenes in rapid succession tracing Jones's life up to his assumption of power over the tropical island. He tries on his Pullman-car uniform and then goes to the Baptist church to bid farewell to his friends. Singing "Now Let Me Fly," he is called by a train whistle and leaves for the city, where he quickly forgets his sweetheart back home and becomes involved with his co-worker Jeff's girlfriend. After singing "Little Gal," he enters into business deals, takes up gambling, and quickly kills Jeff in a fight. Working as a member of a chain gang, he sings "Water Boy" before killing a guard and then fleeing the country to an island where, we are told, "Ain't nothing there but trouble."

Most of the play's first scene remains intact and is performed reasonably well by Robeson and Dudley Diggs. But once they escape into the forest, Jones, O'Neill, and the play are soon lost. Earlier Smithers has said the jungle gives him the "creeps," but the viewer doesn't share this response when beholding a Hollywood-manufactured studio set, not even as believable as a low-budget "Tarzan" film. Worse yet are the transparent visions Jones sees, which appear as double exposures without any sense of immediacy or danger. They do not carry Jones back to a primal state but simply review moments already seen in the long preamble. The Witch Doctor can be mistaken for a large spider, and the crocodile looks as if it had been borrowed from a production of *Peter Pan*. And when the church scene is reenacted behind a scrim, Robeson is allowed to sing one more spiritual, "Didn't My Lord Deliver Daniel?" After being shot on screen by a silver bullet, he stumbles about, finally falling dead at Smither's feet. The crudeness of the movie makes it laughable, of interest only for the presence of Paul Robeson who, in spite of his imposing size, great voice, and emotional gifts, still cannot make the role his own. It is largely a vehicle for a number of his favorite songs. However, when Robeson played the role on the stage in the United States and in London and, as late as 1939, in summer stock, he created a memorable Brutus Jones that Hollywood proved unable to duplicate.

THE EMPEROR JONES AS MARIONETTE THEATRE

Perhaps the most unusual adaptations were the marionette versions that played in New York and California. Jerome Magon had been designing scenery at Provincetown when he saw Fannie Goldsmith Engle's *The Chinese Nightingale* and immediately entered the field of puppetry: "When I later decided to produce my own show, I was irresistibly drawn to Eugene O'Neill, whose plays have always held a strange fascination for me." (10) He had directed a production of *Jones* with live actors and believed, "The play was still in my bones, and I felt that its eerie, unearthly theatricality would make it an ideal vehicle for marionettes." (11) He used a revolving stage in an expressionistic production that opened at the New School for Social Research in the late 1930s. Performances went well except for the defective gun: "at every climax, when poor Brutus Jones raised his revolver to shoot at some new apparition in the forest, all of us took a deep breath and prayed inwardly." (12) The successful production elicited praise from the author, who sent Magon an inscribed copy of the play.

On the West Coast, another version had been playing since 1928. Ralph Chesse, its creator, considered *Jones* "a perfect play for marionettes." (13) When in 1937 he became the local director of the Marionette Project of the Federal Theatre Project, he obtained performance rights from O'Neill to produce the play royalty free. His production followed the text closely, striving for "stark and vivid terror." (14) Eight settings were required, and to ensure the effectiveness of the gun he placed a black-shrouded stagehand among the trees on stage so that the shots would emanate directly from the marionette Emperor. All figures were hand carved and decorated: the Witch Doctor carried a bone in one hand and a wooden rattle in the other; the Crocodile God had shining eyes and teeth that sparkled fiercely. When Hallie Flanagan visited O'Neill to report on the Federal Theatre Project's cycle of his plays, he expressed particular interest in this production. (15)

These versions were intended for adult audiences and,

surprisingly enough in a country that traditionally considers marionette shows the province of children, both were popular. Chesse included *Jones* in his repertory for more than forty years, along with his productions of *Hamlet* and *Macbeth*.

THE EMPEROR JONES AS MODERN DANCE

Jose Limon, the great Mexican-born dancer and choreographer, moved to the United States with his family when he was eight years old. Following the examples of his parents, he pursued music and played several instruments. But as his education advanced, he became more interested in painting, which eventually led him to New York City, where he saw his first dance concert and at once decided to become a dancer. He auditioned for two major figures in the modern dance movement, Doris Humphry and Charles Weidman, who jointly operated a school to which he was immediately admitted. He soon joined their company, with which he danced professionally for the next ten years. After World War II, he formed his own company, which continues today even though Limon died in 1972. His most famous work, *The Moor's Pavane* (1949), based on Shakespeare's tragedy of *Othello*, demonstrated his gifts for adapting and distilling the essence of a dramatic masterpiece to the requirements of modern dance. Setting it to music by Heitor Villa-Lobos, he choreographed his version of O'Neill's play; it was first performed on July 12, 1956, and quickly took its place as a major work in Limon's repertory.

The dance may be viewed in the Dance Collection of the Lincoln Center Library of the Performing Arts in several film versions, performed by Limon and others. The stage is bare except for the large throne that dominates the action; this is a wide, low-seated abstract form, consisting of four legs that resemble those of a kneeling deer. The high back is shaped as four extending arms, each ending in an opened hand of claw-like fingers. The seat is much too large for one person and envelopes Jones so that at times he seems to live within it, dancing on, around, and over it. Here the throne has become the entire palace of the play.

At the opening, Jones sits, distraught that the natives he once led in rebellion are now turning upon him. His stylized uniform proclaims his self-image: a jacket molded in the shape of a proud puffed-out chest, covered in gothic designs of heavy metallic braid, with exaggerated shoulders adorned with gleaming gold epaulets and a high freestanding collar. Huge cuffs, fringed boots, and a Napoleonic hat with plumes covering the top and trailing from the back suggest a circus lion-tamer more than a rebellious leader. Yet, as O'Neill demands, "there is something not altogether ridiculous about his grandeur. He has a way of carrying it off." (16)

Six men materialize out of darkness and dance Jones's disturbed thoughts until he asserts himself and drives them off to perform a solo section proclaiming that he is still the Emperor. He is angered when the White Man, the second leading role and Limon's major change from the original, hangs his Panama hat on the throne. Insulted, Jones hurls the hat to the ground and flourishes a glistening oversized pistol. Undeterred, the White Man begins to tilt the throne, rocking and turning it, to suggest its imminent collapse. Jones recognizes the warning and flees into the forest.

Now the chase begins as the frightened Emperor moves around three trees (made from large curved shields carried by the dancers, who in the semidarkness menacingly project an arm or a leg as Jones passes). Following the original text, a series of scenes unfolds, reflecting Jones's past. The same six male dancers play the roles of slaves, members of the chain gang, and the Demons, as Limon named them. On each appearance, Jones is more tattered and finally is seen bare-chested as he is driven by the frightful figures of his past. In panic, he kills a man he meets and is further tormented by the shadows closing in upon him. Soon a creature of many legs and arms appears, followed by the White Man, now ensconced upon the throne. At the end, the slaves bear the dead body of Jones, throwing it about with disdain, finally leaving it crumpled on the throne. Over the near-naked corpse, they haphazardly discard the jacket and the hat, which gleam resplendently and ironically in the fading light.

One critic said Limon "gave a magnificent performance" as "the swaggering, self-made Negro emperor, faced by the revolt of his subjects ... [and] Lucas Hoving, as the symbol of the power of the white man, created an effectively sinister characterization." (17) Without drum beats, Limon still projected the psychological destruction of a demigod in a dance that lasted just over twenty minutes. With his high cheekbones and the angular features of the Mexican Indian, Limon proved that Jones need not be portrayed as a black man.

THE EMPEROR JONES AS A COMMERCIAL RECORDING

In 1971, Caedmon issued an album of two long-playing records with James Earl Jones as Brutus Jones. Jones had recently triumphed on Broadway in *The Great White Hope* and, as the preeminent black actor of the day, undoubtedly appeared to be the ideal choice for the

Emperor. But, as he makes clear in a discussion that follows the performance and often seems to apologize for it, he was reluctant to take the role. The recording includes a rehearsal for the album as part of the final version, which suggests that Caedmon may have had doubts about the project; it is also possible that the star required that his strong feelings about the racist tone of the play be made known to the public. This was recorded at a time when America was undergoing social changes that had resulted from the protests of the 1960s and was still suffering from the loss of Dr. Martin Luther King, Jr., whose assassination had taken place only three years earlier.

The "rehearsal" turns out to be a discussion between Jones and director Theodore Mann of the Circle-in-the-Square Theatre, the Off-Broadway company associated with O'Neill revivals since its landmark production of *The Iceman Cometh* in 1956. Mann tells the listener that they discovered early in rehearsals that what appears to be a simple play is in fact a deceptively complicated work that is very significant "for a black man in today's society." (18) He invites listeners to join in "the creative process we all participated in to make this recording." Then Jones is heard reading O'Neill's first description of the Emperor: "He is a tall, powerfully-built, full-blooded negro of middle age. His features are typically negroid, yet there is something decidedly distinctive about his face--an underlying strength of will, a hardy self-reliant confidence in himself that inspires respect." The word "yet" disturbs the actor and compels the next twenty minutes of analysis. To Jones, the word represents "that insidious prejudice that all white men had, and most still do, about black people." He accuses O'Neill of using "Niggerisms" to make the play palatable to white audiences of the 1920s and speaks of the Emperor's "full-out character" that borders on caricature, the black man as a "fun image."

When Mann reminds him that audiences don't see stage directions, Jones replies that, even so, "I can't ignore those facts, as great as O'Neill was." The play offends middle-class blacks, according to the actor, because they perceive the character as, what he terms, "a 'dis' and 'dat' Nigger" in manner and style although he acknowledges that young blacks would be more apt to see the play as a "study of power" and accept it. Without resolving his dilemma but still not forgetting it ("Why didn't he choose another word?" "And" instead of "Yet" would make all the difference, he later suggests), the actor and director discuss O'Neill's belief that materialism will be the destruction of the American people just as it is of Jones in the play. "Brutus Jones is carrying white society on his back," says Mann, who sees the Emperor as the victim of a culture in which "God is the dollar" and the desire for possession is "dedication to something that doesn't mean a god-damned thing." Jones, the actor, agrees that "the god of capitalism is misleading us."

The era in which this recording was made demanded a lengthy explanation of the play in order to safeguard reputations, especially because, when one listens to the performance, one discovers that Jones, in covering the wide emotional and vocal range of the character, makes the most of what he terms "Niggerisms" at every chance. His interpretation is unabashedly and unapologetically that of "a 'dis' and 'dat' Nigger" and, ironically enough, in so doing he makes the character powerfully human and sympathetic and never a stereotype. He creates a sense of panic the listener shares as that great stentorian voice turns into a truly tragic whimpering cry: "Oh, Lawd! Mercy! Mercy on dis po' sinner."

The recording, which is still available, also demonstrates that the text, when shorn of all its theatrical accouterments save sound, is able to stand by itself without African Witch Doctor, crocodile, and little Formless Fears. When the actor sees them, as happens here, we all see them.

OTHER PRODUCTIONS OF INTEREST

A complete performance history would give attention to many more productions than can be mentioned here. Certainly, the one at the Yale Drama School in 1931 would interest students of O'Neill for it was directed by his former teacher, the great traditionalist George Pierce Baker, and designed by Donald Oenslager, one of Broadway's foremost scene designers. It was the second half of a double bill that also included *Bound East for Cardiff*, directed by Alexander Dean.

Just as *Porgy and Bess*, which for similar charges of racism had not been seen in a major production since the 1950s, began to reemerge in the 1970s, so did *Jones*, specifically at the Perry Street Theatre, an Off-Broadway playhouse in Greenwich Village only a few blocks from where it was first produced. One critic claimed "the play itself is neither dated nor timely" and suggested theatregoers in 1977 should still find it worth seeing. Mel Gussow commented, "One would have expected that, in revival, *The Emperor Jones* would seem dated, but in this swift, understated production, counterpointed by our own memories of recent politics (would Idi Amin permit a staging in Uganda?), the play takes on a renewed relevance." (19)

In 1984 a musical version was presented by the Pepsico Summerfare, the International Performing Arts Festival of the State University of New York at Purchase, starring stage, film, and television star Cleavon Little. An artistic disaster, the production made no attempt to integrate music and drama, with the consequence that the dances (there were no songs as such) merely interrupted O'Neill's text. One could identify with the original audiences at the Provincetown who complained of waiting several minutes during scene changes, for here the drama halted each time the dancers performed and then awkwardly started again. However flawed the production, it, and not the text, suffered the brunt of critical damnation.

Today [1988], the temptation to collaborate remains as great as ever. How timely it would be if the play were translated into Spanish and set in Central America with a pocked-faced Emperor who remains in power no matter how many forces try to remove him. Only psychological fears, extending from his drug-dealing past to his Spanish and Indian heritage, can force him to flee into the arms of a Witch Doctor who, rising out of the Panama Canal, is not only red as O'Neill required, but also white and blue and looks like Uncle Sam.

O'Neill himself was unable to resist experimentation with his own play. Writing twelve years after the original production, he expressed new ideas: "All the figures in Jones's flight through the forest should be masked. Masks would dramatically stress their phantasmal quality, as contrasted with the unmasked Jones, intensify the supernatural menace of the tom-tom, give the play a more complete and vivid expression." (20)

The past decades, in spite of vastly changing tastes and social reforms, in spite of experimentations that failed and because of the many that succeeded, prove that collaborators are ever ready to reassess and reexpress O'Neill's still challenging theatrical myth. I am certain we will discover this to be true yet again when we see the Chinese production tonight. (21)

NOTES

1. Oscar Cargill, N. Bryllion, and William J. Fisher, eds., *O'Neill and His Plays: Four Decades of Criticism* (New York: New York University Press, 1961), 146.

2. Cargill, 146.

3. Cargill, 146.

4. Arthur and Barbara Gelb, *O'Neill* (New York: Harper and Row, 1962), 438.

5. Olin Downes, "*Emperor Jones* in West," *New York Times*, 5 November 1933.

6. Cargill, 199.

7. Jo Mielziner, *Designing for the Theatre* (New York: Bramhall House, 1965), 77.

8. Cargill, 199.

9. Cargill, 199.

10. Paul McPharlin, *Puppetry: An International Yearbook of Puppetry and Marionettes, 1939* (Detroit: Puppetry Imprints, 1939), 19.

11. McPharlin, 19.

12. McPharlin, 19.

13. Ted Salter, "Caricature: Ralph Chesse," *Puppetry Journal* 32, 6 (May-June 1981): 23.

14. Leslie White, "Eugene O'Neill and the Federal Theatre Project," diss., New York University, 1986, 197.

15. White, 204.

16. Eugene O'Neill, *The Emperor Jones*, in *Nine Plays* (New York: Modern Library, 1921), 6.

17. Mel Gordon, "Eugene O'Neill's Jungle Movie Tragedy," *Villager*, 29 September 1977, 135.

18. Eugene O'Neill, *The Emperor Jones*, with James Earl Jones as the Emperor, dir. Theodore Mann, Caedmon, TRS 341 (two records), New York, 1971.

19. Mel Gussow, "Classics Today, Visions Tomorrow," *New York Times*, 23 September 1977.

20. Cargill, 119.

21. For a description of this production, see my Introduction to this book.

22

The Iceman Cometh Twice:
A Comparison of the 1946 and
1956 New York Productions

Daniel J. Watermeier

The Iceman Cometh was the last play of Eugene O'Neill's to be produced in New York during his lifetime. Presented by the Theatre Guild, it opened on Broadway at the Martin Beck Theatre on October 9, 1946. It was the first O'Neill play to have been presented on the New York stage for twelve years, and undoubtedly its arrival had been eagerly anticipated by both critics and audiences. Generally, however, despite the reputation of the Theatre Guild, the experience of director Eddie Dowling and designer Robert Edmond Jones, and a talented cast, the production was not particularly well received.

Ten years passed before an O'Neill play would be staged again in New York; it was a revival of *The Iceman Cometh*. Mounted on Off-Broadway by the Circle-in-the-Square theatre company, this 1956 production is generally considered a landmark in the stage history of O'Neill's plays since World War II. Not only was the production a critical and popular success, but also it propelled director Jose Quintero and actor Jason Robards into successful careers as O'Neill interpreters and stimulated an immediate revival of interest in O'Neill's work, particularly in his late plays.

Why was the 1946 production a relative failure, while the 1956 revival was a success? The answer to this question provides a case study of the complex interrelationships among a play, its production, the theatrical and cultural tendencies of the time, and its critical and popular reception.

For patriotic and personal reasons, O'Neill would not allow any of his new plays to be produced during the war years. However, in the summer of 1944, O'Neill and Lawrence Langner, the Theatre Guild's co-producer, reportedly began discussing the possibility of staging *The Iceman Cometh* "a year or so after the peace." O'Neill felt that if the play were produced immediately after the war its "pessimism . . . would run counter to public optimism and would result in a bad reception by the audience," but thought that "a year or so after the peace, there would be considerable disillusionment, and that the public would then be more inclined to listen to what he had to say in his play." (1)

Despite these reservations, by the early months of 1946, less than a year after the German and Japanese surrendered, on May 7 and August 14, 1945, respectively, the Guild was already preparing a production of *The Iceman Cometh* for a fall opening.

One can only guess why O'Neill went against what would prove to be his better instincts in agreeing to this premature production of *The Iceman Cometh*. His renewed contact with the theatre after moving back to New York from California in the fall of 1945 may have motivated a change of mind. Langner may also have pressured him for an early production to revitalize the Theatre Guild, whose reputation had been waning for a number of years. Indeed, for this very reason, as Louis Sheaffer reports, Carlotta had urged caution on O'Neill in renewing his association with the Guild. (2)

With O'Neill's generally enthusiastic support, the Guild selected Dowling to direct and also to play Hickey. (Later the impracticality of this plan was realized, and James Barton was cast as Hickey.) Jones was commissioned to design the set. O'Neill undoubtedly would have preferred director Phillip Moeller, who had staged his earlier Guild productions, most notably *Strange Interlude* and *Mourning Becomes Electra*, but Moeller, following a dispute with board members, had resigned from the Guild in 1941.

Sheaffer writes that "few plays in the Guild's history were cast with as much care." It took almost a year to cast all the roles, with O'Neill having considerable authority in the final selection. The rehearsal process, however, seems to have been fraught with difficulties and tensions. O'Neill reportedly attended afternoon rehearsals, but his presence was not always welcomed by Dowling. At first Dowling tried to enliven the leisurely drama with some appropriate stage movement and pieces of "business," but every afternoon the playwright eliminated what the director had introduced in the morning. O'Neill wanted no inessential action that might distract, even momentarily, from his words. After being told by the Guild management to follow the text scrupulously--no stage business unless specified in the script--Dowling, according to cast members, was "cowed . . . like a whipped child . . . afraid to suggest anything." Dowling himself confided to stage manager Karl Nielsen: "I dread their (the O'Neills) coming in the afternoon." For his part, O'Neill was never satisfied with Dowling's direction. Actors later recalled that the rehearsals were "solemn and heavy" or "a real ordeal." (3)

O'Neill had opposed a pre-Broadway tryout period, but Actor's Equity had granted an extra, fifth week to rehearse the play. Even with this extra rehearsal week and the protracted prerehearsal planning, the final rehearsal ended at 3:00 P.M. on October 9, only an hour and a half before the opening curtain. Clearly the production was barely ready to open.

Sensing that the critics might be disturbed by the unusual length of *The Iceman Cometh*, the Theatre Guild had sent them copies of the play in advance of opening night. Perhaps familiarity with the text would mitigate the length of the performance or at least encourage increased critical attentiveness to the play despite its length. The Theatre Guild also invited the critics to a pre-curtain dinner; so, as Robert Garland of the *Journal American* (October 10, 1946) wrote, the critics "could assess, well-fed and all unhurried, the merits or demerits of *The Iceman Cometh*." The curtain arose at 4:30 P.M. and the performance ran until 10:00 P.M., with a dinner interval from 6:00 to 7:00 P.M. (Subsequently performances began at 5:30 P.M. and ran until about 11:00 P.M.)

Contrary to Langner's assertion that the critics "gave the play the greatest acclaim" and despite the rather unusual steps on the part of a producing organization to influence critical reaction, most of the critics were not especially enthusiastic about either the play or its production. Garland, for example, pronounced it "neither good Broadway, good Theatre Guild nor good Eugene O'Neill." Most critics complained principally about the length of the play, its somber, depressing content, Dowling's competent but stilted, uninspired direction, and James Barton's unimpressive performance as Hickey. Louis Kronenberger of *PM* (October 11, 1946), for example, confessed disappointment complaining about "its great length, its often static tone, [and] its often repetitious incident." He thought that "philosophically" the play was "more long windedly explicit" than "in any way profound."

Ward Morehouse of *The Sun* (October 10, 1946) described the play as "stark," "disturbing," "powerful," and "intense," but also "too slow" and "too long winded." In a similar vein Howard Barnes of the *Herald Tribune* (October 10, 1946) thought the play had "a savage undertone and moments of bleak and tragic majesty," but that it remained "essentially earthbound and monotonous" and dramatically confused. In an unusually long and acerbic essay in *Time* magazine (October 21, 1946) the play was described as "a thick (though much too fatty) slice of life--a somber, sardonic, year long comic strip with a comic strip's microscopic variations." The anonymous *Time* critic complained that "O'Neill's bums" were "flat" and that "they never grew more complex, they only grew incredibly familiar, like chickens seen turning over and over on a spit." The play was "static" and "enormously protracted," and its philosophy was "scarcely deeper than a puddle."

Even those critics who were most receptive to the play, like Brooks Atkinson of the *New York Times* (October 10, 1946), and Richard Watts, Jr., of the *Post* (October 10, 1946), still noted its "garrulousness." Moreover, some of Atkinson's descriptive passages, although accurate and well-intentioned, probably did little to promote ticket sales. For example, at one point in his review he referred to the barroom setting as "a gloomy charnel-house"; and at another, he described the play as moving "across the stage as methodically and resolutely as a heavy battle attack overrunning strategic points with a kind of lumbering precision."

The critics universally admired Jones's setting, which Stark Young of the *New Republic* (October 21, 1946) praised as "austere, elegant and elusively poetic, and uncannily right for the realistic poetic quality of the play." They also generally admired the acting, particularly veteran actor Dudley Digges' rendition of Harry Hope, which was variously described as "magnificent," "expert," and "fine." Indeed, the cast was comprised of a number of experienced and talented performers. Garland called them "gifted," and Young wrote that it was "a relief to see so many expert actors instead of the usual run of technically indifferent players we so often get on Broadway nowadays."

The critics, however, were not entirely impressed by James Barton in the pivotal role of Hickey. Kronenberger, for example, "damning with faint praise," described Barton's performance as "competent." Barnes wrote that he played "the final stanzas with less knowledge than rather bewildered intensity." Indeed, Barton, during Hickey's important but lengthy last-act monologue, "went-up" so badly that he had to ask the prompter for assistance. According to Ward Morehouse of *The Sun* (October 10, 1946), "the audience shuddered"; but when he "recovered bravely," they gave him an ovation. But the mood of the scene was clearly damaged. Several critics pointed that they would have preferred to see director Dowling in the role. (Dowling had in the previous season given an inspired, impressive performance as Tom in *The Glass Menagerie*, which he also directed.) Watts, for example, wrote that Dowling "would have been far more touching and impressive in the role" than Barton. While Morehouse called Dowling "the ideal actor" for Hickey, Young believed that Barton played Hickey "as Dowling would have played it" but was ultimately dissatisfied with the performance. He thought that Russell Collins who played James Cameron would have given the role more of what it needed--"much more inner concentration, depth, projection, and unbroken emotional fluency."

Dowling's direction, like his imagined performance as Hickey, was generally found to be "sympathetic," "understanding," and workmanlike, but on the whole uninspired. Perhaps Young was most perceptive about the flaw in Dowling's direction. He wrote that Dowling's method "consists largely in a certain smooth security, an effect of competence, of keeping things professional and steady, and often doing pretty much nothing at all." There was, he noted, "a considerable degree of stylized performance, actors sitting motionless while another character or other groups take the stage." While such an approach might be justified by the "stylized structure" of the play, Young thought that the play would have gained by direction characterized by "more pressure, more intensity and a far darker and richer texture."

Despite such reviews and the length of the performance (about three and one-half hours), the O'Neill mystique was apparently strong enough to attract audiences, although how large they were is not known. Reportedly, about 10 percent of the audiences tended not to return after the dinner interval. Langner tried but failed to persuade O'Neill to significantly cut the play, although, as Vena has documented, some textual modifications were affected in rehearsals, including line deletions. About two months into the run the dinner interval was eliminated, with the performance beginning at 7:30 P.M. and ending at 11:20 P.M. with about "fifteen minutes cut from the original time by quickening the pace." While this new schedule pleased O'Neill, it did not please Langner, who felt "it put too severe a strain on the audience." (4)

The play continued to play for six performances a week (two less than normal) for almost a half year, closing on March 15, 1947--a total of 136 performances. It was not a notable run, but it was respectable, particularly considering the competition during the 1946-47 season. For example, the night before *Iceman* opened, Jose Ferrer opened in a subsequently acclaimed performance as *Cyrano de Bergerac* that ran for 195 performances. Although they had opened in earlier seasons, *Oklahoma!, Life with Father, Harvey, Born Yesterday, O Mistress Mine* starring the Lunts, *Annie Get Your Gun*, and *State of the Union*, all now considered "classics" of the American stage, were still running. During its run *Iceman* also faced stiff competition from a visually splendid production of Oscar Wilde's *Lady Windermere's Fan* (227 performances), Noel Coward's *Present Laughter* (158 performances), Maxwell Anderson's *Joan of Lorraine* with Ingrid Bergman (198 performances), Lillian Hellman's *Another Part of the Forest* (182 performances), Ruth Gordon's *Years Ago* with Frederic March and Florence Eldridge (199 performances), and Arthur Miller's *All My Sons*, which played through the next season--to name just a few of the over eighty new plays and revivals opening on Broadway in 1946-47.

Judging, moreover, from the productions mounted during the 1945-46 and 1946-47 seasons, light comedies, musicals, romantic historical dramas, and melodramas, especially those featuring "stars" and lavish scenery and costumes, were overwhelmingly the staple fare of Broadway. A somber almost four-hour drama, set in a seedy Bowery saloon, featuring an assortment of desperate drunks, regardless of its inherent dramatic value, hardly reflected the interests or temperament of immediate postwar America. The disillusionment that O'Neill so presciently predicted had not yet set in. Despite labor unrest, an uneasy peace with strained relationships between the Soviet Union and the United States and political instability in other parts of the world, and the clear and present danger of nuclear holocaust, Americans were still caught up in an end-of-the-war euphoria. That *Iceman* played for as long as it did, may say more about general interest in or curiosity about O'Neill, the legendary playwright, or about Langner's commitment as a producer--for surely his financial profits must have been relatively small, if there was any profit at all--than about interest in the play or about American theatrical tastes at the time. (5)

Regardless of the length of the run and Langner's support, O'Neill was clearly dissatisfied with the production of *Iceman*. Following an abortive effort to mount *A Moon for the Misbegotten* in 1947, he refused permission to stage any of his unproduced plays. By the time of his death in 1953, his plays had been virtually forgotten by the "living" theatre.

THE 1956 REVIVAL

In 1956, director Jose Quintero and producer Ted Mann succeeded in getting permission from Carlotta Monterey O'Neill to produce *The Iceman Cometh* for their Circle-in-the-Square Theatre. (6)

In contrast to the 1946 production, this production was staged not in a large Broadway theatre (the Martin Beck had a 1200-seat capacity) with a traditional proscenium stage, but in small, 177-seat theatre with a narrow thrust stage surrounded by audience on three sides. Brooks Atkinson in the *New York Times* (May 9, 1956) described designer David Hayes's set as "a few tables and chairs, a squalid bar, a flimsy door leading into the street, a handful of fly blown chandeliers and a few ranks of benches for the audience." Indeed, despite the compelling poetic realism of Robert Edmond Jones's setting for the 1946 production, the audience, by nature of the auditorium-stage relationship of the Martin Beck theatre, remained separated, even distanced, from the action. The configuration of the Circle-in-the-Square, however, and Hayes's design, as Atkinson indicated, created a sense of intimacy between actors, action, and audience. This intimacy contributed significantly to audience and critical response to the play. An actor in the company, Addison Powell, thought the "space was fifty percent of the success of that production." (7)

Unlike the protracted production schedule of the Theatre Guild *Iceman*, Quintero operated very quickly. As he has written, he cast all of the characters, except for the pivotal role of Hickey, in four weeks of interviewing about four hundred actors and actresses. (In fact, he probably cast the play in less than four weeks, and even the number of performers interviewed is suspect.) Many of the cast, much to the astonishment of several, were cast solely on the basis of their interview, without an audition. In some cases Quintero knew them, but in some instances he seems to have cast mainly on the basis of physical appearance and his own intuition.

Although the various accounts of how Robards was cast as Hickey are somewhat different, he did audition for the role, probably reading Hickey's last-act monologue for Quintero. The director later would describe the cast as "oddly assorted and most unorthodox . . . ranging from highly trained and experienced actors to ones who were beginning their careers at the age of fifty. Some had never been in a play before."

The production was rehearsed over a four-week period in the theatre, as there was no separate rehearsal space. Both Quintero and the cast seemed to have adapted naturally to the thrust configuration. Addison Powell remembered "the staging seemed to flow . . . everything kind of grew organically." (8) Quintero with limited rehearsal time for this long, complex play, seems to have trusted his casting and his "environmental" setting. He kept a loose rein over the rehearsals, encouraging or inspiring the performers, rarely explaining or "intellectualizing," but allowing the play and the cast to develop on their own. Unlike Eddie Dowling, however, Quintero was clearly in authority as director.

The critical reaction to the production, to Hayes's setting, Quintero's pacing, the ensemble acting, and particularly Robards'

Hickey was universally laudatory.

Brooks Atkinson noted that in Hayes's setting, the audience has "the sensation of participating." (9) Actors and audience were "all part of the same setting and closely related on that account." He praised Quintero for this "major production of a major theatre work," for telling "the story simply and spontaneously" and for "bringing every part of it alive in the theatre." He compared Quintero to "a versatile conductor who knows how to vary his attack with changes in volume and rhythm; he knows how to orchestrate a performance." Robards's Hickey, he thought, far surpassed James Barton's performance: "His unction, condescension and piety introduce an element of moral affectation that clarifies the perspective of the drama as a whole. His heartiness, his aura of good fellowship give the character of Hickey a feeling of evil mischief it did not have before."

Robert Hatch of *The Nation* (May 26, 1956) observed that the production was "excellent" and that the performers seemed "completely saturated in the coma of defeat" and they became "increasingly convincing as the evening wore on." He also thought the staging was "well-suited to the sprawling structure of the play," and "it puts us all in the saloon which is the point." Lee Strasberg wrote that the lumbering style of the original production was replaced by a "raffish aliveness," so that the play's "intrinsic power, rugged strength and sardonic humor . . . appeared in its true significance." (10) (Indeed, the 1946 production seems to have been devoid of humor.)

Richard Hayes of *The Commonweal* (August 24, 1956) vividly described the impact of Quintero's direction, writing that he "subtly and with surpassing control . . . has preserved both the play's rigorously inflexible structure, and the tidal movement of awareness which washes and breaks against this. Yet he has lightened the drama's oppressive singleness of mood with pools and eddies of personal feeling: humor that is not harsh but wryly grotesque and touching, with a fearful undertow of despair; transient scenes of finely-wrought portraiture which stand out like patches of color against the bleak lithography of this dead world." Hayes thought that Robards gave Hickey "an unctuous, evangelical fervor, an unnerving jauntiness, which subtly cracks to disclose the corruptions of circumstance and will" which rooted the character "firmly in the American experience." In Robards's hands, "Hickey's disintegration in the last act--at first barely perceptible, then accelerating with a terrible momentum--" was "the most appalling portrait of personal extinction in our theatre since Lloyd Nolan's performance in Herman Wouk's *The Caine Mutiny Court Martial*. (11)

The production eventually ran for over two years, for one year without Robards, who by that time was playing in the Broadway production of *Long Day's Journey into Night*. Quintero won a Vernon Rice Award for his direction, and the production itself received a Rice Award for the best Off-Broadway production of the season.

Without diminishing the vital importance of Quintero's direction, of the setting, or of the performances, particularly Robards's Hickey, one must also consider what part the venue and the times played in making this production of *The Iceman Cometh* such a critical and popular success.

That *The Iceman Cometh* achieved success in an Off-Broadway theatre, particularly the Circle-in-the-Square, is not insignificant. In the postwar period, Off-Broadway had more and more become identified as the venue to produce new European plays, revivals of classics and of important American plays that had been commercially unsuccessful on Broadway, and new experimental plays--types of drama that Broadway was no longer capable of or interested in mounting. By the mid-fifties Off-Broadway was well established and officially recognized by the various trade unions and theatrical reviewers and journals. Circle-in-the-Square, in particular, had achieved, as Stuart W. Little has written, a reputation as "a theatre of respected professionals instead of a studio for out-of-work actors and hopeful theatre artists." (12) In large part, this reputation was achieved with its highly successful revival of Williams's *Summer and Smoke* in 1954. The Off-Broadway location and the reputation of Circle-in-the Square for productions of high artistic quality undoubtedly provided a foundation, a psychological "set," for the enthusiastic critical reception that *The Iceman Cometh* received.

Furthermore, the American temperament of 1956 was different from that of 1946. The hopefulness of the immediate postwar years had dwindled over the decade. Despite relative economic and political stability, the mid-fifties were not happy. For many Americans, it was period fraught with a sense of negativism and defeatism, of personal powerlessness, a sense, as Lee Strasberg remembered, "that man is a failure and the universe he inhabits meaningless." (13) It was a vision reflected in the plays of Tennessee Williams, particularly *Camino Real* (1953) and *Cat on a Hot Tin Roof* (1955), and in Arthur Miller's *The Crucible* (1958) and *Death of a Salesman* (1949), in the novels and poems of the "Beat Generation," and in such films as *On the Waterfront* (1954) and *Rebel without a Cause* (1955).

In the throes of this general "Cold War" mentality, American critics and audiences of 1956 were undoubtedly more attuned to the bleak existential resonances of *The Iceman Cometh* than they had been in 1946. Indeed, in 1946 the critics had most often compared *The Iceman*

Cometh to Gorky's *The Lower Depths* and to a lesser extent to Saroyan's Depression-era drama *The Time of Your Life* (presented in New York in 1939, the same year that O'Neill wrote *The Iceman Cometh*). In 1956, however, it was most often compared to Beckett's *Waiting for Godot*, which, directed by Herbert Berghof with Bert Lahr and E.G. Marshall as Gogo and Didi, had opened the month before on April 19 at the John Golden Theatre on Broadway. Although *Godot* only ran for fifty-nine performances, it was critically well-received and voted one of the best plays of the season. Several critics in their reviews alluded to *The Iceman Cometh* as a "Waiting for Hickey." Richard Hayes of *The Commonweal* was especially struck by the thematic similarities between *The Iceman Cometh* and postwar existential visions as reflected in the writings of Albert Camus. He described both *The Iceman Cometh* and *Long Day's Journey into Night*, which had been published in 1956, in terms of their "massive concentration of . . . solitude," their illumination of the abyss and of the "cruelties of reality and solace of illusion," and "their absence of the sense of possibility." In such an intellectual and social climate, *The Iceman Cometh* would seem particularly relevant.

In the late summer and autumn of 1985, Jose Quintero and Jason Robards reunited for a revival of *The Iceman Cometh*. After playing for a month at the Kennedy Center in Washington, D.C., it transferred to Broadway's Lunt-Fontanne Theatre on September 29. In addition to Robards, the generally strong cast included such prominent performers as Barnard Hughes, who played Harry Hope, and Donald Moffat as Larry.

With a few notable exceptions, the critics were as enthusiastic about this production as they had been about the 1956 production. *New York Times* critic Frank Rich called it (September 30, 1985) "as stirring a production of O'Neill's masterwork as one might hope to see." Edwin Wilson in *The Wall Street Journal* (October 4, 1985) praised the "superb performances" especially Robards's, while William A. Henry III in *Time* (October 14, 1985) described the revival as a "triumph."

Despite the positive critical reaction, the stellar performances, and the reputation of Quintero and Robards, the production closed after only sixty-two performances. Later in the season, a distinguished revival of *Long Day's Journey into Night* directed by Jonathan Miller with Jack Lemmon as James Tyrone closed after sixty performances.

The Broadway audience of the mid-1980s, like that of the mid-1940s reflected itself in entertaining but shallow musicals like *Tango Argentina, Cats,* and *Singin' in the Rain* or in Neil Simon comedies like *Biloxi Blues*. O'Neill's harrowing, tragic analyses of lost American dreams were more relevant than ever, but American audiences, at least on Broadway, were clearly not receptive to their message.

NOTES

1. Lawrence Langner, *The Magic Curtain* (New York: E. P. Dutton & Co., 1951), 400, 402. For this account, I have drawn in part on Gary Vena's recent, detailed history, *O'Neill's The Iceman Cometh: Reconstructing the Premiere* (London and Ann Arbor: UMI Research Press, 1988).

2. Louis Sheaffer, *O'Neill: Son and Artist* (Boston: Little, Brown and Company, 1973), 551.

3. Sheaffer, 573-74.

4. Vena, 47-50; Sheaffer, 585; and Langner, 406.

5. According to Vena, in O'Neill's *The Iceman Cometh*, p. 10, the Theatre Guild had a substantial advance sale for *Iceman*. There was a box office advance sale of $133,000, Theatre Guild subscriptions of $58,000, and theatre party bookings of $71,000. This advance could have kept the production going for several months. The production cost $50,000, a fairly large cost at the time for a "straight" drama. The cost of the Theatre Guild production of *Othello* in 1944, for example, was $50,057.94   (from notes in the Webster Papers at the Library of Congress).

6. Quintero has recounted how the production rights were secured in his autobiography, *If You Don't Dance They Beat You* (Boston: Little, Brown and Company, 1974), and in an earlier article in *Theatre Arts* (April 1957): 27-29 and 88, entitled "Postscript to a Journey." An unpublished doctoral dissertation by Edwin J. McDonough "Quintero Directs O'Neill: An Examination of Eleven Plays of Eugene O'Neill staged by Jose Quintero in New York City, 1956-1981," New York University, 1985, also supplements Quintero's account with information derived from interviews with other production participants. (McDonough's study, somewhat revised, is now published by UMI Research Press.) See also Sheila Hickey Garvey, "The Origins of the O'Neill Renaissance: A History of the 1956 Productions of *The Iceman Cometh* and *Long Day's Journey into Night*," *Theatre Survey* 29 (May 1988): 51-68. Garvey's essay was published after I had completed my study for the O'Neill Conference in Nanjing.

7. McDonough, 43.

8. McDonough, 38.

9. Brooks Atkinson, *New York Times*, 8 November 1956.

10. *Famous American Plays of the 1950s*, introduction (New York: Dell Publishing Co., Inc., 1962), 18.

11. *The Caine Mutiny Court Martial* was presented in 1954.

12. Stuart W. Little, *Off Broadway: The Prophetic Theatre* (New York: Coward, McCann, & Geoghegan, Inc., 1972), 15.

13. Lee Strasberg, introduction, *Famous American Plays of the 1950s*, 9.

23

Directing the Plays of Eugene O'Neill--Style, Substance, and Synthesis

Betty Jean Jones

Eugene O'Neill's plays are a part of living dramatic literature and should be looked upon not only as literature to be read and analyzed but also as blueprints for live, theatrical production. O'Neill continues to be praised by historians, critics, and theorists as the American playwright who first treated drama as literature. Yet in the realm of theatrical practice it is necessary for us to confront directly certain characterizations of his work such as "boring, complex psychological investigations," "long and tiring evenings at the theatre," "morbid visions of the dark side of life"--perennial excuses for avoiding stage productions of works by O'Neill. Myths often originate in human inability to deal with complex truths. Whatever kernels of truth may lie in O'Neill production myths, they are not insurmountable, even for amateurs.

In directing plays of O'Neill one must meet head-on the challenges of interpretation. One must engage in a "production translation" process, by which is meant constructing performance studies techniques as a way of deciphering what is so often perceived as unapproachable material. O'Neill wrote plays to be produced, and inherent within each are some "decoding factors" that will open the work to translation from the page to the stage in a process of meaning, without sacrificing "the magic" of the theatre experience.

Three central areas of investigation should be considered when directing an O'Neill play: style, substance, and synthesis. *Style* is centrally concerned with internal coherence and involves consideration of the physical (actors, sets, costumes, lights, sound) and the metaphysical (transport of meaning from page to stage to audience, themes and thought processes in the text from actor to character to audience, and the impact of the total dramatic vision). General "decoding factors" that run throughout the O'Neill dramatic canon involve (a) narrative techniques (e.g., O'Neill's penchant for heavy exposition and lengthy character and situation descriptions in the stage directions), (b) rhetorical techniques (e.g., language and character evolution), and (c) theatrical techniques (e.g., employing experimental techniques related to theatrical movements such as expressionism and symbolism). Each of these techniques is a vital key to the final determination of style.

Substance, or meaning, in the works of O'Neill is related to considerations of style. Meaning is at the heart of production communication in O'Neill plays, all of which have complex levels of meaning. These levels involve considerations for action, language, character development, theme, and setting, or *mise en scene.* O'Neill as a playwright often uses levels of objectivity in constructing meaning. For example, characters like Larry Slade in *The Iceman Cometh* and Cornelius Melody in the final act of *A Touch of the Poet* engage in detached, self-reflection that at once disarms the listener and at the same time focuses the meaning clearly and directly. O'Neill uses the concept of unmasking to reveal meaning, as in the literal and figurative use of masks in *The Great God Brown* and the heavy symbolism of masks in *All God's Chillun Got Wings, The Hairy Ape,* and *The Emperor Jones.*

Synthesis involves the unity of technique that erases the lines of distinction between style and substance, rendering what appears in production a seamless whole. This unity informs the total dramatic vision and determines the final impact on the audience. O'Neill achieves synthesis in the text of his plays through a mosaic of isolation and blending. Consider the isolated cells of thought in *Strange Interlude,* managed within simultaneous representation of continuous action, and the disjointed yet connected stories of the inhabitants of Harry Hope's bar in *The Iceman Cometh.* The Donald Gallup/Yale University preliminary edition of *The Calms of Capricorn* from O'Neill's unfinished manuscript reveals, for example, a cinematic vision of point-counterpoint conversations on the deck of a ship becalmed in the South Atlantic. The rhythms in *Capricorn* are complex and must therefore be rendered in a manner that allows a certain isolated focus yet maintains a unified, fluid progression of the drama, a task of sizeable proportions for any production team.

The concepts of style, substance, and synthesis as applied to an O'Neill text developed for performance can be well illustrated using *A Touch of the Poet.* Set outside Boston, Massachusetts, in 1848, *Poet* is the first in a cycle of plays meant to dramatize the history of an American family. The cycle was to follow the union of the Melody and Harford families over a one-hundred-year span in America. The Melodys, of Irish-immigrant stock, are represented by Sara Melody, a major character in *Poet*; and the Harfords, of Northeastern Yankee tradition, are represented by Simon Harford, an unseen but strong offstage presence in *Poet*.

Hailed by some critics as one of the major plays of O'Neill's mature period, *Poet* was written over several years, circa 1935-1940, and ranks with the autobiographical *Long Day's Journey into Night* (circa 1939-1941), and the intense character study *The Iceman Cometh* (1939) as an outstanding example of O'Neill's dramatic vision. First published in 1956, the play did not have its first production until March 29, 1957, when the Royal Dramatic Theatre in Stockholm premiered the work. The first American production of *Poet* opened on October 12, 1958, at the Helen Hayes Theatre in New York.

Poet was chosen for "main-stage" production at the University of North Carolina-Greensboro and was presented as an O'Neill centennial commemorative production on November 4-8, 1987. This was the fourth O'Neill drama in my directing career, after university studio productions of *The Iceman Cometh, More Stately Mansions*, and *The Calms of Capricorn* at the University of Wisconsin-Madison. As *Mansions* and *Capricorn* follow *Poet* in chronological sequence in the proposed cycle, my directing of *Poet* can be viewed as a completion of a natural progression.

The first consideration in directing the play was style of production. I determined that the text demands communication of a gritty realism, tinted like an early color photograph, showing an ambience of decline but with a possibility for hope. (1) This seminal statement of my directorial concept was designed to guide the work of the theatrical team in translating the text from page to stage to audience. The key "decoding factors" in the directorial concept are *realism, tinted*, and *photograph*. Techniques of production were developed around these factors for acting, the *mise en scene*, and ultimately the communication of meaning to the audience through synthesis of the total dramatic vision.

Relative to substance (meaning), O'Neill presents Cornelius Melody's struggle within an America that is embarking upon a new age of growth and development. Set in 1828, *Poet* presents the impact of the American nation's transformation through character, action, and setting. Melody's poetic soliloquies are not mere asides, but openings into the character's soul that reveal the clarity of the play's intent, as may be seen in Melody's exchange with himself in the mirror in act one, in which he claims he still bears the stamp of an officer and a gentleman.

Then he looks into the glass and recites lines from Byron's "Childe Harold" in an effort to justify this to himself. Such dramatic moments show Melody's search for meaning amid the conflict of his longing for otherwordliness, and the day-to-day struggle for power and possessions, a personal dilemma concurrent with America's similar struggles during the mid-nineteenth century. Each time Melody performs the Byronesque ritual in front of the mirror, his character is evolving toward the climactic change at the end of the play. The reciting of the poem is another "decoding factor" that illuminates the play for performance as it informs character, setting, and action.

The dramatic conflict is manifested throughout the play in rapid character transitions within the dialogue, a singular challenge for the most experienced of actors. This seeming character fracturing is another "decoding factor" that opens the interpretation of the play. The actor becomes the agent for action, thought, and location in a profound rendering of O'Neill's playwriting mosaic, coupling isolation and blending.

O'Neill carefully constructs dramatic action that is not merely contemplative. He provides at least four major moments of decisive physical action that undergird the psychological conflict, driving the play to its climax and conclusion. These moments of important physical action must be managed with moment-to-moment revelation, while also focusing the meaning clearly and directly for the audience. Three of these dramatic moments take place offstage: (1) the attack on the Harford lawyer Nicholas Gadsby by Melody's bar cronies Roche and O'Dowd; (2) the brawl at the Harford mansion, when Melody and his cousin Cregan try to confront Henry Harford, Simon's father; and (3) the startling twist involving Melody's charging from the tavern with his dueling pistols, in what O'Neill reveals as a murder/suicide/rebirth trinity of revealing impact, when Melody kills his prize horse (the symbol of his own posing as the pompous Major) and then assumes the air of his former peasant heritage. This fourth and final revelation of character and unified dramatic meaning is accomplished through Melody's unmasking. When he returns to the stage after killing the mare, Sara asks him why he did it. In his reply he undergoes a total return to the peasant persona and confesses that the Major intended to kill his horse and then himself. But the shot that killed the horse finished the Major as well, and it would have been a waste of a good bullet to use it on a corpse. Moments later, when Nora, Melody's wife, asks him to go lie down and rest, he replies that he isn't tired but fresh as a newborn man. He says this after a raucous brawl during which he has been severely beaten both physically and psychologically. The tragic moment of seeming defeat leads to knowledge that forges a transformation of almost apocalyptic proportions as Melody summons new courage to assume the Irish peasant persona.

The fourth climactic moment of physical action is the moment in the final act when Melody strikes his daughter Sara, a symbolic double attack that can be read as an act of self-discipline. O'Neill infuses Melody at this point with that strange objectivity that allows the character to engage in detached self-reflection that has catastrophic yet hopeful results. Melody's physical attack on Sara is another "decoding factor" central to the play's meaning. Sara is her father personified. She both loves and loathes the duality of character she has inherited from Melody--her desire for social advancement in Yankee acceptance by marrying Simon Harford and her fiery Irish peasant temperament. Early in act one Sara tells her mother that when her father came to America he had the opportunity to become all the lies he pretends to be. He possessed the education and the money required to rise, and she vows that if ever she had such chances, she would make her dreams come true. This speech by Sara prefigures what we are to assume is a note of hope at the end of the drama.

Sara does not undergo the full transformation back to Irish peasant as does her father. There is no need. She accomplishes a synthesis of character that will allow her to best use both parts of her Irish-American heritage in forging the life she wants. Sara's character development is another "decoding factor" relative to the play's meaning, and her ability to balance the passion and reason of her character is central to the meaning of the play in all its physical and metaphysical aspects. She appears to be at once a woman before her time and a woman of no other time. She accomplishes a synthesis that informs the needed unity in final production impact from page to stage to audience.

Like transitional American dramatic realist and fellow Irish-American James A. Herne (1839-1901), O'Neill founded his drama on an authenticity of place that shaped the characters therein. The world of the drama as described by O'Neill shows levels of physical and spiritual decay. The decay present within Melody's tavern and its inhabitants is one of revelation as much as of diminution. There is a quality of life and light that can be read as hopeful. These sometimes highly contrasting inner and outer states of being are to be managed within a mode of presentation that assumes high levels of verisimilitude, though varying in degree within the course of the drama. The impact of the *mise en scene* is crucial in production, as any theatre event is at first visual, then aural.

University of North Carolina-Greensboro scene designer Lang Reynolds provided a setting he described as: "elegantly empty to facilitate O'Neill's fertility of emotion throughout, serving as a counterpoint to O'Neill's language, character development, and action." (2) The visual effect of the setting is one of wood, space, and various stages of completion, surrounded by black masking that pushes the set forward toward the audience (blending), while fixing it in space (isolation).

Costume Designer Adele Cantor used the "decoding factor" of contrast in appearance that informed the play's meaning. The dramatic text reveals four levels of contrast in appearance: (1) the three bar cronies (O'Dowd, Roche, and Riley), who represent various stages of peasant disrepair, closer to Melody's beginnings; Nora, Melody's wife, belongs in this first category; (2) Deborah Harford (Simon's mother) and her lawyer Nicholas Gadsby, as representatives of the Yankee gentry; (3) the change of Sara from her barmaid's dress (peasant innocence) to her best dress to impress Simon (young seductress); and (4) the striking figure of Cornelius Melody in his old but well-preserved Sixth Dragoon uniform from Wellington's army, and later the beaten and torn Melody in the remnants of the same uniform--a contrast that should be managed with a synthesis of stark transformation while simultaneously representing a logical progression given the events that precede the change.

Using the concepts of style, substance, and synthesis as discussed above was an effective way of producing this important work. The challenge of interpreting O'Neill in production for an audience requires what one might consider the ultimate attempt at synthesis: dramaturgical study of the text, integration of character/action/locale within the limitations of budget, skill levels of personnel, and the unfamiliarity of general audiences with O'Neill works in production.

What were the results of this approach to this production of O'Neill's *A Touch of the Poet*? Our general audiences (composed of both university and community members) were the best barometer. They stayed throughout each performance. They listened with rapt attention. They laughed and gasped at what theatre practitioners may assume to be the correct moments (and at some moments no one could anticipate). They applauded generously at the conclusion of each performance. They sought out production personnel to ask questions, to compliment, to complain about the exposition in act one, and to say that they did not know O'Neill could be so funny, so diverse, so interesting, so relevant today. They want us to do more O'Neill. We hope to do so soon.

(NOTE: Color production plates from the UNCG Theatre production of O'Neill's *A Touch of the Poet* were exhibited at the Conference in Nanjing University Library as part of the "International Exhibit: Books on Drama and Theatre." Complimentary copies of the commemorative program, complete with five essays by O'Neill scholars who assisted with the production and details on the production process and personnel were available at the exhibit as well.)

NOTES

1. Betty Jean Jones, "Director's Promptbook" for UNCG Theatre production of Eugene O'Neill's *A Touch of the Poet* at the University of North Carolina-Greensboro, November 4-8, 1987; Greensboro, North Carolina.

2. Lang Reynolds, "Scene Designer's Analysis Book" for UNCG Theatre production of Eugene O'Neill's *A Touch of the Poet* at the University of North Carolina-Greensboro, November 4-8, 1987; Greensboro, North Carolina.

24

All God's Chillun Play Games

Marcelline Krafchick

In his two-act drama *All God's Chillun Got Wings* (1923), O'Neill focuses on marital war with an intensity that points back to Strindberg and ahead to *Long Day's Journey into Night*. But the racial mixture of the marriage forces Jim and Ella Harris into particular variations on deadly spousal games. By game I mean a way of structuring time wherein the moves are predictable according to the objective of an emotional reward. O'Neill's acute awareness of the limited social possibilities for blacks in his time translates into a discerning and disturbing glimpse of how institutionalized bigotry plays itself out in the individual psyche as it turns to games for emotional survival.

The play's interracial marriage has led many of its first reviewers as well as more recent critics to render simple sociological readings. Ruby Cohn refers to *Chillun* as one of a series of "pretentious and messianic" plays, (1) one that is "so inadequate in its exploration of a black-white relationship that few people cherish it today." (2) Other critics, though, have recognized that race is only the play's surface issue. T. S. Eliot, reviewing an edition of *Chillun* published together with *Desire under the Elms* and *Welded*, found it the most interesting of the three: "[O'Neill] not only understands one aspect of the 'negro problem,' but he succeeds in giving this problem universality, in implying a wider application. In *this* respect, he is more successful than the author of *Othello*, in implying something more universal than the problem of race-- . . . the universal problem of differences which create a mixture of admiration, love, and contempt, with the consequent tension." (3) One wishes Eliot would have elaborated. I think, though, that games are an apt model to investigate both the universality and the tension Eliot refers to in *All God's Chillun*.

Virginia Floyd, in describing O'Neill's ideas for realized and unrealized plays, traces his growing interest in about 1919 in the deterioration of marriage, in the chasm that forms after an idealistic union, with such telling titles as *Man and Wife*. Floyd attributes that interest to O'Neill's ambivalence about his wife, Agnes Boulton. (4) The conflict between a man's career goals and his role as husband is the central idea, for instance, of *The First Man* (1920-21).

Meanwhile, another preoccupation was Joe Smith, a black friend, fellow frequenter, and sometime roommate at the Hell Hole in 1915, who would become realized finally in 1939 as Joe Mott in *Iceman*. O'Neill, who wrote to Smith through the 1920s, urging him not to let "the game" lick him, sketched several attempts at a play about him, even using the name Joe in his 1921 notes. (5)

Another means by which the immediacy of social ills reached O'Neill was his acquaintance with Paul Robeson, whom he discovered with great enthusiasm in 1920. Robeson had made his acting debut at the Harlem YMCA that year and, while studying law at Columbia University, toured England in a play with Mrs. Patrick Campbell. (6) In a 1928 interview Robeson reported, "I was keen to be a lawyer. I thought this gift of getting people to listen to me would probably be a great help." But he was persuaded to act in a play, "just for the fun of it. . . . Well, it happened that Eugene O'Neill, the American dramatist, was in the house. He came round to see me afterwards and told me I should play the part of Emperor Jones in his great play which was to be produced in London. I laughed at the idea, though, of course, I appreciated his interest, and went back to my law work." (F 77) Although Robeson says he was more interested in law, O'Neill, Jimmy Light, and Gig McGee prevailed on him, and his triumph became history.

When Robeson first accepted roles in both *All God's Chillun* and *The Emperor Jones*, the Ku Klux Klan threatened him because a white woman was to kiss his hand in *Chillun*. The Hearst newspapers and the American Legion called for the play to be banned, and there was a general ruckus. The son of a slave, this accomplished debater, opera singer, actor, athlete, and lawyer, while creating a sensation in *Othello* in London and at Carnegie Hall in New York, was, until 1930, refused service at leading hotels in both cities (F 29). Certainly his experience crystallized ideas O'Neill had been discussing in correspondence with W. E. B. DuBois and brought another dimension to the saga of down-and-outer Joe Smith, the phenomenon of talent, versatility, and education being blocked.

In an interview in *The Manchester Guardian* in 1935, Robeson pointed out the special difficulties of educated Negroes. When asked if he had suffered persecution himself, the actor replied with an example from his law career:

> I had to find a solicitor's office to get some practice in my profession. It was likely to be a desperate search, but I was lucky; a white friend of mine liked me because I was a good footballer, and took me into his office. . . . His partners were furious. "What is a Negro doing here?" The American typist refused to take down my dictation. I left the place, and not only the place but the profession, for we Negroes cannot get the necessary experience at the Bar.
>
> Even if I had remained at the profession I could not have defended my brethren the Scottsboro boys. The white judges would not listen to my speech. (F 100)

Here was a man distinct from Smith, one of Harry Hope's losers --this one was blessed with ability, motivation, and mental discipline. Had Robeson not been talented in the arts but merely a capable lawyer, his head would have been pressed flat against the ceiling of opportunity. O'Neill knew these facts well when he created Jim Harris, who tells himself that all he has to do to succeed is to pass the bar exam. The question, "What if he did pass?" bears on Jim's universal game.

Egil Tornqvist has pointed to the recurring game images throughout the plays, such as baseball as "the game of life" in *Abortion*. (7) In *The First Man* the game of hide-and-seek parallels marriage, with the spouses pretending "You are me and I am you!" In *Chillun* O'Neill introduces more than one level of games: (1) overt contests, like marbles and boxing, (2) pretending, such as exchanging identities and attributing understanding to a mask; and (3) the psychological tactic of survival, which is the focus of my study.

On the first level, in the opening scene which Jim later keeps recalling, children are playing marbles; Mickey, the young man who fathers Ella's child, is in the boxing game; society divides visibly into sides of black and white, like teams in a contest. On the second level, as children and as adults, Ella and Jim play "let's pretend," trying to shed their labels Painty Face and Jim Crow. They try to trade colors by means of chalk and shoeblack (it never occurs to them that exchanging places would keep them on opposite sides). And a pretend-face, a mask, becomes a personality that Ella talks to and murderously stabs.

On the third level are the roles Jim and Ella play within their marriage to accommodate to their obstacles: brother-sister, buddies, father-daughter, saint-demon, rescuer-lost soul. Related to this last is the play's most interesting aspect, Jim's game of angel's wings as spiritual one-upmanship. Those who cast him as simply a victim of overt social evil are not listening closely.

"O'Neill's first aim," Timo Tiusenan says of *Chillun*, "was to impress on the minds of his spectators a vision of society as the nemesis of Ella and Jim. After that, he hurried toward the latter half of the play, shaped as a case study in individual psychology." (8) This is true. That is, Jim's game is a product of the uneven clash between the races, but not all blacks play it, and not only blacks play it. It is Jim's way of coping, and it makes him a far more engaging character than a simple victim.

Most people do not play games alone, and Ella's behavior meshes crucially with Jim's. This pair is not out of *West Side Story*. The reason eight-year-old Ella wants to be black has nothing to do with loving Jim. She never defends him against name-calling by other white children. But she deplores her rosy color because the children tease her as "Painty Face," a name she minds "mor'n anything," (9) even the risk of being called "nigger." When they get acquainted years later we see her without resources, ignorant, betrayed, alone. Her illegitimate child has died of illness, and though she has a job in a factory she considers herself "through." "Jump in de river, huh?" Shorty concludes when they meet. (103) Yet even such a woman, because she is white, is superior to Jim in society's mind and, critically, in Jim's.

After Jim and Ella marry, what occurs in the two-year lapse between acts one and two is the delayed start of a sexual relationship. For practical reasons, such as avoiding riots, the audience is kept from seeing the good parts of the Harris marriage. But they exist, according to exposition at the opening of act two. The couple's first year in France was so pleasant that Jim "never thought then we'd ever want to come back here." The two had lived at first, he tells his sister, "like friends-- like a brother and sister." But what prompted Ella to avoid people, first Americans, then French, was their becoming "as close to each other as could be." (115) Sexual intimacy triggered in Ella the residual force of cultural attitudes, shame. To the degree to which she has become loving to Jim, she must hate that loving.

Of course, that way lies madness. When Shorty, grown into pimp and dope-peddler, ignores Ella's call from the window of the Harris home, Ella experiences for herself the quality of Jim's humiliation. Here her sanity slips, and in the next scene (II, iii) the room is distorted.

If Ella's device for coping is to hate her love, Jim's is to love her hatred.

We see in *Iceman*'s Joe Mott that O'Neill's way was not to idealize blacks in propaganda-pieces for social progress, but to include them in a human family beset by delusions. Yet because Jim's white wife abuses him and sabotages his passing the bar exam, *Chillun* has appeared to many readers as just such propaganda. O'Neill regarded this play one of his two most misunderstood, along with *Dynamo*. (10) Though many have praised the play as being ahead of its time in portraying a racially mixed marriage, with its notorious hand-kissing, it is ahead of its time more essentially in O'Neill's dealing evenhandedly with his two demented protagonists. Today we can consider their relationship without having to sentimentalize Jim.

The basis for Frederic I. Carpenter's disappointment in *Chillun* is that it "achieves neither unity, nor dramatic conviction," (11) that Jim is pathetic rather than tragic, and that the ending "rings false." Jim's sudden exaltation "when Ella becomes insane and regresses into a childish dependence upon [him]" troubles Carpenter, but it is entirely plausible in terms of another of Carpenter's observations, that Ella's "feeling of subconscious hatred for him is justified psychologically by his own masochistic self-abasement before her." Carpenter, led by the title's implication of spiritual meaning to expect "tragic understanding and self-transcendence," finds instead "pathetic defeat and self-delusion." (12)   But if, as he says, *Chillun* "points to the major psychological dramas to come," (13) then the phenomenon of survival through delusion ties this early play to *Iceman*, *Hughie*, and *A Moon for the Misbegotten*. And the Congo mask holds the play's psychological center, the nature of the couple's games.

For critics the mask symbolizes, in Michael Hindon's words, "a link to [Jim's] original communal context," (14) and in Carpenter's words, "the racial past of the Negro," so that Ella strikes "to destroy the dark, inner self of her Negro husband." (15) I suggest another view.

O'Neill's schematized counterposing, in the early scenes, of Negro harmony with spring against white repressiveness may foster the notion that O'Neill is, in Cohn's term, "messianic." But the harsh division between Jim and his sister Hattie, who is an outspoken progressive, reveals that the play is not uncritical of Jim, who is out of harmony with a vital element that Hattie introduces to the play. Accused by his peers of "buying" white, Jim has "bought" the notion of becoming "the whitest of the white" by being a full-fledged member of the bar; he buys the metaphor of whiteness as excellence. He even declares that "all love is white." (108) Through Hattie's wedding gift of the Congo mask, pointedly to the bridegroom only, she presents the white bride with her real adversary, not blackness, as is generally understood, but black excellence: strength, beauty, workmanship, tradition, even royalty--qualities that give the lie to whiteness as metaphor for excellence. Hattie describes the mask as "a work of Art by a real artist--as real in his way as your Michael Angelo." (119) Though Ella wants it around to mock it, she connects it to his success, insisting,

"Jim's not going to take any more examinations!" Eventually, she is compelled to stab that royal face, as she is *not* moved to damage the portrait of Jim's conventional black father, which she addresses too, but with disdain. Her reason for "killing" the mask is clear: "If you'd passed, it would have lived in you. Then I'd have had to kill you . . . or it would have killed me." (131) Though Jim would remain black, she hates the authority he wants to earn.

Jim never passes; he has chosen the most efficient vehicle for failure, marriage to Ella. And her revulsion, rather than robbing him of self-esteem, reinforces his "self-abnegation," so that she hands him spiritual superiority.

O'Neill wives, like Ruth Mayo and Martha Jayson, are often victims of their men's selfishness. Ella's madness is an effect not only of her guilt born of social stereotypes but also of Jim's un-selfishness; she agonizes much as Hickey does over his Evelyn's unbearable forgiveness. Sainthood is the devil to live with.

Jim is beset from all sides: (1) His black schoolmate Joe attacks him for "swellin' out grand" and denying his race in front of whites. Joe allows Jim to attend high school graduation only after he admits to being a "nigger," and Jim apologizes to Joe for graduating: "This is my second try. I didn't pass last year." (97) (2) Mickey, Ella's white lover, displays classic antiblack brutality. (3) Mrs. Harris opposes her son's marriage to a white woman out of her own pride and prudence. (4) Hattie rejects her brother's eager "self-abnegation."

Jim is also assaulted by his own fear of the social consequences of success. When we see him study, perspiring and repeating a line from Blackstone, we have reason to suspect that passing the bar, that is, entering "God's country" (130), has so much illusion resting on it that he cannot afford to accomplish it.

Like Hickey, Jim believes that he can attain truth and freedom and that the only way to become free is to face the truth. (116) "Once I become a Member of the Bar [O'Neill capitalizes 'Member']--then I win, too! We're both free--by our own fighting down our own weakness! We're both really, truly free!" (123) Jim's flunking, then, is associated not so much with his intelligence as with cosmic justice.

Jim clings to the opening scene, when justice seemed accessible and Mickey declared him the winner in a game. When the adult Mickey says that Ella now "hates de sight of a coon," Jim replies, "I--I know--but once she didn't mind--we were kids together--." Mickey: "Aw, ferget dat! Dis is *now*!" (99) When Jim asks her why she hasn't spoken to him for years, she says they have "nothing in common any more." He replies, "Maybe not any more--but--right on this corner--do you remember once--?" That conversation nine years earlier suffices for Jim to confront Ella's lover and offer her friendship despite her present rudeness.

When Ella apologizes five years later for "the rotten way" she used to treat Jim, he again fixes on the scene fourteen years earlier: "But before that--way back so high--you treated me good (He smiles)." (107) And in his mother's house: "Don't you remember playing here with us sometimes as a kid?" Ella recalls only "playing marbles one night--but that was on the street." (117) The innocence that appeared to him as justice cannot be revived, but Jim had pinned all his hopes on it.

For most people who fear success, the hazard is independence, which is experienced as abandonment. In Jim's case, victory as a full-fledged member of the bar would be pyrrhic; it would not bring him acceptance as a white man. He must not pass and face that. The pain of masochism is the price one is willing to pay in order to avoid the nightmare of helplessness. Jim is not a simple victim, and his universal game is turned to by many in the human family.

Robeson wrote, "If ever there was a broad, liberal-minded man, [Gene O'Neill] is one. He has had Negro friends and appreciated them for their true worth." (F 71) In the same article, he described *All God's Chillun* as a play "mocking all petty prejudice, emphasizing the humanness, and in Mr. O'Neill's words, the 'oneness' of mankind." (F 70)

NOTES

Chillun was written during a period of several multiscene one-acts. In its uncommon two-act structure, the first half stresses environmental pressures from society at large, the second half the psychological effects of these pressures, made visual through the use of stage design that features a shrinking room. The play's central scene (four) at the end of act one presents a hellish wedding with opposite sides, black and white, staring at each other with loathing, while Jim is gripped by hysterical hope.

1. Ruby Cohn, *Dialogue in American Drama* (Bloomington: Indiana University Press, 1971), 67.

2. Cohn, 67.

3. T. S. Eliot, "Books of the Quarter," *The New Criterion* 4 (April 1926): 395.

4. Virginia Floyd, *Eugene O'Neill at Work: Newly Released Ideas for Plays* (New York: Frederick Ungar, Inc., 1981), 29.

5. Floyd, 176n.

6. Philip S. Foner, ed., *Paul Robeson Speaks: Writings, Speeches, Interviews, 1918-1974* (New York: Brunner/Mazel, 1978), 28.

(Subsequently cited as *F* with page numbers.)

7. Egil Tornqvist, *A Drama of Souls* (New Haven: Yale University, 1969), 149.

8. Timo Tiusenan, *O'Neill's Scenic Images* (Princeton, N. J.: Princeton U. Press, 1969), 177.

9. Eugene O'Neill, *All God's Chillun Got Wings*, in *Nine Plays by Eugene O'Neill* (New York: Random House, 1952), 93. (All subsequent page references are to this edition.)

10. Louis Sheaffer, *O'Neill: Son and Artist* (Boston: Little, Brown and Co., 1973), 325. For an account of the hate campaign against the play, and O'Neill's defense of it, see 134-35.

11. Frederic I. Carpenter, *Eugene O'Neill* (New York: Twayne, 1964), 104.

12. Carpenter, 104-5.

13. Carpenter, 103.

14. Michael Hinden, "The Transitional Nature of AGCGW," *Eugene O'Neill Newsletter* 4 (1980): 3-5.

15. Carpenter, 105.

Part Five

O'Neill Abroad

25

Ingmar Bergman and
Long Day's Journey into Night

Egil Tornqvist

O'Neill's most memorable drama, the finest American drama ever written, produced by one of the foremost directors of our time at the theatre that has cared more for O'Neill's plays than any other, including those in his native country--the success of Ingmar Bergman's recent production of *Long Day's Journey into Night*, opening at the Royal Dramatic Theatre in Stockholm on April 16, 1988, seemed guaranteed. And indeed, the production has been praised in all quarters.

It is, surprisingly enough, the first time that Bergman has staged an O'Neill play. Surprising, in view of his obvious affinity, via their common "spiritual father" Strindberg, with the American playwright. After reading Bergman's revealing autobiography, *Laterna Magica* (1987), one understands even better why the Swedish director has felt attracted especially to *Long Day's Journey*. In both cases we deal with artists who in play after play, film after film have been unusually autobiographical (as was Strindberg!), be it in disguised form. Suddenly, in these late works, they give us a key to all that has gone before. O'Neill, we all know, would have become one hundred this year. Bergman has just turned seventy. They certainly do not belong to the same generation, but the gap between the two is not so great that it cannot easily be bridged. And of course Bergman is now older than O'Neill ever became. This explains perhaps why Bergman in his production of *Long Day's Journey* has stressed the "deep pity and understanding and forgiveness for all the four haunted Tyrones" that O'Neill speaks of in the dedication to his wife that precedes the play, a statement that seems to be an echo of the pity for suffering mankind that forms the central theme of Strindberg's *Dream Play*, staged by Bergman no less than four times.

As I have already indicated, the Royal Dramatic Theatre in Stockholm has a very special relationship to O'Neill. It was there that many of his plays were performed in that period of his life when his own country seemed to turn its back on him. A few weeks before he died, O'Neill told his wife Carlotta that he did not want an American theatre to do *Long Day's Journey*, that he wanted it done at the Royal Dramatic Theatre in Stockholm "in gratitude for the excellent performances they had given his plays over the years." (1)

The leading director in Sweden at that time, Olof Molander, who had earlier done *Mourning Becomes Electra*, was the logical person to stage the play; but when Molander was rejected in his attempt to have his favorite actress, Tora Teje, perform the part of Mary Tyrone, he refused to do the play altogether. Instead the young and promising Bengt Ekerot was asked to direct the play.

The world premiere took place on February 10, 1956. It was a tremendous success. In fact, it is doubtful whether the Royal Dramatic Theatre has ever launched a better production. The impact was shattering. To an audience familiar with Strindberg's revelations of complex and painful family relations--in, for example, *The Father*, *The Dance of Death* (one of O'Neill's favorite plays), *The Ghost Sonata*--Ekerot's *Long Day's Journey* in many ways seemed a more realistic, more recognizable reenactment of what takes place in those plays.

O'Neill's dialogue was followed to the letter, resulting in a performance lasting close to four and one-half hours. Also the stage directions were carefully adhered to; spectators were introduced to a very realistic New England living room. The actors were the best the country could boast: Lars Hanson as Tyrone, Inga Tidblad as his wife Mary, Ulf Palme as the elder son Jamie, and Jarl Kulle as the younger Edmund, O'Neill's alter ego. The actors wonderfully matched one another, so that the spectator's interest could be equally divided between them, a matter of utmost importance in this play where we are asked to sense the playwright's willingness to understand *all* four.

As it happens, I saw this production when it was revived in 1962 for a tour in the United States. Lars Hanson had then been replaced by another outstanding actor, Georg Rydeberg. Still a very impressive production, it made an indelible impression on Sweden's most important contemporary playwright, Lars Noren, who recognized much of the interaction in his own family in that of the Tyrones. It may well be that this devastating experience encouraged Noren to write plays. I can think of no playwright today who comes closer to O'Neill in the obsession with which he deals with one and the same family in play after play, trying to understand *all* the family members, as O'Neill did.

The head of the Royal Dramatic Theater at the time of the world premiere of O'Neill's play, Karl Ragnar Gierow, has said that "the dialogue is written in such a way that a group of actors who do not stick closely to the text will not manage the task." (2)   Florence Eldridge, similarly, who did the part of Mary Tyrone in the first Broadway production, has praised O'Neill's widow Carlotta for rejecting all talk of the play's being repetitious and for refusing to have a single word cut. "The more one worked on the play," Eldridge says, "the more one realized that it was a symphony. Each character had a theme and the 'repetitions' were the variations on the themes." (3) Obviously, no one would think of abbreviating a Bruckner or Mahler symphony with the argument that it is too repetitious!

Now, more than thirty years later, the play is not so sacrosanct as it was in 1956, and Bergman has omitted quite a bit of the dialogue. Reducing the number of literary allusions, he limits the antithesis between Tyrone and Edmund to one between Shakespeare and Nietzsche. The initial, allegorical pig story is omitted, as are some peripheral jokes and remarks. Although some of the 1912 atmosphere and some of the Irish fragrance has thereby disappeared, none of the critics have found that these omissions have been harmful to the play. (We must here realize, of course, that we are dealing with a Swedish, not an American production.) The omissions seem wholly in line with Bergman's reductive tendency, his desire to make the truly important aspects stand out by doing away with all environmental paraphernalia.

In contrast to the realistic 1956 production, Bergman presents an existential version of universal significance. This appears most significantly in the extremely sparse scenery, designed by Gunilla Palmstierna-Weiss, who told me she had made seven models before she arrived at the final one. Instead of a recognizable New England living room, we are faced with a black "raft"--a square, raised stage, sloping toward the auditorium--surrounded by blackness, insisting that although the sun may enter the living room when the play opens, darkness surrounds it. Or, as Tyrone's Shakespeare has it, that our little life is rounded with a sleep. The blackness of O'Neill's back parlor has, as it were, been extended.

What I have just called a raft may also be seen as a jetty, the two columns at the back of the stage corresponding to piles or a dock; it was by jumping from a dock that Mary had once tried to commit suicide. The stage thus in a sense visualizes the past, which is, in her words, "the present" and "the future, too."

From another, more technical point of view the scenery may be compared to the black interior of an old-fashioned, funnel-shaped gramophone; an acoustic box, where every whisper can be heard, was the image the director and the scenographer had in mind.

Bergman's version is decidedly a dream-play, stressing the unreality of life; he is exceedingly cinematic in his concentration on the four characters, on their gestures, their movements, and above all their faces, and in his sparse use of projections. First we see the facade of the house, dreamlike in its low-angle perspective, as though floating in air: exterior and interior in one and the same stage picture. Then emerges a projection of the window in the spare room in which Mary's relapse takes place, that is, a visualization of what is on the mind of the men. Then a closed double doorway, telling us that no escape, no exit is possible. Subsequently, a grotesquely big wallpaper pattern invites the audience to enter into the fantasy world of the four characters as they succumb to dreams and drunkenness.

To the left on the raised stage a worn brown armchair, to the right a round table surrounded by four chairs of different shape: four different human fates.

Largely abstaining from atmospheric light, Bergman throughout the play had the characters brightly illuminated, as though they were put on a dissecting table or exposed to X-rays. The lighting in this sense visualizes their attempts to get at the naked, unashamed truth with each other and their sense of being painfully stripped of their consoling masks with regard to themselves.

In O'Neill's stage directions the mask-face dichotomy of the characters, their facade mentality, is visualized in the contrast between the neat and at times brilliantly lit front parlor and the black back parlor. In Bergman's version this has its counterpart in the projection in the first act of the facade of the Monte Cristo cottage in New London, the summer home of the O'Neills and the dramatist's model for the setting of the play. There is also an ironical reference to the facade mentality in the classical Greek (imitation) column (cf. the house facade in *Mourning Becomes Electra*), which later is shown to hide a liquor cabinet. If this piece of property relates especially to the men's tendency to embellish their weaknesses, another column, on which a Madonna and a votive candle have been placed, visualizes Mary's inclination to cling to an empty faith. Empty, because when the stage is revolved in the latter part, the sculpture is shown to be not as three-dimensional as we would have expected, but flat and provided with a support at the back. (One is reminded of Bergman's woodworm-eaten Madonna in his film *The Touch*.)

In a wider, existential sense, the Greek column with its Dionysian content (the liquor) is obviously an (ironic) reference to Edmund's (O'Neill's) Nietzschean craving for a rebirth of the Greek spirit, the Greek sense of tragedy--this is his "religion"--whereas the Holy Virgin clearly represents an alternative (Christian/Catholic) faith. But, as we have seen, both properties are *hollow*; the four characters are doomed to move restlessly between what used to be the two cornerstones of western civilization; toward the end we see them, not unlike Becket's four figures, resigned, in frozen positions, waiting for --death.

The inclusion of a worshipped Virgin Mary in the scenery reminds us of Mary Tyrone's attempt to gain back her lost faith. At the same time, the sculpture is a reminder of the men's worship of the Virgin's namesake, Mary Tyrone. It is significant that their discovery of her relapse into morphine addiction more or less coincides with *our* discovery that the back of the sculpture is flat, hollow.

In the play text there is an interesting contrast between "the four somewhat dissociated lamps in the living room representing the living present" and "the five united" front parlor bulbs reminding us of the harmony that might have been, (4) (i.e. *all* the Tyrones including the dead Eugene, who is very present in their minds).

Abstaining from this lamp symbolism, Bergman nevertheless retains it in a way by opening his performance with a little pantomime, a device he had sometimes earlier resorted to, notably in *Hedda Gabler*. The four Tyrones slowly enter the black platform, form a group, a *tableau vivant*, in which each one of them touches someone else, a group suggesting closeness, intimacy, tenderness, love. Then the group is dissolved and the play begins. In the subsequent action we will never see them together like this. At most there are brief moments of tenderness and love between individual members of the family.

This initial pantomimic tableau may be seen in different ways. We may see it as a pose, a facade, an expression of how the family is trying to keep up appearances, a visualization of how it wishes to be seen by others. We may see it as an expression of wish-fulfillment, visualizing their common dream of how everything might have been. Or--and this I find the most satisfactory interpretation--we may see it as an image of the love that binds the four together in spite of everything, as an expression of the fact that the author's understanding for them has its counterpart in their understanding for one another. Indeed, as the play gradually reveals, their conflicts with one another should not be taken at face value. They are primarily projections of conflicts within each one of them. The dissolution at the end is caused primarily by their inability to accept themselves.

At the end, which is clearly designed as a contrast to the initial togetherness, the four disappear in different directions, escaping each other: the unity is dissolved. Or to put it in more existential terms, one after the other they leave the lighted "raft" of life and depart into the surrounding darkness, as we are all doomed once to leave this life *alone* on our "journey into night." Edmund is the last to disappear. Before he leaves the stage a radiant tree is double-projected on the cyclorama. It is both a complicated net of nerves visualizing the entangled relationships between the characters and a token that out of these entangled relationships a soul is being born. When Edmund picks up his black notebook shortly before he exits, it is an indication that, like another Trigorin--Bergman many years ago staged Chekhov's *The Seagull*--he will record what he has experienced around him. Actually, Edmund is less akin to Trigorin than to Konstantin, the young writer who kills first the seagull, then himself (cf. Edmund's death wish combined with his desire to have been born a seagull). The black notebook provides a link between the 1912 situation we have just partaken of on the stage and the play Edmund's alter ego some thirty years later was to write, *Long Day's Journey*. Was it perhaps a dream, a fantasy of the burgeoning young playwright, that which we have just seen enacted? (We are not very far from Bergman's interpretation of *A Dream Play*, in his famous 1970 production, turning the Poet into the dreamer of that play.)

Edmund's part--played by Peter Stormare, Bergman's favorite actor at the moment, is perhaps the most difficult one in the play. He has less of a past, less of a profile than the other family members. This might be because O'Neill was closest to him. But the reason may also be that Edmund is the one we most easily can identify with; he is the character who bridges the distance between stage and auditorium. At least this is the impression one gets from Bergman's version, which in many ways resembles his production of Strindberg's *Ghost Sonata* fifteen years earlier. In this play Strindberg, via his alter ego the young Student, leads us inward from the beautiful facade of the house representing the world to the imperfections of humanity and life within. In *The Ghost Sonata* the disillusioned older generation is pitted against the still hopeful younger one. Our view of life, Strindberg seems to say, is very much a matter of age, how far we have come on our journey through life, how much we have seen of it, and how tainted we have become by it.

This same difference between generations can be sensed in *Long Day's Journey*, in which Edmund is relatively innocent because he is still young. But whereas Bergman's production of *The Ghost Sonata*, for all its blackness, ended with a kind of holy family trinity, stressing the director's belief in the power of human love, his way of ending *Long Day's Journey* indicates something else: certainly not the absence of human love but more the powerlessness of it.

In Bergman's version, James Tyrone, played by Jarl Kulle (best known abroad, perhaps, for his part in Bergman's film *Fanny and Alexander*) is a big, boisterous child, in need of a mother, as his first entrance together with Mary clarifies. He is also an actor who is play-acting at home, as he no longer has a stage on which he can perform. Kulle performs the part brilliantly in his own way. But, as other Tyrones have demonstrated, it can be done differently, and perhaps with more depth. Take the scene in which Tyrone tells Edmund about the poverty of his youth. In Bergman's version, he is significantly costumed in a dressing gown that bears witness to his glorious past. In Lars Hanson's interpretation this was a very introverted scene, the confession of a broken man. Fredric March, in the original Broadway production, turned it into just one more whiskey-impregnated anecdote, while Laurence Olivier made it a forceful apology by a professional actor, a kind of "Brutus is an honorable man" speech. Kulle's version is yet another variation.

The focal character in the play is decidedly the wife and mother Mary. Like the other characters, she is dressed according to the fashion in 1912. When she hands to her husband her bridal gown, the symbol of her youthful and loving self, the family loses its center and binding force. This is why her relapse into drugs is so feared by them all. Bibi Andersson, who performs this part, is very impressive, but she does not display the nervous frailty and oversensitiveness of Inga Tidblad. Like her husband, this Mary seems to be acting a part; it is hard to believe that she is as worried as she says she is.

Jamie's sarcastic comment on her final entrance--"The Mad Scene. Enter Ophelia!"--was cut by Bergman; presumably it seemed superfluous to the Stockholm audience, which could easily provide a link between Bergman's barefoot Ophelia in his recent production of *Hamlet* and his, at this point, barefoot Mary. This kind of autobiographical intertextuality is common with Bergman.

The most impressive of the four actors is undoubtedly Thommy Berggren, who does the part of the elder brother, Jamie. Jamie is an actor just like his father, but in contrast to him he is merely a ham-actor. As in several of his films, Bergman here utilizes the contrast between (reasonably respected) stage actors and (discriminated against) clowns. Thommy Berggren's Jamie, the least loved of the four, is clownesque, hiding his true self behind the mask of a grinning clown. And yet the marvelous thing with Berggren's interpretation is that we sense that behind the clown's facade, behind his snobbish and vulgar Broadway wise-guy appearance, there is a very sensitive human being, more gifted, perhaps, and probing than any of the other Tyrones. Admittedly, Berggren in the last act to a great extent steals the show, for our balance of sympathy is upset in his favor.

Play-acting or role-playing is the common denominator of the Tyrones. They sense the need of putting on masks, which others accept and which they accept themselves. Here we are very close both to the playwright who wrote *The Great God Brown* and to the filmmaker who wrote and shot *Persona*. As *The Great God Brown* on a symbolic-existential level dramatizes much the same situation, and much the same conflicts as *Long Day's Journey*, one might even say that Bergman has directed the latter play in the spirit of the former one, while permeating it with his own vision.

Recently Bergman turned *Hamlet* into a transparent counterpart of himself as a young playwright-director. The same actor who incarnated Bergman's Hamlet (Peter Stormare), in *Long Day's Journey* performs the part of Edmund, enough to indicate the proximity of this character not only to O'Neill but also to Bergman.

If it may be said that Bergman's production cautiously stresses Edmund's quality of being an outsider--not the least in his positions and movements--his version is nevertheless essentially an attempt to strike a balance between the four characters, to understand them all, as Bergman in his autobiography tries to do with regard to his own family. We are invited to partake of an existential, post-Brechtian drama emphasizing--as Strindberg does in his chamber plays--the fundamental representation of a fateful family interaction.

NOTES

I wish to thank Ms. Gunilla Palmstierna-Weiss for her readiness to inform me about the scenic aspects of Bergman's production, at a meeting in May 1988.

1. Tom J. A. Olsson, *O'Neill och Dramaten* (Stockholm: Akademilitteratur, 1977), 103.

2. Karl Ragnar Gierow, "Lang dags fard till London," *Svenska Dagbladet*, 16 February 1972.

3. Florence Eldridge, "Reflections on *Long Day's Journey into Night*: First Curtain Call for Mary Tyrone," *Eugene O'Neill: A World View*, ed. by Virginia Floyd (New York: Frederick Ungar Publishing Co., 1979), 287.

4. Egil Tornqvist, *A Drama of Souls: Studies in O'Neill's Supernaturalistic Technique* (Uppsala: Almavist & Wiksell, 1969), 101.

26

How Does O'Neill Fare in China?

Wenpei Long

Eugene O'Neill casts a long shadow not only on the American theatre, but also on modern Chinese drama. O'Neill was introduced to the Chinese public in the late 1920s, when he was at the height of his career. Since then, O'Neill has undergone fluctuations in popularity in the United States; and in China, too, opinions have gone through drastic changes.

So, historically, how does O'Neill fare in China? This topic will be dealt with in three parts.

I. The period between the 1920s and 1940s witnessed the first crest of popular interest in O'Neill in China. Among the plays translated and published then were *Beyond the Horizon, Anna Christie, The Emperor Jones, Strange Interlude, Mourning Becomes Electra, Ah, Wilderness!, Days Without End,* and several one-act plays. Six plays were staged in Beiping (now Beijing), Shanghai, or Nanjing: *Ile, Bound East for Cardiff, In the Zone, Beyond the Horizon, The Emperor Jones,* and *Before Breakfast.* Some fifty critical essays written about O'Neill appeared in Chinese newspapers and periodicals. Several critics looked upon him as "a poet, an observer of human nature," (1) who "inspires man in his striving upward and to seek light even in crimes and insults." (2) Other critics observed that his plays were different from those written by Ibsen and Shaw, who portrayed their characters in terms of social relationships while O'Neill depicted his as isolated entities. Still others regarded O'Neill as "an important promoter" in the history of American drama, who "has smashed many of the set rules of the stage, but never violated the fundamental principles of drama." (3)

These criticisms are sound and to the point. Despite the fact that the critics did not have the opportunity then to read O'Neill's late plays (to be published in the 1950s) or to become acquainted with the latter-day literary trends of the West, they had an intuitive grasp of the essence of most of O'Neill's plays. However, they did not go into detailed analysis, nor did they try to expound their findings on a theoretical level. Even with this historical limitation, their work can by no means be ignored. They were trail-blazers who discovered O'Neill for Chinese literary circles, thus enabling Chinese dramatists to learn of his valuable experience in playwriting.

II. The second period, the 1950s through the mid-1970s, saw O'Neill's popularity in temporary suspension in China. Because of the international political situation in the 1950s, the channels of cultural exchange between China and the West narrowed, and criticism of Western literature became biased. All contemporary Western writers whose works were not obviously directed against capitalism were largely ignored. For instance, of all American writers only Walt Whitman, Mark Twain, Jack London, Theodore Dreiser, John Steinbeck, and a few others were published and studied. O'Neill's plays were laid aside and neglected. None of his later plays were translated, nor were his critical essays published, to say nothing of producing his plays on the Chinese stage. News of the publication of his posthumous dramas was carried in the *Reference Material for Foreign Literature*, but this was almost all that could be read about O'Neill in China during this period. Ironically, O'Neill was given an entry in the 1961 trial edition of *Cihai* (Encyclopedia). Here he was referred to as "a well- known and prolific American playwright, his outstanding plays include *Beyond the Horizon, The Emperor Jones, The Hairy Ape*, and *Strange Interlude*. These plays reflect various problems of American capitalist society, such as murder, poverty, power of money and racial prejudice. However, these plays are extremely pessimistic and despairing, full of decadent sentiments." (4) Obviously this comment failed to do justice either to O'Neill or to his plays.

III. The third period, the late 1970s to the present, constitutes the second crest of O'Neill's popularity in China. During this period great changes took place in our objective and subjective worlds. The policy of openness and reform adopted by the Chinese government since 1979 has put an end to the period of a closed society and ushered in a new stage. Since then, China has been a scene of bustling activity in literary and art circles. With the improvement in Sino-American relations, cultural exchanges between the two countries, after more than twenty years of stagnation, have been revived. We O'Neill fans once again have access to most of his plays and to research literature by scholars from various parts of the world. Riding the waves of this Sino-American rapprochement are a great number of Chinese artists and scholars who have either visited America or taken part in O'Neill conferences and symposiums. American experts and scholars also have visited China. Among them is George C. White, the president of the Eugene O'Neill Theatre Center, who directed *Andy* (an adapted version of *Anna Christie*) in Beijing. Another is Professor Normand Berlin, who visited China in 1987 and lectured on O'Neill in Shanghai and Nanjing.

As a result of this new spirit of exchange, there has appeared an O'Neill boom, in which his plays have been translated and produced with unprecedented enthusiasm. Since 1979, we have translated or retranslated more than twenty O'Neill plays (four different translations alone of *Long Day's Journey into Night*). About one hundred critical essays on O'Neill have appeared in various publications throughout China. Plays such as *Anna Christie, Beyond the Horizon, Desire under the Elms,* and *Homecoming* (one part of the trilogy *Mourning Becomes Electra*) have become standard theatrical fare in such cities as Beijing, Shanghai, Shenyang, Dalian, Harbin, Changchun, and Taiyuan. Three plays have been televised nationwide, thereby achieving unprecedented coverage in China.

Apart from this, O'Neill has been included in the curricula of Chinese universities. Wherever there is a course in American literature, there is a chapter for O'Neill; and some universities offer "O'Neill and contemporary American drama" as an elective course. Quite a number of students, both graduate and undergraduate, have selected O'Neill as the subject of their theses. The Chinese Theatre Association sponsored symposia in 1981 and 1982, in which promising young and middle-aged playwrights from around the country took part. The prominent Chinese dramatist Cao Yu lectured on both occasions on O'Neill's dramatic art. Participants at these sessions were greatly moved by O'Neill's persistent pursuit of the meaning of life and his courageous attempts at reforming American drama. Young Chinese playwrights, in particular, have benefited from these lectures and consequently, have written a number of plays full of original ideas. We might say they owe their achievements in part to O'Neill, for he has shown them a theatre of unlimited possibilities.

Chinese students of O'Neill now have a deeper understanding of this great playwright. First of all, in our evaluation we have abandoned the vulgarized social approach and so avoided imposing our biases on the playwright and his works. Now we are paying more attention to the plays themselves, in an attempt to look for the original perception of the author. In the past, whenever *The Emperor Jones* came up for discussion, we would attach much importance to Jones's words: "For de little stealin' dey gits you in jail soon or late. For de big stealin' dey makes you Emperor and puts you in the Hall o' Fame when you croaks." From these words we would draw the conclusion that the corrupting influence of American society is the cause of his downfall. This analysis, of course, is relevant to the simple surface structure. But a careful reading of *The Emperor Jones* will lead us to the "force behind" that actually shatters the dream of Jones. It is quite obvious that the author has never ascribed the defeat of Jones to his rebellious pursuers, who, as a matter of fact, did not enter the forest until the last scene, whereas Jones has made every preparation for his escape and nothing seems to stand in his way. He fails for he is bogged down by his subconscious guilt and fear. The drums of his pursuers bring to consciousness the social and psychic sediments accumulated from primordial times. It is guilt, fear and superstition that have deprived Jones of his self-control and loose him like a blind man in a dark forest of destruction. In discussions of *The Hairy Ape*, formerly our attention was centered on Yank's class attributes and on how the play dealt with the social position of workers in capitalist countries. This approach, in a sense, is understandable. However, we must go deeper. In O'Neill's opinion, Yank is "a symbol of man, who has lost his old harmony with nature, the harmony which he used to have as an animal and has not yet acquired in a spiritual way." (5) This is the dilemma of modern man as seen by O'Neill. It is in this sense that O'Neill said, "Yank is really yourself and myself. He is every human being." (6) Here is the lesson: we must penetrate the surface of apparent actions and plots to go to the deep structure of the work in question, or we will fail to understand the real intention of the playwright.

The subject of "human nature" is no longer off-limits with us; the viewpoint that "literature is the study of man" is now reaffirmed. O'Neill was a serious writer who persistently pursued the true meaning of life. His concerns were always man's fate and dilemma in the contemporary world. After the catastrophe of World War I and the great depression of the 1930s, O'Neill was shocked by the holocaust that befell man in World War II, which intensified his realization of the predicament in which man found himself. This realization flows through his late plays, which have become, in a sense, a record of the soul of a generation in America. The pity is that this record was mistaken by some Chinese critics as pessimistic and despairing and therefore decadent. It is not until recent years that a just evaluation was accorded O'Neill and his works.

We have discarded the view that realism is the only effective artistic approach in favor of an unbiased attitude towards various artistic forms. Apart from being a persistent pursuer of the meaning of life, O'Neill was also an indefatigable experimenter in the art of the theatre. His contributions in this respect are greater than any of his predecessors in the annals of American theatre. His early plays, an attempt at facing up to naked life, led American drama in breaking away from commercialism and escapism, thus guiding it to merge with the mainstream in American literature. Following this, he experimented with European expressionism, symbolism, stream of consciousness, and so on, to reveal the inner world and inner conflicts of his characters. With these explorations, he adopted an effective form conducive to his own vision and emerged in his late plays with a style that was uniquely his own. It was a new realistic approach which assimilated the achievements of his experiments in the 1920s and early 1930s. It was an artistic synthesis on a higher level.

Today, Chinese playwrights are following a course similar to that of O'Neill's, a direct result of the spirit of reform and an unbiased approach towards various schools of art. In recent years, the Chinese stage has witnessed a series of outstanding "exploration plays," such as *A Visit from the Dead, Barbarians, The Magic Cube, The Nirvana of Grandpa Doggie,* and *The Chronicle of Mulberry Green* (which was adapted from a novel of the same title and produced by the Central Academy of Drama in Beijing). These plays are unique in both matter and form, and they all point to a common tendency to break new ground for new expression. We are glad to see that many playwrights, directors, actors, and actresses as well as stage designers have original ideas and insight. They are discriminating "borrowers." It is my firm belief that there will be playwrights in China who, like O'Neill and other outstanding dramatists, will make their contributions to the treasure house of world drama.

Three hundred years ago, Ben Jonson, the famous English dramatist, said of Shakespeare in a panegyric poem, "He was not of an age, but for all time." History has borne out the truthfulness of his prediction, to which, however, an addition may not be irrelevant: all great writers of the world transcend time and space. On this occasion of celebrating the centennial of Eugene O'Neill, let us offer our hearty thanks to the great American playwright whose efforts have vastly enriched the cultural treasury of the world and whose artistic achievements are a bridge between Chinese and American cultures. It is the duty of all of us here to work to reinforce this cultural bridge and make it play a more effective role in facilitating exchanges and promoting friendship and understanding between our two nations.

NOTES

1. Jiazhu Zhang, "O'Neill," *The New Moon* (January 1929), No.

ll, vol. I.

2. Zhongyi Gu, "O'Neill, the Playwright," *Modern Times* (October 1934), No. 6, vol. 5.

3. Zhongyi.

4. *Cihai*, trial ed. (Beijing: Zhonghua Book Company, 1961), 206.

5. Doris Falk, *Eugene O'Neill and the Tragic Tension* (New Jersey: Rutgers University Press, 1958), 34.

6. Arthur and Barbara Gelb, *O'Neill* (New York: Harper and Row Publishers, 1973), 499.

27

Two Popular O'Neill Plays Staged in Japan: *Ah, Wilderness!* and *Desire under the Elms*

Yasuko Ikeuchi

It would be ridiculous as well as unfair for any critic to comment on a staged play without having viewed the production. Having failed to see the play performed, one can only guess what the actual production was like. Some documents, however, such as the director's plans for the play, would surely tell why the play was chosen to be staged at a particular time, and to a certain degree some reviews could tell how the production was received. From such limited sources, any statement I might make here would of course lack authority and completeness, but even so, I believe an important aspect of modern Japanese culture can be brought to light with this discussion. Before discussing two Japanese productions of O'Neill plays, I would like to quote Horst Frenz, who has written about translations, productions, and studies of O'Neill by Japanese scholars or theatre groups:

Although translations of Eugene O'Neill's plays existed in Japan before 1924, none of his plays was performed on the Japanese stage until that year. It was through the Tsukiji Little Theatre that the American playwright found a first hearing before a Japanese audience, and, between 1924 and 1929, six of his plays became part of the Tsukiji repertoire. The first Japanese production of any O'Neill play, *Beyond the Horizon*, took place in October, 1924. (1)

Further investigation by a Japanese scholar, (2) however, shows that the first Japanese production was not *Beyond the Horizon* but *Ile*, performed by a little theatre group called Geijutsu Kyokai at Kobe Takarazuka Little Theatre in 1923. According to a list made by Hisae Tada, *Ile* was produced four times, *The Long Voyage Home* three times, and *Anna Christie* also three times, to name a few in order of popularity.

The so-called Little Theatre Movement, in which the Tsukiji was very important, aimed to create a modern Japanese theatre that would exist independent of traditional Japanese theatre forms such as Noh, Kabuki, and Kyogen. They introduced Ibsen, Chekhov, and contemporary German Expressionists as well as Shakespeare to the public. The 1920s in Japan saw the same sort of theatre movement as the Provincetown Players had created in America about ten years before, one that was passionately opposed to the nineteenth century conventional and commercial theatre.

In the 1930s, however, Japan invaded China and rushed into World War II, and one of the domestic developments of this new situation was the complete suppression of all innovative artistic movements. It was difficult for theatre artists to introduce American drama to the Japanese public as well as for native Japanese playwrights to write plays other than ones that would support the expansionist national spirit. In this context my interest lies in the struggle of Japanese theatre artists to survive the war. An adaptation of O'Neill's *Ah, Wilderness!* by Tomoyoshi Murayama, a playwright and director, serves as one of the best examples of resistance to the military regime of that period. What Murayama wanted to express by his adaptation can show, conversely, what the original, *Ah, Wilderness!*, is really about.

According to Michinori Hirose's comparative study (3) of Murayama's adaptation of the O'Neill play, Murayama happened to see *The Emperor Jones* and *The Hairy Ape* performed by the Tsukiji in 1927, and these performances inspired in him an interest in O'Neill. In 1932 Murayama was arrested for the first of several times by security police on the charge of disturbing public peace and order; and he was released on condition that he never again write anything that might be considered as critical of the imperial power of Japan or that contained any socialist ideology. He was also made to promise never to promote any theatre activity designated exclusively for the working class. The left-wing theatre Murayama had joined was forcefully dissolved while he was imprisoned. After being released, he proposed that all theatre artists or groups unite regardless of their differences either in politics or artistic beliefs, and in consequence he managed to organize a new federation of theatre groups in 1934. Under stern surveillance Murayama selected *Ah, Wilderness!*, a play that, though not typical of O'Neill, he found moving because of its depiction of a family in which each individual member communicates equally and freely within an atmosphere of spontaneity, affection, and harmony. It was partly because of cruel censorship and also because of the repressive Japanese family system that Murayama decided to change O'Neill's depiction of a typical American middle-class family of the early twentieth century into that of an imaginary Japanese family not likely to be found anywhere in Japan at that time, so that it could be a sort of daring, bold resistance to the Japanese family system of the time. His adaptation, entitled *First Love*, was criticized for subverting traditional values and the patriarchal hierarchy within the family. In the prewar days *First Love* was performed twice, once in 1937 and again in 1938. These productions were part of the reasons that Murayama was imprisoned again in 1940. In 1941 Japan expanded its reckless imperialist war by attacking Pearl Harbor, and thereafter no production of O'Neill's plays or other American works was allowed in Japan. Just after the war, in 1946, *First Love* was performed again with Murayama's open remarks made to criticize the traditional Japanese family system. In his essay on the production of *First Love*, Murayama wrote that the so-called beautiful family system peculiar to Japan and championed by the authorities was nothing more than a fictitious belief, a kind of myth, idealized, romanticized, and beautified, which benefited only the big landowners and capitalists. (4) *Ah, Wilderness!* was performed in the original by the Haiyuza in 1947 and found a favorable reception.

Compared with the original, *First Love* was condensed somewhat and its fictional world was made smaller, though its formal structure was the same four-act one as in the original. Murayama cut out a scene where Richard gets drunk with a prostitute partly for economic reasons and partly because of censorship. He also cut the harbor scene in which Richard makes up with Muriel and the two kiss as they dream about their future. Instead, in the adaptation the young couple only talk through the window of the Millers' house without embracing or kissing, making the scene more modest and in keeping with typical Japanese love scenes of that period. *Ah, Wilderness!* ends with a lovely scene in which the elderly couple compares their love to autumn in contrast to the flowering springlike love of the young couple, but Murayama's adaptation finishes with an exchange of but a few flat words by the elderly couple.

A striking difference between the original and the adaptation is that in the latter they do not discuss politics so openly as they do in the former. Whereas a young rebel, Richard, criticizes American capitalism, his counterpart, Teiji, does not criticize the Japanese social system directly. He mentions the Spanish Civil War, but in an obscure, roundabout way:

TEIJI.   (Richard) To hell with the festival! I am not in the

	mood while people are being killed and wounded and bleeding all over the place in Spain!
IKUJIRO.	(the counterpart of Sid) What has Spain got to do with you?
TEIJI.	A lot! To me Spain has got a lot more to do with me than your bloody mine in Hokkaido! (5)

Teiji's comment on the current situation of Spain obviously reveals Murayama's sense of crisis about the Spanish War, where democracy was at stake. It also seems to show that Murayama avoided topics related to the harsh realities of his contemporary Japan because of censorship. Among his favorite writers, however, Teiji mentions not only Dostoevski and Whitman but also Takeo Arishima, a Japanese writer who experienced the wave of democracy that swept through Japan in the Taisho era (1912-1925) and committed a double suicide with another man's wife, and Takuboku Ishikawa, a rebellious Japanese poet. These Japanese writers are representatives of the most liberal, progressive, and intelligent people, though they seem indecent, blasphemous, and even scandalous to Teiji's mother.

In spite of certain trivial differences between the two plays, the result of Murayama's avoidance of direct confrontation with the ruling political powers of his day, they are in essence identical. The humor and cheerfulness of the dinner scene in act two, filled as it is with the father's lovable repeated boast about saving a child's life in the river when he himself was a little child, his wife's continuously tricking him into eating bluefish despite his repeatedly expressed dislike of the fish as it gave him indigestion, and the uncle's drunken, uncontrollable, and tremendously funny jokes, are retained. This scene reveals the essence of the original's world, the funny, lovely, and affectionate family situation, which is kept intact in the adaptation. No matter how the adaptation was cut, it remains as pungent, pure, and precious as the original. It represents "an ideal of domestic mutuality." (6)

In the postwar era the most popular O'Neill play staged in Japan has been *Desire under the Elms*, which has been performed four times, and it is followed by the four productions of the one-act *Before Breakfast*. The O'Neill revival of the late 1950s in America led to Japanese productions in the 1960s of his masterpieces, *Long Day's Journey into Night* and *The Iceman Cometh*, both of which attracted fair-sized audiences. My interest here, however, also lies in the postwar Japanese cultural situation, which experienced a liberation from the dominant values of the cruel, oppressive, and authoritarian ruling power of Japan. It was not until the end of the war that we could express ourselves and pursue our individual aspirations freely. In the democratic postwar Japanese society, individual desire has not been generally deemed in need of suppression, which is perhaps the greatest change in values since the war. "Never Say 'We Want' until We Win!" was the notorious slogan of that war period in Japan. This explains partly why *Desire under the Elms* has proved particularly popular since the end of the war. Desire is both the key term for accurately interpreting O'Neill's play and a key word for understanding the essence of postwar Japanese popular culture, a culture that has witnessed various kinds of explicit, outspoken, and affirmative expressions of desire.

Tsuneari Fukuda reviewed the production of *Desire under the Elms* by the Mingei Theatre Group in 1958 and declared it a kind of misfire that made the audience feel frustrated because it lacked a climactic explosion of sexual and earthly desire at the end of the play. (7) Fukuda criticized Taku Sugawara's direction, which drew too many harmonious gestures, moves, or expressions from all the actors that were similar to those of a sentimental traditional Japanese theatre form called "Shinpa." Abbie, according to Fukuda, is the central character of the play, whose desire is to come out from her innermost core, and therefore she could have expressed her desire for Eben all the more passionately if she had acted as if she had never paid any attention to his existence. In dealing with modern tragedy as powerfully structured as O'Neill's, says Fukuda, the main characters should be drawn as solitary, isolated, and uncompromising existences. In other words, each individual character has the power and capacity to put a tragedy in motion. In this context Fukuda reacted favorably to the performance of Shu Takizawa, who had acted the role of Ephraim Cabot. But he added that at the end the stage set and props had regrettably hindered Takizawa from standing alone as a defeated but uncompromising man. Fukuda concludes with other critical remarks, finding, for example, the reconciliation between Abbie and Eben to fall short of the intended final affirmation of the truth of their love. Their relationship, he says, is marred by the sentimental acting conventions used in that production.

There were some favorable reviews as well. Shin'ichiro Nakamura found the Mingei production powerful because in that performance he felt he could see the root of Greek myth. (8) The most recent Japanese production of *Desire under the Elms* was directed by Koichi Kimura in 1982. In the playbill Kimura explains that he chose the play for its affirmation of the struggle to pursue the truth of human nature despite the fact that the struggle is cast in a negative light by all the main characters becoming alienated from themselves. Kimura points out that life is always a losing battle in O'Neill's tragic dramas because the destructive force is always shown to be inherent in people's dreams and desires. This, says Kimura, is O'Neill's generalization about the human endeavor, that it is the price human beings have to pay as they struggle through their lives. According to Kimura, no matter how dreams or desires destroy people in O'Neill's tragic dramas, the meaning of their struggle, conversely, is that human beings have a good, highly developed, and very strong life force within them.

Of the other Japanese productions of *Desire under the Elms*, Kimura felt that the naturalistic treatment sometimes resulted in melodrama centered on the entanglement of sexual and earthly desires, while in others he found fault with their old-fashioned, realistic handling, as if the play were merely a vehicle for delineating rural problems. Through his own production, Kimura wanted to see the spontaneous, unsophisticated, and transcendental intuition that is connected with desire in O'Neill's tragedy in the larger perspective of the world view of Thoreau and Emerson, both of whom interpreted intuition as that which is most characteristic of human existence. Kimura says Eben stays at the farm not so much because of his greedy, earthly desire to possess it as because of his spontaneous, intuitional response to the beauty of nature. Ephraim Cabot also sticks to barren and stony land not so much because of his grossly material desire as because of his response to the will of God, which he sees in the sterile, stony soil. In this context Kimura is giving an entirely new interpretation of the play, especially when he views desire as positive in terms of the wild, rough, and unpolished nature of the life force, a force that seems to have been lost in contemporary human existence. Kimura argues that today we live in what has been called the "plastic age," in which our desires or aspirations are reduced to a banal, stereotyped kind, completely different from the wild, natural, and untamed desires depicted in *Desire under the Elms*. In the world today, says Kimura, people have become pessimistic about human possibility, and by contrast, the characters in the play seem all the more human, courageous and beautiful for their persistence in the pursuit of the truth of their desire, even if they ultimately lose their battle.

Kimura's production received mixed reviews. One, which appeared in the newspaper *The Mainichi*, says favorably that Kiwako Taichi played the complicated and varied role of Abbie well. (9) This Abbie is at one moment a woman who tries to possess the house and the farm by intrigue while at another she is a woman who loves Eben regardless of her financial interest and who goes even so far as to commit infanticide to prove that love. This review is also complimentary about Kimura's directing and especially praises his skillful treatment of space: the farmhouse, set in a tray-like space, revolves itself to show first the exterior of the house, then the living room, and then the bedroom in succeeding scenes.

In another review, which appeared in *The Hochi*, Eiichi Adachi says that the performance shows the conflicting struggle between characters who steadfastly stick to their own desires or fixed ideas to the last. (10) He could discern Kimura's intention to criticize by contrast the contemporary world where people seem to have lost both their self-confidence and their connections to the powerful life force that gives meaning to their everyday lives. The critic, however, adds that the actual performance was only halfway successful. Even despite the sensibility Kimura brought to his interpretation of the play, he still was not able to explore the full range of the tragic world of the play.

Koji Ozaki, in *The Yomiuri*, criticizes Kiwako Taichi's acting for being superficial and simply an excuse to exaggerate her sensuality. Ozaki found the actual performance failed to show the powerful life force that drives and controls all the characters. (11)

Because I did not see Kimura's production, I have nothing to add to these critical comments. As I mentioned earlier, however, my interest here lies in the interpretation of the key term "desire," in the thematic context of the play and in its context within postwar Japanese culture.

When Kimura says he finds the main characters more human and more beautiful, as compared with his contemporaries, who seem to have lost confidence in their ability to achieve anything worthwhile and who become pessimistic about all human possibility in contemporary society, he touches upon the core of *Desire under the Elms*. None of the main characters in the play gives up his or her struggle halfway: Ephraim Cabot clings to the barren, stony land in the hope of changing it into a farm that will pay; Eben claims his right to the farm over that of his father in order to avenge the death of his mother, Cabot's second wife, a woman Eben thought had been worked to death by his father; and Abbie wants to have the farm and the house when she marries old Cabot because she had had an unhappy married life with her drunken first husband and had experienced as well the dissatisfaction of working in another's house. The triangle between the three characters, borrowed from Greek myth as presented in Euripides's *Hippolytus*, reveals, however, another kind of struggle, different from that of Greek myth, and principles current in mid-nineteenth century America. Many critics have pointed out O'Neill's use in this tragic drama of both Freudian theory and Puritanism. Normand Berlin comments on "the Freudian pattern" (12) or "Freudian determinism" (13) in his concise analysis of what O'Neill calls "sinister maternity": (14)

Mother as female principle, Mother as the demands of the past, Mother as avenging spirit, Mother as lover. In human form, Mother is

Ephraim's second wife (soft, good-natured, worked to death by
Ephraim) and Abbie (who takes Eben's mother's place in the home and
his affection) and Min (the prostitute shared by father and son): in
animal form, Mother is cows that Ephraim must visit; in the form of
animated nature, Mother is the elms, darkly rooted, maternally
protective and oppressive, creating shadows and hidden corners,
informing the play's action. (15)

      We see not only maternal principles but also the patriarchal
power structure worked into the dramatic structure. In this context, if we
focus on only the religious aspect of Puritanism, we fail to see the
essence of its relation to the maintenance of patriarchal rule: Cabot has
his farm, does anything to keep it, and wants a son to whom he will
pass on the property. Ephraim despises his other two sons, who go to
California for "easy riches" (16) and an escape from the hard work on
the stony land, and his youngest son Eben for being soft and
good-natured. "Ephraim is the stern apostle of a hard, demanding God,
and he embodies a New England Puritan tradition that is biblical and
oppressive." (17) He becomes estranged from himself as well as his
family in this hard, stoic struggle and ironically goes to his cows often
for the warmth. He piles up stones to make a wall to separate his farm
from others, and he has become as sterile and cold as the stones he
works with. This is a battle, in which the father keeps his farm for
himself as long as possible and finally selects one of his sons as the heir
to whom the farm will pass. From the perspective of patriarchal
hierarchy, especially shown in such a puritanical, rigid, and stoic way
as Ephraim's, he cannot afford a spontaneous, affectionate, and
harmonious family world: he has lost mutual understanding, warmth,
and communal feeling in his family relationships. This is what Abbie
wanted to have in her relationship with Eben. They are attracted to
each other both physically and spiritually because they can share the
same things: innocent and spontaneous affection, a sense of the beauty of
nature, and a response to the mysterious power of nature. They exist
closest to nature when they join in a passionate sexual union. After this
natural, happy union, the naive Eben humorously shows his good-
naturedness by saying suddenly to his father: "Yew 'n' me is quits. Let's
shake hands." (18) Abbie also forgets about her early scheme to possess
the farm and moves beyond the boundary of earthly desire. When, near
the end of the play, Eben expresses doubt as to the genuineness of Abbie's
love for him, she kills her son, whom Ephraim believes is his son and is
his heir, but who is in fact Eben's. Inhuman as it is, infanticide has the
symbolic significance here of destroying the bonds holding Abbie and
Eben within the patriarchal family system. In this system, woman is
regarded as a mere tool for producing a son who is to inherit the

property. That Eben shares full responsibility for this infanticide with Abbie means that he, as well as she, stands beyond the rule of patriarchal powers, though both of them, it is clear, will pay for their act with their own lives. They refuse to be trapped within patriarchal hierarchy.

This battle of two principles is simplified as one between the father, who is literally and figuratively the patriarchal head, and the mother, who is the female principle in harmony with nature. In O'Neill's depiction, however, the female principle is not idealized or beautified. Though sometimes too simplified and schematic, woman's suppressed feelings and desires take form under the pressure of the puritanical, patriarchal hierarchy. In *Desire under the Elms*, the main characters' individual struggles show how those characters' desires are interrelated dramatically within the larger framework of the modern world. This simplification and schematization of desires also makes clear to us contemporaries the kinds of battles that are taking place in this drama. O'Neill creates the final affirmation of love beyond the world of puritanical, patriarchal, and oppressive power in terms of "desire" as a key concept. If we produce *Desire under the Elms* for the audience of today, we can emphasize this new interpretation more than anything else.

NOTES

1. Horst Frenz, "Eugene O'Neill in Japan," *Modern Drama* 3, no. 3 (December 1960): 306.

2. Hisae Tada, "The First Production of O'Neill in Japan," *Kyoritsu Review*, no. 8 (1980).

3. Michinori Hirose, "An Adaptation of O'Neill," *Comparative Culture* no. 14 (October 1971). Saneatsu Asada also wrote about Tomoyoshi Murayama's adaptation of O'Neill in *European and American Writers and Japanese Modern Literature*, vol. 1 (Tokyo: Kyouiku Shutsupan Center, 1974).

4. Tomoyoshi Murayama, "*First Love* and Japanese Family System," *The Complete Works of Showa*, vol. 24, *An Anthology of Showa Plays* (Tokyo: Kadokawa, 1953), 247-48.

5. Murayama, 229.

6. Tom Scanlan, *Family, Drama, and American Dreams* (Westport, Conn.: Greenwood Press, 1978), 109.

7. Tsuneari Hukuda, "Erroneous Ways of Directing," *Geijutsu Shincho*, January 1958, 129-32.

8. Shin'ichiro Nakamura, "A Review of Three Plays,"

Shingeki, January 1958, 89.

9. Anonymous review, *The Mainichi,* 17 February 1982.

10. Eiichi Adachi, rev., *The Hochi,* 9 February 1982.

11. Koji Ozaki, rev., *The Yomiuri,* 21 February 1982.

12. Normand Berlin, *Eugene O'Neill* (New York: Grove Press, Inc., 1982), 80.

13. Berlin, 80.

14. Eugene O'Neill, *Desire under the Elms,* in *Nine Plays by Eugene O'Neill* (New York: Modern Library, 1959), 136.

15. Berlin, 73.

16. Berlin, 74.

17. Berlin, 72.

18. O'Neill, 181.

28

Directing *Mourning Becomes Electra* in Japan

Yoshiteru Kurokawa

Japanese theatre started to produce Western drama in 1906 with Shakespearean plays by traditional Kabuki actors or newly trained amateur actors. In the list of productions that followed, we find such dramatists as Ibsen, Wedekind, Chekhov, Gorki, Gogol, Maeterlinck, Lady Gregory, Hauptmann, Schnitzler, and others until we come to the name of Eugene O'Neill, the first American playwright produced in Japan. His first production was *The Emperor Jones* in 1924, then *Ile, The Long Voyage Home, Before Breakfast, The Hairy Ape*, and *Thirst* in 1927.

After World War II and after the O'Neill revival in the West in the mid-1950s, we saw several more plays in Japan: *Ah Wilderness!, Desire under the Elms, Long Day's Journey into Night*, and *The Iceman Cometh*.

Today, American plays are fairly popular among Japanese audiences because most of the Broadway "hit" shows are produced in translation. Of the American playwrights, Tennessee Williams is the best liked, then follows Arthur Miller, although his plays have been less regularly seen in recent years.

The year 1988 seemed appropriate as the best occasion for the second O'Neill revival or at least for presenting a contemporary view of O'Neill. Otherwise, the name could be forgotten forever except in academic circles.

I selected *Mourning Becomes Electra* as my first choice. Neither *Mourning Becomes Electra* nor *Strange Interlude* had been produced for audiences. While I had seen *Strange Interlude* in London with Glenda Jackson as Nina (in which the technique of "spoken thought" worked well, much to my surprise) and found it challenging, I preferred a play that was more theatrical, spectacular, and imaginative. Even so, I did not want to direct *Mourning Becomes Electra* as a theatrical spectacle. Instead, I wanted to cut down as much as possible the melodramatic elements to make it realistic to our audiences's taste while retaining its inherent theatricality.

The first and most difficult step was to determine how to deal with the length of the performance. If all three parts were spoken in literal translation, the play would take more than nine hours with several ten-minute intervals in between. Audience endurance apparently has changed since the 1930s because today the Japanese can sit in a theatre for three hours at most. Moreover, a policy regulates the closing time of theatre doors at 9:30 P.M., and they can only open at 6:30 or 7:00 P.M. because of the general working hours.

There were two alternatives: to choose one of the three parts and make it a little shorter or to condense the entire play to nearly one-third of its original length. I followed the latter course, which seemed almost impossible at the time. I know scholars will disagree with my vandalism, but I wanted to show even a touch of the play to the Japanese audience.

As a result, I made the play three acts with fourteen scenes instead of thirteen acts in three parts, which meant all the scenes were to be staged.

My method of pruning the text was to focus on four points: (1) cutting repetition from the lines, even though they are important for expressing strong passions or anxieties; (2) cutting explanatory lines or actions so that audiences would be forced to use their imagination; (3) cutting sequences that sounded too melodramatic or too obvious; and (4) cutting chorus portions at the beginning of each of the three parts and replacing them for part one and part two by scenes with Seth, the gardener, and with a woman I created based on a minor character in the play.

Here are examples of my methods. In act one of part one *Homecoming*, Brant mentions "the Blessed Isles" to Lavinia, a theme which runs through the entire play and affects each character:

Unless you've seen it, you can't picture the green beauty of their land set in the blue of the sea: The clouds look down on the mountain tops, the sun drowsing in your blood, and always the surf on the barrier reef singing a croon in your ears like a lullaby!

We hear Orin speak something similar in act two of *The Hunted*. He has just returned wounded from the war and tells his dream about his mother. "The Blessed Isles" reflects Brant's past experience as a seaman, but the "South Sea Islands" Orin imagines come from his reading Melville's *Typee*. Orin says:

> There was no one there but you and me. And yet I never saw you, that's the funny part. I only felt you all around me. The breaking of the waves was your voice. The sky was the same color as your eyes. The warm sand was like your skin. The whole island was you.

After their mother's death, Lavinia takes Orin on a long voyage to the East to let him forget the past. On the way, they land on the "South Sea Islands" and spend a month there. According to Orin, "they turned out to be Vinnie's islands, . . . They only made me sick." Lavinia dreamily tells Peter of the islands soon after she and Orin return from the trip, "--the warm earth in the moonlight--the trade wind in the coco palms--the surf on the reef--the fires at night and the drum throbbing in my heart. . . . " For Orin the image of the "South Sea Islands" has failed, but for Lavinia it promises freedom from the past, from all the deaths she has faced.

This idealistic image of the far away islands is somewhat shared even by Ezra. Confessing his real feeling for their marriage, he urges Christine to start a new life together. "I've a notion if we'd leave the children and go off on a voyage together--to the other side of the world--find some island where we could be alone a while. You'll find I have changed, Christine."

I find the first lines of Brant to Lavinia are rather obtrusive because they make him sound cheap. He must be the romantic captain whom Lavinia hates for his affair with her mother, but whom she loves unconsciously. She must realize that his love for Christine is motivated in revenge upon the Mannons for his mother's hardship and miserable death. Even so, he must not look cheap and mean. The romantic talk on the beach in the moonlight is necessary for Lavinia to become charmed and fascinated by the captain. Obsessed as he is with the image of "the Blessed Isles," he cannot help repeating it when he becomes extremely passionate. But I thought his enchanted memory of Lavinia that night needs to be touched upon, if only briefly. Otherwise, the reiteration of the image of "the Isles" would sound rather pointless and repetitious. All in all, sequences of this image must be carefully dealt with because long lines charged with such high tension do not always make strong, effective impressions on today's audience.

Here is an example of method number two: omission of the explanatory lines and actions. At the beginning of act three of *The Haunted*, Lavinia comes alone into the sitting room from the study, where in the previous act she has been told by Orin that he is writing a "true history of all the family crimes, beginning with Grandfather Abe's" and that he finds her "the most interesting criminal" of them all. Then she speaks aloud to herself: "I can't bear it! Why does he keep putting his death on my head: He would be better off if--Why hasn't he the courage--? . . . Oh, God, don't let me have such thoughts! You know I love Orin! Show me the way to save him! Don't let me think of death! I couldn't bear another death! Please! Please!" She addressed the last half to the portraits of the Mannons hanging on the wall.

Here she has revealed her secret anticipation of his death. But this should not yet be hinted at because, when this long soliloquy is omitted, her later outburst of hatred and rage to Orin is unexpected and thus far more dramatic.

Method number three applies to sequences such as the medicine-box business employed at the end of *Homecoming* and in the scene with Ezra's body laid out on a bier in act three of *The Hunted*. In the latter, Lavinia places the box on her father's body over his heart to watch Christine's reaction. On seeing the box, Christine "starts back with a stifled scream and stares at it with guilty fear." This medicine-box business seems too old-fashioned and ineffectual to appeal to the audience today. As Professor Normand Berlin points out, Ezra's dying scene is very melodramatic with his finger pointing at Christine. He gasps forth, "She's guilty--not medicine!" It is enough for Lavinia to assume what she thinks is true especially when the audience knows what really happened in this scene. Lavinia should not be certain that Christine has poisoned Ezra. So I cut out the medicine-box sequences and Ezra's dying last line in my version.

As for drastically cutting chorus parts, I have Seth and his cousin Minnie from another port town on the New England coast take their place. She visits Seth once a year, and he introduces her to the Mannon estate at the beginning of *Homecoming*. At the beginning of *The Haunted*, she visits Seth a year later and becomes curious to see the ghosts of the Mannons, about which the townspeople have told her. Whether or not O'Neill intended it, I used Seth and Minnie for comic relief in this everlastingly heavy drama.

With these revisions, right or wrong, I went into rehearsal and met great difficulties with the many scene changes. Our set designer had made a device by which the house could be divided into three parts and easily moved. For interior scenes, the three parts were turned around and set up as a sitting room, a bedroom, and a study. During the many rapid scene changes, I employed old American sea songs I had heard on records. The stage was in half light with a strong shaft of light coming down like a heavenly power.

The reception of the production was generally good from critics and audiences alike, but financially it lost money.

29

O'Neill in a Chinese Classroom: *Before Breakfast-- A Good Starting Point*

Jianqui Sun

With all O'Neill's masterpieces having been introduced into China over the years, why do I choose for my course "Drama in English" a one-act play, *Before Breakfast*, written in 1916 when the playwright was still learning his trade?

The play is selected because it is accessible to Chinese students for its subject matter, as it deals with a husband-and-wife relationship. O'Neill's apparent concern for the theme of the family stems from his Irish immigrant background. In Ireland, as in China, the family is the basic focal point, the fundamental social structural unit, and hence the center of human drama. O'Neill's anxiety over the problems of keeping the family together in a new environment paralleled the problems Chinese artists and intellectuals faced in the cities in the 1930s and 1940s as industry developed. Because of this similarity, it is no accident that the play was one of the first to be translated into Chinese. Translated by Fan Fang in 1927, it was performed by Bai Yang, a noted film star, in Shanghai in the 1930s.

As the play is short and relatively simple and is written in the form of a monologue, it is easy to present in class. My students are business majors with very little exposure to Western literature or drama. But my experience of analyzing the play with them has been extremely rewarding.

I first explain the stage setting, stressing the imaginary bedroom by using the classroom door for the purpose, and locating the kitchen on the platform where I am standing. Then I read with feeling some important passages making sure the students get tired of the wife's berating and taunting of her husband. I act out the last part of the play:

Alfred! Why don't you answer me? (. . . *something crashes heavily to the floor. She stands, trembling with fright.*)
Alfred! Alfred! Answer me! What is it you knocked over? Are you still drunk? (*Unable to stand the tension a second longer she rushes to the door of the bedroom.*)
Alfred! (. . . *transfixed with horror. Then she shrieks wildly and frenziedly.* . . .)

The class would mutter, "The husband must have killed himself," or "He committed suicide." The atmosphere was extremely tense. I waited for the tragic feeling to strike home and then started discussion from the following three aspects: the theme, the use of imaginary space and offstage sound, and the form of monologue.

THEME

Thematically, the play deals with the human need for understanding and the despair that arises without it. It focuses on the basic household conflicts between husband and wife, using family as the microcosmic picture of society.

Synopsis: The play is set in a flat of an American slum early one morning. While the wife, Mrs. Rowland, is preparing breakfast, she urges her husband in the bedroom to get up for breakfast and to go out and look for work. However, her husband does not leave. Unable to cope with his unrelieved poverty, the failure of his literary career, his mistress's pregnancy, and his wife's nagging, Mr. Rowland reaches a state where alcohol has ceased to offer any solace and has left him without a shred of dignity. He commits suicide. In the play, factors of unemployment, starvation, and the realization that no one appreciates his poetry all join together to destroy the poet. He is unwilling to go on, yet he is powerless to change. After a futile inner struggle, he seeks escape in death.

Through this plot, O'Neill establishes his eternal theme of the human need for understanding and the despair occasioned by its absence. Although the play is short--its entire duration is only about thirty minutes--O'Neill successfully tackles, through this cameo of domestic life, the great universal human conflicts, which will foreshadow almost all the basic conflicts in his later plays. These conflicts include hope and disenchantment, materialism and art, pride and humility, human responsibility and failure to fulfill it, self-love and self-loathing, understanding and alienation, the idyllic past and the harsh present, alcoholism as a temporary escape and death as the final one.

These pairs of conflicts form the themes of many of O'Neill's great plays, and they reveal his dark and deep vision of life and point to his interest in larger outside forces.

To enhance the theme of human despair, O'Neill uses thematic devices such as time and alcoholism. He employs real time to achieve emotional impact. Mrs. Roland's screams that announce her husband's death suddenly make the audience realize they have been the unknowing witnesses to a suicide. This shock increases their emotional involvement in the play.

The theme of alcoholism is worth special mention because it reflects the basic attitude of many of O'Neill's characters. In the play the wife relies on liquor to make her hard life easier. The husband seeks relief outside his home to avoid confrontation, and when he is home, his drunkenness saves him from having to deal with his wife directly. However, the more he drinks, the fiercer his wife's tongue lashes out at him. Although he endures life by seeking refuge in drunken oblivion, alcohol is not the final escape for him. Once his illusion is shattered, life is worse than death. In this sense, *Before Breakfast* carries much the same weight in expressing the theme of despair through alcoholism as O'Neill's later masterpieces, *Long Day's Journey* and *The Iceman Cometh*.

IMAGINARY SPACE AND OFF-STAGE SOUND

A stage, however large, has limited space, but the imaginary space knows no bounds. O'Neill easily breaks the spatial limit of the stage and guides the audience's imagination to a wider space. His method is to set aside a certain area on or off the stage to create a difference between the actual stage space and that which he wants the audience to feel. The difference produces strong tension and, as a result, an imaginary space. In *Before Breakfast* he allots the offstage area to the bedroom. Although the play is set in a kitchen, the audience's attention throughout the play is focused on the bedroom behind. With every line Mrs. Roland delivers, one wonders what her husband is doing there. The spectators have to imagine for themselves every movement and action of the man inside that unseen room. Because Mr. Rowland never appears on stage, he never comes into the kitchen, and the audience's attention must move between the visible kitchen and the invisible bedroom. When the wife berates the husband for his clumsiness and inability to hold a bowl of water steadily, the audience is imagining the husband's awkward movements. Thus the drama is going on simultaneously in two rooms, and the space is at least doubled.

O'Neill's successful experimentation at the early stage of his career prepares the ground for the more stunning use of the technique in many of his later plays.

Chinese audiences in 1983 saw Arthur Miller's *Death of a Salesman*. They were deeply impressed by his "modern" treatment of putting on stage the inner state of mind of a mentally sick, tired salesman. One side of the stage represented reality; the other, unlit, symbolized the other world from which Willy's dead brother called the salesman to join him in death. Miller's treatment of stage space was outstanding. But as early as 1916, in presenting a dying man's last struggle, O'Neill had already used the method in *Before Breakfast*. Having learned this, the students would better understand O'Neill's contribution to American drama.

O'Neill's use of imaginary space in *Before Breakfast* and in his later plays, such as *The Emperor Jones*, finds its echoes even in Chinese theatre. In his *Wilderness* (1937), the playwright Cao Yu devoted a whole act (act three) to chase scenes in which the chasers are offstage, out of view, but the threat of their possible appearance keeps the audience in suspense. In the audience's imagination, the stage extends to the very end of some primitive forest and becomes limitless in space. Indeed, once the audience is stimulated to use its imagination, where can it not reach? In another modern Chinese drama, *The Apeman* (1984) by Xinjian Gao, the setting shifts freely from city to mountain, from bedroom to wilderness, without bothering about changing sets; and the result is stunning and spectacular. But the principle the dramatist abides by is the same as that O'Neill employs in *Before Breakfast*: exploring imaginary space.

O'Neill's use of offstage sound is another method of establishing imaginary space. The dislocation between sound and visual image once again forces the audience's attention to travel. His plays, mostly tragedies, are filled with stifling, unbearable tension. As his characters are trapped in a stalemate, unable to move forward or backward, time often seems to have stopped. Often O'Neill employs offstage sound to disrupt overwhelming tension and to provide an impetus for further conversation, adding richness and subtle details to his characterization.

In *Before Breakfast* O'Neill plays a trick of deliberate ambiguity in the drip drop of "liquid." Both the audience and Mrs. Rowland think it is the tipped-over water. Even after Mr. Rowland has bled to death, the wife remains ignorant. O'Neill has used some auditory clues to inform her, to alarm her, and to frighten her. She is unaware that the echoing drip marks the slow progression of death, and so O'Neill succeeds in stressing her role as an insensitive and inattentive wife.

MONOLOGUE

O'Neill advocates the clearest, most economical dramatic devices to reveal the deeply hidden human conflict. Knowing well Browning's art and influenced by what Strindberg had done in *The Stronger*, O'Neill carries on his own experiment. He lets an unattractive housewife speak to an unresponsive offstage husband for thirty minutes without any significant interruption. Because this is a shrewish wife humiliating her husband and goading him to look for work, it is only appropriate for her not to leave room for her husband to retort. The dramatic situation allows and justifies the monologue form.

A monologue reveals the complex inner world of the speaker. Yet the speaker in this case is not at all complex. If O'Neill invites the audience to gain insight only in the simple and flat character of Mrs. Rowland, the play would be dreary, but the charm with which he sustains the audience lies elsewhere.

His drama takes place not on the stage but behind it. The minds of the audience react in such a way that they constantly supply lines for the silent husband. They draw a detailed portrait of this man as being delicate, supersensitive, romantic, sentimental, and poetic, but at the same time timid, cowardly, vain, lazy, henpecked, and deceitful. The man has reached a point where life does not matter to him any more because it has become a heavy burden. Why talk? He sees no need, as all the accusations against him are facts, and he knows no way to change them. The only thing he can do is to impart what he feels through silence to the audience. Actually, O'Neill is presenting the antithesis of what interests him most. Mrs. Rowland's lines are the shavings carved out by the sculptor for the purpose of shaping what remains. O'Neill cleverly builds the character of the wordless husband into the verbose wife's lines. This is a great accomplishment that shows the talent and virtuosity of the fledgling dramatist.

O'Neill's fondness for monologue is determined by his deep understanding of human psychology and human tragedy. Knowing that alienation is one of the most deep-rooted of modern man's problems, he resorts to this one-sided conversation to communicate the message of loneliness and isolation. The impact of this dramatic device on the Chinese audience and readers is truly strong. The impact is not only emotional but also moral, because the accused has no chance to defend himself, a fact that shifts our sympathy and compassion toward the silent one in our moral judgments.

We know the wife has to work hard to support her alcoholic, jobless husband; we know she has every reason to complain and win our sympathy; but we cannot give all our sympathy and compassion to her. The husband deserves all the blame, and yet we do not want to blame him before we hear his side of the story. In a society where artists go hungry, the individual is not to blame. The audience still waits. After discussing these techniques, I followed Professor G. B. Baker's workshop method and asked the students to write down the possible responses of Mr. Roland toward his wife's speech. The students could respond in a monologue or in the form of a dialogue. The results were interesting and surprising, revealing the students' full understanding of O'Neill's tragic vision and dark view of life.

Short as it is, *Before Breakfast* contains much of the budding brilliance that will mature in later O'Neill. It gives a taste of O'Neill's theme, of his concern and anxiety over the family, and a glimpse of his dramatic techniques and experimentation. With these as a foundation, the Chinese students will be able to handle his masterpieces later on.

30

Panel Discussion on the Nanjing O'Neill Theatre Festival

Jiaoru Qian: Fellow participants, we now begin the last session of the conference, a panel discussion on the four productions we watched over the past three nights. I am Jiaoru Qian of Nanjing University. I would first like to introduce the panelists to you. This is Professor Zongjiang Huang, a noted dramatist and filmwriter in China. He has been a four-time guest at the Eugene O'Neill Theatre Center and has written a number of film scripts such as *The Story of Willow Castle, Sea Soul,* and *The Serfs*. He also adapted *Anna Christie* with a Chinese setting for George White's production in Beijing in 1984.

Next to Mr. Huang is Mrs. Judith Johnston-Weston, executive producer of the Eugene O'Neill Theatre Festival of Los Angeles. Next is Mr. Changnian Feng, a director from Jiangsu Art Theatre, who directed the performance of *The Emperor Jones*. On my right is Mr. Guodong Xiong, also a director from Jiangsu Art Theatre; he directed *Beyond the Horizon*. Next is Mr. Tom McDermott, co-founder and artistic director of the Eugene O'Neill Theatre Festival. He has directed award-winning productions in Los Angeles, San Francisco, and New York. And he is the director of the *Hughie* we saw last night. Sitting over there is Mr. Yuan Yao, artistic director of Qianxian Theatre, which produced the *Long Day's Journey into Night*.

Also I would like to introduce Professor Ralph Ranald and Professor Margaret Ranald, who have graciously volunteered to be the recorders of this session.

I'd also like to introduce our interpreters. Mr. Jie Fei, a senior student of our department, graduating next month, and Assistant Professor Yongli Yang.

Before questions are asked, each panelist will give us a ten-minute briefing of the production of their respective plays. Mr. Huang and Mrs. Johnston-Weston will talk about some other things.

Huang: I am not an expert or scholar on O'Neill like you. I am only a fan of Eugene O'Neill. When a high school student, I read the early translations of O'Neill's sea plays and *Beyond the Horizon* by Mr. Yuocheng Gu. How I dreamed of going beyond the horizon! Then I went to college but did not finish it, just like Eugene O'Neill. I went onto the stage, became a professional actor, then a sailor, again following in the footsteps of Eugene O'Neill. (Laughter) There was World War II, of course. Patriotism. But I became a sailor mainly because of Eugene O'Neill. When the war was over in 1946, I went back to college, but was still unable to finish. I got TB, just like O'Neill. (Laughter)

When my first play was published and performed, I thought I was a Chinese O'Neill. (Applause) Then came the Liberation in 1949. We were isolated. You call it iron curtain or bamboo curtain; anyway there was a curtain. So, I accused and condemned Eugene O'Neill in this or that way. Then came the Cultural Revolution. I was persecuted, of course, as you can understand. The chief crime I was accused of was my worship for Eugene O'Neill. Then, when the Cultural Revolution was over, I was invited to visit the United States. It so happened that the sponsor of my trip was the Eugene O'Neill Theatre Center in Connecticut.

You might wonder what we accused or condemned Eugene O'Neill of in those years. The first thing was his fatalism. The second was his pessimism. But it seems to us now, whether a fatalist or not, whether a pessimist or an optimist, O'Neill depicted life sincerely. I think the most important thing we have learned from Eugene O'Neill is that we are still learning. Another accusation was that O'Neill is not a realist in his art. Probably you cannot even understand why that was a problem in China. You know we advocated revolutionary realism. If you were not a realist, you were not a revolutionary; you were a counterrevolutionary. I think O'Neill used expressionism, symbolism, modernism, even absurdism, to make the reality he presented more real. Again, what we have learned from O'Neill is the fact that we are still learning.

That is my, or *our*, long voyage home from beyond the horizon, my life's journey into day. It is such a bright day now that we can have this bright international conference. I think you know what it means to me, to you, and to the whole world.

Pardon me, my English is broken and pidgin. (Applause)

Qian: Thank you, Mr. Huang, for this talk. And I'd like to congratulate you on having arrived on such a bright day from beyond the horizon. Next is Mrs. Johnston-Weston.

Johnston-Weston: We're very honored to be here and to share in this international celebration of Eugene O'Neill and his realism. All of our experiences have just been overwhelming.

I'd like to speak a bit about mounting productions of O'Neill in the United States and emphasize again what a pleasure and honor it is to be here particularly. In the United States we have literally been faced with the question, "Why O'Neill?" and "Why China?" And when we arrived here and got off the train and had such a warm welcome and saw in town the banners and the enthusiasm about O'Neill, we knew why O'Neill and why China. (Applause)

Back in 1985 Tom McDermott, Stan Weston, and I got together and decided to honor Eugene O'Neill in his centennial year, 1988. Since that time, our dream has grown and it's now our desire to continue doing Eugene O'Neill as long as we can. Each year, we'd very much like to produce some of his plays somewhere in the world, particularly in the United States.

And I'd like to talk about the United States just a bit. Back in 1986, we had the opening of our Eugene O'Neill Theatre Festival. We opened in Los Angeles with three plays: *A Touch of the Poet, Before Breakfast,* and *Hughie,* with *Before Breakfast* and *Hughie* playing together in an evening. We had a nine-week run in Hollywood, Melrose Theatre, a very small theatre, a ninety-nine seat Equity-waiver house. That was quite an experience. It was an experience in that, in talking about Eugene O'Neill, there were times when people would say, "Who was Eugene O'Neill?" "I don't know who he is." Others would say, "O'Neill, he must be related to Tatum, or Ryan O'Neal." (Laughter) And we'd say, "No. No. He's America's greatest playwright." Very honestly, it was difficult to find people who really understood O'Neill, much harder than finding people who knew who he was.

I must tell a small joke that was both on us and, I think, on O'Neill. During *Poet, Before Breakfast,* and *Hughie,* we had posters made up for our productions. We had them hanging throughout the theatre as well as throughout the Hollywood area in Los Angeles. After one performance of *Poet,* someone walked up to me and said, "The posters are quite nice. But isn't it a little arrogant of Stan Weston to have his face plastered everywhere?" He had no idea this was Eugene O'Neill. (Laughter) I explained to him this was not Stan Weston, although I know Stan would be flattered, and that this was indeed Eugene O'Neill. (Laughter) After the performance of *Hughie,* Tom was approached by a Hollywood agent who said that he really enjoyed the production and really thanked Tom for writing it. (Laughter) So, you see, there are a few obstacles in the United States to overcome in terms of education about our greatest playwright.

It is our greatest hope that with this international cultural exchange with China, we can strengthen the love for O'Neill back in our own country. We will be taking the experiences back with us, on film as well as in our heart, and sharing them with Americans. As I said, we want to continue to do everything we can to foster the international production of Eugene O'Neill and to foster cultural exchange along this line.

I thank the Eugene O'Neill Society and all of you for this overwhelming experience. Thank you.

Qian: Now Mr. McDermott.

McDermott: I'll speak briefly about *Hughie*, tell you what I feel about it, and how I worked on it. But before I do, I'd like to thank Judith for bringing us here. I gave this trip up six months ago because it seemed too difficult. And if it wasn't for her work, none of this would have happened for us. This is a personal thing, I know, but I want you to help me applaud her. (Applause) Thank you.

Hughie is a deeply consummate play, a two-character play, with two lonely men searching for a way to make life larger, in search of their hopeless hopes. This play is surrounded by death. And the central image I gave to my actors is that this is a dance, a courtship dance where each of them dances around one another, never really reaching the other. In the end, they come together. It's a consummation, not a sexual, but a spiritual consummation between the two. They help each other to live. Erie cannot go up to his room. He knows if he gets to his room, he is finished. Something keeps him there, keeps him speaking about the ghosts, the ghost of Hughie, the ghost of love.

The play presents two tremendous challenges to its director and actors. The first is the immensity of the role of Erie Smith. He talks nonstop for an hour. In order for the play to have depth, movement, and structure, the role must be played by an actor of extraordinary talent and imagination. I am blessed to have Stan Weston. Together he and I analyzed the play line by line so that we could break it down and make sense of it.

Then there was the Night Clerk with his silent thoughts and fantasies, with which I am afraid I will never be totally satisfied. The first time I directed this, I chose to have the thoughts silent. I just had sound out there. The actor sort of pantomimed what he was feeling.

Then I added the monologue where he speaks about Arnold Rothstein. Film is not a new idea. Ms. Krafchick wrote a paper on it, which was very interesting. Unfortunately, it is very expensive to get that for the stage. So, I was unable to try it out, but I also fear that if you make those thoughts too strong, you also break the rhythm of the monologue which is going on at the same time. It's a terrible problem. But it's one that challenges directors to try different ways. Perhaps, with its flaws it's like life, like what O'Neill talks about life. And maybe that's good and maybe it will never be perfect. I think it makes art wonderful that we are imperfect, that every production can be different. So, I hope next time I do *Hughie* I'll try something else.

The actor playing Charlie Hughes must constantly be working. I want him to be alive the whole time. When I first approached this play, someone said, "Well, it doesn't matter who you cast for it. The Night Clerk just sits there and has a few lines." But I looked at the play and said, "No. It's a two-character play." People complain to me sometimes that I am upstaging the role by having the guy staring out or being too active. But I think that's what the play is about.

Underneath it all, this is a play about love, perhaps a different phase of love than what we are used to seeing, but love just the same. I believe Erie discovers in the existential moment of time that he did love Hughie, who was perhaps the only person he really had ever cared for. And this love is in effect his own belief in himself, his confidence.

Here we have two characters, a Gambler and a Night Clerk, stuck in this heady existence. But tonight, the Night Clerk takes the chance. He reaches out to Erie in the end. He speaks out, and Erie laps it up like it was duck soup or dope or heroin. In the end, perhaps, they are fooling themselves. But what the hell? And O'Neill says, "Truth. What's the truth? Nothing, pal. Not a thing." It is this passionate love that I most want to express to my actors so that we can give it to the audience. And it's been gratifying for me to see that the soul of China has responded to the passionate soul of O'Neill. The mark of true artistic geniuses is that they transcend various times, cultures, languages, and policies. And I am honored to have witnessed here in the past few days a resurrection. This is a real resurrection in which the discovery of a great artist has happened. This is something special. (Applause)

Qian: We had a wonderful performance last night. And we had a wonderful talk this morning. I think, with Mr. McDermott's explanation of his ideas behind the staging of *Hughie*, we now understand it better. Now we can move onto this side of the table. Mr.

Xiong, please.

Xiong: First of all, on behalf of the entire cast and staff of *Beyond the Horizon*, I'd like to express thanks to all the scholars and experts who are here from both within and beyond the horizon. Your participation in the festival has added much to this old city of Nanjing. (Applause)

For the cast and staff, this is our first experience with an O'Neill play. I should say we had a spiritual meeting with Eugene O'Neill. In staging this play, we found not only O'Neill but also ourselves. Whenever I read the play, I always had a strange feeling as if I saw O'Neill standing beyond the horizon looking at me, and sometimes as if I were standing over there looking at him. I came to see that each of us stands at once on both this side of the horizon and beyond it. From this revelation, I decided to adapt the play to a Chinese background, by putting it in the milieu of a rural village in the low reaches of the Yangtse River and let each of the characters bear a Chinese name. I hope that by doing so, it can help eliminate the distance between my Chinese audience and the American play.

It is my understanding that although the play is entitled *Beyond the Horizon*, the real emphasis is laid on this side of the horizon. It portrays successfully many true-to-life characters. So, I said to my cast and staff that we should do likewise on the Chinese stage. We strive to represent quite realistically Chinese rural life. That is why we use so many authentic stage properties and costumes. In fact, the cast and staff spent several weeks in a village in the Yangtze Delta experiencing daily life before we actually began rehearsals.

People in different cultures behave differently. The ways to show love and hatred vary from culture to culture. So, we have made a lot of changes from the original script. We read each scene in O'Neill's play again and again and tried to make out what O'Neill meant by this or that, and then figured out ways to render it in the language of the Chinese theatre.

Qian: Thank you for your exposition of the play that you directed so successfully. Our next speaker will be Mr. Changnian Feng, who directed *The Emperor Jones*.

Feng: I have always been an admirer of Eugene O'Neill. I had the idea of producing *The Emperor Jones* even when I was a student at a drama school. So, this production has fulfilled my long-cherished dream. (Applause)

The Emperor Jones is a play with a long production history both in China and in the West. So, the crucial thing for me is to find a new theatrical approach. Whenever I read the play, I am always struck by the horror of the dark, primitive forest, the suffocating drumbeat of the African tom-tom, the mysterious atmosphere and the simple grandeur of the play. I am also fascinated by the play's deep probe into the psyche of its characters, the elaborate sets of symbols, and the philosophical and psychological ramifications of the play. It seems to me that a realistic, conventional theatrical approach is absolutely inadequate. So, I felt I had to use more expressive means to do the play justice. Hence the new form--pantomime-dance--of this production.

Another consideration in choosing this form is the Chinese audience. Since the form is a good mixture of action, pantomime, music and dance, it is in a sense similar to the form of Peking Opera, though our performance is much more abstract and modern than the traditional art. I think, therefore, it is an effective way to bring O'Neill to the Chinese theatregoers.

To put it in a nutshell, the main emphasis of our performance is the overall mood and atmosphere created by the pantomime-dance based on the psychological truth of the protagonist Emperor Jones, which can be very different from the logic of our day-to-day life. For example, in certain scenes, we see human bodies or clotheslines hanging from tree branches. This is used to reflect Jones' state of mind. It is expressionistic, rather than realistic.

The second emphasis of our production is the symbols; for instance, the use of the cross in two scenes. The third emphasis lies in the treatment of time and space. At times, we try to blur the line between reality and illusion, or to juxtapose the real and the illusory, so as to effectively show the reality in Jones' illusion and the illusion in his reality. An example comes from the scene in which the Emperor is encircled by the natives running at a dizzying speed, each with a flaming torch in hand. Another point is that throughout the performance we try to maintain a delicate balance between pantomime and dance, relying on the traditional language of the theatre and our real life.

Finally, I would like to take this opportunity to acknowledge with deep gratitude that in mounting this production we benefited a great deal from our literary adviser Professor Haiping Liu's careful explication of the original script. (Applause) And also from our guest choreographer Shijin Su's very innovative and original work. (Applause)

Qian: Finally, we will have Mr. Yuan Yoa talking about *Long Day's Journey into Night.*

Yao: I feel honored to attend this international conference. First of all, I'd like to talk a bit about Qianxian Theatre. The history of this group, one of the best-known performing companies of the People's Liberation Army, can be traced back to the Chinese War of Resistance against Japanese Aggression (1937-1945). In its early years, this group often marched with the Army and performed close to the battlefields. Most of its members were originally field soldiers and officers and propagandists of the revolutionary war. Given this background, it was natural that it should have developed some unique tradition and style of performance.

We feel proud that this is the first American play ever done by our company, and it also marks the premiere of *Long Day's Journey into Night* in China. I believe the Nanjing/Shanghai O'Neill Theatre Festival and this production will have great impact on Chinese life. With his integrity and insight as a true artist, O'Neill helped create the American drama and thus won high respect from people all over the world. Though China and the United States have different social systems and different political faiths, the Americans and the Chinese belong to the same human race. We are all thinking of ways to solve our common problems. Human beings have always been seeking light in darkness. It is the good artist, intellectuals, and so on, who hold the torches to light the human path. And Eugene O'Neill is one of them. It is based on this knowledge that we present O'Neill's masterpiece, *Long Day's Journey into Night* on the Chinese stage. (Applause)

Qian: Thank you, Mr. Yao. Now we invite questions from the audience.

Jackson Bryer: I'd like to say something to all of you. I don't think you people in China realize how unusual it is for us to come to China as O'Neill scholars and to see productions of all these plays. The only way I convey the importance of this festival to you is to tell you something about my own experience. I have been reading and teaching and studying and writing about O'Neill for thirty years. Last night was the first time I've ever seen a production of *The Emperor Jones*. When I go to Shanghai tomorrow, it will be the first time I ever see a production of *The Great God Brown*. I have lived most of my life in New York and Washington, two cities in which theatre is given every night by hundreds and hundreds of theatre companies. I go to theatre forty to fifty times a year. So, that will give you an example of what our country feels about these plays and this playwright. Beatrice Laufer, who wrote the music and lyrics for the opera *Ile*, which all of you are going to see in Shanghai this week, has been trying for twenty years to get that opera done in the United States. It has had two productions. So, when we come half way around the world, and you thank us for coming, I think it is important for you to know we thank you. (Applause)

Rolf Fjelde: I was a college student in 1946 when I went to the production that has been much talked about of *The Iceman Cometh*. And that evening was a very long evening. At the end, there was a general breaking-up of the audience. And then there was a sudden tremor that went through everyone. They said, "He is here! He's here!" And I saw this figure unfold out of one of the aisle seats and make his way up. His cavernous eyes, the prodigious sorrow in them, parchment-red face, those spidery trembling fingers of O'Neill. He walked up the aisle past all of us. The whole house was totally hushed. I have had the good fortune of meeting many people of eminence, but that sense of human greatness, and human compassion and emotion, was absolutely overwhelming. And I think, as I remember that face, what it would have meant to him, having been disappointed with that production, to know what is being done here: it would have been a magnificent experience for him. So, I can only say again, in a humble way, through that experience, I'd like to thank you, our Chinese hosts. (Applause)

Betty Jean Jones: I'd like, too, to begin by saying that we thank you for all you have given us. (Applause) I hope that China will understand that we in the West have so much to learn from you. (Applause) And especially in the theatrical sense. There's much we can learn from all of you in the way you produce your own theatre as well as the theatre of the West. It has been an extraordinary experience for all of us. Because I represent a three-fold theatre interest --as a director, scholar and former actress--I must say that I have learned so much from watching your work. I thank you for that.

I'd like to speak generally of the productions that we saw. There were three important things that struck me about them that, I think, would please any theatregoer looking at these works, whether Western or Eastern, and that certainly would please O'Neill. First, the fresh new approach that was brought to all of them, that is, no fear of the material. Secondly, the kinship to the work, conveying the sense that O'Neill belongs to the world, to all of us. That was in all of the work. And finally, in every case a sincerity of performance. I know these people, every character. I understand Mary. And I understand Andrew and Robert. I understand the Emperor Jones. That sincerity of performance was true, and we thank you for that.

Thomas Pawley: I'd like to ask some questions. I want to ask the director of *The Emperor Jones* about his rationale for omitting scenes one and eight.

Feng: In the production, we use the form of pantomime-dance, something between pantomime and dance. It is difficult for us to present the two scenes that are the realistic story frames of the expressionist play. So, we change scene one to a scene of a dream and scene eight to a highly stylized symbol.

Pawley: In the first scene of the script there are three characters, two men and an old woman. Those three characters disappeared in your scene. Could you have brought them into pantomime-dance, too?

Feng: Yes, it is possible. I think the emphasis of *The Emperor Jones* is laid in the forest, in Jones' psychology, fear and emotions, and so on. So, I think our treatment of the first scene is more in harmony with the scenes that follow. But I will take it into consideration in our revival in the future.

Jean Chothia: In *Beyond the Horizon*, the audience applauded particularly, I think, at moments of strange activity. The audience all laughed and clapped. Was it because of that unusual realism?

Xiong: Exactly. People laughed because they found it surprisingly realistic.

Robert Sarlos: I'd like to make two comments about *The Emperor Jones*. I am particularly impressed with the scenery, which was very imaginative, very evocative. The second is that I wonder whether the music could not have helped the climax more. The music was very exciting and very much involving. Could we start it, have it started, at a slower speed as O'Neill himself suggested, and then have it accelerate?

Feng: Yesterday after the performance, some critics and experts questioned me about the treatment of the drumbeat. They don't think it should be stopped during the performance and that it is very important. It will be easy for us to improve this.

McDermott: I am presumptuous to defend my colleague. He's a director, he has the right to a concept. I think you're missing a point here. (To the interpreter) I hope you will translate this to Mr. Feng. I am a director, and I know what he is talking about. He is not interested in literally showing the play. If you look at it, you see that it's almost like Christ before he is on the cross. He has a dream of what's to come, then he acts it inside him. It's the inner workings of the man that he wanted to show. So, he didn't have to stay within the scope of the play as written. This is a directoral concept. He used *The Emperor Jones* to get deeper inside the play from his own standpoint. I think it was brilliant. I would like you to tell him to stay with his concept because it's right there. It's very important that we, as supposed scholars of O'Neill, not try to impose upon him that perhaps he made a mistake.

Egil Tornqvist: I don't think we are talking about whether it is faithful to O'Neill's text. I think we are talking about the effect and what is most effective to the audience. And that is quite a problem to discuss. For instance, I am not worried about the fastness of the drumbeat but more perhaps the problem of the scene shifts and the music and the musical interludes. I could imagine using the drumbeat shifting the scenes, and keeping the drumbeat throughout with variations so that we keep the audience spellbound. That's the most important thing. How can you keep the audience most effectively in your grip, without having too great a monotony?

Feng: Frankly, I am not very satisfied with the sound effect myself. I think I can accept the suggestion that we should deepen the drumbeat throughout the play.

James Robinson: I've two questions, one to the director of *Long Day's Journey into Night*, the other to the director of *The Emperor Jones*. In *Long Day's Journey into Night* the set design was very interesting to me, because of its modern or contemporary nature; and also the costumes seemed contemporary for the boys, but old-fashioned for Mary. I think I can understand the reason for that. But, as part of the set design, there were faces by the bookcase. There was a picture of Shakespeare above the bookcase. Also on the panel up above, facing the audience, was an eye, a closing eye and a nose. I thought I detected it in another place somewhere between the portrait of Shakespeare and the panel above. I was wondering what the rationale for that was?

Jianping Li (assistant director of *Long Day's Journey*: The director and the set designer of our production of *Long Day's Journey into Night* wanted to emphasize another important character in the play-- fog. They used masks to reveal the symbolic meaning of the fog.

The fog is very obscure, which represents the obscure relationship among the family members.

Robinson: My second question is for the director of *The Emperor Jones*. First of all, like all of us, I liked it extremely well. So, my congratulations to the director and all the cast. (Applause) My question is why did you add sexuality to *The Emperor Jones*? That's not what I understand the play is about. That's not in the text. I found it very interesting that the witch doctor was cast as a woman. And there were very short interludes containing highly sexual hints. I am wondering what the rationale was?

Feng: My reason for this is that Jones is a very lively man, and when he is on his deathbed, he has various desires and dreams. So, I think, sexuality is reasonable. Though I cast the witch doctor as a female, I simply wanted to make it a symbol of fate, or a symbol of death, rather than emphasizing sexuality.

Dongling Zhu (Professor of Chinese, Suzhou University): I'd also like to make some brief comments on *The Emperor Jones*. I have read the play many, many times and have always been wondering what might be the best form to present it on the stage. After seeing the performance last night, I think Jiangsu Art Theatre has indeed found a perfect form for the play. I believe we can say the production is the cumulative result of two significant trends, or movements, in China, namely, the experimental theatre and the cultural retrospection. Another point is the religious dimension of the production. I don't think it is just limited to Christianity. I find an element of Oriental religion in it as well. The role of the dual-sex witch doctor, for example, can be found in Buddhism. By stressing the religious dimension, I think the production has been able to bring the play to a more sublime level.

Jones: I have a question about *Beyond the Horizon*. The ending seems to be deliberately hopeful, that the sun is rising and there's good feeling and hope, which is not quite like the text. Is there some particular reason for the director doing that?

Xiong: I just follow the stage directions of the translated script. The sun is rising, but it is only a symbol, it is not the reality.

Haiping Liu: I'd like to make some comments on the American production of *Hughie*. First, I want to congratulate the Eugene O'Neill Theatre Festival from Los Angeles on their highly successful production last night. It was so hot, stuffy, and humid in the theatre. People would usually stop going to theatre on days like this in China. But last night I noticed few in the audience left their seats during the performance, which is really extraordinary. And, also, I don't think most of the Chinese in the audience, except the participants of our conference, know much English. It would be hard to imagine they could follow the monologues of the play, which we know are full of the argot and slang of New York in the 1920s. As translator of the play, I know only too well how difficult it is for Chinese even to read the play. But the audience last night looked very attentive and interested. This shows how gripping the performance was. It also points, of course, to the general interest the Chinese people hold in American theatre.

The Eugene O'Neill Theatre Festival is the only American theatre company participating in this festival of ours. In a few days, they will go to Shanghai and present this production on the same stage with a Chinese version of *Hughie* by the Shanghai Youth Theatre. This exciting event is unprecedented in the history of Chinese theatre. So, I think, we should really thank Judith, Tom, Stan, and Charles for bringing this wonderful performance across the Pacific Ocean to China. (Applause)

Marcus Konick: Like everybody else, I think *The Emperor Jones* is an extremely beautiful performance. The only thing that worries me very much is religion. There are some Catholic symbols in the production, but actually Jones is a Baptist. I'd like to understand the rationale for that.

Feng: My understanding of the play is that O'Neill aims at exploring what he called "big themes." So, it's not appropriate to deal with Jones as a real figure or to deal with some concrete religious problems or racial problems.

Pawley: I have exactly the opposite reaction to that scene, as I have already told the director. Apparently, the person who carries Christ's cross is Simon, a Cyrenian, a black man. I thought it was a black man taking up Christ's cross. In one scene I saw Christ being carried on his hip. I don't know if it was really intentional to do that. Jones says, "I carry my Jesus in my hip pocket," you remember? And I thought I saw that being done at one point. A crucifix is a Christian symbol. And he's a "good Baptist." And the black Baptist ministers I know wear the crucifix.

Feng: Yes, it is intentional. The text says that Jones is a Baptist, and it's very symbolic that he carries the cross.

Virginia Floyd: I want to congratulate you on *The Emperor Jones*. I thought it was a very daring, dramatic, and exciting piece of drama. I consider *The Emperor Jones* something like a Greek play. And in Greek plays, you always have a king in a very high position and the tragedy is in his downfall. Therefore, I suggest that you have one brief shot of him in the opening scene on the throne as a king so that when he loses everything, it will be much more dramatic. I don't know if this can be done.

As for *Long Day's Journey into Night*, I think that is extraordinary. I've seen productions of this play in the United States and in Stockholm, Sweden. We often hear the love-hate relationship between the Tyrones or the O'Neills. And here I saw, in this production, love and affection, while in most productions the hatred comes out. I found that very moving. I talked to a wonderful translator here of *Long Day's Journey into Night* who told me a bit of the last scene has been cut. I wonder why some of the dialogue was omitted?

Yao: It's the habit of Chinese audiences that a play should last no longer than two hours, so we have cut some very long speeches. The director has cut only parts that might be difficult for the Chinese to understand and that do not affect the whole structure and characterization of the play.

Floyd: At least, there's some new direction in the production. Currently in New York, Jack Lemmon's production of *Long Day's Journey into Night* was cut to three hours, but it was not good and the acting was not good either. One thing I'd like to comment on is that O'Neill, as you know, never allowed a line changed in his plays. Since O'Neill himself had planned to turn *Marco Millions* and *Lazarus Laughed* into musicals, I think he would be pleased with *The Emperor Jones* with music and pantomime.

Feng: Thank you.

Qian: If we have time, I'm sure, there will be many more interesting questions and comments to come. Before we break up, Mrs. Johnston-Weston would like to say a few words.

Johnston-Weston: I'd like to say that honoring O'Neill is a tremendous opportunity to bring all of us together, and it's a privilege to be on this panel with such distinguished directors, producers, and artists who have inspired us and given us some ideas as to how O'Neill can be represented.

In honoring O'Neill, though, I think there's someone else we need very much to acknowledge, a man of tremendous vision, of tremendous heart, and of the ability to transcend cultural boundaries. I know he's been working for over two years to do this. And I just want all to stand and honor Professor Haiping Liu. (Long applause)

Qian: A lady over there wants to say a few words.

Rongjin Xie (Editor, *Foreign Theatre Journal*, Beijing): I'm not going to ask any questions. But I'm going to supply you with a little piece of information, that is, at the end of September or at the beginning of October, the centennial celebration of Eugene O'Neill will continue in Beijing. And all of you are welcome to attend. (Applause)

Qian: I realize that the air-conditioning is turned off, and we are really overtime. Thank you very, very much. Thank you. *Xie-xie.* (Applause)

> [Transcribed by Yu Zhao from the tape recordings of the panel discussion with the aid of the detailed notes taken by Ralph and Margaret Ranald.]

O'Neill: An International Perspective-- A Bibliographic Note

The most complete international bibliographical survey of O'Neill's plays in translation and of O'Neill criticism appeared in 1984 in *Eugene O'Neill's Critics: Voices from Abroad,* edited by Horst Frenz and Susan Tuck (Carbondale: Southern Illinois University Press). Translations are listed from the following countries: Argentina, Brazil, Bulgaria, Chile, China, Czechoslovakia, Denmark, Finland, France, Greece, Hungary, India, Iran, Iraq, Israel, Italy, Japan, Korea, Netherlands, Norway, Pakistan, Poland, Portugal, Rumania, Spain, Sweden, Thailand, Turkey, United Arab Republic, Uruguay, USSR, and Yugoslavia. Critical essays reprinted in the volume represent, Argentina, Austria, China, Czechoslovakia, Denmark, England, Finland, France, Germany, Hungary, Ireland, Italy, Japan, Poland, Spain, Sweden, and the USSR. Among the critical voices included here are those of Hugo von Hofmannsthal, Lennox Robinson, Alexander Tairov, Sean O'Casey, Per Hallstrom, Gabriel Marcel, St. John Irvine, Toshio Kimura, Kenneth Tynan, and Timo Tiusanen.

Eugene O'Neill: A World View, edited by Virginia Floyd (New York: Frederick Ungar, 1979), offers no general bibliography; however, most articles conclude with extensive notes. The volume contains nineteen articles from Europe and the United States by, among others, Tom Olsson (Sweden), Timo Tiusanen (Finland), Clifford Leech (England), Marta Sienicka (Poland), Peter Egri (Hungary), and Maya Koreneva (USSR). American authors include John Henry Raleigh, Frederick Wilkins, Albert Bermel, and Esther Jackson. Several essays by actors and directors Florence Eldridge, Arvin Brown and Ingrid Bergman offer reflections on problems performing O'Neill.

James A. Robinson's *Eugene O'Neill and Oriental Thought: A Divided Vision* (Carbondale: Southern Illinois University Press, 1982) examines O'Neill's fascination with Oriental philosophies and their influence upon such plays as *The Fountain, Marco Millions, The Great God Brown, Lazarus Laughed, Strange Interlude, Dynamo,* and the late plays. The extensive bibliography includes works on Oriental thought known to have been in O'Neill's personal library.

Ward B. Lewis in his *Eugene O'Neill: The German Reception of America's First Dramatist* (New York: Peter Lang, 1984) traces the introduction of O'Neill upon German stages beginning with *Anna Christie, The Emperor Jones* and *The Hairy Ape.* He examines the playwright's recognition and acclaim in the 1920s with *Desire under the Elms, The Great God Brown,* and *Strange Interlude,* then looks at the early postwar years when *Mourning Becomes Electra* and *Ah, Wilderness!* were first produced. The study concludes with a survey of the reception of the late plays. An extensive German-language bibliography follows, along with fifty pages of notes.

Critical Essays on Eugene O'Neill, edited by James J. Martine (Boston: G. K. Hall, 1984) contains an essay by Peter Egri of Hungary, as well as those by such American O'Neill scholars as Jackson R. Bryer, Lisa M. Schwerdt, Michael Manheim, Steven F. Bloom, and Susan Tuck.

In *Chekhov and O'Neill: The Uses of the Short Story in Chekhov's and O'Neill's Plays* (Budapest: Akademiai Kaido, 1986), Peter Egri, professor of English at Eotvos University in Budapest, examines the types of connections between the short story and the drama of Chekhov and O'Neill. Among the O'Neill plays analyzed are *Hughie, A Moon for the Misbegotten, Mourning Becomes Electra, A Touch of the Poet, The Iceman Cometh,* and *Long Day's Journey into Night.* Bibliographical references are given in twenty-six pages of notes.

Edward L. Shaughnessy's *Eugene O'Neill in Ireland: The Critical Reception* (New York: Greenwood Press, 1988) is a history of O'Neill production and critical reaction in Ireland as well as an anthology of major opinions from 1926 to 1988. Representative newspaper coverage is included along with essays by Sir John Ervine and Dennis Donoghue. An appendix lists all O'Neill productions in the Republic of Ireland and Northern Ireland between 1922 and 1987. The bibliography covers general background books on Irish theatre, book reviews, and articles related to O'Neill in performance and in Irish critical thought.

Chinese-American Cultural Dialogue through Drama--Eugene O'Neill and China by Haiping Liu and Dongling Zhu (Nanjing: Nanjing University Press, 1988), provides a bibliography of O'Neill's plays translated, published, and produced in China, along with the Chinese reviews and criticism of his drama over the past sixty years. The book studies the cultural background of the Chinese responses to his plays and his influence on modern Chinese theatre as well as his indebtedness to ancient Chinese philosophy. Also included are a number of photographs of stage performances. The book is available only in Chinese.

Eugene O'Neill as Contemporary Theatre edited by Yoshiteru Kurokawa (Tokyo: Hosei University Press, 1990), is the proceedings of an international O'Neill conference (June 11-13, 1988) sponsored by Hosei University and directed by Yoshiteru Kurokawa. It contains twenty papers contributed by Japanese, Chinese, European, and American scholars. The book is published in Japanese.

The Recorder, a journal of the American Irish Historical Society, dedicated an issue to the O'Neill centenary with what it called "an International Celebration" (Volume 3, Number 1, Summer 1989, The American Irish Historical Society, 991 Fifth Avenue, New York, New York, 10028). Edited by New York University professors Terence Moran and Lowell Swortzell, this issue contains eighteen articles by such well-known scholars as Virginia Floyd (USA), Father Paschal Onunwa (Nigeria), Marc Maufort (Belgium), Peter Egri (Hungary), Jean Chothia (Great Britain), Tom Olsson (Sweden), Yasuko Ikeuchi (Japan), and Zhao Yu (China). The volume is divided into four sections: "O'Neill the Irishman," "O'Neill the Dramatist," "O'Neill the Theatrical Genius," and "O'Neill the Classroom Subject."

Eugene O'Neill's Century: Centennial Views on America's Foremost Tragic Dramatist, edited by Richard F. Moorton, Jr. (New York: Greenwood Press, 1991) contains papers from a festival held at Connecticut College in New London "so that international O'Neill centennial conferences at Stockholm, Sweden, and Nanjing, China, might be complemented by a yearlong festival of performance and scholarship commemorating New London's gifted son on the playwright's native ground." The thirteen articles selected for publication are divided into three sections entitled: "O'Neill's Tragic Art," "Art and Life--The Wellsprings of Genius," and "O'Neill

Onstage."   Of particular interest to international readers is "A Spokesman for America: O'Neill in Translation" by Rita Terras, who begins her overview with the ironic but true statement: "Eugene O'Neill's work has been staged more often and has had larger audiences in Europe than anywhere else in the world including the United States." Other articles of interest are "Searching for Home in O'Neill's America" by Kristin Pfefferkorn, "'Get My Goat': O'Neill's Attitude toward Children and Adolescents in His Life and Art" by Lowell Swortzell, and two by the editor, a classicist who reexamines O'Neill's understanding and use of the *Eumenides* and then looks at *Mourning Becomes Electra* as veiled autobiograpy.

The Eugene O'Neill Review, under the editorship of Professor Frederick C. Wilkins, Department of English, Suffolk University, Boston, MA., 02114-4280, regularly contains articles and reviews of international interest. The *Review* is indexed annually. Among the contributors to the *Review* (and its predecessor, *The Eugene O'Neill Newsletter*) are many of the scholars represented in this volume.

Index

About the Editors and Contributors

JUDITH E. BARLOW is an associate professor of English and associate professor of Women's Studies at the State University of New York at Albany. She is the author of *Final Acts: The Creation of Three Late O'Neill Plays* and editor of *Plays By American Women, 1900-1930.*

JEAN CHOTHIA is a Fellow of Selwyn College and University Lecturer of English, Cambridge University. She recently completed a study of the work of the French director Andre Antoine. Her *Forging a Language: A Study of the Plays of Eugene O'Neill* was published in 1979.

WILLIAM R. ELWOOD has published in the areas of nineteenth and twentieth-century continental theatre and drama. His specialization is German theatre history and drama with a special focus on German expressionism. He was professor of Theatre and Drama at the University of Wisconsin-Madison and Chair of that department from 1978-1988. Currently, he is Dean of Graduate Studies at Emerson College, Boston.

ROLF FJELDE, the foremost translator of Ibsen into English, is founding president of the Ibsen Society of America. He has published and lectured extensively on modern drama here and abroad and his Ibsen play texts have enjoyed over 500 productions on the English-speaking stage. Professor of English and Drama at Pratt Institute in New York City, he was three-time playwright-in-residence at the Eugene O'Neill Theatre Conference. In 1991, he received the Royal Medal of St. Olav from Norway's king for excellence of service to Ibsen's art.

VIRGINIA FLOYD annotated and edited *Eugene O'Neill at Work: Newly Released Ideas for Plays* and *Eugene O'Neill: The Unfinished Plays*, edited *Eugene O'Neill: A World View*, and wrote *The Plays of Eugene O'Neill: A New Assessment.*

MARIKO HORI is an assistant professor of English in the Department of Economics, Aoyama Gakuin University in Tokyo. Her main research area is Modern British and American Drama. Recent articles in print include the study of Eugene O'Neill and Samuel Beckett.

YASUKO IKEUCHI is an associate professor of English at Ritsumeikan University, Kyoto, Japan. In 1983-1984, she was a Fulbright Scholar at the Yale School of Drama. She is the author of "O'Neill and America: A Shared Adolescence--A Study of *The Emperor Jones* and *The Hairy Ape*," "The Survival Game in *Hughie*" (delivered at the 1984 and 1986 O'Neill conferences, respectively), "*The Iceman Cometh*: What a Salesman Failed to Sell" (1980), and "Two Families, Two 'Wildernesses': *Ah, Wilderness!* and *Long Day's Journey Into Night*" (1981). Her article, "De-mythification of Femininity in *Strange Interlude*" was published in 1989.

BETTY JEAN JONES is a professor of Theatre at the University of North Carolina at Greensboro, where she is also director of graduate studies in Theatre. Her areas of specialization are American Theatre and Drama and American Film Studies. As a director at Greensboro, she has staged several works by Eugene O'Neill.

ALBERT E. KALSON teaches drama and film at Purdue University. He is the author of a book on J. B. Priestly and articles on dramatists from Shakespeare to Alan Ayckbourn.

MARCUS KONICK was teaching at the University of Nanjing as a guest professor in the Department of Foreign Languages at the time of the conference *Eugene O'Neill: World Playwright*. He has since returned to his home in Lock Haven, Pennsylvania, where in retirement he continues to investigate aspects of Puritanism in modern literature.

MAYA KORENEVA, a senior researcher, Gorky Institute of World Literature, Moscow, is the author of numerous articles on problems in American literature and individual authors, editor of three collections of essays on different periods of history of American literature, and several collections of short stories, poetry, and drama in translation. She has also translated works by American, British, and Irish authors: William Faulkner, D. H. Lawrence, Eugene O'Neill, Samuel Beckett, Dylan Thomas, Denise Levertov, and Edward Albee. She is writing a book on Eugene O'Neill.

MARCELLINE KRAFCHICK is an associate professor of English at California State University, Hayward. A former Carolina Playmaker, she teaches drama and mythology. She has published books on rhetoric and fiction and has presented and published papers on mythology, Henry James, and O'Neill.

YOSHITERU KUROKAWA, playwright-director, is a professor of American drama at Hosei University, Tokyo, and currently is teaching Japanese literature and language at Nanjing University, China. He was the organizer of 1988 Hosei University International Symposium, "Eugene O'Neill as Contemporary Theatre."

WARD B. LEWIS is an associate professor of German at the University of Georgia, where he pursues interests in twentieth century drama, exile literature, and American-German literary relations.

GANG LI is now a translator of technical English at a paper mill in northeast China. He was a graduate student at Nankai University when he co-organized a conference on Eugene O'Neill for graduate students in Tianjin, May 5-7, 1988.

HAIPING LIU is professor and chairman of English at Nanjing University, China. The organizer of the festival and conference *Eugene O'Neill: World Playwright* held in China in June 1988, he has published books and articles on O'Neill in both English and Chinese, including *Eugene O'Neill on Drama* (1988).

FELICIA HARDISON LONDRE is Curators' Professor of Theatre at the University of Missouri-Kansas City and dramaturg for Missouri Repertory Theatre. She recently published *The History of World Theatre: From the English Restoration to the Present* (1991), a narrative study. Earlier works include *Federico Garcia Lorca, Tom Stoppard*, and *Tennessee Williams* .

WENPEI LONG is a retired professor of American Literature at Fudan University, Shanghai. She has published a number of books and essays on O'Neill and has translated several of his plays into Chinese.

MARC MAUFORT holds a postdoctoral research appointment with the National Fund for Scientific Research in Belgium. His articles on O'Neill have appeared or are forthcoming in volumes of essays and such periodicals as *The Eugene O'Neill Newsletter, Revue Belge de Philologie et d'Histoire, The Theatre Annual, Theatre Survey,* and *The Recorder.* In 1988, he organized an international conference in Belgium to celebrate the 100th anniversary of O'Neill's birth. The proceedings of this conference were published in 1989 in Amsterdam.

JAMES S. MOY is associate professor of Theatre and Drama at the University of Wisconsin-Madison. A specialist in nineteenth-century American theatre, he also teaches theatre history and theory.

THOMAS D. PAWLEY is Curators' Distinguished Professor Emeritus of Speech and Theatre at Lincoln University, Jefferson City, Missouri. Co-editor with William Reardon of *The Black Teacher and the Dramatic Arts,* he is also the author of two published plays and numerous articles on the theatre and a Fellow of the American Theatre.

ZHIJI REN is professor of English at Fudan University, Shanghai, where he teaches English and American literature at both the graduate and undergraduate levels.

JAMES A. ROBINSON, professor of English Literature at the University of Maryland, wrote *Eugene O'Neill and Oriental Thought: A Divided Vision,* published in 1982, which explores O'Neill's fascination with Hinduism, Buddhism, and Taoism and their influences upon his plays.

ROBERT K. SARLOS teaches at the University of California, Davis, and directs the doctoral program in Dramatic Art. His publications range from Elizabethan-Jacobean to American theatre and drama, with an emphasis on methodology. His *Jig Cook and the Provincetown Players: Theatre in Ferment* received the 1983 Hewitt Award for distinguished achievement in theatre history.

LISA M. SCHWERDT teaches writing and literature at the University of Central Florida and Rollins College. She is the author of

Isherwood's Fiction: The Self and Technique as well as articles on Joyce, Fowles, and O'Neill.

JIANQUI SUN is associate professor of English at Beijing Economics and Trade University, where she teaches English as a second language and offers a drama course in English.

LOWELL SWORTZELL is professor of Educational Theatre at New York University. His publications on O'Neill and other subjects in drama and theatre have appeared in professional journals and collections. A specialist in children's theatre, he is editor of several play collections and author of books in that field, including the *International Guide to Children's Theatre and Educational Theatre* (Greenwood Press, 1990), winner of the Distinguished Book award of the American Alliance for Theatre and Education and named a *Choice* Outstanding Academic Book.

EGIL TORNQVIST has been a professor of Scandinavian studies at the University of Amsterdam (Holland) since 1969. His publications include *A Drama of Souls: Studies in O'Neill's Super-naturalistic Technique* (1968), *Strindbergian Drama: Themes and Structure* (1982), and (together with Barry Jacobs) *Strindberg's Miss Julie: A Play and Its Transpositions* (1988).

PAUL VOELKER is professor of English at the University of Wisconsin-Richland and past president of the American Drama Society. He has served as director and dramaturg of O'Neill productions, published essays on O'Neill in *American Literature* and *Modern Drama*, and presented papers at O'Neill Centenary conferences in Belgium, Sweden, and the United States, as well as in China.

DANIEL J. WATERMEIER is professor of Theatre and Film at the University of Toledo. He has contributed articles on American theatre and drama and Shakespearean stage history, as well as numerous book and theatre reviews to such journals and books as *The Cambridge Guide to World Theatre, Theatre History Studies, Theatre Research International, Shakespeare Quarterly,* and *Modern Drama*. In 1980-1981, he was the recipient of a John Simon Guggenheim Fellowship.

JEAN ANNE WATERSTRADT is a professor of English at Brigham Young University, Provo, Utah, where she teaches Shakespeare, modern drama, and a biennial O'Neill seminar. She has organized and directed two O'Neill symposia. She is the editor of *Encyclia*, the journal of the Utah Academy of Sciences, Arts, and Letters.